THE END OF HUMAN RIGHTS

THE END OF HUMAN RIGHTS

CRITICAL LEGAL THOUGHT AT THE TURN OF THE CENTURY

COSTAS DOUZINAS

·HART·
PUBLISHING

OXFORD

2000

Hart Publishing
Oxford and Portland, Oregon

Published in North America (US and Canada) by
Hart Publishing c/o
International Specialized Book Services
5804 NE Hassalo Street
Portland, Oregon
97213-3644
USA

Distributed in the Netherlands, Belgium and Luxembourg by
Intersentia, Churchillaan 108
B2900 Schoten
Antwerpen
Belgium

Hart Publishing Ltd is a specialist legal publisher based in Oxford, England.
To order further copies of this book or to request a list of other
publications please write to:

Hart Publishing Ltd, Salter's Boatyard,
Folly Bridge, Abingdon Road, Oxford OX1 4LB
Telephone: +44 (0)1865 245533 or Fax: +44 (0)1865 794882
e-mail: mail@hartpub.co.uk

British Library Cataloguing in Publication Data
Data Available
ISBN 1 901362–91–4 (cloth)
ISBN 1 84113–000–1 (paperback)

Typeset by Hope Services (Abingdon) Ltd.
Printed in Great Britain on acid-free paper
by Biddles Ltd, www.Biddles.co.uk

Contents

Preface

This is the final part of a trilogy that Ronnie Warrington and myself planned in the late 1980s. The first two volumes *Postmodern Jurisprudence* and *Justice Miscarried* were published in 1991 and 1994 and contributed to the creation of a distinct British critical legal movement and to the turn of legal scholarship towards ethical concerns. This final volume of the trilogy completes the intellectual journey Ronnie and I started with the aim of reconstructing legal theory for a new world of cultural pluralism, intellectual openness and ethical awareness. Fate ordained that I would not have the privilege of discussing ideas, disputing arguments and writing this book with Ronnie. *The End of Human Rights* is dedicated to him.

When I started my career, my then Head of Department told me that if I persisted with my theoretical interests, my academic future would be limited. A few years later, an article of Ronnie and myself was rejected by a learned law journal because it used words like 'deconstruction' and 'logocentrism', which could not be found in the OED. How things have now changed. Our article was eventually published and went on to be translated in five languages, a rather unique achievement in law. The word 'deconstruction' appears commonly in law textbooks and articles. An interest in theory is a positive advantage for young scholars applying for academic posts.

Legal education has been experiencing recently something of a Renaissance, which has put it back where it belongs, at the heart of the academy. The Critical Legal Studies movement was pivotal in this development. But I should add that for me the greatest achievement of critical lawyers is that they teach, research and write under the guiding principle that a law without justice is a body without soul and a legal education that teaches rules without spirit is intellectually barren and morally bankrupt. This book, a critique of legal humanism inspired by a love of humanity, belongs to that climate. It aims to offer an advanced textbook of legal theory and human rights for the melancholic lawyer at the end of the most atrocious century in the history of humankind.

I had the amazing good fortune to be involved in the establishment and phenomenal success of the Birkbeck Law School in the early 1990s. This success would not have been possible without the extraordinary group of committed academics and imaginative scholars, my former and current colleagues, who made Birkbeck the best little law school in Britain. I owe many intellectual debts to all of them and in particular to Peter Goodrich and Nicola Lacey, my predecessors as Heads of the Birkbeck Law School. Peter's historical sensitivity, fiery imagination and acerbic sense of humour have contributed to the writing of this book and the wider critical legal project in many ways, many conscious and acknowledged, others unconscious and opaque. Nicola's gracious wisdom and friendly advice in relation to this and many other projects has been invaluable. Critical legal studies would not have been such an influential movement without those two charismatic friends.

Many colleagues and friends have contributed to the writing of this book over the last two years. I cannot mention them all. But I have great pleasure in thanking some friends, whose contributions are close to the surface of the text. I should like to thank in particular Alexandra Bakalaki, Bill Bowring, Julia Chryssostali, Lindsay Farmer, Peter Fitzpatrick, Rolando Gaete, Adam Gearey, Shaun McVeigh, Les Moran, Tim Murphy and Adam Tomkins. The students of the Human Rights course at the Birkbeck Law School have contributed to this book through both their huge enthusiasm and commitment to human rights and their suspicions towards all grandiose statements by the powerful. Over the years, I learned more from them than they possibly learnt from me.

Research for this book was greatly facilitated by various grants and fellowships. Birkbeck College gave me a long sabbatical leave after the completion of the establishment of the Law School. Part of the research was carried out at the European University Institute, Florence and at the Universities of Princeton and the Cardozo Law School, New York, where I held various fellowships in 1997 and 1998. Yiota Cravaritou was a great help and inspiration at Florence, Jeanne Schroeder and David Carlson were important sources of edification in New York, while Kostis Douzinas and Nancy Rauch provided the most wonderful hospitality and animated discussions in New York. Natasja Smiljanic and Maria Kyriakou were invaluable research assistants at various points of the project. My daughter Phaedra suffered seriously in the summers of 1998 and 1999 when rather than going swimming with her, I kept writing and being an

unsociable and irritable companion. Nicos and Anna Tsigonia provided inspiration and challenged ideas. Finally, my deepest thanks go
to Joanna Bourke who, throughout her *annus mirabilis* of 1999, kept
being a resourceful and tolerant company and altogether fabulous.

Dryos, Paros, August 1999

PART I

THE GENEALOGY OF
HUMAN RIGHTS

1

The Triumph of Human Rights

A new ideal has triumphed on the world stage: human rights. It unites left and right, the pulpit and the state, the minister and the rebel, the developing world and the liberals of Hampstead and Manhattan. Human rights have become the principle of liberation from oppression and domination, the rallying cry of the homeless and the dispossessed, the political programme of revolutionaries and dissidents. But their appeal is not confined to the wretched of the earth. Alternative lifestyles, greedy consumers of goods and culture, the pleasure-seekers and playboys of the Western world, the owner of Harrods, the former managing director of Guinness Plc as well as the former King of Greece have all glossed their claims in the language of human rights.[1] Human rights are the fate of postmodernity, the energy of our societies, the fulfilment of the Enlightenment promise of emancipation and self-realisation. We have been blessed – or condemned – to fight the twilight battles of the millennium of Western dominance and the opening skirmishes of the new period under the dual banners of humanity and right. Human rights are trumpeted as the noblest creation of our philosophy and jurisprudence and as the best proof of the universal aspirations of our modernity, which had to await our postmodern global culture for its justly deserved acknowledgement.

Human rights were initially linked with specific class interests and were the ideological and political weapons in the fight of the rising bourgeoisie against despotic political power and static social organisation. But their ontological presuppositions, the principles of human equality and freedom, and their political corollary, the claim that political power must be subjected to the demands of reason and law, have now become part of the staple ideology of most contemporary regimes and their partiality has been transcended. The collapse of

---

[1] *Fayed* v. *UK* (1994) 18 EHRR 393; *Saunders* v. *UK* (1997) 23 EHRR 242; *The Former King Constantine of Greece* v. *Greece* Appl. 25701/94. Declared admissible 21 April 1998.

communism and the elimination of apartheid marked the end of the last two world movements which challenged liberal democracy. Human rights have won the ideological battles of modernity. Their universal application and full triumph appears to be a matter of time and of adjustment between the spirit of the age and a few recalcitrant regimes. Its victory is none other that the completion of the promise of the Enlightenment, of emancipation through reason. Human rights are the ideology after the end, the defeat of ideologies, or to adopt a voguish term the ideology at the "end of history".

And yet many doubts persist.[2] The record of human rights violations since their ringing declarations at the end of the eighteenth century is quite appalling. "It is an undeniable fact" writes Gabriel Marcel "that human life has never been as universally treated as a vile and perishable commodity as during our own era".[3] If the twentieth century is the epoch of human rights, their triumph is, to say the least, something of a paradox. Our age has witnessed more violations of their principles than any of the previous and less "enlightened" epochs. The twentieth century is the century of massacre, genocide, ethnic cleansing, the age of the Holocaust. At no point in human history has there been a greater gap between the poor and the rich in the Western world and between the north and the south globally. "No degree of progress allows one to ignore that never before in absolute figures, have so many men, women, and children been subjugated, starved, or exterminated on earth".[4] No wonder then why the grandiose statements of concern by governments and international organisations are often treated with popular derision and scepticism. But should our experience of the huge gap between the theory and practice of human rights make us doubt their principle and question the promise of emancipation through reason and law when it seems to be close to its final victory?

---

[2] Despite the enormous amount of books on human rights, the jurisprudence of rights is dominated by neo-Kantian liberals. There are a few notable exceptions. Rolando Gaete's *Human Rights and the Limits of Critical Reason* (Aldershot, Dartmouth, 1993) is a powerful expression of the doubts about human rights demagoguery and the limitations of reason's emancipatory ability. From a legal and historical perspective, the most far-going criticism of human rights is the small classic by Michel Villey, *Le Droit et les droits de l'homme* (Paris, P.U.F., 1983). Bernard Bourgeois, *Philosophie et droits de l'homme: de Kant à Marx* (Paris, P.U.F., 1990), is the best critical introduction to the classical philosophy of human rights. In a more political vein, the recent collection *Human Rights: Fifty Years On* edited by Tony Evans (Manchester, Manchester University Press, 1998) explores some of the most widespread concerns about the state of international human rights law.

[3] Gabriel Marcel, *Creative Fidelity*, 94 (R. Rosthal trans.), New York: Farrar, Strauss, 1964.

[4] Jacques Derrida, *Spectres for Marx* (P. Kamuf trans.) (London, Routledge, 1994) 85.

Two preliminary points are in order. The first concerns the concept of critique. Critique today usually takes the form of the "critique of ideology", of an external attack on the provenance, premises or internal coherence of its target. But its original Kantian aim was to explore the philosophical presuppositions, the necessary and sufficient "conditions of existence" of a particular discourse or practice. This is the type of critique this book aims to exercise first before turning to the critique of ideology or criticism of human rights. What historical trajectory links classical natural law with human rights? Which historical circumstances led to the emergence of natural and later human rights? What are the philosophical premises of the discourse of rights? What is today the nature, function and action of human rights, according to liberalism and its many philosophical critics? Are human rights a form of politics? Are they the postmodern answer to the exhaustion of the grand theories and grandiose political utopias of modernity? Our aim is not to deny the predominantly liberal provenance and the many achievements of the tradition of rights. Whatever the reservations of communitarians, feminists or cultural relativists, rights have become a major component of our philosophical landscape, of our political environment and our imaginary aspirations and their significance cannot be easily dismissed. But while political liberalism was the progenitor of rights, its philosophy has been less successful in explaining their nature. The liberal jurisprudence of rights has been extremely voluminous but little has been added to the canonical texts of Hobbes and Kant. Despite the political triumph of rights, its jurisprudence has disappointedly veered between the celebratory and legitimatory and the repetitive and banal.

Take the problem of human nature and of the subject, a central concern of this book, which could also be described as a long essay on the (legal) subject. The human nature assumed by liberal philosophy is pre-moral. According to Immanuel Kant, the transcendental self, the precondition of action and ground of meaning and value, is a creature of absolute moral duty and lacks any earthly attributes. The assumption of the autonomous and self-disciplining subject is shared by moral philosophy and jurisprudence, but has been turned in neo-Kantianism, from a transcendental presupposition into a heuristic device (Rawls) or a constructive assumption that appears to offer the best description of legal practice (Dworkin). As a result, we are left with "the notion of the human subject as a sovereign agent of choice, a creature whose ends are chosen rather then given, who comes by his aims and purposes by acts of will, as opposed, say, to acts of cognition".[5] This atomocentric approach may offer a premium to liberal politics and law but it is cognitively limited and morally impoverished. Our strategy differs. We will examine from liberal and non-liberal perspectives the main building blocks of the concept of human rights: the human, the subject, the legal person, freedom and right among others. Burke, Hegel, Marx, Heidegger, Sartre, psychoanalytical, deconstructive, semiotic and ethical approaches will be used, first, to deepen our understanding of rights and then to criticise aspects of their operation. No grand synthesis can arise from such a cornucopia of philosophical thought and not much common ground exists between Hegel and Heidegger or Sartre and Lacan. And yet despite the absence of a final and definitive theory of rights a number of common themes emerge, one of which is precisely that there can be no general theory of human rights. The hope is that by following the philosophical critics of liberalism, Kant's original definition of "critique" can be revived and our understanding of human rights rescued from the boredom of analytical common-sense and its evacuation of political vision and moral purpose. This is a textbook for the critical mind and the fiery heart.

Human rights can be examined from two related but relatively distinct main perspectives, a subjective and an institutional. First, they help constitute the (legal) subject as both free and subjected to law. But human rights are also a powerful discourse and practice in domestic and international law. Our approach is predominantly theoretical but it will often be complemented by historical narrative and political and legal commentaries on the contemporary record of human rights. To be sure, criticisms based on the widespread violations of human rights are not easily reconcilable with philosophical critique. Philosophy explores the essence or the meaning of a theme or concept, it constructs indissoluble distinctions and seeks solid grounds,[6] while empirical evidence is soiled with the impurities of contingency, the peculiarities of context and the idiosyncrasies of the observer. On the other, empiricist, hand, human rights were from their inception the political experience of freedom, the expression of the battle to free individuals from external constraint and allow their self-realisation. In this sense, they do not depend on abstract concepts

---

[5] Gaete, op. cit., supra n.2, 125.

[6] For a general discussion of the relationship between continental and Anglo-American philosophy in relation to the concept of freedom, see Jean-Luc Nancy *The Experience of Freedom* (Stanford, Stanford University Press, 1993).

and grounds. For continental philosophy, freedom is, as Marx memorably put it, the "insight into necessity"; for Anglo-American civil libertarians, freedom is resistance against necessity. The theory of civil liberties has moved happily along a limited spectrum ranging from optimistic rationalism to unthinking empiricism. It may be, that the "posthistorical" character of human rights should be sought in this paradox of the triumph of their spirit which has been drowned in universal disbelief about their practice.

But, secondly, have we arrived at the end of history?[7] Over two centuries ago, Kant's *Critiques*, the early manifestos of the Enlightenment, launched philosophical modernity through reason's investigation of its own operation. From that point, Western self-understanding has been dominated by the idea of historical progress through reason. Emancipation means for the moderns the progressive abandonment of myth and prejudice in all areas of life and their replacement by reason. In terms of political organisation, liberation means the subjection of power to the reason of law. Kant's schema was excessively metaphysical and laboriously avoided direct confrontation with the "pathological" empirical reality or with active politics. But Hegel's announcement that the rational and the real coincide identified reason with world history and established a strong link between philosophy, history and politics. Hegel himself vacillated between his early belief that Napoleon personified the world spirit on horseback and his later identification of the end of history in the Prussian State. And while the Hegelian system remained fiercely metaphysical, it was used, most notably by Marx, to establish a (dialectical) link between concepts and abstract determinations and events in the world with the purpose of not just interpreting but changing it.

Hegelianism can easily mutate into a kind of intellectual journalism: the philosophical equivalent of a broadsheet column in which the requirements of reason are declared either to have been fulfilled historically (as in right-wing Hegelians and more recently the musings of Fukuyama) or to be still missing (as in messianic versions of Marxism). In both, the conflict between reason and myth, the two opposing principles of the Enlightenment, will come to an end when human rights, the principle of reason, becomes the realised myth of

---

[7] See Francis Fukuyama, *The End of History and the Last Man* (London, Penguin, 1992) and Derrida's critical comments in *Spectres for Marx*, op.cit., supra n. 4. The German debate is reviewed in Lutz Niethammer, *Posthistoire. Has History Come to an End?* (London, Verso, 1992).

postmodern societies. Myths of course belong to particular communities, traditions and histories; their operation validates through repetition and memory, a genealogical principle of legitimation and the narrative of belonging. Reason and human rights, on the other hand, are universal, they are supposed to transcend geographical and historical differences. If myth gets its legitimatory potential from stories of origin, reason's legitimation is found in the promise of progress expounded in philosophies of history. A forward direction is detected in history which inexorably leads to human emancipation. If myth looks to beginnings, the narrative of reason and human rights looks to *teloi* and ends.

In postmodernity, the idea of history as a single unified process which moves towards the aim of human liberation is no longer credible,[8] and the discourse of rights has lost its earlier coherence and universalism.[9] The widespread popular cynicism about the claims of governments and international organisations about human rights was shared by some of the greatest political and legal philosophers of the twentieth century. Nietzsche's melancholic diagnosis that we have entered the twilight of reason, Adorno and Horkheimer's despair in the *Dialectics of the Enlightenment*[10] and Foucault's statement that modern "man" was a mere drawing on the sands of the ocean of history about to be swept away, appear more realistic than Fukuyama's triumphalism. The Frankfurt sages argued that the conflict between *logos* and *mythos* could not lead to the promised land of freedom, because instrumental reason, one facet of the reason of modernity, had turned into its destructive myth. The dialectic no longer represents the voyage of homecoming of the spirit. Reason's inexorable march and its attempt to pacify the three modern forms of conflict, conflict within self, conflict with others and conflict with nature, led to psychological manipulation and the Gulags, to political totalitarianism and Auschwitz, finally to the nuclear bomb and ecological catastrophe. As a new tragedy unfolds daily in east and west, in Kosovo and East Timor, in Turkey and Iraq, it looks as if mourning more than celebrations becomes the end of the millennium.

Unfortunately political philosophy has abandoned its classical vocation of exploring the theory and history of the good society and

[8] Gianni Vattimo, *The End of Modernity* (Cambridge, Cambridge University Press 1988) *passim*; *The Transparent Society* (Cambridge, Polity 1992) Chapter 1.

[9] Costas Douzinas and Ronnie Warrington with Shaun McVeigh, *Postmodern Jurisprudence. The law of text in the texts of law* (London, Routledge, 1991) Chapters 1 and 5.

[10] (London, Verso, 1979).

has gradually deteriorated into behavioural political science and the doctrinaire jurisprudence of rights. On the side of practice, it is arguable that Home Secretaries should come from the ranks of ex-prisoners or refugees, Social Security Secretaries should have some experience of homelessness and life on the dole, and that Finance Ministers should have suffered the infamy of bankruptcy. Despite the consistent privileging of experience over theory, this is unlikely to happen. Official thinking and action on human rights has been entrusted in the hands of triumphalist column writers, bored diplomats and rich international lawyers in New York and Geneva, people whose experience of human rights violations is confined to being served a bad bottle of wine. In the process, human rights have been turned from a discourse of rebellion and dissent into that of state legitimacy.

At this time of uncertainty and confusion between triumph and disaster, we should take stock of the tradition of human rights. But can we doubt the principle of human rights and question the promise of emancipation of humanity through reason and law, when it seems to be close to its final victory? It should be added immediately that the claim that power relations can be translated fully in the language of law and rights was never fully credible and is now more threadbare than ever. We are always caught in relations of force and answer to the demands of power which, as Foucault argued forcefully, are both carried out and disguised in legal forms. Recent military conflicts and financial upheavals have shown that relations of force and political, class and national struggles have acquired an even more pervasive importance in our globalised world, while democracy and the rule of law are increasingly used to ensure that economic and technological forces are subjected to no other end from that of their continuous expansion. Indeed, one of the reasons that gives normative jurisprudence the unreality, about which law students so often complain, is its total neglect of the role of law in sustaining relations of power and its descent into uninteresting exegesis and apologia for legal technique.

At the time of their birth, human rights, following the radical tradition of natural law, were a transcendent ground of critique against the oppressive and commonsensical. In the 1980s too, in Poland, Czechoslovakia, East Germany, Romania, Russia and elsewhere, the term "human rights" acquired again, for a brief moment, the tonality of dissent, rebellion and reform associated with Thomas Paine, the French revolutionaries, the reform and early socialist movements.

Soon, however, the popular re-definition of human rights was blanked out by diplomats, politicians and international lawyers meeting in Vienna, Beijing and other human rights jamborees to reclaim the discourse from the streets for treaties, conventions and experts. The energy released through the collapse of communism was bottled up again by the new governments and the new mafias in the East which look the same as the governments and mafias of the West.

Against this background, it is highly topical to ask whether the state of human rights is the outcome of intrinsic traits or whether it is a contingent development which will be overcome as the few rogue regimes around the world come to accept the principles of civilised life. To be sure, such enquiries are often treated with incredulity, if not outright hostility; for many, to question human rights is to side with the inhuman, the anti-human and the evil. But if human rights have become the realised myth of postmodern societies, their history demands that we re-assess their promise away from the self-satisfied arrogance of states and liberal apologists and attempt to discover political strategies and moral principles that do not depend exclusively on the universality of the law, the archaeology of myth or the imperialism of reason.

★★★

The tradition of natural law was exhausted well before our century, although it has recently enjoyed something of a revival. Contemporary jurisprudence examines natural law as part of the history of ideas, as an intellectual movement and political doctrine that came to a deserved end in Enlightenment's assault on myth, religion and prejudice. Standard textbooks start the examination of natural law with Antigone's "unwritten laws" and move to the Stoics for whom natural law embodied the "elementary principles of justice which are apparent, they believed, to the 'eye of reason' alone".[11] Cicero enters briefly: "there is a true law, right reason, in accordance with nature; it is unalterable and eternal". He is accompanied, in cameo appearances, by Aquinas, Grotius and Blackstone, whose statement that "natural law is binding all over the globe; no human laws have any validity if contrary to it" is explained in a rather embarrassed fashion.[12] For all these writers, the right and the natural are united in some unclear fashion, although the definition of nature and

---

[11] Maurice Cranston, *What are Human Rights?* (London, Bodley Head, 1973) 10–11. H. McCoubrey, *The Development of Naturalist Legal Theory* (London, Croom Helm, 1987) is a good example of this whistle-tour style of jurisprudence.
[12] Cranston ibid., 11.

the identity of its author differ widely, changing from the purposive cosmos to God, reason, human nature and individual self-interest. The mutation of natural law into natural rights in the seventeenth century is hailed as the first victory of modern reason over the medieval witches and Locke and Bentham, the English contributors to the debate, are acknowledged as the early precursors of human rights. Locke is the modern revitaliser of the moribund tradition, while Bentham is the definitive debunker of any remaining "nonsense on stilts". The potted history of natural law ends with the introduction of the Universal Declaration of Human Rights in 1948, which turned naturalistic "nonsense" into hard-nosed positive rights. For the first time in history, those unwritten, unalterable, eternal, God-given or rational fictions can stop being embarrassed. They have been fully recognised and legislated and enjoy the dignity of law, albeit of a somewhat soft kind. God may have died, according to Nietszche, but at least we have international law. More recently, a new jurisprudence of rights, the explicit purpose of which is to mitigate the moral poverty of legal positivism, has quietly acknowledged the natural law as part of its genealogy.[13]

Like all simplified history, this standard presentation of natural law has some elements of truth, but suffers also from a number of crippling philosophical and historical defects. Its overall perspective is that of evolutionary progressivism: the present is always and necessarily superior over the past, history is the forward march of all-conquering reason, which erases mistakes and combats the prejudices of intellectual positions and political movements. The history of natural law is a typical example of Whig historiography, in which every idea or epoch is inexorably moving towards the present. In this version, the international recognition of human rights marks the end of the ignorant past while retaining and realising, at the same time, its potential for individual freedom and equality. There is an obvious empirical difficulty with this approach: more human rights violations have been committed in this rights-obsessed century than at any other point in history. But it is the philosophical question of historicism that concerns us here.

The problem with historicism can be stated simply: if all historical movement is relentlessly progressive and all thought inescapably historical, in that it can only arise or acquire validity if it becomes

---

[13] Anthony Lisska, *Aquinas's Theory of Natural Law* (Oxford, Clarendon, 1996) Chapters 1, 2 and 3 offer a comprehensive review of the recent return of naturalism in legal and political philosophy.

generally accepted at a particular historical period, no ideals or standards exist outside the historical process and no principle can judge history and its terror. According to the political philosopher Leo Strauss, historicism argues that "all human thought is historical and hence unable to grasp anything eternal".[14] Strauss has argued forcefully that, political philosophy since Macchiavelli, has suffered from an extreme historicism, in which the ideal has been consistently and perilously identified with the real and has lost its critical purchase. Historicism is exemplified by the Hegelian claim that the real and the rational coincide and, in jurisprudence, by the rise of positivism.[15]

For the classical legal tradition, nature was a quasi-objective standard against which law and convention could be criticised. But the cognitive and normative positivisation of modernity has expelled historical transcendence or exteriority. The ceaseless demand that all tradition, order or rule be in accord with human freedom has led to the total demystification not just of the mythical and religious aspects of the world, but of all attempts to judge history from a non-immanent position. In law, this trend is apparent in a number of developments which undermined and eventually destroyed the pre-modern legal cosmos: the abandonment of substantive concepts of justice and their replacement with proceduralist and formal ones; the identification of law with rules posited by the state and the destruction of the older tradition according to which law (*dikaion* or *jus*) is what leads to a just outcome in the relations amongst citizens; the replacement of the idea of a right according to nature by natural and human rights which, as attributes of the subject, are individual and subjective and can hardly establish a strong community. A society based on rights does not recognise duties; it acknowledges only responsibilities arising from the reciprocal nature of rights in the form of limits on rights for the protection of the rights of others.

If the value of human thought is relative to its context and all is doomed to pass with historical progress, human rights too are infected with transience and cannot be protected from change. Only those rights adopted by law (domestic or international) have been introduced into the history of the political institution and can be used, for as long as they last, to defend individuals. The legalism of rights goes hand in hand with the voluntarism of positivism and becomes a very restricted protection against the all-devouring state

---

[14] Leo Strauss, *Natural Law and History* (Chicago, University of Chicago Press, 1965) Chapters 1 and 2 and at 12.

[15] ibid., 319.

legislative and administrative power. Claims about the existence of non-legislated rights are "nonsense upon stilts" and fictions like the "belief in witches and unicorns."[16] As a result, "far from the historical having to be judged by the criteria of rights and of the law, history itself, as we know, becomes the 'tribunal of the world', and right itself must be thought of as based on its insertion in historicity".[17] The symptom of the disease is homoeopathetically declared to also be its cure but, like many less respectable therapies, it leads to an even greater malady.

When nature is no longer the standard of right, all individual desires can be turned into rights. From a subjective perspective, rights in postmodernity have become predications or extensions of self, an elaborate collection of masks the subject places on the face under the imperative to be authentic, "to be herself", to follow her chosen version of identity. Rights are the legal recognition of individual will. People acquire their concrete nature, their humanity and subjectivity by having rights. From the legal point of view, the general agreement that a desire or interest is constitutive of "humanity" suffices for the creation of a new right. In this way, is and ought are collapsed, rights are reduced to the facts and agreements expressed in legislation or, in a more critical vein, to the disciplinary priorities of power and domination.[18] As Strauss puts it starkly, criticising the replacement of transcendent natural right by the socially immanent general will, "if the ultimate criterion of justice becomes the general will, i.e. the will of a free society, cannibalism is as just as its opposite. Every institution hallowed by a folk-mind has to be regarded as sacred".[19]

Legal humanism by uniting right and fact on the terrain of human nature has undoubtedly contributed to the rise of legal positivism and historicism. Historicism is the indispensable companion of individualism and, the fascination with history, the paradoxical result of our obsession with the present. We are interested in history, because we want to understand and control our age and because we believe that history can make humanity transparent to its self-reflection. History is an – inadequate – antidote for those philosophies of suspicion which declared the human finitude and opaqueness. Today, it is

---

[16] Jeremy Bentham, *Anarchical Fallacies* in J. Waldron (ed.), *Nonsense upon Stilts* (London, Methuen, 1987) 53.

[17] Luc Ferry and Alain Renaut, *From the Rights of Man to the Republican Idea* (F. Philip trans.) (Chicago, University of Chicago Press, 1992) 31.

[18] See, Villey, op.cit., supra n. 2, Chapters 1 and 2 *passim*.

[19] Leo Strauss, *What is Political Philosophy* (Chicago, University of Chicago Press, 1959) 51.

impossible not to be historicist, not to believe that everything happens and is validated in history; it is almost impossible not to believe that right is coeval with legal rights. These objections have led to the recent proliferation of theories, which try to rescue the realm of rights from the relativism of historicism by presenting them as the immanent structure of Western societies, the inescapable demands of moral reason or both.[20] Yet a theory of human rights which places all trust in governments, international institutions, judges and other centres of public or private power, including the inchoate values of a society, defies their *raison d'être*, which was precisely to defend people from those institutions and powers. But is a strong theory of rights possible in our highly historicised world? The claim that human rights are universal, transcultural and absolute is counter-intuitive and vulnerable to accusations of cultural imperialism; on the other hand, the assertion that they are the creations of European culture, while historically accurate, deprives them of any transcendent value. From the perspective of late modernity, one can be neither a universalist nor a cultural relativist.

Here we reach the greatest political and ethical problem of our era: if the critique of reason has destroyed the belief in the inexorable march of progress, if the critique of ideology has swept away most remnants of metaphysical credulity, does the necessary survival of transcendence depend on the non-convincing absolutisation of the liberal concept of rights through its immunisation from history? Or, are we condemned to eternal cynicism, in the face of imperial universals and murderous particulars? Sloterdijk has argued that the dominant ideology of postmodernity is cynicism, an *"enlightened false consciousness*. It is that modernised, unhappy consciousness, on which enlightenment has laboured both successfully and in vain. . .Well-off and miserable at the same time, this consciousness no longer feels affected by any critique of ideology; its falseness is already reflexively buffered".[21] The gap between the triumph of human rights ideology and the disaster of their practice is the best expression of postmodern cynicism, the combination of enlightenment with resignation and apathy and, with a strong feeling of political impasse and existential claustrophobia, of an exitlessness in the midst of the most mobile society. The only recommendation offered by a critic of human rights is to adopt ironical distance towards those who ask us to take

---

[20] See Chapter 9 below.
[21] Peter Sloterdijk, *Critique of Cynical Reason* (M. Eldred trans.) (London, Verso, 1988) 5.

rights seriously and to accept the "contingency, uncertainty and painful responsibility" for forms of "civil life and civilisation that will eventually perish".[22] Irony of course is one of the most potent weapons of the cynicism and self-serving nihilism of power and power-holders and can hardly be used on its own as a political pro-gramme of resistance to cynicism. But can there be an ethics that respects the pluralism of values and communities? Can we discover in history a non-absolute conception of the good, that could be used as a quasi-transcendent principle of critique? The last part of this book begins this most difficult and pressing of tasks, of seeking in history a standpoint critical of historicism.

The meaning of history and of historical determination frames a second and subsidiary question. What is the link, if any, between the classical tradition of natural law and the modern tradition of natural and human rights?[23] The French Declaration of Rights started a trend by proclaiming these rights as "natural, inalienable and sacred". It was followed by the American Declaration of Independence, according to which "all men are created equal, [and] are endowed by their Creator with unalienable Rights", a statement repeated verbatim by Article 1 of the 1948 Universal Declaration of Human Rights. These rather extreme statements present natural and human rights as a direct continuation of the classical law tradition. They have received wide support from liberal philosophers. John Finnis claims that rights are extrapolations from "principles always inherent in the natural law tradition".[24] Alan Gewirth believes that all human beings, by virtue of their humanity, recognise in themselves and others, rights to free-dom and well-being. He goes on to argue that rights exist even if they do not receive "clear or explicit recognition or elucidation".[25] Jack Donnelly argues that while human rights were conceived in the sev-enteenth and eighteenth centuries, they enjoy a universal character

---

[22] Gaete, op. cit., supra n. 2, 172

[23] V. Black, "On connecting natural rights with natural law", Persona y Derecho 1990, 183–209. Fred Miller has recently argued that Aristotle's theory of justice has an implicit doctrine of natural rights, in F. Miller, Nature, Justice, and Right in Aristotle's Politics (Oxford University Press, 1995). Brian Tierney has also argued that a natural rights theory could be formulated in Aristotelian language but it was not. Tierney claims that natural rights theo-ries developed, first in the early Middle Age well before the generally accepted opinion that they hail from the seventeenth century. Brian Tierney, The Idea of Natural Rights (Atlanta Georgia, Scholars Press, 1997) Chapters 1 and 11. See Chapters 2,3 and 4 below.

[24] John Finnis, Natural Law and Natural Rights (Oxford, Clarendon, 1980) passim.

[25] Alan Gewirth, Reason and Morality (University of Chicago Press, 1978) 99; and Human Rights (University of Chicago Press, 1982) Introduction and Chapter 1.

that makes them applicable to all societies.[26] For Michael Perry, finally, the idea of human rights is "ineliminably religious" and indissolubly linked with Catholic and scholastic versions of natural law.[27]

Leo Strauss, Michel Villey and Alasdair MacIntyre deny the connection. For the neo-Aristotelians, the political philosophers of the seventeenth century created a radically new moral and political discourse based on individual rights which destroyed the classical tradition of natural law. Natural rights are creations of modernity and their origins are successively placed in the early Middle Ages (Tierney), the fourteenth century (Villey), or the seventeenth (MacPherson, MacIntyre, Shapiro and pretty much everyone else).[28] Again, the philosopher credited with the crucial step in the transformation from natural law to natural rights varies from William of Ockham to Grotius, Hobbes or Locke. Behind this periodisation and accreditation lies the famous quarrel between the "ancients and moderns". Strauss, Villey and MacIntyre believe that the passage from the ancients to the moderns was catastrophic. For MacIntyre, "natural or human rights are fictions" inventions of modern individualism and should be discarded.[29] Kenneth Minogue, Maurice Cranston and John Finnis, on the other hand, see this radical change as a necessary stage in the process of human emancipation.

Throughout this book, it will be argued that perhaps both the relativism of historicism and the ahistorical universalism of liberal theorists, for whom all societies and cultures have been or must be subjected to the discipline of rights, are wrong. Historicism does not accept that history can be judged; for the rights fanatics, history ends in the universal acceptance of human rights which turn political conflict into technical litigation. For the former, the hope of transcendence of the present has been banned while, for the latter, transcendence still survives in the outposts of empire in the form of the aspiration to achieve a Western-type individualist consumer society. To defend the idea of transcendence without abandoning the discipline of history, we need to re-examine the origin and trajectory of natural law.

---

[26] Jack Donnelly, *Universal Human Rights in Theory and Practice* (Ithaca, Cornell University Press, 1989) 88–106; Louis Henkin, *The Age of Rights* (New York, Columbia University Press, 1990) Introduction and Chapter 1.

[27] Michael Perry, *The Idea of Human Rights* (New York, Oxford University Press, 1998) Chapter 1.

[28] See below Chapters 3 and 4.

[29] Alasdair MacIntyre, *After Virtue* (London, Duckworth, 1980) 70.

From this perspective, the next four chapters offer a genealogy of human rights, in the form of an alternative history of natural law, for which the promise of human dignity and social justice has not been met and can never be fully realised. Our main guides will be the conservative political philosopher Leo Strauss, the Catholic legal philosopher and historian Michel Villey, and the Marxist philosopher Ernst Bloch. Natural law represents a constant in the history of ideas, namely the struggle for human dignity in freedom against the infamies, degradations and humiliations visited on people by established powers, institutions and laws. The political philosophers Luc Ferry and Alain Renaut have accused Strauss and Villey of extreme anti-modernism and have claimed that their work amounts to a call for a return to a pre-modern Aristotelian universe.[30] The idea of a return to the ancients is meaningless and cannot be imputed, I believe, to our authors. In any case, the premise behind our brief history is neither the superiority of the past nor the inevitably progressive present, but the promise of the future. Young Marx wrote that the task of philosophy is to achieve "a humanised nature and a naturalised humanity". This is also the unfulfilled potential of natural law and human rights which, to use Ernst Bloch's evocative phrase, expresses the "forward-pressing, not-yet-determined nature of human being".[31] The re-telling of the history of natural law tries to follow Bloch's impulse and tease out of the tradition its often concealed concern for the unfinished person of the future for whom justice matters. Natural right was written out of modern law because of its critical potential. Its tradition unites critics and dissidents more than any other philosophy or political programme. Natural law is too important to leave to theologians and historians of ideas and the narrative in the first part aims to rescue from the tradition those elements, often suppressed in the "official" histories, which link natural law and contemporary human rights struggles. The substantive and methodological stakes are high: is there a place for transcendence in a disenchanted world? What type of rights and by extension of social bond can a critical attitude adopt after the exhaustion of the great modern narratives of liberation?

★★★

The triumph of human rights was declared after the collapse of communism. Paradoxically however this coincided with the "death of

[30] Ferry and Renaut, op.cit., supra n. 17, Chapter 1.

[31] Ernst Bloch, *Natural Law and Human Dignity* (Dennis J. Schmidt trans.) (Cambridge Mass, MIT Press, 1988) xviii.

man" as the sovereign centre of the world announced, in the seventies and early 1980s, by social theory and philosophy. In that period, the highly influential thought of Marx, Nietzsche and Freud and their followers, the great philosophers of "suspicion" according to Paul Ricoeur, successfully challenged the assumptions of liberal humanism, "the philosophy of the progressive realisation of the 'whole man' throughout history".[32] Humanism explores what is right according to human nature, in its natural dignity or scientific objectivity and turns "man" into the end of historical evolution, the standard of right reason and the principle of political and social institutions. According to humanism, humanity has two unique characteristics: it can determine its own destiny and, secondly, it is fully conscious of itself, transparent to itself through self-observation and reflection. Both premises were seriously undermined by the great critics of modernity. Marx debunked the belief, always a little suspect to European ears, that irrespective of social and economic background, people can acquire riches and control their destiny through the operations of the market. Nietzsche and his disciples Heidegger and Foucault, destroyed the claim that the enlightenment values of rigorous method, bourgeois self-reliance and Christian piety could lead to endless progress, harmonise humanity and its environment and make knowledge a universal human good. Finally, the psychoanalysis of Freud and his epigones fatally undermined the belief that we have mastery and control over our selves. If anything, the "self is split" and lacking, the creation of forces and influences beyond our control and even comprehension. From the social and economic environment to the structures of language and communication to the unconscious, our century has re-discovered fate in the form of finitude and opaqueness: destiny has been re-interpreted as social determination or individual necessity and, individual freedom has been placed in a permanent state of siege, threatened not so much by dictators of left or right but by elements and forces which either have a constitutive role in the creation of individuals or lurk in the recesses of self, making themselves known when reason sleeps, in dreams, jokes and linguistic slips. "Opaque with regard to itself, and finding itself thrown into a world founded on other principles, the subject – thought by early modern philosophy to be the foundation both of itself and of reality – was shattered. With it were undermined the val-

---

[32] Lucien Seve, *Man in Marxist Theory* (Sussex, Harvester Press, 1978) 65.

ues of humanism: self-foundation, consciousness, mastery, free will, autonomy."[33]

But the announcement of the "death of man" has been accompanied by the most protracted campaign to re-claim the individual, as the triumphant centre of our postmodern world and to declare freedom, in the form of autonomy or self-determination, as the organising ideal of our legal and political systems. We have seen this in the endlessly proclaimed return of (to) the subject, in the importance of identity and identity-related politics, in the return of morality to politics and of humanism to law. In liberal jurisprudence, the return to the subject is evident, on the right, in the recent domination of rights theories and, on the left, in the moralism of political correctness. While philosophy and social theory insist on the social construction of self and on the role of structure, system and language in the organisation of the world, the desire to return to a pristine condition of selfhood and to re-instate its freedom and propriety, deconstructed and demystified by the philosophies of suspicion, returned dramatically to law. But can the sovereign subject of rights be squared with the deconstruction of subjectivity?

This is not an idle question. Rights were the first public acknowledgement of the sovereignty of the subject and influenced strongly the modern "metaphysics of subjectivity".[34] The "anti-humanist" philosophers did not discuss human rights at great length, with a few exceptions.[35] On the other hand, from Adorno to Arendt and from Lyotard to Levinas, they all commented on the way in which humanism can be turned into the inhuman, its dream of a rationally emancipated society transformed into the nightmare of totalitarian administration or bureaucratic technocracy. Foucault, Lyotard and Derrida became repeatedly involved with political and human rights

[33] Alain Renaut, *The Era of the Individual: A Contribution to a History of Subjectivity* (M.B. DeBeviose and F. Philip trans.) (Princeton NJ, Princeton University Press, 1997) xxvii.

[34] See Chapters 7 and 8.

[35] Michel Foucault is the most obvious. He was equally critical of the philosophy of subjectivity and of the legal and contractual presentation of power. Foucault argued that the theory of right disguised disciplinary practices and domination and hoped to show "how right is, in a general way, the instrument of this domination – which scarcely needs saying – but also to show the extent to which and the forms on which right . . . transmits and brings into play not relations of sovereignty but of domination. My general project has been, in essence, to reverse the mode of analysis followed by the entire discourse of right . . . to invert it, to show . . . how force relations have been naturalised in the name of right". Michel Foucault, "Two Lectures: Lecture Two: 14 January 1976" in *Power/Knowledge* C. Gordon ed. (K. Soper trans.) New York: Pantheon, 1980, 95–6. On the other hand, Foucault more than many a philosopher was closely and continuously involved with diverse rights struggles.

campaigns. It looks as if philosophical anti-humanism and the defence of the human are natural allies. But this linkage of the most severe critique of humanism with the intellectual and political struggles for dignity and equality infuriated liberals. Alain Renaut, a French liberal political philosopher who, with Luc Ferry, spearheaded a number of ill-mannered political attacks on poststructuralist philosophers, admitted light-heartedly about his accusations that "though we have often insisted on rigorously examining the problem of subjectivity with reference to human rights, we did not mean to judge all possible philosophies by a sort of 'litmus test' that would measure their compatibility with the 1789 Declaration of the Rights of Man – posing, as it were, as intellectual magistrates awarding certificates of civic responsibility".[36]

And yet these paradoxical links and superficially unnatural alliances could perhaps be explained. This is a main task of this book. "Human rights" is a combined term. They refer to the human, to humanity or human nature and are indissolubly linked with the movement of humanism and its legal form. But the reference to "rights" indicates their implication with the discipline of law, with its archaic traditions and quaint procedures. Legal institutions occasionally move in tandem with the aspirations of political philosophy or the plans of political science but more often the two diverge. The "rights of man" entered the world scene when the two traditions came together for a brief symbolic moment in early modernity, represented by the writings of Hobbes, Locke and Rousseau, by the French Declaration of the Rights of Man and Citizen and by the American Declaration of Independence and Bill of Rights. The convergence of political philosophy and constitution-making established political and legal modernity, but it was short-lived. Philosophy, law and science soon diverged and moved in different directions to re-combine again, after the Second World War, in the new configuration of human rights.

Legal systems are obsessed with the story of their origins, the foundational moment which endows them with validity and consistency. Peter Goodrich has distinguished between "ideational" and institutional sources of law. Ideational sources refer to the claims a legal system makes to "an external and absolute justification for legal regulation".[37] Institutional sources, on the other hand, are empirically verifiable institutions, such as custom, statute, constitution and prece-

---

[36] Renaut, op. cit., supra n. 33, xxviii.
[37] Peter Goodrich, *Reading the Law* (Oxford, Blackwell, 1988) Chapter 1.

dent. The introduction of human nature and its rights in the legal discourse of the eighteenth century marked a new ideational source.
The legal institution with its history, tradition and logic had to
accommodate the extravagant claims of this revolutionary idea. An
important consequence of this new combination of philosophy, history and legal practice was that the concept of human nature is pulled
towards two contradictory positions. It is asked to form the principle
of law and politics, in other words, to become the new ideational
source of law, to come before and found the law. But the entitlements of empirical people remain the grant and their concrete nature
the creation of the legal system. Hobbes remarked in the *Leviathan*
that "*Persona* in latine signifies the *disguise, or outward appearance of* a
man, counterfeited on the Stage; and sometimes more particularly
that part of it, which disguiseth the face, a mask or Visard: And from
the Stage, hath been translated to any Representer of speech and
action, as well in Tribunalls, as Theaters . . . in which sense Cicero
useth it where he saies, *Unus sustineo tres Personas; Mei, Adversarii &
Judicis*".[38] People must be brought before the law in order to acquire
rights, duties, powers and competencies which give the subject legal
personality. The legal person is the creation of legal or theatrical artifice, the product of an institutional performance. In the discourse of
human rights, this *persona* or mask, the creation of law, must be transformed into law's progenitor or principle, the subject who comes to
life on the stage of law must also come before the law and support its
maker. The three persons of Cicero, the "me" or ego, the legal subject and the judge are the three facets who, fused in one, will form
the holy trinity of the human, the law and its subjects, and create the
ground principle of modern man, father and son, *devant la loi*, both
before and after the law.[39]

In this sense, human rights are both creations and creators of
modernity, the greatest political and legal invention of modern
political philosophy and jurisprudence. Their modern character can
be traced in all the essential characteristics. First, they mark a profound turn in political thought from duty to right, from *civitas* and
communitas to civilisation and humanity. Secondly, they reverse the
traditional priority between the individual and society. While classical and medieval natural law expressed the right order of the *cosmos*

---

[38] Hobbes, *Leviathan* (Richard Tuck ed.) (Cambridge University Press, 1996) Chapter 16,
112.

[39] Jacques Derrida, "Devant la Loi", in A. Edoff (ed.), *Kafka and the Contemporary Critical
Performance: Centenary Readings* (Bloomington, Indiana University Press) 1989.

and of human communities within it, an order that gave the citizen his place, time and dignity, modernity emancipates the human person, turns him from citizen to individual and establishes him at the centre of social and political organisation and activity. The citizen comes of age when he is released from traditional bonds and commitments to act as an individual, who follows his desires and applies his will to the natural and social world. This release of human will and its enthronement as the organising principle of the world had a number of important political implications. Unconstrained freedom can destroy itself. Freed will must be restrained by laws and sanctions, the only limits it understands. These are not intrinsic or integral to it but empirical and external. Freedom and coercion, law and violence are born in the same act. It was the great achievement of Hobbes, the first and probably the best theorist of liberalism and modern natural rights, to realise that when human nature becomes sovereign and unfettered, it needs as its counterpoint a public power which shares in all particulars the characteristics of the undivided and singular free will of the individual and literalises his metaphorical unlimited power. The sovereignty of unshackled will finds its perfect complement and mirror image in the sovereignty of the state. The Leviathan is the mirror image and the perfect, all too perfect partner of emancipated man.

The road from classical natural law to contemporary human rights is therefore marked by two analytically independent but historically linked developments. The first transferred the standard of right from nature to history and eventually to humanity or civilisation. This process can be called the positivisation of nature. Its reverse side is the – incomplete – legalisation of politics which made positive law the terrain of both power and its critique. The second trend, closely linked with the first, was the legalisation of desire. Man was made the centre of the world, his free will became the principle of social organisation, his infinite and unstoppable desire was given public recognition. This twin process determined the trajectory which linked historically but separated politically the classical discourse of nature and the contemporary practice of human rights. But human rights are also the weapon of resistance to state omnipotence and an important antidote to the inherent ability of sovereign power to negate the autonomy of the individuals in whose name it came into existence. Human rights are internally fissured: they are used as the defence of the individual against a state power built in the image of an individual with absolute rights. It is this paradox at the heart of human rights which both moves their history and makes their realisation impossible. Human Rights have "only paradoxes to offer"; their energy comes from their aporetic nature.[40]

[40] The phrase comes from a letter of Olympe de Gouges, the author of the 1791 Declaration of the Rights of Woman and Citizen. Joanne Scott in *Only Paradoxes to Offer: French Feminists and the Rights of Man* (Cambridge, Mass., Harvard University Press, 1996) at 4, uses the expression to describe the position of women in revolutionary France. Our point is more general: the whole field of human rights is characterised by paradoxes and aporias.

2

A Brief History of Natural Law:
I. The Classical Beginnings

Despite wars, genocides, holocausts, the ever more atrocious and imaginative ways oppression and exploitation discover, humanity still believes that a state of individual and social grace exists, even when, particularly when, the wolfish part of man is at its worse. This quest for the just society has been associated from classical times with natural law, the "unwritten laws" of Antigone.

Natural law is a notoriously open-ended concept and its understanding is clouded in historical and moral uncertainty. According to Erik Wolf, there have been some seventeen meanings of the word *naturale* and fifteen of *jus* and their permutations lead to some 255 definitions of natural law.[1] But whatever its different meanings, natural law was for many centuries the capital city of the province of jurisprudence and political philosophy. Its thinking was profoundly hermeneutical, it attended to ends and purposes, meanings and values, virtue and duty. Today nature and law, concepts inextricably twinned for most of the Western tradition, have been radically separated and assigned to different even opposing fields. Classical nature has been replaced by a meaningless natural world which has been draped with the "dignity" of objectivity and the stubbornness of facts. Its study by the natural sciences enjoys a status and legitimacy which eludes the social sciences, philosophy or jurisprudence. Nature itself, however, has been reduced to inert matter, the unresponsive target for human intervention and control.

The modern laws of nature are universal, immutable and eternal, a set of regularities or of repeated patterns. The law of gravity or the second law of thermodynamics are followed in practice, in the sense that one cannot choose to disobey them. They are there, brute facts, verifiable or falsifiable logical abstractions deriving from common observations of natural phenomena. If natural law is of the same

[1] Brian Tierney, *The Idea of Natural Rights* (Atlanta, Scholars Press, 1997) 48.

order, its norms would be something like an independent logical and moral ensemble, a set of norms that both is and ought to be obeyed by people. Natural law would be an objective order of rules or norms something like the natural laws of modern science. Its application, the observable pattern of phenomena that can be subsumed under the concept of law, would link external nature, social and political institutions and the inner life of individuals. Did the Greeks, who first introduced the idea into the universe of political philosophy and jurisprudence, understand natural law as an immutable set of rules? What is the meaning of natural law for the philosophical imagination of the Greeks and the juristic creativity of the Romans?

I. NATURE AND JUSTICE IN CLASSICAL GREECE

Greek philosophy offers a convenient starting point for exploring the genealogy of human right. The surviving philosophical fragments of the Presocratics, the earliest philosophers, are full of references to justice, injustice and right. Heracleitos believed that things regarded as opposites are in fact united and cannot exist without their contrary. There is no upward path without the downward (fr. 69), there would be no heat if there were no cold (fr. 39), justice would be unknown were it not for injustice (fr. 60).[2] And in his most famous fragment, Heracleitos tells us that "war is universal and justice is strife". But if justice is strife, its cessation would mean the end of the world. The oldest extant text of Western philosophy is a fragment by Anaximander on justice, which has become the subject of an important philosophical and philological debate culminating in a famous essay by Heidegger.[3] The fragment reads: "but where things have their origin, there too their passing away occurs according to necessity; for they are judged and make reparation (*didonai diken*) to one another for their injustice (*adikia*) according to the ordinance of time".[4] An archaic, original injustice, an *adikia* that comes before

---

[2] Hayek believes that Heracleitos is the earliest philosopher to emphasise the primary character of injustice. However this is inaccurate as the Anaximander fragment is earlier. F. A. Hayek, *Law, Legislation, Liberty*, Vol. 2 (London, Routledge and Kegan Paul, 1976) 162, n.9 and see J. Burnet, *Early Greek Philosophy* (4th ed., London, A & C Black, 1930) 166.

[3] Martin Heidegger, "The Anaximander Fragment" in *Early Greek Thinking* (D. F. Crell and F. Capuzzi trans.) (New York: Harper and Row, 1975).

[4] This is our translation and emphasises the legal and moral aspects of the fragment. Heidegger's essay discusses the various (mis)translations of the fragment. Nietzsche in his early but posthumously published *Philosophy in the Tragic Age of the Greeks* (M. Cowan trans.)

time marks the beginning of beings and imposes a debt or culpability on people, things and institutions. History (the ordinance of time) is the field in which the reparation or restitution of the originary injustice will be attempted and will fail as everything will return of necessity to its original injustice. But while injustices were clearly felt, in Homeric times, the development of a theory of justice had to wait the discovery of nature.

Archaic Greece did not distinguish between law and convention or right and custom. Custom is a strong cement, it binds families and communities firmly but it can also numb. Without external standards, the development of a critical approach towards traditional authority is impossible, the given goes unchallenged and the slaves stay in line, a view expressed by Heracleitos, who said that justice and injustice are man-made and God does not care about either. Leo Strauss has argued that "originally, the authority par excellence or the root of all authority is the ancestral. Through the discovery of nature, the claim of the ancestral is uprooted; philosophy appeals from the ancestral to the good, to that which is good intrinsically, to that which is good by nature".[5] Greek philosophy, nature and the idea of the just were born together in an act of resistance against traditional authority and its injustices. This development is apparent in the history of the word *dike*, the key Greek term for a cluster of concepts and words connoting the rightful, lawful or just. In archaic Greek, *dike* meant the primordial order, the way of the world.[6] It included *nomoi* and *thesmoi,* customs and norms of conduct which, according to Parmenides, were binding on both gods and mortals. *Nomos*, the word later used for law, originally had the same meaning as *ethos*. As

(Chicago, Regnery, 1962) translates it thus: "Whence things have their origin, they must also pass away according to necessity; for they must pay the penalty and be judged for their injustice according to the ordinance of time". The classical translation of *Fragment of Presocratics* by Diels states that "but where things have their origin, there too their passing away occurs according to necessity; for they pay recompense and penalty to one another for their recklessness, according to firmly established time" quoted in Heidegger, op.cit., supra n.3, 41. Finally J. M. Robinson, *An Introduction to Early Greek Philosophy* (Boston, Houghton Mifflin, 1968) p.34 translates it as follows: "Into those things from which existing things have their coming into being, their passing away too, takes place according to what must be; for they make reparation to one another for their injustice according to the ordinance of time".

[5] Leo Strauss, *Natural Law and History* (Chicago, University of Chicago Press, 1965) 91.

[6] For Heidegger *dike* is "not justice but the overpowering structure of Being; it emerges and shines in its permanent presence as *physis* and is gathered together in its collectedness as *logos*", Costas Douzinas and Ronnie Warrington, *Justice Miscarried* (Edinburgh, Edinburgh University Press, 1994) 88. Heidegger discusses *dike, physis* and *nomos* in Martin Heidegger, *An Introduction to Metaphysics* (R. Mannheim trans.) (New York, Doubleday Anchor, 1961).

Heidegger has shown, the *nomoi* were initially the pastures of horses and wandering for pasturage, later the word took on he meaning of possession and regular usage, indicating both habit and accepted practice and movement, before settling in its classical legal meaning. By the time of the classical period, the meaning of *dike* too had changed to rightful judgment, *dikaion* was the right and just and *dikaios* the rightful person.[7]

The passage from the archaic concept of *dike* and *nomos* to the classical *dikaion* and *physikos nomos* (natural law) is punctuated by the discovery of nature. *Physis* as a normative and legal concept is not used in the extant literature before the fourth century. Sophocles in *Antigone* uses instead the term unwritten laws.[8] The idea of natural law appeared fully developed, for the first time, in Aristotle who in his *Rhetoric* wrote that:

> by law I mean on the one hand particular law and on the other general law, special being that defined by each group in relation to itself, this being either unwritten or written down, and the general law being that of nature. For there is something of which we all have an inkling, being a naturally universal right and wrong, even if there is no community between the two parties nor contract, to which Sophocles' *Antigone* seems to be referring.[9]

---

[7] According to Liddell and Scott, *Greek-English Lexicon* (6th ed., Oxford, Clarendon, 1992) *dike* means custom, usage; right as depends on custom, law; a judgment; (later) lawsuit, the trial of a case. *Dikaion* means a regular way of living; due form; (later) rightful, lawful, just.

[8] It wasn't Zeus, not in the least
who made this proclamation, not to me
Nor did that Justice (*Dike*), dwelling with the gods
beneath the earth, ordain such laws for men.
Nor did I think your [Creon's] edicts had such force
that you, a mere man could override
the great unwritten and certain laws of the gods.
They are alive, not just today or yesterday;
they live forever, and no one knows.
when they were first legislated.
Sophocles, *Antigone* in *Three Theban Plays* (R. Fagles trans.) (London, Penguin, 1984) 446–57. The term *physis* is first related to law, in Demosthenes' oration *"Peri Stephanou"* (On the Crown, C. Vince and J. Vince trans.) (London, Heinemann, 1974). A similar formulation is found in Aristotle, *The Art of Rhetoric* (H.C. Lawson-Tancred trans.) (London, Penguin, 1991) A 1368b: "The law is either particular or common. By particular law I mean that written down in a constitution, and by general I mean those unwritten laws which are held to be agreed by all". This and the quotation immediately below are the earliest references to link the common, unwritten laws with nature.

[9] ibid., 1373b.

Nature as a critical concept acquired philosophical currency in the fifth century when it was used by the Sophists against custom and law and, by Socrates and Plato in order to combat their moral relativism and restore the authority of reason. The Sophists represented the privileged youth of Athens who, in equal measure, despised the old religious taboos and the constant training for war. They set *physis* against *nomos* and individual opinion against tradition and gave *physis* a normative meaning, in which "to reason" meant to "criticise".[10] They argued that the *nomoi* are social conventions and laws and not part of the natural order. Nature as the highest norm justifies, in a rather eclectic way, whatever the instincts lead humans to desire.[11] Callicles in *Gorgias* and Thrasymachus in the *Republic* anticipated Nietzsche, when they argued that human laws were an invention of the weak in order to protect themselves from the strong. The nature of the Sophists combined the savage with the universal and stood both for the right of the strongest and for equality for all. With the Sophists, the critique of law and the figure of the naturally free and self-serving individual entered the historical scene.

Plato's response to the sophist challenge was to re-define the normative character of nature by showing that, far from contradicting law, it sets the fundamental norm of each being. Plato's late dialogue, the *Laws*, extended the concept of *physis* to include the whole cosmos. But this was not a return to the pre-classical *dike*. The new order was that of the soul and of the transcendent spiritual world it inhabits; it was the highest and most natural order and animated the empirical cosmos.[12] The distinction between the two natures followed the Platonic opposition between the worlds of forms and reality but acquired political significance much later. As Louis Dupré argues, it "laid the philosophical basis for the later attempts to integrate the classical concept of nature with that of a Hebrew-Christian Creator beyond nature".[13] But that had to wait. The significance of the debate between Plato and the Sophists was that by juxtaposing *physis*

---

[10] Ernst Bloch, *Natural Law and Human Dignity* (D. J. Schmidt trans.) (Cambridge, Mass, MIT Press, 1988) 7–9.

[11] The classical treatment of *nomos* in Greek thought is Jacqueline de Romilly, *La Loi dans la pensée Grecque: des origines à Aristote*, (Paris: Les Belles Lettres, 1971); see also Martha Nussbaum, "The Betrayal of Convention: A reading of Euripides' *Hecuba*", in *The Fragility of Goodness* (Cambridge, Cambridge University Press, 1986) 397–421.

[12] Plato, *The Laws* (T. J. Saunders trans.) (London, Penguin, 1988): "When [the ignorant] use the term 'nature', they mean the process by which the primary substances were created. But if it can be shown that soul came first, not fire or air, and that it was one of the first things to be created, it will be quite correct to say that soul is preeminently natural", 892 c.

[13] Louis Dupré, *Passage to Modernity* (New Haven, Yale University Press, 1993) 17.

and *nomos* in their various meanings, it opened the whole basis of classical civilisation and institutional existence to radical questioning and innovation and gave rise to political philosophy and jurisprudence. Turning nature into norm or into the standard of right was the greatest early step of civilisation but also a cunning trick against priests and rulers.[14] To this day, when knowledge and reason are subjected to authority they are called "theology" or "legal learning" but they cannot be the philosophy practised by the Greeks.[15]

Classical natural right was radically anti-historicist, or to use a term anachronistically, it had something "objective" about it. But as the radical split between the subject and object, a mainstay of modernity, had not occurred yet, the right reason revealed in nature had none of its modern characteristics. Unlike "objective" statements, natural right was neither static, nor certain, nor did it mirror an inert nature. To understand its meaning, we need to bracket our contemporary assumptions about nature and culture and place it within the teleological cosmos of antiquity.

Classical ontology believed that the cosmos, the universe and everything in it, animate or inanimate, has a purpose, *telos* or end. The Greek cosmos included the *physis* of beings, the *ethos* of social mores, the *nomos* of customs and laws and, most importantly, the *logos* or rational foundation of all that exists, which founded the cosmos as a closed but harmonious and ordered universe. Entities were arranged in a hierarchical way, each holding its unique and differential place within the overall scheme according to its proper degree of perfection, "at the top the incorruptible imponderable luminous spheres, at the bottom, the heavy, opaque material bodies".[16] The end of a being determined its place in the whole and was identical with its nature. "The nature of each is his purpose" wrote Aristotle and Aquinas, in his *Commentary on Aristotle's Physics*, repeated that

---

[14] The French political philosophers Ferry and Renaut have argued that Strauss is an extreme anti-modernist who advocates the return to classical culture. They have totally missed however the critical intent of Strauss' analysis. This is necessary for their argument, according to which, Strauss' naturalism is a rather sterile authoritarianism and cannot be rescued from Aristotelian cosmology. Luc Ferry and Alain Renaut, *From the Rights of Man to the Republican Idea* (Franklin Philip trans.) (Chicago, University of Chicago Press, 1992) 32–4. For a response to their peculiar Heideggerian liberalism, see Bernard Bourgeois, *Philosophie et droits de l'homme* (Paris, P.U.F., 1990).

[15] Strauss, op.cit., supra n. 5, 92.

[16] Blandine Barret-Kriegel, *Les Droits de l'homme et le droit naturel* (Paris, P.U.F., 1989) 46. It should be emphasised here that this cosmology is intrinsically linked with the inegalitarian nature of classical natural right and of its societies. For Aristotle, slavery was natural and therefore not an affront to natural right.

nature acts for an end.[17] The nature of a thing or being is, first, its efficient cause, its *energeia* or potential for perfection, secondly, its developing essence and, finally, its end or aim, the purpose towards which it moves, its actualised potential when it matures and becomes a perfect specimen of its kind.[18] The end or *telos* is a state of existence at which disposition or potency reaches fulfilment or perfection. The nature of the acorn, for example, is to become a mature oak tree, the purpose of the vine to produce sweet-tasting grapes. Similarly, the purpose of a human is to achieve his potential, to pass from the nascent to his fully developed state: a child's end is to become a virtuous adult, a carpenter's to produce excellent tables, a cobbler's the perfect sandals. Aristotle's concept of nature was therefore rich and complex: both the efficient and final cause, the germ present at birth and the aim beings tend to realise naturally.

But if the nature of a thing or being is its state of fulfilment or perfection and every stage in life is a station from its transient presence to its natural end, being cannot be distinguished from becoming and essence from existence. Nature itself, unlike the inert matter of modern science, represents the principle of motion in a purposeful cosmos, in which acorns, lambs and infants can only be understood as a developing order of meaningful and future-looking interrelations. For Aristotle, *physis* was motion, "a source or cause of being moved and of being at rest in that to which it belongs primarily in virtue of itself".[19] Being was always on the way, in a journey that will never end, because perfection was always a step too far, a state always still to come.

Observing the nature of the cosmos and of things and beings in it involves imputing on them aims, purposes and ends politically, in the *polis*, always in conjunction with other things and beings. These teloi are not arbitrary; they are determined by the dispositional characteristics of each being, by its order of needs and wants which, by pointing to its natural constitution, creates a strong moral duty to strive and achieve it. The good of an entity is the completion of the move towards its end, the ever-deferred transition from potency to actuality. A being's nature corresponds to its specific operation or work; a

---

[17] An account of Aristotle's teleology is found in Alan Gothhelf, "Aristotle's Conception of Final Causality", 30/2 *Review of Metaphysics*, 226–54, 1976. For Aquinas's Aristotelianism, see Anthony Lisska, *Aquinas's Theory of Natural Law* (Oxford, Clarendon, 1996) Chapter 4.

[18] Aristotle, *Metaphysics* (D. Bosctock trans.) (Oxford, Clarendon, 1994) 4.4, 1051a7; *Politics* (H. Rakham trans.) (Cambridge Mass, Loeb, 1990) I, 1, 1252a.

[19] *Physics* (D. Bosctock trans.) (Oxford, Oxford University Press, 1996) II, 1,192b, 21–3.

being is good if it does its proper work well, if it follows its nature. Its perfection constitutes its well being or *eu zein* and offers precise guidance in ethical and practical matters. In this sense, the good life is life according to nature and no separation between is and ought exists. The natural teleology of the ancients, their purposeful nature, could thus become the basis of a strong ethics of virtue and value. Right according to nature is what contributes to the being's perfection, what keeps it moving towards its end; wrong or unjust is what violently removes it from its place, disrupts its natural trajectory and "prevents it from being what it is".[20] Natural right is therefore both transcendent to reality, an "ideal", and can be confidently discovered through observation and reasoning, although this does not make it "objective" in the modern sense. The idea of an eternal inert nature is totally alien to early natural law.

Within this broad framework, the various schools of classical philosophy interpreted nature differently. For the Sophists, *physis* was the essence of things which was not sacred or solemn, but simply what endures through change and remains constant behind diversity. Their philosophical successors, the Cynics and the Hedonists, associated nature with the simplicity of animality and the indulgence of private pleasures. The Cynics fought tradition and artifice in its many forms and attacked all institutional invention, from luxurious living to property, family and the polis. The Hedonists taught pleasure; against the dog-life of Diogenes, Aristippus led a life of luxury and preached that natural is what contributes to happiness, the only criterion for judging the value of institutions. Depending on whether the character of innate nature was meant to suffer or enjoy, frugality and pleasure became the twin aims of natural law. To this day, the Cynics and the Hedonists are the forefathers of many revolutionary movements, although preaching the universal right to pleasure without hypocrisy is more dangerous, for the rich and powerful, and harder to fulfil than the message of meagre frugality of the Cynics.[21]

Many times in the history of natural law, an initially revolutionary idea was co-opted by the established powers, tamed and domesticated. Epicurus turned the hedonist pleasures of the flesh with their revolutionary potential into the private and tranquil enjoyment of the philosopher and made a life in contemplation the prerequisite of human dignity. His insistence on the privacy of the undisturbed delights of the mind led him to doubt the sacred origin of the polis;

---

[20] Ferry and Renaut, op.cit., supra n. 14, 34.
[21] Bloch, op.cit., supra n. 10, 9.

he taught, instead, that cities were established through a contract of free and equal individuals who entered it to protect their security. The purpose of the polis and the basis of obligations that carry the force of natural law is utility; the aim of the law is to prevent mutual injury and harm. But despite the individualistic character of Epicureanism, its suspicion of public powers and its critique of injustice, nature and its pleasures remained totally private and had no immediate effect on the social organisation which was sustained by slaves with no obvious stake in the realm of happiness.

The final and most dramatic mutation in the early relationship between *physis* and *nomos* was introduced by the Stoics. The Stoics remained faithful to the superiority of a private life of tranquillity and reflection. They preached and practised *ataraxia* or imperturbability, the supreme duty of self-control over passions and irrationality. But while for Epicurus, happiness according to nature led to a life of dignity, the Stoics made well-being the outcome of a life dignified by the pride of being human. The dignified person was someone whose "head was held high . . . the person who held himself upright, who from the outset related to natural right . . . A pride that was universally formal set an all-encompassing attitude of kinship on the autonomous individual".[22] The Sophists had set *physis* against *nomos*; the Stoics expanded *nomos* into the necessary bond of the universe and identified the two. The new natural law was universal and even divine, its sacred character communed a sublime pathos to its followers. This passion against passions transgressed class divides for the first time and united slave (Epictetus) and emperor (Marcus Aurelius). The Stoics kept referring to a golden age, governed by unwritten laws whose content was the innate equality and unity of all in a rational empire of love. "An extremely anthropocentric, yet divinely sublime, nature governed by necessity was held over positive society and became the sole criterion of valid law".[23]

While the Stoics were not particularly interested in jurisprudence, and their quietism allowed them to accept both democracy and monarchy, they made a lasting contribution to legal thought. Their universal humanity, based on the rational essence of man and equal rights for the whole human race, was a dramatic departure from the Greek world of free and slaves or Hellenes and barbarians. "The contact with the ancient prophets of Israel, who were the first to lay claim to an analogous position, was a singular event full of

[22] ibid., 12.
[23] ibid., 13.

consequence. The unity of the human race, the natural right to peace, formal democracy, mutual aid . . . came to be the beginnings of a more or less definite concept".[24] But these revolutionary ideas were initially confined to the inward looking and austere gaze of the philosopher or the idealised but absent perfection of the hellenistic world. Their more concrete application would have to wait for the law of the Roman Empire and the political declarations of early modernity.

We can conclude, that despite their differences, classical philosophers saw nature as a standard, which must be discovered because it is occluded by a combination of convention and ancestral authority. Philosophy starts when it distinguishes between the truths about a topic given by law, convention or the received opinion (*doxa*) and the truth or the good arrived at through the dialogical critique of received wisdom and the observation of its nature. For the classical philosophers, nature was not just the physical world, the "way things are" or everything that exists but, a term of distinction, a norm or standard used to separate the work of philosophical and political thought from what obstructs or hides it. Nature was philosophy's weapon, the unsettling and revolutionary promethean fire used in its revolt against authority and the law. Its "discovery" and elevation into an axiological standard against convention emancipated reason from the tutelage of power and gave rise to natural right.

The possibility of judging the real in the name of the ideal can only start when what is right by nature confronts the rightful by custom or past practice. The concept of right was freed from its subjection to history or common opinion and became an independent tool for critique. The autonomisation of right was the necessary precondition for the development of a theory of justice from which current arrangements can be criticised. Thus nature was used against culture to create the most cultured of concepts. But if nature was a tactical move motivated by the need to combat the claims of authority which ruled early Greek society, its "discovery" was not so much a revelation or unveiling but an invention or creation. Nature must present itself as what was occluded by culture because philosophy cannot come into existence or survive, if it submits to ancestral or conventional authority. In this sense, the origins of philosophy and the discovery of nature were revolutionary gestures, directed against the claims to authority of the past and of law-as-custom and giving rise to critique in the name of justice.

[24] ibid., 16.

II. PLATO AND JUSTICE AS IDEAL

The cunning and manipulative oratory of the Sophists, the simple or the luxurious life of Cynics and Hedonists, the inward looking Epicurean or the philosophically egalitarian Stoic did not detract from the central methodological and substantive position of the classics. Observing the natural constitution of humans indicates that people live in cities or *poleis*, they are Aristotle's political animals *zoa politica*. No bare individual human nature exists outside of the group, no separate individuals can be found in a natural condition, except for monsters. Love and affection, pity and friendship form the natural kernel of natural right, because pleasure is achieved in association with others. Human nature can be perfected only in the political community and, as a result, the virtue of justice acquired central importance. Individual happiness was to achieve one's "standards of excellence" and political activity aimed to facilitate perfection and the realisation of virtue. A citizen can become excellent only in a just city and a city can become just only if its citizens live a life of virtue. Accordingly, personal morality and political ethics had the same end, peaceful activity in furtherance of virtue. The perfect natural order encompassed the perfect political order. Nature included the germ of law.

Justice, the natural aim of political life and the topic of paramount importance in classical philosophy, was a necessary accompaniment of natural right. The enquiry about justice involved two inter-related dimensions, which can be analytically distinguished: one concerned the political order, the other was more specifically legal. The first is associated with Plato and later the Stoics, the second with Aristotle. Taken together, they present a thoroughgoing use of the method of natural right in the consideration of the social bond. We will examine them in turn, emphasising those aspects of the classical doctrines which are mostly relevant to the genealogy of human rights.

The philosophy of Plato is preoccupied with the question of justice. His *Republic* remains to this day one of the most sustained discussions of the topic in world literature. The quest is conducted in the form of a dialogue between Socrates, the defender of justice as the right order in the city, and various Sophists, presented as purveyors of common-sensical opinions. The dialogue proceeds through the refutation of various definitions and arguments about justice, which Socrates shows to be wrong and to describe injustice rather than justice.[25] The Socratic quest for true justice is a refutation of injustice through reason.

Socrates starts by dismissing conventional theories which present justice as giving people their due, telling the truth and paying one's debts or finally doing good to friends and harm to enemies. He then turns to the main challenge. The cynical view of the Sophist Thrasymachus, that what passes for "justice" is the expression of the interests of the rulers, the wealthy and the strong and, as a result, the truly righteous man always loses out.[26] It is in the interest of the virtuous, accordingly, to act unjustly and promote his own profit since injustice gives more strength, freedom and mastery than the misnomer "justice". The challenge of Thrasymachus goes to the heart of the rationalist dialectic. He chides Socrates to stop "playing to the gallery by refuting others . . . It's easier to ask questions than to answer them. Give us an answer yourself, and tell us what you think justice is".[27] But while Socrates shows that the position of Thrasymachus is logically contradictory and morally untenable, he ends the exchange by admitting that he does not know the meaning of justice. He holds to the belief, however, that justice is good and injustice evil and that justice is always more advantageous than injustice.[28] Reason commands that it is better to suffer an injustice than to commit one.

But Socrates soon admitted that while philosophy is committed to the rule of reason, reasoning alone cannot prove the superiority of justice. He was the first to understand one of the great conundrums of moral philosophy, namely that moral knowledge does not necessarily and automatically lead to moral action. As Ovid put it later, *video meliora proboque; deteriora sequor* (I know the good and approve of it, but I follow evil). To persuade his audience, therefore, Socrates supplements his argument with a number of non-rational claims: righteousness should be practised because it brings happiness, an argument which is both close to Thrasymachus' detested utilitarianism and is acceptable only to those already righteous. Although he dismisses the theory of justice as retribution, he narrates the religious myths of Radamanthus and Er with their threats of divine retribution for evil deeds in the afterlife. Finally, he admits that while philosophy,

[25] Hayek, op.cit., supra n. 2, Vol. 2, 162.

[26] The Sophist Callicles in *Gorgias* had argued, in a proto-Nietzschean manner, that men are divided by nature into the strong and the weak and that law and convention are the creations of inferiors who use the talk of justice to drag their superiors to their own low level. Plato, *Gorgias* (W. Hamilton trans.) (London, Penguin, 1960).

[27] Plato, *Republic* (D. Lee trans.) (London, Penguin, 1974) 336c.

[28] ibid., 354b.

the practice of wisdom and knowledge, is the best teacher of conscience and the city, the external authority of parents and legislators may be the only realistic source available for teaching virtue to the many.

The philosophical Republic is a programme for the best polity, a quasi-constitution for the city that practices justice. It must be constructed by the philosopher who, in using reason, clarifies and promotes the requirements of human excellence according to nature. But the Socratic quest also pays attention to the exigencies and contingencies of the historical situation. No polity can survive or acquire legitimacy, if it does not acknowledge the importance and take account of the "unenlightened" opinions of its citizens, their conventions and customs. The success of the Republic, the application of natural right to politics in other words, depends on the uncertain and always fragile acceptance of the philosopher's design by his fellow citizens and on a large measure of chance.[29] It is a utopia, it does not exist in the present, and its realisation in the future cannot be guaranteed. Natural right revealed in reason is the necessary precondition of the just polity, but it is not sufficient. It must be adjusted to practical and political circumstances and considerations, it must restrain its rationalism and tailor its truth to the opinions and emotions of the many.

The other striking characteristic of the dialogue is that despite the many rational and non-rational arguments canvassed, Socrates offers no definition of justice. Justice is first replaced by reason, later by the idea of the good, which is presented as its substance and ultimate value. But while the good of the individual and of the *polis* provide the necessary criteria for choosing between competing courses of action, the good itself is not accessible to reason. Similarly with justice: Socrates affirmed repeatedly that justice and the good exist and are the highest value. But every attempt to define or describe them was soon abandoned as the dialogue circled around justice and the good without resolution. The closest we come to the meaning of justice is when Socrates compares the constitutions of the ideal city and of the soul. They both follow the principle of "doing one's own and proper task" *suum agere*. The right constitution leads to a balanced relationship between the three classes of citizens in the city and the three parts of the soul in man. The perfection of the parts and their harmonious and proportionate relationship makes the city just and

---

[29] Strauss, op.cit., supra n. 5, 139.

the citizen virtuous. But *suum agere* is a totally formal principle, and can scarcely determine what is to count as proper and as due to each. But this only sustained attempt to describe the characteristics of justice was soon abandoned, when Socrates acknowledged that the comparison of state and soul may not be appropriate.[30]

This endless and inconclusive circling around justice and the good leads eventually to the recognition that the good may be *epekeina ousias,* beyond Being and essence, at the other side of knowledge and reason. As Plato admitted in his seventh Epistle, we can never fully know the good "for it does not admit of verbal expression like other branches of knowledge".[31] Justice too, the political expression of the good, cannot be discovered in laws and in written treatises, as it has no essence or its essence lies beyond immediate life in the "city in the sky". But, while it cannot be rationally defined, justice exists and reveals itself to philosophers and lawgivers in mysteriously divine ways. The quest for justice exemplifies the paradox of reason, formulated by Socrates "in the most extreme manner: reasoning leads to unreason. Faith surfaces three times and in three forms: faith in otherworldly justice, faith in authority, and faith in revelation".[32] Behind the meandering dialogues lies Socrates' ultimate argument for justice: his sacrifice on the altar of a justice that cannot be defined or its superiority proven rationally but which must be acted upon, even at the greatest of costs. Socrates' death is the strongest argument about the inherent injustice of the law. After his sacrifice the burden of proof lies with those who believe in law's justice.

The Republic is the first attempt to raise justice into a universal ethical idea, totally independent of its historical context. People must leave the cave or prison of empirical existence and enter the ideal world of forms before they can grasp the operation of the good and of justice. What is most remarkable in the dialogue, however, is its unswerving attack on all conventional and traditional views. The truth about justice may not be accessible at all, in which case we have an obligation to remain silent in these matters.[33] It may be that the only contribution philosophy can make is to denounce the many

---

[30] *Republic,* n. 27 supra, 435.

[31] Plato, "Epistle VII" in *Phaedrus and Epistles VII and* VIII, (W. Hamilton trans.) (London, Penguin, 1973) 341c. For a full discussion of the Platonic search for the meaning of justice and the good and his admission of defeat, see Hans Kelsen, "The Metamorphoses of the Idea of Justice" in P. Sayre, *Interpretations of Modern Legal Philosophies* (New York, Oxford University Press) 1947.

[32] Agnes Heller, *Beyond Justice* (Oxford, Blackwell, 1987) 73.

[33] Plato, *Epistle VII*, 337.

injustices, to refute the falsehoods of the common sense and to make it understand the natural purpose of the *polis*. At the end, Socrates seems to accept that as no rational argument can conclusively justify his theory of justice, he must offer his own sacrifice as ultimate proof and the gravest offence against reason. In doing so, his arguments and his action are joined in a paradoxical formulation which may be called the *aporia of justice*: to be just means to act justly, to be committed to a frame of mind and follow a course of action that must be accepted before conclusive rational justification.[34]

The classical theory of justice can be described therefore as an ethical and political doctrine, which aims to bring about through debate, persuasion and political action the "best polity or regime" in which human perfection and virtue in association with others can be achieved. Its methodological tools are the observation of nature and rational argument. But it would be misleading to say that this regime is "given" or "found" in nature. Natural right offers an alternative to historical determinism and to conventional and authoritative opinion. Because justice is by definition critical of what exists, philosophy adopts nature as the source of its prescriptions and claims a natural "objectivity" for its right. But this ideal is not given by God, revelation or even an immutable natural order. It is a construction of thought and its actualisation is deeply political. From Anaximander to Socrates, early philosophy claimed that men need and have a sense of injustice. They unceasingly build legal and moral systems to achieve justice but justice is not fully of this world. The rightful individual and social order strive to transcend the infamies of present but, justice is accessible to human thought in a limited way and its realisation is very difficult, even improbable. As Strauss put it, "the best regime, which is according to nature, was perhaps never actual; there is no reason to assume that it is actual at present; and it may never become actual . . . in a word, the best regime is . . . a 'utopia' ".[35] Justice is thus caught in an unceasing movement between knowledge and passion, reason and action, this world and the next, rationalism and metaphysics.

---

[34] The aporia of reason and justice is even stronger in the Jewish tradition. To be just, the Jew must obey the law, without any reason or justification. For Buber, Jews act in order to understand while Levinas denounces what he calls the western "temptation of temptation", the – "Greek" – demand to subordinate every act to knowledge and to overcome the "purity" and "innocence" of the act. Emmanuel Levinas, *Nine Talmudic Readings* (Bloomington, Indiana University Press, 1990) 30–50.

[35] Strauss, op.cit., supra n. 5, 139.

III. ARISTOTLE AND LEGAL JUSTICE

Aristotle's *Nicomachean Ethics* and, in particular, its chapter on Justice are foundational texts for Western law.[36] The discipline of law *stricto sensu* was enunciated in the *Ethics* and juridical activity was presented, for the first time, as relatively autonomous from morals or politics. According to the legal historian Michel Villey, very little can or has been added to legal theory or to the idea of justice presented there.[37] Aristotle starts by distinguishing between general and particular justice. Justice belongs to the virtues, not as one of them but as the totality of virtue. General justice is the "moral disposition which renders men apt to do just things, and which causes them to act justly and to wish what is just". It has two characteristics: first, it is identified with the whole of virtue as exercised in the *polis* and, secondly, it is addressed to the "good of others" *allotrion agathon*. [38] But general justice is much more than the morality of the moderns. Aristotle's *dikaios aner,* the just man, has all the virtues and exercises them for the good of the others and the city. In this sense, general justice resembles the Platonic definition without the strong metaphysical element. It has elements of political and social morality and it is related to the law but is wider than either. As the law covers many aspects of human existence, the just and the lawful may coincide. The "unjust" man is first a law-breaker, secondly, he who takes more than his due. But Aristotle adds, in an early corrective to legalism, that law-breaking is unjust, only if the law is "rightly enacted".[39] The prime example of an unjust law is that which does not foster the other-regarding good.

But it is particular or legal justice which opens a wholly new way of looking at legal relations. To understand its strange to modern ears nature, we should start by examining the end and nature of law. Justice today is a principle or ideal towards which societies aspire, the (absent) soul of the body of laws. For Aristotle, however, this distinction between law and justice did not exist. The word used to express this intimately connected cluster of ethical, legal and political concepts was *dikaion*. The *dikaion* means the right or just state of

[36] For a discussion of Aristotle's ethics see W.F.R. Hardie, *Aristotle's Ethical Theory* (Oxford, Oxford University Press, 1980), J.O. Urmson, *Aristotle's Ethics* (Oxford, Blackwell, 1988).

[37] Michel Villey, *Le droit et les droits de l'homme* (Paris, P.U.F., 1983) Chapter 4.

[38] Aristotle, *Nicomachean Ethics* (J.A.K. Thomson trans.) (London, Penguin, 1976) Bk V, 1129b30–1130a18.

[39] ibid., 1129b14.

affairs in a particular situation or conflict, according to the nature of that case. Particular justice exists in cities; when its demands are contested by two parties, it requires the intervention of a third disinterested person, the *dikastes* or judge. His judgment is the *dikaion,* the lawful and the just solution. The *dikaion* is therefore the object of judicial decision-making, the action of the just man and the end of law. It is a state of affairs in the world, a distribution of things or the just share decided by the judge and, as the object of justice, the aim of human acts and the outcome of judicial consideration. As juridical art, the *dikaion* aims at the right proportion between things or "an external relation to be established between persons on the basis of things".[40] The rightful judgment distributes proportionately things to people, gives them their fair or just share according to the pattern of right relationships. The jurist is not concerned with upholding individual entitlements or rights but with observing the cosmic and civic order, from which he derives guidance. The way of things and of the world teaches the judge patterns of proportionate distributions, which he must respect and promote. The idea of proportion is crucial; it brings justice close to the aesthetic beauty immanent in the harmony of the world.

The *dikaion* should not be confused with morality or general justice and it does not result from the application of moral precepts or legal rules. Greek cities had moral rules and Antigone's unwritten laws fall into that category, but these were clearly distinguished from legal justice. The idea of law as commandment or rule accompanied by sanctions originated in Jewish and later Christian concepts of law and was not of great importance in classical Greece.[41] Particular justice, the art of the judge, was not about morality, utility or truth but about the sharing of external goods, of benefits, burdens and rewards. It was concerned with distribution and retribution and constituted the proper object of the juridical art. The task of the judge was precisely to reach the right outcome in the sharing of external goods. Plato too wrote that the aim of the juridical art (*dikastike*) is to discover the *dikaion* and not to study the laws, which are only supplementary to this task; an unjust law is not law properly speaking, because the role of the jurist is to find the just solution.[42] The judge,

---

[40] Ralph McInerny, "Natural Law and Natural Rights" in *Aquinas on Human Action* (Washington, D.C., Catholic University of America Press, 1992) 217.

[41] Michel Villey, "Dikaion-Torah" in *Seize Essais de Philosophie du Droit* (Paris, Dalloz, 1969).

[42] Plato, *The Laws,* supra n. 12, IV, 715.

like all citizens, must seek the good and the judicial vocation is justice.

Aristotle's description of the judicial art is detailed and practical and follows the method of natural right. A just distribution involves two elements: a recognition of a state of affairs, of an equitable proportion subsisting amongst things, and a distribution of the disputed things according to this arrangement. First, observation; for classical philosophy, the source of natural law was the natural organisation of the cosmos. The just outcome is already inscribed in the nature of things and relationships, in the cosmic order of interrelated purposes and ends and awaits its recognition and pronouncement by the judge. The cosmos and everything in it, including the *polis*, are part of a universal harmony, the various parts and constituents are properly balanced. The city does not enjoy perfect justice, of course. But families, social groups and cities, which have come into being spontaneously and, gradually developed their political relations, values and constitutions, are prefigurations of the perfect order. They can serve as models because the hope of the perfectly just city presupposes that we can extract the idea of justice from its existing imperfect approximations. Observing reality is the first step to the discovery of the just solution.

The judge acts like a botanist or anthropologist: he observes the connections and relations amongst his fellow citizens, the way in which they arrange their affairs, in particular the way in which they distribute benefits and burdens. But the just decision is always provisional and experimental, transient and dynamic in the same way that human nature is always on the move, between the actual and the potential and continuously adjusts to changes, new circumstances and contingencies. Finding the *dikaion* is the aim of the classical jurist but that is never fully and finally achieved; it remains always a step away, full justice is deferred, not yet here and never fully done. In this sense, seeking the just involves the observation of the external world as well as a futural or transcendent element. "If we understand the word law as synonymous to a formulated rule, there is no natural law" writes Villey.[43] Natural right is a methodological principle that helps in the discovery of the just solution, not in our conscience or some strict set of rules, but in the external world of human relations. The natural law is an unwritten law, its content is never fully known; it has nothing to do with the idea of a positive rule or commandment prevalent in modernity.

---

[43] Michel Villey, *Lecons d'Histoire de la Philosophie du Droit* (Paris, Dalloz, 1962) 240.

Furthermore, finding the just solution was a discursive practice and a political act. It involved the learned choice of the judge who considers all the circumstances of the case and the particular conditions persisting at the time.[44] The jurist discovers the *dikaion* by using the art of law: its key principle is *audem alteram partem*: there are always at least two conflicting parties who must be heard and that makes the style of argument rhetorical and the method dialectical. The dialectic was an integral part of classical thought; until the Renaissance, it was the main scholarly method in theology, philosophy and law. The dialectically just solution is not deduced from a general rule, nor is it the outcome of a logical exercise but the application of knowledge about the nature of things. It will be discovered in reality, through a consideration of arguments, examples and an observation of the relationship amongst the parties. The judge considers the pleadings of the parties and compares their conflicting and contradicting opinions as partial expressions of reality. By putting terms and arguments to debate, judges arrive at their decisions dialectically: not the only or truthful opinion but the best in the circumstances. The final ingredient was political: in decision-making, the legislator or judge supplements the observation of nature, the dialectical confrontation and the rational justification with an act of will which cannot be fully theorised. Dialectics is always provisional, open to new arguments, experiences and concerns. Legal judgment, conducted in the realms of *praxis* and *techne* rather than science, *episteme*, is always accompanied by a degree of uncertainty, which is brought to an end by the decision. The *dikaion* is therefore an act of judicial will which, starting from a combination of natural observation and argumentative confrontation, adds a precise meaning and determination (the punishment for such a tort is the sacrifice of two goats) and brings the issue to a close.

In Roman civil law, the method became explicitly casuistical, it started and finished with the case at hand. The casuists stayed close to the facts of the case from which they extracted the solution (*ex facto jus oritur*). They explored existing opinions relating to the case, they looked at doctrinal authorities, at opinions of jurisconsults and at available rules. Examples from the past, unjust outcomes, hypotheticals and cases previously considered, were used to illuminate the present situation. The authorities were not treated as true or binding, they had persuasive only power. The judge intervened by

---

[44] "One cannot know in advance the content of positive justice; it depends on the free decision of the law-giver", Aristotle, *Ethics*, op.cit., supra n. 36, VII. 6.1.

confronting the contradictory claims of the parties, clarifying words and terms, putting the litigants in direct confrontation. This polyphonic procedure in which litigants and authorities, witnesses and precedents, opinions, reasons and arguments, "the sic and the nunc", are brought into dialogue is the gist of the dialectic, and the way through which *jus* emerged. And as social shares were part of the wider cosmic order, a just distribution was politically and ethically right but also a beautiful expression of the wider cosmic harmony.

Finally, Aristotle's theory of justice cannot be understood outside its intricate connection with *phronesis* or practical wisdom. For Aristotle, virtue is the geometrical mean between excess and lack or defect. The moral agent is the prudent man or *phronimos* who acquires his moral sense and discrimination in the course of a life full of experience. His practical judgment is always situated in the concrete circumstances of the case at hand. Aristotle argued that equity, *epieikeia,* is the rectification of legal justice *nomos* in so far as the law is defective. Laws are general but "the raw material of human behaviour" is such that it is often impossible to pronounce in general terms. Thus "justice and equity coincide, and both are good, [but] equity is superior".[45] As people and life have an "irregular shape" the law should be like the leaden Lesbian rule: "just as this rule is not rigid but is adapted to the shape of the stone, so the ordinance is framed to fit the circumstances".[46] There is no model or blueprint to guide the judge, his true vocation is often to decide the just without criteria or rules. The variety of circumstances and the unique situation in each case means that, to achieve equity, the judge must decide from case to case without resort to strict criteria. To be just, the judge must develop and fine tune the art of evaluating the conflicting forces, relations and claims. The mean, so central in Aristotelian ethics, cannot be defined outside each specific situation. Justice is the work of the just, but whether the judge is just or not cannot be judged prior to his judgment. Particular justice as the art of evaluation, calculation and distribution cannot be theoretically specified outside of its context.

This is why Leo Strauss, more interested in the political than legal aspect of justice, found Aristotle less important than Plato. Strauss believed that the Aristotelian emphasis on circumstance and situation turned justice and natural right into concrete judgments and actions and turned them away from general schemes and theories. But Strauss

---

[45] Aristotle, *Ethics*, op.cit., supra n. 36, V, x, 1137a35–b24.
[46] ibid., V, xi, 1137b24–1138a11.

too agreed that for both Plato and Aristotle natural law had a changeable character and recognised the variability of the demands of justice.[47] "There is a universally valid hierarchy of ends, but there are
no universally valid rules of action", Strauss concluded. While the
hierarchy of ends is sufficient for passing judgment on the "level of
the nobility of individuals and groups and of actions and institutions
. . . it is insufficient for guiding our actions".[48] General justice, the
"whole of virtue", which demands the "good of the other" remains
an elusive, always deferred horizon against which legal judgment and
political plan must be precariously conducted. It may be that
Lyotard's verdict that "it is impossible to produce a learned discourse
upon what justice is" applies equally to classic and modern efforts to
create a theory of justice.[49] The reservations of Strauss remain important nonetheless. "The only thematic treatment of natural right
which is certainly by Aristotle and which certainly expresses
Aristotle's own view covers barely one page of the Nicomachean
Ethics".[50]

Aristotle is a theorist of justice and, despite Villey's attempts to
identify the two, natural right and justice follow different and often
conflicting paths. Their invention in classical Greece at around the
same time helped their confusion but, their later trajectory separated
them. In normal times, justice remains a virtue imposed from above.
Even in its Aristotelian prudent and equitable version, justice uses a
number of elements which distance it from natural right. First, legal
justice, rather than challenging existing hierarchies, presupposes a
natural and institutional equilibrium which acts as the empirical and
logical background of proportional judgments. Secondly, Aristotelian
judges are prudent patriarchs. The golden age of Stoics, on the other
hand, had no authority or judge and, Themis, the goddess of custom,
had no use of scales for weighing people and things. Justice was central for those who try to devise the best, most acceptable, form of
exercising power, not for philosophers concerned with dissent and
opposition to established customs or laws. As Bloch argued, "Plato

---

[47] Strauss, op.cit., supra n. 5, 31 57.

[48] ibid., 162–3.

[49] Lyotard states that "I am closest to Aristotle, insofar as he recognises – and he does so
explicitly in the *Rhetoric*, as well as in the *Nicomachean Ethics*, that a judge worthy of the name
has no true model to guide his judgments, and that the true nature of the judge is to pronounce judgments and therefore prescriptions, just so, without criteria", Jean-François
Lyotard and Jean-Loup Thébaud, *Just Gaming* (W. Glodzich trans.) (Manchester, Manchester
University Press, 1985) 26.

[50] Strauss, op.cit., supra n. 5, 156.

and Aristotle made out of justice that which Stoicism never made out of nature, namely, the genius of domination".[51] For Plato, justice regulates the soul as much as the city, it has a disciplining function: it co-ordinates and subjugates the faculties of the person and ensures that each citizen carries out his alotted duties and responsibilities. Despite its utopian element, Platonic justice remained philosophically aloof and politically authoritarian.

Aristotle's pragmatic politics made him less authoritarian, but justice as a legal virtue was scarcely likely to send the slaves marching to the *agora* of Athens. Stoic natural law, with its philosophical quietism, did not do that either; it laid however a possible foundation for future rebellion. In the hierarchical Aristotelian cosmos, classes and people were assigned their exact value and cosmic significance by their natural state but, at the same time, they were constrained to that state alone. Individual justice and the just man had an independent place in Aristotle, but his actions did not refer to intentions, emotions and passions. It was rather an external quality which could be decided, as Villey put it, objectively. Judicial impartiality was its model, alongside the situated and flexible objectivity of nature. Both were necessary for deciding what the citizen's share was. Very little in the standards of law, virtue or value could change under such a concept of justice. They remain the measure of dominant relations which, justice, with its mathematical aptitude, could calculate and weigh exactly. From the perspective of radical natural right, justice was not a critique but a critical apology of positive law. There is considerable distance between this patriarchal conception of justice and the *physis* that philosopher and rebel set precisely against the assignments and distributions of law.

We can conclude that the discovery of nature and the method of natural right was the rebellion of philosophy against the weight of custom and of the past. Natural right claimed the truth of nature against common sense and the dignity of argument and dialectic against the banality and oppression of received opinion. But as the nature of the classical teleological world was a dynamic concept, never finished or perfected but always on the move, natural right, the outcome of the observation of nature and of the dialectical confrontation of opinions, was also provisional and changeable according to new contingencies. As the dictate of observed nature, natural right was quasi-objective; as the outcome of dialectics, it was deeply

[51] Bloch, op.cit., supra n. 10, 39.

interpretative and political. Both objective and constructed, natural right became a non historicist but deeply historical and cultural standard for judging the world.

When this method is applied to the polity, justice is shown to have two aspects, a political and a legal. Political justice explores the overall organisation of the *polis* and tries to imagine the perfect constitution, the most beautiful and harmonious arrangement of the social bond. But justice or the just is also the end, both the aim and outcome, of legal action. Justice as an ideal, is never fully of this world; it forms the horizon against which current practices are judged and found lacking. The just as the outcome of the juridical process is both present and future-looking. The concept of justice is therefore split: an ideal or general justice which promises a future perfection and judges reality in its name and, a legal or particular justice which upholds and redresses proportional equality in the everyday dealings of citizens, but also reproduces the existing balance between free citizens and slaves, men and women, Greeks and barbarians. Legal justice could also face both ways, its provisional judgments reached against the horizon of a purposeful order and a perfect justice always deferred to the future. But this will have to wait. The Greeks were indebted to philosophers, tragedians and dissidents, rather than to judges, for upholding natural right against the justice from above. They remain to this day a powerful lens that helps see through the hazy air of oppressive and unquestioning received opinion into a truth which is both future-looking and timely. Occasionally, we need a remote satellite in order to get the best view of our own earth.

A Brief History of Natural Law:
II. From Natural Law to Natural Rights

I. THE STOICS AND NATURAL RIGHT

The Romans adopted the Greek approach to justice and Roman law developed into the most advanced ancient legal system. The Latin words for justice and law derive from the same root, their semantic field is the same in Greek and Latin (*dikaion* and *jus* for right/law; *dikaiosyne* and *justitia* for justice). The Roman *jus,* like the Greek *dikaion,* was both the lawful and the just,[1] the aim of the jurist in each dispute was to serve justice by aiming at the just solution (*jus, id quod justum est* and *jus objectum justitiae*).[2] The first lines of the Digest state that *justitia est constans and perpetua voluntas jus suum cuique tribuendi* and that law derives from justice: *est autem a justitia appelatum jus.*[3] And when the Digest says that *jus est ars boni et aequi* or that the object of justice is *honeste vivere, alterum non laedere, suum cuique tribuere,*[4] it follows the Aristotelian conception of particular justice.

For the Roman jurist, as for the Greek, the *jus* was not a collection of rules but the just and rightful outcome of a dispute. The Digest says that "our proper civil law is not written but consists solely of the interpretations of the jurists".[5] The opinions of the jurisconsults started being written and eventually acquired a persuasive force for

---

[1] Some legal historians derive the etymology of *jus* from the Latin *jussum* and *jubeo*, to order. This possible association has been used to link *jus* with legal positivism. But *jubere* does not mean commandment in Latin. The semantic field of the Greek *dikaion* with its link between just and lawful influenced the Latin and led to a similar link. See Michel Villey, *Le droit et les droits de l'homme* (Paris, P.U.F., 1983) 39, 48.

[2] Thomas Aquinas, *Summa Theologiae,* 2.2ae.57.1.

[3] *Digest* 1.1.10 Ulpian; *Institutes* I.I.I.

[4] The full passage is: "*Justitia est constans et perpetua voluntas jus suum cuique tribuendi: 1) Juris praecepta sunt haec: honeste vivere, alterum non laedere, suum cuique tribuere; 2) juris-pudentia est divinarum atque humanorum rerum notitia, justi atque injusti scientia*". *Digest* I,I, 10, Ulpian.

[5] "*Aut est proprium jus civile, quod sine scripto in sola prudentium intepretatione consistit*". *Digest,* I, 2. 2, Pomponius.

later cases but the method remained dialectical and casuistical.
"Starting from the study of just and unjust determinations, jurisprudence rises to general knowledge and comes to formulate 'definitions', 'rules', 'verdicts' – opinions of the jurisconsults".[6] The *jus civile*
is a collection of just decisions and jurisprudential rules, of the procedural decrees of the magistrates and, later, of the decrees of jurists
of the imperial court and has little affinity with contemporary systems
of law, except with the common law before the assault of the
European codifying spirit. The Digest states clearly that "the rule
describes a reality briefly. The *jus* does not derive from the rule but
the *jus* that exists creates the rule".[7] The *jus* designates the just share
of each citizen in his relationship with others. The *jura* are not individual rights but real entities in the world, "objective" relations
amongst citizens. They are often things and especially incorporeals
but they include also institutions, such as the marriage, paternity or
trade. Gaius lists amongst the *jura* "the *jus* of building houses higher
and obstructing the light of neighbouring houses, or not doing so,
because it obstructs their light; the *jus* of streams and gutters, that is
of a neighbour taking a stream or gutter overflow through his yard or
house".[8] Cutting through the contemporary distinction between
rights and duties, the *jura* refer also to citizens' civic duties and burdens. The duty to serve in the army, for example, is a *jus* and, the
brutal execution of a parricide is also called the murderer's *jus*. But
predominantly, *jus* is the just outcome of distribution, the calculation
of the just proportion amongst external things shared by the citizens.
It is also the end of the just act or judgment, the aim of the art of law
(*id ad quod terminatus actus justititae*). For the classical lawyers, "*jura* are
plainly not rights in the modern sense".[9] As Michel Villey has argued,
in Ulpian's definition of justice as *suum jus cuique tribuere*, the *jus* refers
not to an individual right but to the just share or due determined
within an established structure of relationships and varying with each
person's status and role.[10] Like the Greek *dikaion*, therefore, the *jus*

---

[6] Villey, op.cit., supra n. 1, 66.

[7] "*Regula est quae rem quae est breviter enarrant. Jus non a regula sumatur sed a jure, quod est,
regula fiat*". *Digest*, 50, 17, I Paul.

[8] *The Institutes of Gaius* (F. De Zalueta ed., Oxford, 1946), I.

[9] Richard Tuck, *Natural Rights Theories* (Cambridge, Cambridge University Press, 1979)
9.

[10] Michel Villey, "Les Origines de la notion du droit subjective" in *Leçons d'histoire de la
philosophie du droit* (Paris, Dalloz 1962) 221–57; *La Formation de la Pensée Juridique Moderne*
(Paris, Montchrétien, 1968). It has been argued that the concept of the Romans and early
glossators closest to individual right is not *jus* but *dominium* with its implications of property,
possession and control and to that extent Villey is wrong. For a review of this debate, see

differs both from a moral code and from a system of positive laws regulating conduct.

Aristotelian concepts of legal justice survived and thrived in Rome,
where the Stoic ideas of natural law, simplified and transformed by
Cicero, were also applied for the first time. As the Greek city-states
started dissolving, first in the Macedonian and later in the Roman
Empires, the idea of a law common to all imperial subjects, of a *jus
gentium*, started to take hold. The Stoics had stayed away from direct
political involvement, but the morality of universal humanity, which
they espoused and based on norms deriving from rational human
nature, could be used equally well to restrain the irrational passions
of individuals and ethnic and local nationalisms, in favour of a new
cosmopolitanism. The Stoic Chryssipus, for example, described universal humanity as a nation, while for Posidonius, the world was "the
commonwealth of gods and men".[11] But it was Cicero, an eclectic
Stoic and a pragmatic lawyer and politician, who turned the rational
universality of Stoicism into the legal ideology of Rome.

Cicero rationalised Roman law and claimed that many of its central tenets could be traced back to universal rational norms. In the
process, the Stoic "common notions", through which men partook
of universal reason and became aware of its dictates, were psycholo-
gised. The *orthos logos* or right reason of the Greeks, which united
natural necessity with the laws of reason, was turned into the *recta ratio*
of good sense, "though of course as a common sense that has become
the supreme source of law".[12] When the Roman jurists spoke of *jus
naturale* or used nature to explain or qualify legal concepts, their terms
had less of an Aristotelian tint and more of a practical import: "For
'natural' was to them not only what followed from physical qualities
of men and things, but also what, within the framework of that

Tuck ibid., 5–39. Michel Villey's response was that while *dominium* meant mastery over
words or things, it was not a legal construct but a pre-legal reality restricted by law. For
Villey, the whole structure of language in Rome was built around concepts different from
ours in which the concepts of the subject and subjective rights had no place. See *Le droit et
les droits de l'homme* op.cit., supra n. 1, 74–104. Tuck agreed that the "classical Romans did
not have a theory about legal relationships in which the modern notion of a subjective right
played any part", ibid. at 12. He differs from Villey, however, who believed that subjective
rights were introduced after the nominalist revolution in the 14th century, and argues that
the first glossators collapsed the concepts of *jus* and *dominium* in the 12th century and created the origins of a theory of rights. For an exhaustive review of the debate, see Brian
Tierney, *The Idea of Natural Rights* (Atlanta, Scholars Press, 1997) Chapter I.

[11] Quoted in Ernst Bloch, *Natural Law and Human Dignity* (D. J. Schmidt trans.)
(Cambridge, Mass, MIT Press, 1988) 14.

[12] ibid., 20.

system, seemed to square with the normal and reasonable order of human interests and, for this reason, not in need of further evidence".[13] Still, the Roman *jus* continued to signify a set of objective relations in the world and, like Greek law, did not have a concept of individual rights. And while Aristotle and universal legality may have pragmatically coincided for a brief period, through the needs of the Roman Empire, they soon diverged again. Aristotelian justice made its last grand appearance in the writings of Thomas Aquinas and then gradually descended into positivism. The natural right tradition, on the other hand, influenced by Stoicism and Christianity, moved towards a command-theory of law and a subject-based interpretation of right and prepared the modern conception of human rights. Let us examine closer some of the main elements of Stoic thought which, misdigested and eclectically revised by Cicero, exerted such immense influence on later political and legal thought.[14]

The Stoic teaching radically changed both the classical method of arguing about the naturally right and the content of nature, the source of law. Nature became the source of a definite set of rules and norms, of a legal code, and stopped being a way of arguing against institutional crystallisations and common opinions. The Stoics were the first pagans to believe that natural law was the expression of a divine reason which pervaded the world and made human law one of its aspects. Cicero's famous quotation from the Republic is worth quoting at length:

> The true law, is the law of reason, in accordance with nature known to all, unchangeable and imperishable, it should call men to their duties by its precepts and deter them from wrongdoing with its prohibitions . . . To curtail this law is unholy, to amend it illicit, to repeal it impossible; nor can we be dispensed from it by the order either of senate or of popular assembly; nor need we look for anyone to clarify or interpret it; nor will it be one law in Rome and a different one in Athens, nor otherwise tomorrow than it is today; but one and the same law, eternal and unchangeable will bind all people and all ages; and God, its designer, expounder and enacter, will be the sole and universal ruler and governor of all things.[15]

This God-given, eternal and absolute natural law had little to do with the natural right of the Sophists or of Plato and Aristotle.

---

[13] Erns Levy, "Natural Law in Roman Thought", 1949 *Studia et Documenta Historiae et Juris* 15 at 7.

[14] Michel Villey, *Histoire de la Philosophie du Droit*, Paris (4th ed., 1975) 428–80.

[15] Cicero, *Republic* (N. Rudd trans.) (Oxford, Oxford University Press, 1998) III, 22.

Next, the concept of nature. The Aristotelian nature was a normative concept which combined the essence of a thing with its potential for growth and perfection, the efficient and final end of the cosmos and of all beings and things. Stoic nature was much more static. Its normative character was retained but became an omnipresent and determining spirit (*pneuma*), the *logos* or reason found as seedling in everything. This omnipotent *logos* unites man and world; in humans, it acts like the artist's fire:[16] it begets and sculpts the body and makes it cohere by assembling its components (*logos spermatikos*).[17] But it also commands the whole world, in the same way that the emperor commands his empire. Diogenes Laertius wrote that nature "is the force which constrains the world . . . a stable force which derives from itself, produces the seminal reasons and contains what comes from it".[18] Nature was therefore ontologised and spiritualised: it became the creative spirit or life principle which, in its pure state, is God while in man resides in the soul. The soul, Cicero's *vis innata*, is an internal force which unites human with divine *logos* and makes them discern the law of nature, which they are bound to observe.

Natura initium juris said Cicero.[19] The law, human institutions, rules and all worldly order proceed from a single source, all-powerful nature, the sole *fons legum et juris*[20] and *logos* discloses them to man. Nature commands, it is a moral precept which orders men to obey the sovereign *logos* which rules history. Natural right became a matter of introspection and revelation rather than of rational contemplation and dialectical confrontation and led to an abstract morality of precepts which anticipated Kant. As a result, two possibilities were opened. In the first, nature, with its principles of human dignity and social equality, was retained as a category of social and legal opposition and as the content of right. The second and dominant, however, equated natural with positive law and the real with the rational and anticipated Hegel. It privileged the passive and private morality of the happy soul and sanctioned existing institutions, social hierarchies and inequalities with the imprimatur of reason and nature. *Physis*, which had started its career in opposition to *nomos*, came finally to be identified with it.

[16] Cicero, *De natura deorum* (R. W. Walsh trans.) (Oxford, Clarendon, 1997) II. 22. 57.
[17] ibid., II. 11.29; II.22.58.
[18] Diogenes Laertius, VII. 148, quoted in Villey, supra n. 14, p.440.
[19] Cicero, *De inventione* (H. M. Hubbell trans.) (London, Heinemann, 1949) II, 22, 65.
[20] Cicero, *De Legibus* (N. Rudd trans.) (Oxford, Oxford University Press, 1998) I, 5.

How could one find the content of this natural law? The right reason or *recta ratio* proceeds from the God of *logos* and its commands are placed in the conscience, through the "common notions" mentioned above. The logos has been inscribed on the soul and the paramount duty is to follow its commands. The sage does not need to observe nature or the city but only to listen to his inner voice. Stoicism became a religion with reason its god and law, and with natural right closer to the private morality of conscience than to the classical legal method. The Stoic concepts of nature and law had more in common with Christianity than with Aristotle and led directly to the modern idea of human nature. Let us summarise some Stoic innovations which paved the way to the legal humanism of the moderns.

The law no longer derives from external but from human nature, man's reason. Man is celebrated as a rational being and is given a preeminent position above the rest of nature, against Aristotelian physics, in which the force of nature harmonised and hierarchised humans and animals.[21] As a result, while nature and reason were initially closely connected, reason eventually came to replace nature as the principal source of law. Following its commands is to follow our nature. But reason is also rationed and not everyone had equal access to it; the surest guide to its commands is the reason of sages (*ratio mensque sapientis*).[22] Thus, the idea that the legislator or judge is the mouthpiece of the spirit or reason of law entered the historical stage.[23] Finally, law and the just reside in the collection of legal and moral rules discovered by the human spirit. The *dikaion* of the Greeks and the *jus* of the Romans became identified with a set of laws *leges* and became a system of rational rules, discovered by the reason of the sages.

Jacques Derrida has called the dominant tradition of Western metaphysics, "logocentric".[24] In the Stoics, we find the first expression of a philosophical and ideological construction we have called "logonomocentrism".[25] It identifies the *logos* as reason with the law

---

[21] Cicero provides a further similarity: prefiguring Grotius, Puffendorf and the 17th century naturalists, he starts with human nature in order to explain the nature of society and law. In *De Legibus*, I. 5 and in *De Officiis* (M.T. Griffin and E. M. Atkins trans.) (Cambridge, Cambridge University Press, 1991) I. IV.11, Cicero gives a legally relevant list of human traits and inclinations which include, *ala* Hobbes, self-preservation, etc.

[22] *De Legibus*, II. 4.

[23] Cicero claims in *De Legibus* that the universal reason and the rules of the sages come from Jupiter (II. 4).

[24] Jacques Derrida, *Of Grammatology* (G. Spivak trans.) (Baltimore, The Johns Hopkins University Press,1974).

[25] Costas Douzinas and Ronnie Warrington with Shaun McVeigh, *Postmodern Jurisprudence* (Routledge, 1991) 25–8.

and presents rational rule as the foundation and spirit of community. Being is equated with presence, with what is present in consciousness, and with the primacy of *logos* as *nomos*. Indeed, being is present in law and this immanence gives rational law an ontological pre-eminence. Rationalism, the cult of the legislator and of rules associated with legal positivism, the celebration of individual rights which derive from human nature, they all appear for the first time together in late Stoic thought and Cicero. But law's ontological dimension also promotes ideas of human dignity and social equality. The law as reason that begets the world pushes towards an, admittedly abstract, fraternity of all humankind. In this latter aspect, Stoic natural law remains one of the most honourable chapters in the history of ideas and is linked with the later theories of natural and human rights.

But the main force moving the law towards a theory of natural rights was its gradual christianisation. Jewish cosmology did not possess an inclusive and purposive concept of the cosmos. For the Jewish religion, the universe is the creation of God. It displays his omnipotence and presence precisely through his absence and, as such, it cannot acquire the autarchic normative weight of the Greek *physis*. Similarly, Christianity claimed that the world had been created *ex nihilo* through the free act of God. Nature, the invention of Greek philosophical imagination, was turned into the creation of an all-powerful being. The cosmos was reduced to the natural universe; the natural ends given to all things and beings were turned into their providential position in the plan of salvation, and teleology became eschatology. Nature retained a limited only normative character "expressing in time what from all eternity resides in God" and confirming and complementing divine law.[26]

The seeds of Christian natural law could be found perhaps in St. Paul's statement, inspired by Stoic teachings, that God has placed a natural law in our hearts (Rom 11.15). This was the beginning of the idea that conscience is the rule of God ingrained in the heart. After the victory of Christianity, the *jus* became intertwined with morality and took the form of a set of commandments or rules, the paradigmatically Jewish type of legality. Eventually, the Christian Fathers, commenting on the Bible, started using the term *jus* to mean divine command and, natural law to signify the Decalogue. Gratian's *Decretum,* published in the twelfth century, stated that the natural law is contained in the Gospels and is "antecedent both in point of time

---

[26] Louis Dupré, *Passage to Modernity* (New Haven, Yale University Press, 1993) 30.

and in point of rank to all things. For whatever has been adopted as custom, or prescribed in writing, if contrary to natural law is to held null and void . . . Thus both ecclesiastical and secular statutes, if they are shown to be contrary to natural law, are to be altogether rejected".[27] This usage was adopted by the medieval canonists and, finally, in the fourteenth century, *jus* came to mean individual power or subjective right.

A crucial link in the christianisation of law must be sought in Augustine's theory of justice which combined some of the characteristic difficulties of Plato's metaphysics and Aristotle's rationalism. Aristotle believed that a secularised version of *dike,* the order of the world, still existed and just laws and constitutions were part of it. His identification of law with justice was therefore a way of strengthening the authority of law, while retaining the dynamic character of justice according to nature. Augustine, on the other hand, equated the two in order to undermine the authority of law of the still pagan Roman Empire. He defined justice, like Aristotle, as *tribuere suum cuique*. But while for Aristotle, a man's due was determined by the *ethos* of his *polis* and the judgments of the practically prudent, for the Christian bishop, man's due was to serve God. The virtue of justice was defined as *ordo amoris*, the love of order: by attributing to each his proper degree of dignity, justice leads men to an ideal state in which the soul is subjected to God and the body to the soul. When this order is absent, man, law and state are unjust. Justice is therefore the love of the highest good or God.

> Where, then is the justice of the man, when he deserts the true God and yields himself to impure demons (as the romans do)? . . . Is he who keeps back a piece of ground from the purchaser, and gives it to a man who has no right to it, unjust, while he who keeps back himself from the God who made him, and serves wicked spirits, is just? . . . Hence, when a man does not serve God, what justice can we ascribe to him . . . And if there is no justice in such an individual, certainly there can be none in a community composed of such persons.[28]

Unjust law is no law and an unjust state is no state. Without justice, states become great robberies. "Where there is no true justice there can be no law. For what is done by law is justly done, and what is unjustly done cannot be done by law. For the unjust inventions of

---

[27] *Decretum,* D. 8, 2, 9.

[28] *De Civitate Dei* (M.Dods, J.J. Smith and G. Wilson trans.) (Edinburgh, 1872) Bk IV, Ch. 4.

men are neither to be considered nor spoken of as rights."[29] Augustine's denunciation of the injustice of the pagan state and its law was a consequence of his deep pessimism about the human condition. The original sin and the fall made it impossible for secular law and justice to redeem people from evil. We can never know fully God's wishes, and justice will always remain a promise that cannot be fulfilled in this life. Justice is a divine attribute which does not belong to this world. Indeed, our fallen nature is so ignorant that we cannot fully understand even fellow humans. Christian princes and judges, despite good intentions, cannot expect therefore to understand people well enough to pass correct judgments. Secular justice is a misnomer and a poor approximation for the justice of God and, while necessary, its success will always be limited. As Judith Shklar puts it:

> justice fails on two grounds, cognitive and practical, and the realm of injustice is revealed to be so extensive that it is quite beyond the cures of even effective political law and order . . . In the Augustinian vision injustice embraces more than those social ills that justice might alleviate. It is the sum of our moral failures as sinful people, which from the outset dooms us to being unjust.[30]

But while injustices are denounced, the earthly city is called the *civitas diaboli*. Its laws come into existence and are called just out of necessity. The function of states and laws is to coerce men, restrain their *cupiditas* or infinite desire and keep the peace in these cities of the devil. The state has no intrinsic legitimacy therefore and even the most successful nations are certain to decline and fall. Its limited utility is to meet internal and external violence with violence. Against the classical tradition, Augustine argued, that not only does "the removal of justice not lead to the breaking up of a state, but in fact there never has been a state that was maintained by justice".[31] The few predestined to be saved will stay in *the civitas terrena* as *peregrini*, itinerant foreigners, until they join the realm of true justice in the city of God after this life.

Augustine gave religious expression to the strengths and difficulties of classical theories of justice. He agreed with Plato that we can neither fully know nor achieve justice in this world. But while all attempts are bound to fail, we must continue the doomed quest

---

[29] ibid., Bk XIX, Ch. 21.

[30] Judith Shklar, *The Faces of Injustice* (New Haven, Yale University Press, 1990) 26.

[31] Dino Bigongiari, "The Political Ideas of St. Augustine", in St. Augustine, *The Political Writings* (Henry Paolucci ed.) (Washington D.C., Gateway, 1962) 346.

through laws and institutions which will never achieve what they promise. With Aristotle, Augustine accepted that justice is *suum cuique*. But the love of God replaced the *politically* situated love of justice and judgments lost their flexibility. They became both more certain, in an attempt to imitate God's absolute justice, and impossible since the gap between God and humanity is unbridgeable. Justice, identified with God's love, does not belong to this world; injustice becomes the condition of humanity. And yet, Augustine's inward turn to the self in his *Confessions*, his emphasis on the justice of a sovereign legislator and on the coercive role of state power prefigure the jurisprudence of modernity. At the same time, his city of God redefined the idea of utopia for a Christian audience, as a place of unblemished well-being. The Stoics had placed their utopia in a mythical past, while the city of God belongs to an unknown but predetermined and certain future. Augustine has been called a "prophetic utopian", the "chief source of that ideal of a world order which is haunting the minds of so many today" but also a "Macchiavelian".[32] If we bracket his Christian metaphysics, he is the first political philosopher who both accepted and legitimised the might of the state and proposed a higher justice which state law flagrantly violates. Augustine's Christian peregrines were asked not to contrast the two but "to tolerate even the worst, and if need be, the most atrocious form of polity".[33] But the juxtaposition between heaven and earth and their sharp separation had created the conditions for their eventual comparison and combination. As the two-world metaphysics was gradually weakened, the time came when the principles of heaven were made to justify first and to condemn later the infamies of earth.

II. THE RELATIVE NATURAL LAW OF THOMAS AQUINAS

The classical theory of *dikaion/jus* survived in part in the work of Thomas Aquinas. Ulpian had defined jurisprudence as the search for just solutions carried out through the knowledge of things[34] and Aquinas' theory of right faithfully followed this definition.[35] Michel

---

[32] Etienne Gilson quoted in "Introduction" to *The Political Writings*, op. cit., supra n. 31, vii.

[33] *De Civitate Dei*, op.cit., supra n. 28, XVIII, 2.

[34] *Digest*, I.I.10.

[35] The First Article in *Summa's* chapter on Justice states categorically that the object of *jus* is the just or right and offers the Philosopher (Aristotle) as main evidence for the

Villey has forcefully argued that, despite the Christian influence, Aquinas remained an Aristotelian in many respects. Villey finds Aquinas' specific contribution to jurisprudence not in the often cited chapter on Law of the *Summa Theologiae* but in the less frequently examined chapter on Justice. The similarities between Aristotle's general justice and Aquinas' *justum* are striking.

> [T]hat which is correct in the works of justice, in addition to the direct reference to the agent [which pertains to all the other virtues], is constituted by a reference to the other person. It is the case, therefore, that in our works, what responds to the other, according to the demands of a certain equality *aequalitatem* is what is called right *justum*.[36]

The strong link remains when we move from general to particular justice. The various Aristotelian meanings of *dikaion/jus* are retained: *jus* is the lawful and the just, justice, as a juridical activity, is the art through which the just becomes known and which tends towards establishing a just state of affairs. As the object of justice, *jus* is again a legal quality inherent in a external entity, an objective state of affairs rather than a subjective right, for which Aquinas has no word or concept. The *jus* as just outcome is an arrangement of things amongst people that respects, promotes or establishes the proportion or equality inherent in them, and these proper relations are observable in the external world. *Res justa, id quod justum est*, writes Aquinas and, *ipsam rem justam*, the just thing itself.[37]

In all these respects, Aquinas followed the teachings of the "Philosopher", whom he endlessly quoted. But his most important and novel contribution to jurisprudence was the fourfold distinction between eternal, natural, divine and human law with its religious overtones, found in the *Summa*'s chapter on *Lex*. Here the law has none of the uncertainties and hesitations associated with Aristotle and the classics. Natural law is definite, certain and simple. No doubt is expressed about its harmony with civil society and the "immutable character of its fundamental propositions", formulated by God the lawgiver in the "Second Table of the decalogue".[38] These principles of divine law suffer no exception in the abstract and, their universal

proposition. ST II-II, Q. 57; Saint Thomas Aquinas, *On Law, Morality and Politics* (W. Baumgarth and R. Regan eds) (Indianapolis, Hackett, 1988) 137. See generally, Anthony Lisska, *Aquinas's Theory of Natural Law* (Oxford, Clarendon, 1996).

[36] ibid.

[37] ibid., 138.

[38] Leo Strauss, *Natural Law and History* (Chicago, University of Chicago Press, 1965) 144.

validity is emphasised by their inscription in human conscience. At
the same time, the natural law revealed in the Decalogue presupposed
a fallen humanity and a sinful nature and, as a divine remedy against
sin, it became flexible and relative. *Natura hominis est mutabilis*, wrote
Thomas, and this flexibility can lead to amendments not just in positive law but in the *jus naturale* itself. Natural law cannot be legislated
in rules or canons of behaviour and does not accept a rigid or fixed
formulation. It offers only general directions as to the character of
people and the action of the law. These are supple and flexible,
imprecise and provisional, context dependent and situation following. To be sure, this God-ordained and newly-found flexibility
allowed state authorities a large degree of discretion.

Aquinas succeeded in integrating law and state into the divine
order through the mediation of relative natural law: while the state
was the result of the original sin, it was also justified because it served
the hierarchical celestial order as its human part. State law and its
coercion were necessary punishment and indispensable remedy for
sins (*poena et remedii peccati*) and they were open to criticism only if
they did not follow the edicts of the Church. At the same time, the
state was responsible for the well-being and security of its citizens
and, the Decalogue, the "compendium of relative natural law", furnished it with the necessary rules. Thus in equating the Decalogue
with natural law, Thomas helped turn it into a "technical, rational
canon of positive law",[39] a way of interpreting and justifying reality,
an almost experimental method.[40]

And while Thomas separated natural and eternal law and assigned
them respectively into the here and the here-after, he also linked
them through a series of hierarchised divine mediations. "Now, all
men know the truth to a certain extent, at least as to the common
principles of natural law . . . and in this respect are more or less cog-
nisant of the eternal law".[41] Justice is the canonical form of this mediation and a principle of gradual participation in the divine order.
"Even an unjust law, insofar as it retains some appearance of law
through being framed by one who is in power, is derived from the
eternal law, since all power is from the Lord God, according to
Romans".[42] Natural law and justice came again together and justice

[39] Bloch, op.cit., supra n. 11, 27.
[40] Michel Villey, "Abrégé du droit naturel classique" in 6 *Archives de Philosophie du Droit*,
27–72, (1961), 50; *La Formation*, op.cit., supra n. 10, 126–30.
[41] *Summa Theologiae*, ST I-II, Q. 93, 3d Art. (38).
[42] ibid.

"in giving to each his due – whether that be a requital in the form of punishment or reward, or distributive according to merit – it expressed a gradation, namely, that architectonic hierarchy which Thomism had erected as the mediation between earth and heaven, heaven and earth".[43] In this way, Thomism justified fully the medieval order, once its rulers and masters had accepted the dominance of the Church. The Stoic golden age as well as Augustine's City of God, the mythical past and the unknown but certain future, were partially present in the medieval city and the relativised natural law lost its ability to oppose positive law. Michel Villey distinguished between Aquinas' concepts of *jus* and *lex* and presented the former as the legal concept *par excellence* while restricting *lex* to moral law and its commands. But Aquinas, following standard practice, occasionally distinguished and at other times equated the two terms.[44] Villey's sharp distinction between the classical and Thomist *jus/dikaion* and the Judaeo-Christian *torah* or *lex* cannot be sustained, because the two were complementary. The just and objective share of external goods, was often determined through the application of *lex*, of law or precept.

But the greatest problem with Aquinas, from the perspective of the natural law tradition, lies in Aquinas' definition of justice. Justice turned into a category of natural law and expressed the advantage of church and feudal hierarchy; its demands were satisfied as long as the law was administered without prejudice and exception. This type of justice represented the inauthentic and relative natural law which repressed sins and atoned for guilt. Classical natural law, on the other hand, was not about the just application of existing laws. It was a rational and dialectical confrontation of institutional and political common sense. The Thomistic *suum cuique tribuere* allowed the scholastics to combine Aristotle and the Old Testament concept of justice as retribution, in a way that retained both Greek class hierarchies and the Judaic patriarchal principle, itself alien to social divisions. Maimonides brilliantly combined severity of form and relativity of content in his definition of justice: "Justice consists in granting his right to everyone who has a right, and in giving to each living being that which he should receive according to his rights".[45] But this justice which completes relative natural law, as its highest virtue and ideal, is very different from classical natural law. Freedom,

---

[43] Bloch, op.cit., supra n. 11, 28.
[44] Tierney, op.cit., supra n. 10, 22–27.
[45] *Guide for the Perplexed*, III, Chapter 53.

communal property and abundance ruled the Stoic edenic age, but for the Christian Father natural law became, after the fall, the law of retribution, accompanied necessarily by courts, punishments and the authority of the sword. Thus, the Church abandoned the Stoic positions on rational freedom and human dignity and "in this way the worst *embarrassment* of natural law, namely, oppression was founded upon natural law itself as something that had been relativised".[46] It was handed down from above, it was based on inequality and domination and underpinned and promoted social differentiation. "Distributive justice gives to each that which corresponds to his degree of importance (*principalitas*) within the community".[47] This hierarchical justice becomes the foundation of an unjust rule. It was represented throughout medieval Europe in the form of *Justitia,* a severe woman whose scales weigh each person's dues, whose sword decapitates the enemies of order and Church and whose blindfolded eyes, added in the late Middle Ages, symbolise the impartiality of justice.[48] As Bloch pithily observed, this is not "a category that thought, justifiably dissatisfied, could consider its own".[49]

Thomas was the last thinker in the Aristotelian legal tradition of *jus naturale* and the most prominent of the new religious naturalism (*lex naturale*). Historians will argue about the relative prominence of *jus* or *lex* and of the legal or religious-moral aspects of his work. But as a direct result of his teachings, the new legislative powers of Church and state were legitimised and, natural law teaching was absorbed by theology. The religious re-definition of natural law profoundly undermined the political and prudential character of the classical doctrines of justice and the critical emphasis of natural law. The ideal city of the future, which for the Greeks and Romans would be built through rational contemplation and political action, was replaced by the non-negotiable other-worldly city of God. God, the lawgiver, infuses his commands with absolute certainty; natural law is no longer concerned with the construction of the ideal moral and political order and the just legal solution, but with the interpretation and confirmation of God's law. After Aquinas, justice largely abandoned its critical potential for jurisprudence. With its pathos vacated and its role as primordial standard gone, it turned into a "cold virtue". The

---

[46] Bloch, op.cit., supra n. 11, 26.

[47] *Summa Theologiae*, II-2, Q. 61, 2nd Article (166–7).

[48] Martin Jay, "Must Justice be Blind", in Costas Douzinas and Lynda Nead, *Law and the Image* (Chicago, University of Chicago Press, 1999) Chapter 1.

[49] Bloch, op.cit., supra n. 11, 38.

word survives but "its supremacy in natural law disappears, and above all, the undeniable moment of condescension and acquiescence, inherent in the severity that the word confers upon itself, disappears".[50] Rousseau defined it as "the love of man derived from the love of oneself"[51] and in this formulation, as social justice, it migrated from law to economics and socialism. Freedom and equality, not justice, will be the rallying cries of modern natural law.

III. THE INVENTION OF THE INDIVIDUAL

There is one final and crucial aspect in the genealogy of human rights, without which we cannot understand the jurisprudence of modernity. This is the process through which the classical and medieval tradition of objective *jus* turned into that of subjective rights and the sovereign individual was born. John Finnis has argued that the transition from Aquinas' *jus* defined as "that which is *just in a given situation*" to that of Suarez as "something beneficial – a *power – which a person has*" was a "watershed".[52] It re-defined the concept of right as a "power" or "liberty" possessed by an individual, a quality that characterises his being. The detailed historical steps leading to this watershed have been examined by Richard Tuck and Michel Villey and more recently by Brian Tierney[53] and there is no need to repeat them here. The remainder of this Chapter will signpost only the main stations in this important transition.

The birth of modern man and of individual rights passes through the theology of Catholic scholasticism, which discovered the principles of natural law in the way God created human beings. The essential nature of man was created by God and all main elements of natural law can be deduced from the morality of the commandments. Moral and political obligations derive from revealed truth and, as a result, Christian love and the *caritas* of providence replaced the quest for the best polity. The first radical step in this direction was taken by the Franciscan nominalists Duns Scotus and William of Ockham. They were the first to argue, in the fourteenth century, against the dominant neo-Platonic views, that the individual form is not a sign

[50] ibid., 43.

[51] Jean Jacques Rousseau, *Emile or on Education* (A. Bloom trans.) (London, Penguin, 1991) IV.

[52] John Finnis, *Natural Law and Natural Rights* (Oxford, Clarendon, 1980) 207.

[53] Richard Tuck, op.cit., supra n. 9; Michel Villey, *La Formation de la Pensée Juridique Moderne*; Brian Tierney, op.cit., supra n. 10, Chapter I.

of contingency nor is the human person the concrete instantiation of the universal. On the contrary, the supreme expression of creation is individuality, as evidenced in the historical incarnation of Christ, and its knowledge takes precedence over that of the universal forms of the classics. Nominalism rejected abstract concepts and denied that general terms like law, justice or the city represented real entities or relations. For William, collectivities, cities or communities, are not natural but artificial. The term "city", for example, refers to the sum total of individual citizens and not to an ensemble of activities, aims and relations, while "law" is a universal word with no discernible empirical referent and has no independent meaning. Society, as Mrs Thatcher a contemporary nominalist would say, does not exist, only individuals do. Medieval science avoided totalities and systems and concentrated on particulars because, argued the nominalists, all general concepts and structures owe their existence to conventional linguistic practices and have no ontological weight or empirical value. Thus, meaning and value became detached from nature and were assigned to separate atoms or particulars, opening the road for the Renaissance concept of the genius, the disciple and partner of God and later for the sovereign individual, the centre of the world.[54]

The legal implications of nominalism cannot be overstated. William argued that the control exercised by private individuals over their lives was of the type of *dominium* or property and, further, that this natural property was not a grant of the law but a basic fact of human life.[55] The absolute power of the individual over his capacities, an early prefiguration of the idea of natural rights, was God's gift to man made in his image. At the same time, the nominalists based their ethics on divine commands and deduced the whole law from their prescriptions. The law was given by the divine legislator whose will is absolute and obligatory for humans *per se* and not because it accorded with nature or reason. Indeed, Duns Scotus argued that God's will has priority over his reason and the good existed because the Omnipotent willed and commanded it and not on account of some other independent quality. In this way, the source and method of the law started changing. It was gradually moved from reason to "Will, pure Will, with no foundation in the nature of things".[56]

---

[54] Ernst Kantorowicz, "The Sovereignty of the Artist: A note on Legal Maxims and Renaissance Theories of Art" in *Selected Studies* (New York, J. J. Augustin, 1965).

[55] Villey, *Histoire de la Philosophie*, op.cit., supra n. 14, 157–265; *Le droit et les droits*, op.cit., supra n. 1, 118–25; Tuck, op.cit., supra n. 9, 15–31.

[56] Rommen quoted in J.M. Kelly, *A Short History of Western Legal Theory* (Oxford University Press, 1992) 145.

Similarly, the jurist's task was no longer to find the just solution but to interpret the legislator's commands for the faithful subjects.

The separation of God from nature and the absolutisation of will prepared the ground for God's retreat and eventual removal from earthly matters. The celebration of an omnipotent and unquestionable will was both the prelude for the full abdication of divine right and the foundation stone of secular omnipotent sovereignty. Legal positivism and untrammelled state authoritarianism found their early precursor in those devout defenders of the power of God. And in a move that was to be repeated by the political philosophers of the seventeenth century, the Franciscans combined absolute legislative will with the nominalist claim that only individuals exist. The combination "led pretty directly to a strongly individualistic political theory which had to undergo only a few modifications to emerge as something very close to the classic rights theories of the seventeenth century".[57] The mutation of objective natural law into subjective individual right, initiated by William, amounted to a cognitive, semantic and eventually political revolution. Villey describes it as a "Copernican moment" emphasising its theoretical and epoch-making affinities with the new scientific world. From that point on, legal and political thought placed at the centre of its attention the sovereign and the individual with their respective rights and powers.

The second scholastic school, argued that natural law is a branch of morality and linked religious rules of conduct with modern reason. The Spanish scholastics totally abandoned the idea of *jus* as an objective state of affairs and adopted fully an individualistic conception of right. A crucial text in this transition was the seventeenth century *De Legibus* by the Spanish Jesuit Franciso Suarez. Suarez argued that the "true, strict and proper meaning" of *jus* is, "a kind of moral power *facultas* which every man has, either over his own property or with respect to that which is due to him".[58] Grotius too saw *jus* as a quality or power possessed by a person. Grotius returned and expanded the Stoic tradition according to which *jus naturale est dictatum retae rationis*.[59] But by asking the law to accord with the rational nature of man, he finally abandoned both the classical and the Christian traditions of natural law. Nature, perceived as solely a physical universe, became radically separated from humanity, it was emptied of the ends

[57] Tuck, op.cit., supra n. 9, 24.
[58] Finnis, op.cit., supra n. 52, 206–7.
[59] Grotius, *De Jure Beli et Pacis Libre Tres* (Law of War and Peace, F. Kelsey trans.) (Indianapolis, Bobbs-Merrill, 1962) vol.I, 9.

and purposes of the classics or the animistic soul of the medievals and stood without meaning value or spirit, a frightening and hostile force. The right, no longer objectively given in nature or the commandment of God's will, follows human reason and becomes subjective and rational. The naturally right becomes individual rights.

The theological influence was still evident in the work of all great philosophers of the seventeenth century. *Omnia sub ratione Dei* was their rallying cry, a slogan destined to a transient but all-important existence. It destroyed the medieval world view but it soon succumbed to its own humanistic tendencies and led to the death of God. Descartes explicitly linked new physics and theology, Hobbes and Locke organised their civil state under the auspices of God. All great philosophers wrote a kind of political theology and believed that God underwrote their systematic efforts. A laicised deism replaced Christ with the God of Reason and eventually with Man become God. But in a different sense the great Enlightenment writers, Descartes, Hobbes, Locke and Rousseau, despite their differing conceptions of natural right and social contract, represented the rebellion of reason against the theocratic organisation of authority. The modern natural rights tradition, which turned violently against ancient cosmology and ontology and redefined the source of right, was a reaction to the co-optation of natural law by religion and the accompanying loss of juridical flexibility, political latitude and imaginative utopianism which characterised the classical tradition. The secular theology of natural rights placed the abstract concept of man at the centre of the Universe and transferred to him the adoration offered by the medievals to God. The forward looking and prudential aspects of the theory of the "best polity" were undermined but, at the same time, the openness of classical natural law became a potential horizon of individual identity and right.

Medieval constitutional theories and utopias had been organised around the ideas of the fall and the divine legislator. But the early modern undermining of the secular power of theology, meant that the relative natural law, which regulated humanity in a state of sin, could no longer be used to justify oppressive social and political regimes. The grace of divine authority and the aura of its earthly representative could not captivate the soul of the people and, in its place, modern natural law attempted to re-construct the constitution using reason alone. Epicurean ideas, according to which the *polis* was the outcome of an original contract, and the Stoic belief that the law should be in harmony with the reason of the world, acquired renewed importance. But this was the natural law of modern merchants and not of ancient sages; it attributed contemporary legal and social arrangements to a primordial assembly and a freely-entered contract.

The idea of an original contract was accompanied by the device of a state of nature in which men lived before entering society or the state. Against the ancients, for whom nature was a standard of critique transcending empirical reality, the nature of Rousseau, Hobbes and Locke was an attempt to discover the common elements of humanity, the lowest common denominator behind the differing individual, social and national characteristics and idiosyncrasies. This quest for the permanent, universal and eternal, had to deduct from empirical people whatever historical, local or contingent factors had added to their "nature". The natural man or *noble savage* was not a primitive forefather of the patrons of Parisian salons or of London merchants but had similarities with them. As species representative, man *qua* man, he was an artificial construct of reason, a naked human being endowed only with logic, strong survival instincts and a sense of morality. According to John Rawls, who famously repeated the mental experiment, natural man toils and contracts behind a "veil of ignorance".[60] The fiction drew its power from the importance contract had acquired in early capitalism. It was only in an emerging market society that all important institutional and personal questions could be addressed through the putative agreements of rational individuals. But despite assurances to the contrary, the man of nature was not totally naked: his "natural" instincts and drives differed widely from one natural lawyer to the next. For some, natural man was competitive and aggressive, for others peaceful and industrious, for others both. Eternal nature seemed to follow current social priorities and political concerns and to be quite close to the preoccupations, hopes and fears of the contemporaries of the theorist.

The fictional contract became a device for philosophical speculations about the nature of the social bond and political obligation, the model constitution and the rights of empirical men in London and Paris. Abstraction, the removal of concrete characteristics, was seen as logically necessary. The philosophical construct was asked to act as a refutation of both feudal society and absolutist government, through the operation of a revolutionary and previously unheard of termination clause which authorised the people to overthrow their

---

[60] John Rawls, *A Theory of Justice* (Oxford University Press, 1972). The veil conceals all the major individualising characteristics from the contractors.

government in case of non-performance of its contractual obligations; and as the blueprint for the constitutional arrangement still to come. In this second function, the contractual device introduced the rationalism of the Enlightenment into the constitution. Legal norms and social relations were shamelessly deduced from axiomatic normative propositions (original evil and desire for security, original goodness and sociability, individual freedom and the need to restrict it, etc.).

The various schools of modern or rational natural law, despite their differences, shared a number of characteristics.[61] First, they all believed that social life and the state are the result of free individual activity. We can detect here the heavy influence of legal mentality. It is deeply pleasing to a lawyer, steeped in the doctrine of contract, to believe that legal forms and free agreements lie at the basis of society. Social contract theories adopted the contract doctrine of "constructive knowledge": the contractors willed all reasonable consequences of their agreement, while what could not have been rationally willed was not willed at all (restrictions on property and capital accumulation, for example, were unreasonable and a political system that enforced them brought the contract's termination clause into operation). Secondly, if the legal and social order derives from an original agreement, it was realised through the power of reason and logic to deduce a complete and gapless system of rules from a few axiomatic principles. The essence of the state was to be rationally reconstructed from its valid elements and justified only by means of reasoned argument, based on its founding principles in the contract; indeed reason was declared the essence of the state. The prestige of the natural sciences was thus transferred to political philosophy and natural law became a pure discourse of deduction modelled on mathematics.

The natural sciences in their quest for predictability and certainty discarded irregularities; natural law followed suit. The methodological purity of mathematics complemented perfectly the belief in universal homogeneous concepts and eternal laws, which became a central tenet of rational natural law. The iron laws and the strict necessity and homogeneity of Newton's mechanical nature were reinterpreted as a normative universality and were co-opted in the fight against the hierarchical society of feudal privilege. Rational natural law and natural rights became the discourse of revolution. The liberal version of Thomas Paine inspired the Americans, the democra-

---

[61] Bloch, op.cit., supra n. 11, 53–60.

tic of Jean-Jacques Rousseau the French. No political philosophy or version of natural law was worthy of the name, if it was not grounded on universal principles or did not aim at universal ends. The great discoveries, the marvellous inventions and the triumph of the mercantile and urban economies, aided by the levelling exchange-value of money, combined to increase the cachet of the universal. But the discourse of the universal soon became the companion of capitalism and the upholder of the market, the place where, according to Marx, human rights and Bentham reign supreme. The rationalism of natural law too, having consigned the classical conception of politics and the search for the "best polity" to the history of ideas, became the legitimatory discourse of utilitarian governments and was used against the emerging socialist and reform movements. A side-effect of this rampant rationalism was the intellectual impoverishment of jurisprudence: the violence at the heart of law and of public and private power, which had helped re-organise the world according to the new political and economic orthodoxies, was written out of the texts of law, which became obsessed with normative questions, with the meaning of rights, sovereignty or representation. Much of the unrealistic rationalism which still bedevils jurisprudence hails from this golden age of natural law. This idealism not only totally obfuscates law's role in the world, it also distorts our understanding of legal operations because:

> it serves no purpose to pick out partial relations and even partial tendencies in real life and insert them into the head as an arithmetical problem . . . in order to come up with a logic that formally is like iron, but remains weaker and unreal from the point of view of content . . . formal necessity, that is, the absence of contradiction in the deduction and form of a proposition, is hardly a criterion of its truth in a dialectical world.[62]

But alongside this law-abiding and sombre nature, which accorded with the bourgeois interests in calculability and certainty, a different conception of a *natura immaculata* lurked below the surface, in the pure and harmonious nature of classicism, the edenic visions of romanticism and the perfectibility of utopian socialists. This marginal conception of a purified and perfect nature linked with the classical tradition of nature as standard and provided a critical and redemptive perspective against the injustices and oppressions which the social system, justified by rational natural law, tolerated and even promoted.

[62] ibid., 191.

This concept of nature would eventually combine with the idea of social utopia and provide the radical side of human rights.

★★★

At the end of this historical journey, it is important to remember that classical natural law was built on the intrinsic connection between natural right and justice. The same terms, *dikaion* and *jus*, connoted both the just and the law, and the business of the classical lawyers was to discover the just solution to a conflict. This linguistic link survives today in the double meaning of the word justice, as the transcendent ideal of law and as the administration of the judicial system. But classical right was not a moral law that lurks in the human conscience as a universal superego and places all under the same moral commands. It was rather a methodological principle which allowed the philosopher to criticise sedimented tradition and the jurist to discover the just solution in the case in hand. Classical natural law contained a passion for justice but it did not coincide with it. Natural right enters the historical agenda, directly or in disguise, every time people struggle "to overthrow all relations in which man is a degraded, enslaved, abandoned or despised being".[63] Justice, on the other hand, has too often been associated with a moralistic, patriarchal attitude, in which distributions and commutation protect the established order and perpetuate the inequalities and oppression natural law tries to redress:

> Genuine natural law, which posits the free will in accord with reason, was the first to reclaim the justice that can only be obtained by struggle; it did not understand justice as something that descends from above and prescribes to each his share, distributing or retaliating, but rather as an active justice of below, one that would make justice itself unnecessary. Natural law never coincided with a mere sense of justice.[64]

For those fighting against injustice and for a society that transcends the present, natural right has been the method and natural law has defined the content of the new. This is the link between natural law, natural and human rights. But the voluntarism of modern natural law cannot provide a sufficient foundation for human rights. Its inevitable intertwining with legal positivism meant that the tradition which created natural and later human rights has also contributed to the repeated and brutal violations of dignity and equality which have accompanied modernity, like its inescapable shadow.

---

[63] Bloch, op.cit., supra n. 11, xxviii–xxix.
[64] ibid., xxx.

4

Natural Right in Hobbes and Locke

From Plato's *Republic* to early modernity, philosophy placed the search for the best polity at its centre. Thomas Hobbes continued this tradition which brought together political thought and legal concerns. His early works were general theories of law. The later *De Cive* and *Leviathan* and the posthumous *Dialogue* changed somehow their emphasis, in an attempt to create a science of politics which according to Arendt, "would make politics as exact a science as the clock did for time". For most commentators, the main achievement of Hobbes lies in his political theory, which has also been denounced by others for its authoritarianism and parochialism. If one could analytically distinguish between political and legal theory, a difficult task for that period, it is arguable that Hobbes made a more lasting contribution to the science of law: in his radically new method of analysing legal foundations, in his re-definition of the traditional juridical concepts of law, right and justice, finally, in his adjustment of traditional sources and ends of law to the concerns of modernity. The influence of Hobbes has waned in politics, with the rise of the purer liberalism of Locke and the democratic tradition of Rousseau. But his re-invention of the juridical world remains unsurpassed. We can summarise his contribution by saying that Hobbes is the founder of the modern tradition of individual rights, the first philosopher to replace fully the concept of justice with the idea of rights. If this aspect of his work is understood, legal positivism becomes the necessary accompaniment and partner of rights discourse and some of the liberal critiques of Hobbes lose much of their validity.

Hobbes' revolutionary contribution to jurisprudence is perfectly illustrated by the following statement from the beginning of the XIV Chapter of *Leviathan*, entitled "Of the first and second Naturall Lawes, and of Contracts", which is worth quoting at length:

> THE RIGHT OF NATURE, which Writers commonly call *Jus Naturale*, is the Liberty each man hath, to use his own power, as he

will himselfe, for the preservation of his own Nature; that is to say, of his own Life; and consequently, of doing any thing, which in his own Judgement, and Reason, hee shall conceive to be the uptest means thereunto.

BY LIBERTY, is understood , according to the proper signification of the word, the absence of externall Impediments: which Impedimens may oft take away part of a mans power to do what hee would; but cannot hinder him from using the power left him, according as his judgement and reason shall dictate to him.

A LAW OF NATURE, (*Lex Naturalis*) is a Precept, or generall Rule, found out be reason, by which a man is forbidden to do, that, which is destructive of his life, or taketh away the means of preserving the same; and to omit, that, by which he thinketh it may be best preserved. For though they that speak of this subject, use to confound *Jus*, and *Lex, Right* and *Law*; yet they ought to be distinguuished; because RIGHT, consisteth in liberty to do, or to forbeare; Whereas LAW, determineth, and bindeth to one of them: so that law, and Right, differ as much, as Obligation and Liberty; which in the same matter are inconsistent.[1]

This concise and epigrammatic statement, is a clear declaration and definition of the modern rights of man. It remains unsurpassed in clarity and precision in the early modern literature of natural rights and clearly indicates its ontology and theology. Like Leviathan himself, this striking statement is Janus-like. It is still in conversation with the Aristotelian tradition which distinguished between right (*dikaion, jus*) and law (*nomos, lex*) and attributed the dignity of nature to the former. But Janus' other face looks to the future. Natural right is not the just resolution of a dispute offered by a harmonious cosmos or God's commands. It derives exclusively from the nature of "each man". The source or basis of right is no longer the observation of natural relations, philosophical speculation about the "best polity" or the interpretation of divine commandments but human nature.

How did this change of source affect the relationship between law and right or justice, the structuring principle of legal activity in the pre-modern world? For the classics, the law *nomos* and the right *dikaion* coincide, and justice, another word for right, was law's object and end. The two concepts were so closely connected that they were often used as synonyms, something Hobbes wanted to avoid. Hobbes

---

[1] Thomas Hobbes, *Leviathan* (Richard Tuck ed.) (Cambridge University Press, 1996) Chapter 14, 91.

occasionally confused the two terms but he also presented the relationship as a clear evolution from the state of nature to civil society. The Hobbesian state of nature, has no organised community and law, except for the natural law of self-preservation. But this law is not "properly law". In a radical move, which will irreversibly change the concept of justice, Hobbes identified right with freedom from law and from all external and social imposition. Laws are not conducive to right because they restrain freedom. But the law of self-preservation is different: it derives from human nature and as such it does not impose external constraints or restrict liberty.

With this move, Hobbes separated the individual from the social order and installed him at the centre, as the subject of modernity and the source of law. The classical tradition discovered the naturally right by observing relationships in human communities. For Aristotle and Aquinas, jurists could find the model of legal organisation and the answers to legal problems in the natural order of their world. This order fell well short of the ideal, but included sufficient elements of the perfect polity to give rise to direct philosophical and legal deliberations about the just solution. Individuals were naturally social and political and no useful conclusions could be reached without the observation of their communities and social interactions. The starting point of Hobbes, a student of Stoicism and nominalism, was precisely the opposite. The eye of the observer is no longer trained on society but on the isolated individual in a pre-social state of nature. Natural right is not to be sought in the harmonious order of the political community but in its opposite, the natural characteristics of a Crusoe-like figure. Human nature, Hobbes believed, has certain common traits, the observation of which will determine what is naturally right. Nature becomes therefore a scientific hypothesis, its law takes the form of observable regularities or common patterns present in all men. Because human nature is objectively given, reason can deduce from an observation of the way men actually behave, a series of natural laws that should be followed by the Commonwealth. Reason has been freed from the metaphysical claims of Stoicism and Christianity, it is no longer a spirit, does not reside in the soul and does not have much to say about the essence of things. "Reason is calculation" writes Hobbes and true reason is part of human nature.[2] In

---

[2] Hobbes, *De Corpore*, I, 2, at 3. Cf "by right reason in the natural state of men, I understand not, as many do, an infallible faculty, but the act of reasoning, that is, the peculiar and true ratiocinations of ecery man concerning these actions of his, which may either redound to the damage or benefit of his neighbours", *De Cive* II,1 at 16.

its new role, reason can discover the best means and co-ordinate their action towards a desired end. This is the calculative, instrumental reason of the moderns and its task in the field of morals and politics is not to guide the conscience but to build a science through the observation of the external world and human nature.

When reason comes to examine human nature and develop the science of politics, it discovers there desire, reason's negation and adversary. Indeed, while the first natural law is unrestricted freedom, the second is the duty to keep promises and the twenty-odd other laws offered from the observation of human nature refer to passions, such as gratitude, sociability, moderation and impartiality (the virtues) or revenge, lack of generosity and arrogance (the vices). The passions, desire, appetite and aversion, are the most powerful human force:

> But whatsoever is the object of any mans Appetite or Desire; that is it, which for his part calleth *Good:* And the object of his Hate and Aversion, Evill; And of his Contempt, *Vile and Inconsiderable* . . . For Morall philosophy is nothing else but the science of what is *Good,* and *Evill,* in the conversation, and Society of man-kind. *Good* and *Evill,* are names that signifie our Appetites, and Aversions; which in different tempers, customes, and doctrines of men, are different.[3]

Desire is stronger than reason. When reason confronts it, it must either acknowledge its impotence or try and recruit the passions to its own – always endangered – advantage. Desire and pleasure, presented as instinctual forces or "drives" in the psychoanalytical terminology, acquire central political and legal significance, and turn the theological nominalism of the medievals into a "scientific" individualism. This radically new concept will provide the idea of individual rights, struggling to emerge in the religiously inspired writings of the scholastics, with a secular and pragmatically fecund foundation. The centrality of the passions, both empirically observed and metaphysically asserted as natural, turns the moral philosophy of Hobbes into a political hedonism and prepares the ground for utilitarianism. The end of law is no longer virtue and justice, but individual pleasure, and reason is the main instrument to this end. This approach makes natural right no longer the fair share of a legal distribution, a state of things in the outside world, but an essential attribute of the subject. Right is a power that belongs to the individual, a subjective quality which logically excludes all duty. This is precisely the basis of the distinction between law and right: the law imposes duties and does not

---

[3] *Leviathan,* supra n. 1, Chapter 6, 39; Chapter 16, 110.

confer powers; this makes it the opposite of right. When right is a share of social goods, it is always part of relationships, it implies duties and is by definition limited. New natural right is the "power of doing any thing", an unlimited and undivided sovereignty of the self.

When we turn from source to form, natural right is defined as the "liberty [of man] of doing any thing as he wille himselfe" and liberty as "the absence of external Impediments".[4] Right means doing; it is an active state of bodily motion guided by will which, against the schools, is no longer defined as rational desire but as the "last appetite in deliberating",[5] desire's final state which puts the body and its appetites into motion and, through their action, realises its end in the world.[6] The Cartesian divide between spirit and body is absent here. Man is treated as a force of nature, an agent of action, motivated by desire and seeking pleasure. Liberty is negative; it is an infinite license, a freedom of motion that has no inherent limitations but only external, empirical constraints, most notably in the liberty of other men to pursue the same ends or to engage in motion that puts them on a collision course.

The natural anthropology of Hobbes is a concise statement of modernity. Following a felicitous and now classical presentation of the move from the ancients to the moderns, man is no longer conceived as a mirror of some superior and external reality but as the lamp, the source and centre of light illuminating the world. Being is no longer the creation of a divine first cause nor does it approach reality as a copy of a pre-existing original. Man is productive, his essence is to be found in his "doing" and "bodily motion", he becomes the creator and cause of actions and the bestower of meaning upon a profane reality. The self as agent recognises himself as the centre of decision making with a power that springs neither from pure emotions nor from pure intelligence. The power of will is unique. This power finds its perfect manifestation in decision. In ending deliberation and taking a decision, the desiring self projects itself in the world and becomes a sovereign agent for Hobbes or an autonomous and responsible subject for Kant. Imagination and art, too, are no longer conceived as resemblances of a transcendent reality of forms, nor is the artist a craftsman imitating the divine *demiourge*. The model of the modern artist is the inventor and

---

[4] ibid., Chapter 14, 91.

[5] ibid., Chapter 6, 44.

[6] Chris Tsaitourides, "Leviathan-Moby Dick: The Physics of Space", VIII/2 *Law and Critique*, 223–243, 1997.

imagination, in its ability to co-ordinate the faculties, becomes itself transcendental. Finally, in the practical realm, agency becomes central. The subject is enthroned as a free agent, as the immediate source of activity and the cause of actions that emanate from it. The modern self fulfils itself in what he does, our actions express our true existence, and as a result we can only know what we make.

But the unencumbered desire and action of natural right creates two difficulties. First, it is shared equally by all. "Nature hath made men so equall, in the faculties of body, and mind . . . the weakest has strength enough to kill the strongest . . . and as to the faculties of the mind, . . . I find yet a greater equality among men than that of strength".[7] This natural equality of desire and strength has nothing in common with the classical hierarchical conception of right and of justice. Traditional political philosophy had claimed that man can perfect himself in political society and had made duty the primary moral fact. From Aristotle to early modernity, the just outcome was determined according to a person's due in a community, *suum jus cuique tribuendum*. In the *polis* or the *civitas*, the natural hierarchy of the parts of the soul or amongst the various classes provided an order, a measure which was also the principle of justice. But when nature is emancipated from the harmonious and hierarchical order of the ancients, it becomes absolute equality, a terrible equivalence of force, which knows only the justice of desire and the constraint of force and law. Secondly, as a result of Hobbes's identification of pleasure with the good and of pain and death with evil, morality cannot distinguish between the different types of pleasures and pains and is unable to create a scheme of values. "The Desires and other Passions of man, are in themselves no Sin. No more are the Actions which proceed from these Passions, till they know a Law that forbids them". It is precisely this combination of unlimited liberty of action, of equality of powers and of the moral indifference of desire and its objects that leads to a "warre of every man against every man".

The political recognition of desire leads to the primacy of right over duty. When the individual becomes the centre of the world, when fear, hate and love[8] are the only ends of action, everyone is entitled to self-preservation and to the means to achieve it. Each man is the sole judge of the right means and every action in pursuit of

---

[7] Leviathan, supra n. 1, Chapter 13, 86.

[8] Hobbes states that what "men Desire, they are also sayd to LOVE: and to HATE those things, for which they have Aversion. So that Desire, and Love, are the same thing", *Leviathan*, supra n. 1, Chapter 6, 38.

desire is by nature just. "To this war of every man against every man, this is also consequent: that nothing can be unjust. The notions of right and wrong, justice and injustice, have there no place. Where there is no common power, there is no law: where no law, no injustice".[9] The primacy of desire leads to the establishment of civil laws (*leges*). Classical and medieval cosmology, the source of natural right, assumed a natural hierarchy of spheres and being. Hobbes turns the cosmology into an anthropology and transfers the hierarchical model from the universe to human desires. Death, the denial of nature, is the most natural of all facts, and the fear of death the most powerful of all passions. Uncontrolled desire finds its limit in the desire and fear of the other and in death. The desire of self-preservation makes men abandon unrestricted freedom in return for the security offered by the commonwealth created through their contractual subjection to the Sovereign.[10] It is not nature therefore but death, as the negation of nature, which is the most natural and strongest of passions. Death is the basis of natural law and the target of civil laws. Because equality is unlimited, because desire is uncontrollable, death becomes the master and the power of the Sovereign must be total and illimitable. The Sovereign is a "Mortall God", its only limit is death, the "absolute master". The law is the outcome of desire and of a death drive which, well before Freud's discovery, linked law, desire and mortality. Unlimited passion creates unlimited sovereignty, violence and its fear are the ground of law. Both natural right and the state entrusted with its limited protection are deathbound. As Leo Strauss put it, in Hobbes "death takes the place of the *telos*".[11]

The impasse created by the free pursuit of desire by equals can only be broken through a covenant that "erects a Common Power" and transfers natural right to it. The object of agreement is to:

> conferre all their power and strength upon one Man, or upon one Assembly of Men, to beare their person; . . . and therein to submit their Wills, every one to his Will, and their Judgements, to his Judgement. This is more than Consent or Concord; it is a real Unitie of them all, in one and the same Person, made by Covenant of every man with every man, in such manner, as if every man should say to every man, *I authorise and give up my Right of Governing my selfe, to this Man, or to this Assembly of men, on this condition, that thy give up thy Right to him, and Authorise all his actions in like manner* . . . the Essence of the

---

[9] ibid., Chapter 13, 90.
[10] ibid.
[11] Strauss, *Natural Law and History* (Chicago, University of Chicago Press, 1965) 181.

Common-Wealth . . . is *One Person of whose Acts a great Multitude, by mutuall Covenants one with another, have made themselves every one the Author, to the end he may use the strength and means of them all, as he shall think expedient, for their Peace and Common Defence.*[12]

The Sovereign created through the covenant takes the characteristics of natural man and his right. The Leviathan has unrestricted power, his sovereignty cannot be forfeited, he is the sole legislator, himself not subjected to the law[13] and, his rights are indivisible, absolute and incommunicable. Civil law is "to every subject, those Rules, which the Common-Wealth hath commanded him, by Word, Writing, or other sufficient Sign of the Will, to make use of, for the Distinction of Right, and Wrong; that is to say, of what is contrary, and what is not contrary to the Rule".[14] These laws, following consistently the earlier analysis, are commands and impositions: "the end of making Lawes, is no other, but such restraint . . . And Law was brought into the World for nothing else, but to limit the naturall liberty of particular men".[15] The creations of absolute legislative power are necessary even though they violate the first natural law of unrestricted freedom because of the uncertainty and insecurity of equal desires and forces. Civil laws are "properly laws".[16] They derive from nature, not as its spontaneous accretions, but as artifices: "we have derived civil rules from nature, which gives us natural laws, through the use of art, assisted by reason, itself natural but able to transform nature and adapt to the needs of a world of sin, adjust them to the circumstances of social life".[17] Civil laws are both natural and the outcome of the public reason of the Sovereign and, unlike unchangeable natural law, adapt to social need, evolve and vary. Natural law did not create property rights, because natural humanity enjoyed resources communally before the fall while, after the fall, uncertainty about goods dominated. Civil laws are necessary therefore for the creation of rights. They distribute riches and create proper property rights:

---

[12] *Leviathan*, supra n. 1, Chapter 18, 120–1.

[13] "For having the power to make, and repeal laws, he may when he pleaseth, free himself from that subjection", *De Cive*, VI, 14, at 83; *Leviathan*, Chapter 26. This is the reason why Hobbes is so hostile to the common law tradition, particularly the claim associated with Sir Edward Coke that common law is superior to the law of king and Parliament. See, *Dialogue between a Philosopher and a Student of the Common Law of England* (J. Crospey ed.) (Chicago, University of Chicago Press, 1997).

[14] *Leviathan*, supra n. 1, Chapter 26, 183.

[15] ibid., 185.

[16] ibid.

[17] ibid., 188.

The distribution of the materials of this nourishment, is the constitution of mine and thine and his; that is in one word propriety; and belongeth in all kinds of commonwealths to the sovereign power . . . The introduction of propriety is an effect of commonwealth which can do nothing but by the person that represents it, it is the act only of the sovereign; and consisteth in the laws, which none can make that have not the sovereign power.[18]

Once the Commonwealth has been established, the natural right that led to its foundation is transferred to the "Ordinances of Souveraign Power". When civil laws, Leviathan's sole responsibility, are given the task of protecting the rights of individuals, natural law in a final feat of trans-substantiation becomes identical with civil law. "The law of Nature and Civill Law, contain each other, and are of equal extent . . . The Law of Nature therefore is a part of the Civill Law in all Common-wealths of the world . . . And therefore Obedience to the Civill Law is also part of the Law of Nature".[19] Civil law and rights are the secular version of natural law. Its source remains the same, a natural reason adapted only to the exigencies of the secular world; but the practical necessities of civil life often lead to commands which contradict natural law. As a result, after the identification of civil and natural law, justice was radically re-defined: First, and in keeping with natural law, "INJUSTICE is no other than *the not Performance of Covenant*. And whosoever is not Unjust, is *Just*".[20] But secondly, "Lawes are the Rules of Just, and Unjust; nothing being reputed Unjust, that is not contrary to some Law".[21] At the end of a long process, natural right was turned into state-given individual rights and justice became obedience to the law. The only principle of justice is conformity with state laws.

At first, contractual consent appears to be the foundation of Leviathan and the modern state. But this is a sleight of hand. The primacy of desire leads inexorably to the social contract, which presents society as the outcome of individual freedom and agreement. To be sure, a covenant based on those premises cannot work unless it is turned into the total subjection of all to the commands of the state. The violence that marked the beginning and the force necessitated by the fear of death, enters civil law and becomes its inescapable condition and supplement. The command of the Sovereign becomes the

[18] ibid., 187.
[19] ibid., 185.
[20] ibid., Chapter 15, 100.
[21] ibid., Chapter 26, 184.

basis of all authority. Laws are laws because of their source and sanctions, not because of their reason. The supremacy of state authority mirrors the natural freedom of the individual; Leviathan, the perfect partner and necessary constraint of the individual, both shares and inaugurates the individual's attributes.[22]

The power of the Sovereign is therefore the result of individual desire and right. Liberalism, the political philosophy which treats rights as the fundamental political fact and eventually identifies the function of the state with their protection, finds its foundational document in Hobbes. Rights are natural while duties conventional; they arise from the contract and, as the contract means total subjection to the state, they ultimately derive from the will of the Sovereign. Legal positivism is the inevitable accompaniment of the individualism of rights. "The Liberty of a Subject, lyeth therefore only in those things, which in regulating their actions, the Sovereign hath praetermitted".[23] Burke complained that "the Parisian philosophers . . . explode or render odious or contemptible, that class of virtues which restrain the appetite . . . In the place of all this, they substitute a virtue which they call humanity or benevolence".[24] But the replacement of virtue and duty with a right deriving logically from human nature and politically from the will of the Sovereign had already been completed in Hobbes. All the elements of political and legal modernity are present in *Leviathan*: individual prior to society; natural and later human rights based on law's recognition of desire; the conventional Sovereign, made in the image of the free individual, whose right establishes individual right; legal positivism and the centrality of will and contract. Most of all, we find in Hobbes the internal link between desire, violence and law.

One could argue, therefore, that the doctrine of sovereignty is a legal doctrine, because all power and rights belongs to the Sovereign not through grant or custom but as of right. According to Strauss, natural public law, the discipline created in the seventeenth century by Macchiavelli and Hobbes, "lowered the goal of politics". Classical political philosophy had distinguished between the ideal of the best polity and that of the legitimate regime. The latter depended for its realisation on the practical wisdom of the statesman, who adjusted the ideal to the exigencies of time and place. Modern natural law answers the problem of the just social order once and for all.

---

[22] Strauss, op cit., supra n. 11, 186 ff.
[23] ibid., Chapter 21, 148.
[24] Burke quoted in Strauss, op.cit., supra n. 11, p. 188.

Though nothing can be immortall, which mortals make; yet, if men had the use of reason they pretend to, their Common-wealths might be secured . . . for by the nature of their Institution, they are designed to live, as long as Mankind, or as the Lawes of Nature, or as Justice is selfe, which gives them life.[25]

The new science of politics, based on the dogmatism of state and rights, is almost identical to the legalisation of political life.[26] It "intends to give a universally valid solution to the political problem as is meant to be universally applicable in practice" and, by necessity, it replaces the idea of the best polity with that of efficient and legitimate government.[27] In legal terms, the study of ends is replaced by the study of means and techniques, while the rights of the Sovereign, as distinguished from their exercise, allow an exact definition without reference to the circumstances of their application; but "this kind of exactness is again inseparable from moral neutrality: right declares what is permitted, as distinguished from what is honourable".[28]

In the new climate, the main task of politics becomes the design of the right institutions. But modern constitution-building bears no relationship to the "best polity" of the classics. The institutions of modern politics should be so value-neutral that, according to Kant, they should be acceptable even to "a nation of devils", guided by reasoned desire and fear. "When commonwealth come to be dissolved, not by external violence, but intestine disorder, the fault is not in men, as they are the *matter*, but as they are the *makers*, and orderers of them".[29] When the business of politics is focused on the efficiency or legitimacy of power rather than its ends and prudent use, all the characteristics of the Sovereign will be visited on its notional progenitor, the individual and his human rights. Power can guarantee the social order by conquering human nature and manipulating its passions. The "mortall God", created in the imaginary image of man the "maker", must now shape man, the "matter", in its own image. An apparent contradiction seems to accompany therefore the creation of Leviathan. As soon as he is born, he destroys the natural rights of his progenitor, of the subjects who contracted to create him. The subjects who voluntarily entered into submission in order to safeguard their rights, must now lay them down and consent to their abolition.

---

[26] "Doctrinairism made its first appearance within political philosophy – for lawyers are altogether in a class by themselves – in the seventeenth century", Strauss, op.cit., supra n. 11, 192.

[27] ibid., 190,191.

[28] ibid., 195.

[29] *Leviathan*, supra n. 1, Chapter 29, 221.

The recognition and protection of natural right prepares its disappearance. To that extent, natural right is always deferred, a mirage or heuristic device which explains the creation of modern politics.

But this is not the whole picture. Even in Hobbes' authoritarian system, natural right survives in two forms. It survives, first, in the person of the Sovereign and in the construction of state power. Sovereign right retains all the characteristics of the individual natural right. Leviathan's unique and infinite right is the civil expression of the absolute right in the state of nature. The Sovereign retains absolute power both in relation to its subjects and the other Sovereigns in international law. The subjects do not give the Sovereign a right or power he does not possess; they simply forfeit their right of resistance. For the nominalist Hobbes, rights belong only to individuals. Communities, multitudes, the people as people can have no right. For sovereignty to become operative and offer its services, it must belong to a singular subject. This happens twice. First, in the fiction of the artificial personality, of Leviathan, the crown or the state. Secondly, in the demand that the real bearer or symbol of sovereignty should be a monarch, a natural person rather than Parliament or the people. Sovereignty is an attribute of individuality, its fictitious construction is necessary because collectivities have no rights.

But the subjects too retain rights. They do not forfeit the right to self-defence and to freedom of conscience. More importantly, they acquire those civil rights which were jeopardised in the state of nature and upon which the moral legitimacy of the state rests. In particular, they acquire the right to property. Hobbes inaugurates a legal system based on the realisation and safeguarding of individual rights. An individual natural right is both the foundation and the outcome of the edifice. Conflicting natural rights lead to the pact, which gives birth to Leviathan, who lays down the law in order to protect and secure individual rights. Civil law is created through the unstoppable advance of individual rights, law's end is the creation of rights. But these are private rights only. Public rights, rights against the state, are totally excluded. The creation and enjoyment of private rights is accompanied by an absence of what we now call human rights. The price for the protection against others is minimal protection against the state. Private rights are the end and value of the system of law, which becomes a system of subjective rights, of their preconditions and consequences: contracts, a strong state and an absolute law.

In this transition from natural right to individual rights, the old link with justice was severed. Hobbes defined justice as the obligations to keep promises and to obey the law. The former is necessary in order to keep the fragile social peace of a society based largely on private agreements, while the latter is the logical consequence of the lack of any rights against the Sovereign. Public and private rights, while formally similar, are clearly distinct. The precondition of individual property rights is the absence of political and human rights, subjection the precondition of freedom. This is the tragedy of individualism, mitigated by the introduction of democracy but still present in the various forms of neo-liberalism. Its attempt to establish law and a system of social relations on their denial, the isolated individual and his rights, can easily end up with their frightening mirror image, an omnipotent state, which destroys rights in their name. Despite jurisprudential claims to the contrary, individual and human are often bitter enemies.

★★★

John Locke's political writings are commonly presented as the early manifesto of liberalism and as the opposite of Hobbes' "totalitarianism". Yet the main assumptions of Locke did not differ radically from his predecessor. The state of nature hypothesis was again at the basis of the political constitution. But the status of natural law is ambiguous. Its rules are not "imprinted on the mind as a duty".[30] On the contrary, conscience is "nothing else but our own opinion or judgement of the moral rectitude or pravity of our own actions".[31] Like Hobbes, however, desire is the mainspring of human nature. "Nature . . . has put into man a desire of happiness, and an aversion to misery; these, indeed, are innate practical principles".[32] The right to pursue happiness is the only innate right, it comes before and founds the law of nature. Men "must be allowed to pursue their happiness, nay, cannot be hindered".[33]

Happiness depends on life and the desire for self-preservation takes precedence over the pursuit of happiness when the two come into conflict. In the state of nature, man is the sole judge of his actions and "may do what he thinks fit". It follows that the natural state is full of fear and danger. Reason wills peace and teaches man what is necessary to that end. The only remedy to the constant conflict of the state of nature is the establishment of civil society or government, and natural law is the sum of its dictates as regards peace and mutual security.

---

[30] John Locke, *An Essay Concerning Human Understanding* P. H. Nidditch (ed.) (Oxford, Clarendon, 1975), I, 3, 3.

[31] ibid., I, 3, 6–9.

[32] ibid., I, 3, 12.

[33] ibid.

But if reason compels the abandonment of the state of nature, it dictates also the powers of the government. Its supreme principle is that all power should emanate from the natural rights of individuals. Locke's social contract was as much one of subjection as that of Hobbes. Every man "puts himself under an obligation to everyone of that society to submit to the determination of the majority, and to be concluded by it". Their "supreme power to remove or alter" the established government does not extend to the contract of subjection of the individual to the community and, while the right of resistance survives the contract, it is dormant and qualified. But while the state of nature appears very similar in Hobbes and Locke, Locke concluded that the right of self-preservation leads to limited government. The best way for safeguarding individual rights is to subordinate the executive to the law, through the medium of the legislature. The pursuit of happiness and self-preservation requires property and, the main purpose of civil society should be the protection of property. As a result, the legislative body should be elected by the wealthy classes solely to ensure that the rights of property were not jeopardised.

The status of property differentiated Hobbes from Locke. While Hobbes inferred the fundaments of the state of nature from an examination of the public law of his time, Locke reconstructed human nature from an observation of the law and the rights of property. The natural right to property follows from the right of self-preservation and is not just the right of motion and "doing". Human nature and desire are directed at objects, at the things which meet man's desires. Meat and drink can be used only if eaten, only if they become appropriated by the individual. Similarly, all other essentials for self-preservation and happiness can be appropriated in order to satisfy man's devouring right. The right to property is based on the natural property each man has over his body and skills, his work and produce. Whenever he makes something with his own labour, he adds to the object a part of himself and acquires property rights over it. "Man, by being master of himself and proprietor of his own person and the actions of labour over it, has in himself the great foundations of property".[34] Admittedly, this natural property right is limited; in the natural state, man can appropriate with his labour only what is useful and necessary for his self-preservation and happiness and must avoid needless waste. After the social contract, however, and the introduction of money, all restrictions upon the right of property are

---

[34] *Second Treatise of Government* (P. Laslett ed.) (Cambridge Univerity Press, 1960) sec. 44.

relaxed. Man can now rightfully and without injury possess more than he can make use of. The introduction of money makes it plain that "men have agreed to disproportionate and unequal possession of the earth, they having by a tacit and voluntary consent found out a way, how a man may fairly possess more land than he himself can use the product of".[35] Civil law allows the possessive individual to amass as much property and money as he wishes because capital accumulation works for the common good. The day-labourer of England, Locke remarks, although divested of his natural right to the fruit of his labour, is better off (feeds, lodges and is clad better) than "the king of a large and fruitful territory" in America.[36] It follows that "the great and chief end therefore of men's uniting in commonwealths and putting themselves under government is the preservation of their property".[37] Capitalism is right and just because natural man is the "absolute lord of his own person and possessions".

Locke's teaching on property was much more revolutionary than his political and constitutional doctrines and had important and unforeseen effects. The individual becomes the centre and origin of the moral and political world because he creates and owes value through his own efforts and is thus emancipated from nature and all social bonds which predated the contract. Self-reliance and creativity become the marks of human achievement, acquisitiveness the mark of self-realisation and dignity. "Understanding and science stand in the same relation to the 'given' in which human labour, called forth to its supreme effort by money, stands to the raw material . . . all knowledge is acquired; all knowledge depends on labour and is labour".[38] Labour is the natural means of escape from nature. This departure from nature through human endeavour leads to happiness and "the greatest happiness [lies] in having those things which produce the greatest pleasures". But since nature cannot be known, no distinctions can be made either between higher and lower pleasures. The only guidance in the absence of the *summum bonum* is the avoidance of the *summum malum*. "Desire is always moved by evil, to fly it" and the highest evil is death. The object of desire and fear coincide. Nature creates the desire of what it fears most. Labour, the art imitating nature, shows that the way to happiness is to turn away and negate nature. And as labour adds value to all things and beings, every

---

[35] John Locke, sec. 50.
[36] ibid., sec. 41.
[37] ibid., 124.
[38] Strauss, op. cit., supra n. 11, 249.

self or thing is malleable and can become the target of conscious intervention and investment. Man can fashion himself through his endeavour as much as he can fashion the physical world. The greatest happiness turns out to be the greatest power to shape and acquire things. Nature, including human nature, which started as the measure of all things, ends up being just matter, to be controlled, exploited and shaped either by the self-fashioning individual or by the all-powerful Sovereign. The fear and desire of the other are united in a new social and political system which makes the desiring individual and the desiring Leviathan the mirror image of each other.

With Locke, the transition from natural law to natural rights and from the purposeful cosmos to human nature was completed. The law's end is no longer to deliver justice as an objective relation amongst people, nor is natural right a warning against sedimented laws and common opinions. Their aim is to serve the individual and promote his "happiness", in other words his desire expressed through his free will. But that means that individuals no longer pursue virtue or strive for the good and politics are not interested in pragmatic approximations and prudent judgments but in the application of truths. The proliferation of many desires destroyed the good, as it had done with the one truth. The emptied place of the good was filled by the (fear of) evil, symbolised by death and broadly interpreted as the non-achievement or frustration of desire. Avoiding the bad has become the end of modern societies: it is the outcome of the enthronement of desire as the principle of individual and social action. The only distant reminders of the old "best polity" are the various utopias, memories of a communal past and promises of a future good society, most of them self-conscious about their impossibility. The human rights announced by the great revolutions of the eighteenth century shared briefly the utopian aspiration. They extended freedom from the private to the public, unlike Hobbes, and they supplemented it with equality, unlike Locke. But these moves were not final or irreversible. The road from the natural rights of the revolutions to the human rights of our age has witnessed the triumph of both individualistic humanism and of the cannibalism of (state and individual) desire. The dialectics of desire inaugurated by Hobbes and Locke, and sanctified by Hegel and Freud, have turned evil and death into the greatest fear and desire. But evil and its fear cannot replace the (pursuit of the) good. Human rights are caught in this continuous see-saw between the best and the worst, between hope for the future and the many oppressions of the present.

5

Revolutions and Declarations:
The Rights of Men, Citizens and a Few Others

The symbolic foundation and starting point of modernity can be timed at the passing of the great revolutionary documents of the eighteenth century: the American Declaration of Independence (1776), the Bill of Rights (1791), the French *Déclaration des Droits de l'Homme et du Citoyen* (1789).[1] Its symbolic closure has been placed at the fall of the Berlin Wall in 1989. In between, the natural rights proclaimed by the eighteenth century declarations mutated into human rights, their scope and jurisdiction expanded from France and the States of the Union to the whole humanity and, their legislators were enlarged from the revolutionary assemblies to the international community and its plenipotentiaries and diplomats in New York, Geneva and Strasbourg. In these two long centuries, the revolutionary ideas both triumphed in the world scene and were violated in the most atrocious and unprecedented ways.

The principles of the declarations were as revolutionary in the history of ideas as were the revolutions in the history of politics. We can follow the themes, concerns and fears of modernity in the trajectory of the rights of man. If modernity is the epoch of the subject, human rights have painted the world in the image and likeness of the individual. The impact of the French Declaration, in particular, has been profound. The Universal Declaration of Human Rights, adopted by the General Assembly of the United Nations in 1948, followed closely the French Declaration, both in substance and form.[2] As a contemporary commentator put it, "the framers of the UN declaration of

---

[1] For a history of the French Declaration, see Lynn Hunt (ed.), *The French Revolution and Human Rights: A Brief Documentary History* (Boston, Bedford Books,19960; Gail Schwab and John Jeanneney (eds), *The French Revolution of 1789 and its Impact* (Westport, Greenwood Press,1995).

[2] See Stephen Marks, "From the 'Single Confused Page' to the 'Decalogue for Six Billion Persons': The Roots of the Universal Declaration of Human Rights in the French Revolution", 20 *Human Rights Quarterly* 459–514, at 461 (1998).

1948 followed the model established by the French Declaration of the Rights of Man and Citizen of 1789, while substituting 'man' for the more ambiguous 'human' throughout".[3]

This Chapter will discuss briefly the eighteenth century revolutionary documents with special emphasis on France. Its main concern is not with the substance of rights but with their philosophical presuppositions, paradoxes and ambiguities, which were enunciated first in these documents and eventually came to dominate the world.

The French Declaration starts as follows:

> The representatives of the French People constituted in National Assembly, Considering that ignorance, forgetfulness or contempt for the rights of man are the sole causes of public misfortune and governmental depravity, Have resolved to expound in a solemn declaration the natural, inalienable and sacred rights of man . . .
> 1. In respect of their rights men are born and remain free and equal. The only permissible basis for social distinctions is public utility.
> 2. The aim of every political association is to preserve the natural and inalienable rights of man. These rights are those of liberty, property, security and resistance to oppression.[4]

The Preamble to the American Declaration of Independence, drafted by Jefferson in 1776, is blunter:

> All men are created equal and are endowed by their creator certain inalienable rights, that among these are Life, Liberty and the pursuit of Happiness. To secure these rights Governments are instituted among Men deriving their just powers from the consent of the governed.

The French Declaration and the American Bill of Rights have many similarities, which can be attributed to the common philosophical influences on the two sides of the Atlantic. Both documents proclaim their rights to be universal and inalienable. They both state that limitations and restrictions on the exercise of rights must be introduced by means of laws legislated by democratically elected bodies. Finally, they both protect similar rights: religious freedom and freedom of expression, the security of the person, due process of law and the presumption of innocence in criminal proceedings. The revolutions were united in their rhetorical (at least) commitment to a political system which guarantees freedom and equality. But the two revolu-

---

[3] Lynn Hunt, "The Revolutionary Origins of Human Rights" op.cit., supra n. 1, 3.

[4] "Declaration of the Rights of Man and the Citizen" in S. Finer, V. Bogdanor and B. Rudden, *Comparing Constitutions* (Oxford: Clarendon, 1995) 208–10.

tions and their documents had also a number of differences and idio-syncrasies. Both similarities and divergences influenced the future course of human rights.

I. A BRIEF HISTORICAL COMPARISON OF FRANCE AND AMERICA

The differences between the political aspirations of the American War of Independence and the social aims of the French social revo-lution have been extensively discussed. The aim of the American documents was to legitimise political independence from Britain, while that of the French, the overthrow of the social order of the *ancien régime*. The Americans used both historical and philosophical arguments to support their newly established rights. They claimed, first, that the natural rights of the declarations were expressions of divine will and a re-statement only of the traditional liberties of the "freeborn Englishman". According to an influential essay by the German jurist Georg Jellinek, the American Declaration and the Bill of Rights, despite their apparent novelty, were inspired by the English charters of right: the Magna Carta, the Habeas Corpus Act of 1679, the Bill of Rights of 1689 and the legal rights to freedom of con-science and religion recognised in the Colonies since the end of the seventeenth century.[5] These historical texts, however, did not con-stitute general declarations about the relations between subjects and political power. Instead, they had established remedies and proce-dures for the protection of predominantly feudal and private rights.

History was complemented by a second naturalist argument, evident in the Declarations of Virginia of 12 June 1776 and Independence of 4 July 1776: the rights of man would be established and best protected, if society is left largely free from state interven-tion. This was typical modern naturalism. Thomas Paine had argued, in the *Rights of Man*,[6] that the revolutionaries must restrict the gov-ernment to a minimum and allow the natural laws of commodity exchange and social labour to operate without regulation or hin-drance. Men obey these laws, whose action coincides with natural rights, because it is in their interest; left free, they would lead to a state

[5] Georg Jellinek, *La Déclaration des droits de l'homme et du citoyen* (G. Fardis trans.) (Paris, 1902).

[6] Thomas Paine, *The Rights of Man, Being an Answer to Mr. Burke's Attack on the French Revolution* (H. Collins ed.) (London, Penguin, 1969).

of social harmony, in which governmental intervention would be all but redundant. The Americans, already pragmatist in outlook, believed that their declarations were both a restatement and clarification of the legal position of their English ancestors and the "common sense" of the matter. Independence from England would allow society to develop its immanent laws, whose workings coincided with the enlightened self-interest of individuals.

The weight of history was made to support the self-evident nature of the laws of free market and the potential conflict between historicism and naturalism was resolved, Gordian knot-like: the contradiction between the two approaches was denied and their results were declared identical. The revolution was not a supreme act of will and its aim was not to construct theoretically and legislate novel rights. It simply cleared the ground for the full implementation of existing laws. These were basically sound and could lead to individual and social happiness, if the influences distorting them were removed. Thus, while the declaration of rights changed the basis of legitimacy of state power, their substance remained largely unaltered. American rights were natural, they already existed and were well-known and the government's job was to apply prudently pre-existing laws to new situations.

In France, the American influence was acknowledged in the parliamentary debates of July and August 1789 but a sharp distinction was drawn between the two Declarations. As Rabaud Saint-Etienne stated in the National Assembly, the first priority for a nation in the process of being born is to destroy the old order and start afresh by establishing a new legislative power. As a result, the need to start with a general declaration of rights was not pressing for the Americans. But for the French nation, which already existed, the first priority was to "constitute rather than just declare the rights since they are an integral part of the Constitution".[7] The different priorities dictated different forms for the two lists of rights: the French prefaced their Constitution with the Declaration making it the ground and legitimation of constitutional reform, while the Bill of Rights was introduced as a series of amendments to the American Constitution.[8]

---

[7] Quoted in Blandine Barret-Kriegel, *Les droits de l'homme et le droit naturel* (Paris, P.U.F., 1989) 35.

[8] According to Barret-Kriegel, a historian of the French Revolution, "in France the declaration of rights provided the basis for government itself and was consequently drafted before the constitution", ibid., 35. Cf Hunt, op.cit., supra n. 1, 15.

The central provision of the French Declaration was the right of resistance to oppression, an expression of the deeply political and social character of the revolution. As Mirabeau declared in the Constituent Assembly, the Declaration was not a list of abstract declarations but "an act of war against tyrants". [9] For the French, the Revolution was an act of supreme popular will, aimed at radically reconstructing the relationship between society and state according to the principles of natural rights. Unlike the Americans, there is nothing obvious or common-sensical about this act and its consequences. The *ancien régime* had degraded nature and corrupted the constitution and it was the task of philosophy to assist in drawing up a rational scheme for the new state, based on the protection of rights. As Habermas put it, the French believed that when philosophical insight and public opinion are separated, "the practical task falls to the *philosophe* to secure political recognition for reason itself by means of his influence on the power of public opinion. The philosophers must propagate the truth, must propagate their unabridged insights publicly". [10] The Revolution took philosophy to the barricades and, once victorious, appointed it its chief adviser.

The public and political nature of the Revolution is evident at all levels. The rights belong to "man" and "citizen" marking a close relationship between humanity and politics; the difference between the natural rights of man and the political rights of the citizen is left unclear; the "Supreme Being" witnesses only and does not legislate or guide the Declaration, which is the act of the representatives of the people acting as the mouthpiece of Rousseau's *volonté générale*. Finally, the proclaimed rights were not an end in themselves but the means used by the Assembly to reconstruct the body politic. Habermas concludes that in America, "it is a matter of setting free the spontaneous forces of self-regulation in harmony with Natural Law, while in [France, the Revolution] seeks to assert for the first time a total constitution in accordance with Natural Law against a depraved society and a human nature which has been corrupted". [11]

---

[9] Quoted in Norberto Bobbio, *The Age of Rights* (Cambridge, Polity, 1996) 87. Cf. "The tone of the Declaration is apparently abstract, but whoever examines the individual liberties listed with a historian's eye, soon realizes that each one represents a polemical antithesis of a specific aspect of society and the state at the time", De Ruggiero, *Storia del Liberalismo Europeo*, quoted in Bobbio, 97, fn. 34.

[10] Jurgen Habermas, *Theory and Practice* (London, Heinemann, 1974) 88.

[11] ibid., 105.

We can detect, in these formulations, the legal expression of the project of the Enlightenment.[12] The new era promised the emancipation of the individual from all forms of political oppression primarily and, potentially, from class or social tutelage. More generally, emancipation meant the progressive abandonment of myth and prejudice in all areas of life and their replacement by reason. Kant's *Critiques*, which launched philosophical modernity through reason's investigation of its own operation, defined the Western world-view as historical progress through reason. Emancipation extends to all aspects of falsity and oppression, from beliefs and superstitions to physical, social and economic needs and insecurities. In political terms, liberation means the subjection of power to the reason of law. The American Declaration adds to emancipation the right to happiness. The "American dream" was already implicit in the foundation of the American State. This second aim, muted at its inception but today as important in the West as emancipation, is the quest for the good life, in the form of self-realisation or self-fulfilment. It is based on the belief that individuals are able to develop their innate imaginative and creative powers through economic improvement and participation in scientific, literary and cultural life. Emancipation enters the world stage as a negative principle or defensive weapon against political oppression and is associated with the value of dignity. Self-fulfilment is a positive force, based on the presumed human potential for improvement and happiness. It soon became associated with the value of equality which aspires to stop domination and enable individuals to shape themselves and the world. "Liberation and dignity are not automatically born of the same act; rather they refer to each other reciprocally" writes Ernst Bloch. "With economic *priority* we find humanistic *primacy*".[13] Both, however, are underpinned by "the massive subjective turn of modern culture, a new form of inwardness in which we come to think of ourselves as beings with inner depths".[14] If emancipation is grounded on the belief in an essential, innate human nature, concealed and overlaid by tradition and cus-

---

[12] See generally Ernst Cassirer, *The Philosophy of the Enlightenment* (F.C.A. Koelln and J.P. Pettegrove trans.) (Princeton NJ, Princeton University Press, 1968) especially Chapter VI; Lucien Goldmann, *The Philosophy of the Enlightenment* (H. Maas trans.) (London, Routledge and Kegan Paul, 1973).

[13] Ernst Bloch, *Natural Law and Human Dignity* (D. J. Schmidt trans.), Cambridge, Mass., MIT Press, 1988) xi.

[14] Charles Taylor, *Multiculturalism: Examining the Politics of Recognition* (Princeton NJ, Princeton University Press, 1994) 29; David Harvey, *Justice, Nature and the Geography of Difference* (Oxford, Blackwell, 1996) 120–50.

tom, self-realisation makes nature the target of conscious intervention. An inherent tension between the two aims is evident from the beginning.

But the two revolutions and their documents were also witness to two alternative strategies for the achievement of their ends. The French is predominantly moral and voluntarist. Human rights are a form of politics committed to a moral sense of history and a proactive belief that collective action can overthrow domination, oppression, and suffering. We make our history and we can therefore judge it, when we come across flagrant instances of persistent historical immorality. The agent of history and the definition of oppression have differed wildly since the eighteenth century: at the collective end, social revolutionaries, anti-colonial rebels and the NATO bombers of Yugoslavia were all involved in political crusades of a moral character. They are accompanied, at the private end, by charity donors, aid contributors and letter writers to The Guardian and, in-between, by human rights campaigns and NGOs. The great political movements of our era which appealed to natural or human rights are the descendants of the French revolutionaries: they include the anti-slavery and decolonisation campaigns, the popular fight against communism, the anti-apartheid movement, protest movements from the suffragettes to the civil rights and from the syndicalist and workers' movements to the various resistances against foreign occupation and domestic oppression.

The American strategy was initially more passive and optimistic. Certain social traits and laws, allowed free action and with some gentle encouragement, will lead inexorably to the establishment and promotion of human rights and the almost natural adjustment between moral demands and empirical realities. Free markets, legal procedures and the rule of national or international law can rectify human rights abuses through their normal operation and impose the principles of dignity and equality on tyrannical as much as on democratic regimes. The huge standard-setting enterprise in the United Nations and other international and regional institutions and the various courts, commissions and human rights procedures for supervising compliance and implementation belong to this second strategy. If, according to Lenin, socialism was the combination of Soviet democracy and electricity, for President Carter, the first great exponent of a moral foreign policy, human rights are the combination of capitalism and the rule of law. Their success depends on barristers not barricades, on reports not rebellions and on protocols and conventions not protests.

From the morality of history to the morality of law, and from the significance of local culture to the predominance of ahistorical values, all the main human rights strategies and arguments were pre-figured in the classical declarations. This radical re-conceptualisation of politics, law and morality had a number of philosophical presuppositions and important consequences, to which we now turn.

II. THE PROCLAMATION OF GROUNDLESS FREEDOM

After the revolutions, every aspect of life was reconstructed in accordance with the principle of free will. The early declarations were the first public expression of the principle and, despite other differences, the American and French Revolutions were united in their declaratory intent. But there is a paradox at the heart of the declarations: they pronounced the rights of "man" in order to rescue them from "ignorance" and "forgetfulness" but, it was the act of declaration itself which established the rights as the ground of the new polity. How can we explain this paradox?

The political philosophy which paved the way to the revolutions believed that natural rights express the immanent laws of society which had been distorted, through lack of representation in America and the unenlightened attitudes of the *ancien régime* in France. These rights promote individual freedom by freeing people to pursue their interests without consideration for substantive moral values. Society should be separated from the state and turn into a morally neutral terrain in which free private activity, commerce, trade and economic transactions take place. The only restrictions placed upon these interest-maximising individuals should be external: positive law divorced from virtue both creates the preconditions of freedom, mainly in contract, and imposes constraints upon individual activity, paradigmatically in criminal law, to allow the reconciliation of conflicting interests. The law of freedom is at the same time the law of coercion, legality may have been separated from morality but has as indispensable companion the police, the prison and the gallows.

Here we may discern a first answer to the paradox. The constitutional assemblies introduced a new type of legislative power and of positive law which, while coercive, was grounded on the assertion that it originated from and established individual freedom. The revolution was legitimised by referring back to the natural autonomy of individuals: their rights are discovered by the rational insight of the

French *philosophe* or the common-sense of the American man of affairs; this way, they both precede the new order and are its legislative creations. Whether through the fictitious original social contract or through the divine derivation and self-evident character of rights, the coercive power of the state is justified by freely entered agreements or the freely arrived insights of autonomous individuals. The declarations construct therefore a new polity under pretext of uncovering or describing it. In linguistic or "speech act" terms, they are performative statements disguised as constative. The text, the supreme expression of revolutionary will, acts on the world and changes it.

The classical declarations claim that human rights belong to "man". They therefore presuppose logically a substratum or *subjectum*, "man", to whom they are given. But the only ontological or methodological precondition of modern philosophy is the equally shared freedom of will, which exists in a pristine form before any predicate or determination. The self-grounding nature of modern man means that his empirical reality is constructed out of the proclaimed rights on condition that they are presented as his eternal entitlements. "Man" in the abstract, legal personhood at large, needs these extravagant assertions in order to ascend to the historical stage and succeed God as the new ground of being and meaning, and human nature is invented as a retrospective justification for the unprecedented rights created by the declarations. As Lyotard put it, "man should have signed the Preamble of the Declaration".[15]

But the reverse seems equally valid: it was the National Assembly, as representative of the French nation, which proclaimed the right of "man" and, in so doing, ushered "man" onto the world scene. The essence of "man" lies in this act of proclamation in which he linguistically asserts and politically legislates without any ground or authority other than himself. Language performs its world-making power and establishes a political system based on a self-referential, groundless freedom. It is in the nature of human rights to be proclaimed, because there is no one outside historical humanity to guarantee them. In the act of proclamation, "man" both recognises and asserts his nature as free will. The revolution is an act of self-foundation, which simultaneously establishes the bearer of right and the power of the legislator, as the historical representative of its own construct, to create all human right *ex nihilo*. From that moment, a new declara-

---

[15] Jean-François Lyotard, *The Differend* (G. van den Abbeele trans.) (Manchester, Manchester University Press, 1988) 145.

tion of rights has a common and immutable element that refers to "man" or human nature and legitimises the legislator and variable contents which open new areas of entitlement and free action.

The paradox we encountered is not unique to the revolutionary documents. It will accompany many new constitutions and human rights enactments which depart from the pre-existing constitutional order. A bill of rights or constitution has two aspects: the enunciation, the act of declaring (performative) and, secondly, the statement, the content of the enunciation (constative). The performative dimension acts out the assertion of the legislators that they are authorised to pronounce rights and, in doing so, it introduces them. The specific claims to "life, liberty and the pursuit of happiness", on the other hand, state these rights and give them substance. The first paradox quickly proliferates into others which will prevent declarations and Bills from ever being fully implemented or from grounding a stable social order. The internal tensions of the original French text are evident everywhere: in the contrast between man and citizen, between principle and exception, between citizen and alien and between men and women, slaves, blacks, colonials, all those excluded from political rights. As a result, contradictions develop "in the instability of the relation between the aporetical character of the text and the conflictual character of the situation in which it arises and which serves as its referent".[16] Similarly, the point of application of the text is also conflictual. As performatives, the declarations carry out their work by being put into effect in the future, in a myriad of situations and circumstances, many unforeseen by the constitutional legislator, many in conflict with its original intentions.[17] Human rights are future looking and indeterminate, they become actual when the act of enunciation performs its effects in various settings which, legitimised by the declaration, put its specifics into practice. As a statement of entitlements, a Bill of Rights creates a forward-looking grammar of action and its applications often differ from the always contested meaning of its sentences.

We will examine below how the performative character of the enunciation anchors a series of claims by groups, initially excluded

---

[16] Etienne Balibar, "The Rights of the Man and the Rights of the Citizen", in *Masses, Classes, Ideas: Studies on Politics and Philosophy before and after Marx* (J. Swanson trans.) (New York, Routledge, 1994) 39–59, 41.

[17] Hans-Georg Gadamer, *Truth and Method* (London, Sheen and Ward, 1975) 324–41; Costas Douzinas and Ronnie Warrington with Shaun McVeigh *Postmodern Jurisprudence: The Law of Text in the Texts of Law* (London, Routledge, 1991) Chapters 2 and 3.

from certain rights.[18] Such claims, if successful, are only indirectly related to the foundational text. We are faced, therefore, with a paradigmatically open text, whose reference is a past conflict and whose performance will help decide future struggles. Interpreting human rights law, which means performing or applying a code or grammar to a conflict, is by definition controversial. The endless, repetitive and rather boring American debate on constitutional interpretation between liberals, strict constructionists and "federalists", who claim to follow the intentions of the founding fathers, is not just about the politics of interpretation.[19] It rather disguises the fact that interpretation is politics because human rights is politics by other means. Both origin and destinations of a Bill of Rights are steeped in conflict. As a result, the text is more than any piece of literature a model of undecidability, and more than any party programme a political manifesto.

The force of the declarations should not be sought therefore in their appeals to fictitious original pacts or divine sources or in the equally mythical institutional rights of the self-governing and self-taxing Englishmen. Indeed, the French declaration makes no reference at all to a social compact. The declarations create and exhaust their own legitimacy in their act of enunciation. There is no need to give any further argument, justification or reason for their genesis besides the proclamatory act which confers upon the legislators both the right to legislate these rights and to claim that they already belong to all "men". But while "man" in the abstract or human nature is the ontological bearer of rights in general, no human right in the abstract, no right to right has been created or developed.[20] Human rights involve always specific claims to free speech, security of the person etc. The ontological ground remains groundless, without substance and determination, an empty vessel which authorises the legislator and receives content and predication from historical acts of lawmaking. Human rights install the radical contingency of linguistic proclamation into the heart of constitutional arrangements.

---

[18] See Chapter 9.

[19] Michelle Rosenberg (ed.), *Constitutionalism, Identity, Difference and Legitimacy* (Durham, Duke University Press, 1994); *Just Interpretations* (Berkeley, University of California Press, 1998).

[20] See Renata Salecl, *The Spoils of Freedom* (London, Routledge, 1994) 123–7.

III. THE EMANCIPATION OF ABSTRACT "MAN"

When "man" replaced God as the ground of meaning and action, the protection of his rights against state power became the legal essence of modernity. But there are many problems with this "man", apparent from the beginning of the human rights tradition. The abstract "man" of philosophy is far too empty. To ground a historical constitution, he must be complemented by other substantive capacities and characteristics, Man as species existence may be the ground of the epistemological revolution of modernity, but the political constitution can scarcely be organised according to such a formal principle. Law is the terrain on which abstract nature acquires concrete form. The legal subject as the vehicle of legal rights mediates between abstract human nature and the concrete human being who travels in life creating her own unique narratives and acting them out on the world. As we will examine in detail below, the recognition of legal subjectivity is our accession to a public sphere of legal rights, limitations and duties, based on the assumption of a shared, abstract and equal essence and of a calculating, antagonistic and fearful existence.[21]

Article 1 of the French *Déclaration*, repeated almost verbatim in the Universal Declaration of Human Rights, states that all "men are born equal in rights and in dignity". Abstract and universal human nature, the essence of the human species, is parcelled out to everyone at birth in equal shares. This is evidently a great fallacy. People are not born equal but totally unequal. Indeed, infancy and childhood are the best examples of human inequality and dependency upon others, upon parents, family members, and community networks, within which human life starts, develops and ends. Once the slightest empirical or historical material is introduced into abstract human nature, once we move from the declarations onto the concrete embodied person, with gender, race, class and age, human nature with its equality and dignity retreats rapidly. This type of affirmative syntax characterises human rights declarations. Rights theorists argue that such statements are normative or aspirational and not statements of fact. They should be read as "all men should become equal in rights and dignity". But this defence is only partially successful. Rights must be presented as constative (as statements of fact) in order to establish their (false) self-

---

[21] See below, Chapters 8 and 9.

evidence and legitimise their legislators: "we are only declaring what has always been your natural condition and entitlements". The statement is false but the gap between its non-existent reality and its future application is the space where human rights develop. To that extent, human rights are a present lie which may be partially verified in the future.

And that future had and still has to wait. Let us examine, briefly, the contents of human nature in its country of origin, France. The Marquis de Condorcet and a few pre-revolutionary philosophers argued that natural rights belong to the abstract man, because " 'they are derived from the nature of man', defined as 'a sensitive being . . . capable of reasoning and of having moral ideas' ".[22] But after sex, colour and ethnicity were added, this abstract disembodied human nature took a very concrete form, that of a white, property-owning man. Men represented humanity because their reason, morality and integrity made them an exact image of the "man" of the declarations. Compared with this prototype of humanity, women's "fleeting feelings" and "natural tendencies precluded their ability to live up to the individual prototype". Any biological, psychological or social difference from the male model were interpreted as handicaps and signs of inferiority:

> Maleness was equated with individuality, and femaleness with otherness in a fixed, hierarchical, and immobile opposition (masculinity was not seen as femininity's other). The political individual was then taken to be both universal and male; the female was not an individual, both because she was non-identical with the human prototype and because she was the other who confirmed the (male) individual's individuality. [23]

As a result, the days following the Revolution were some of the darkest in the history of women.[24] Female nature was caught between the "éternelle malade" of Michelet and the "hysterical woman" of Charcot and was defined as private and practical, her vocation delicate, fragile and emotional, indispensable for domestic tasks but

---

[22] Quoted in Joan Scott, *Only Paradoxes to Offer: French Feminists and the Rights of Man* (Cambridge Mass., Harvard University Press, 1996) 6. For a history of women rights, see P. Hoffman, *La Femme dans la Pensée des Lumières* (Paris, Orphys, 1977); E. Varikas, "Droit naturel, nature féminine et égalité des sexes", *Revue Internationale des Recherches et des Synthèses en Sciences Sociales*, 3–4, 1987.

[23] ibid., 8.

[24] Nicole Arnaud-Duc, "Women Entrapped: from Public Non-existence to Private Protection", in A.-J. Arnaud and E. Kingdom, *Women's Rights and the Rights of Men* (Aberdeen University Press, 1990) 9.

totally unsuitable to the exercise of political and legal rights. In October 1793, the Convention representative Fabre d'Eglantine denounced women who were claiming citizen rights and were not "occupées du soin de leurs ménages, des mères inséparables de leurs enfants ou des filles qui travaillent pour leurs parents et prennent soin de leurs plus jeunes soeurs; mais . . . un sorte des chevaliers errants, . . . des filles émancipées, des grenadiers femelles".[25] Portalis, the main inspiration behind the Code Napoléon, exalted women's "delicate and fine tact, which gives them a sixth sense and which is lost and does not get perfected, except with the exercise of all the virtues, finally, their touching modesty . . . which they cannot lose without becoming more vicious than we, men".[26] As late as 1912, the eminent jurist Maurice Hauriou argued that a woman is not a "null" but a "nonexistent" citizen, like a incestuous or same sex marriage.[27]

Women were not given the right to vote, in France, until 1944. Women's franchise was "the object of a conspiracy of silence, albeit unofficially, on the part of all the revolutionary and post-revolutionary constitutions . . . The pretext is to be found in the substantive reference in the Code to female nature and the necessities of everyday life".[28] Similarly, women's rights to education and work were not recognised until well into the twentieth century and still today they have not been raised to the full status of humanity or of the "man" of the revolution. As a contemporary commentator puts it, we cannot contemplate a declaration of the rights of women because "nous aboutirions alors à la destruction du concept d'être humain".[29] Elizabeth Kingdom concludes that "whatever the general critique of the 1789 Declaration as a social document, its formal constitution of the rights of the citizen could not reliably incorporate the "lost rights" of pre- and post-revolutionary women".[30]

The prototype of human nature was not just male; it was also white. The French Colonies were populated mostly by slaves at the

---

[25] Quoted ibid., 21.

[26] Quoted ibid., 11.

[27] ibid., 14.

[28] A.-J. Arnaud, "Women in the Boudoir, Women at the Pools: 1804, the History of a Confinement", in A.-J. Arnaud and E. Kingdom, *Women's Rights and the Rights of Men* (Aberdeen University Press, 1990) 1.

[29] R. Badinter, *L'Universalité des Droits de l'Homme dans une Monde Pluraliste*, Strasbourg, Conseil d' Europe, 1989, 2.

[30] Elizabeth Kingdom, "Gendering Rights", in A.-J. Arnaud and E. Kingdom, *Women's Rights and the Rights of Men* (Aberdeen University Press, 1990) 99. For definite statements on the current feminist position on rights, see Luce Irigaray, *Thinking the Difference* (K. Montin trans.) (New York, Routledge, 1994); Nicola Lacey, *Unspeakable Subjects* (Oxford, Hart, 1998).

time of the Revolution. Slavery was abolished in metropolitan France, in 1792, and two years later further afield, in an attempt by the revolutionaries to defeat the British in the Caribbean, but this was temporary.[31] It was restored by the Empire, in 1802, and was not abolished again until 1848. Race, like gender equality, was unknown to the Declaration. As Joan Scott concludes, individuality was racially defined. "The superiority of white Western men to their 'savage' counterparts lay in an individuality achieved and expressed through the social and affective divisions of labour formalised by the institution of monogamous marriage".[32]

The historical unreality and emptiness of the concept of "man" and the related incompleteness and indeterminacy of human rights discourse were at the centre of their early critiques from right and left. We will examine below the critiques of Burke and Marx in some detail. But we can anticipate here their attack on "man", as an all too concrete abstraction. "I have met Italians, Russians, Spaniards, Englishmen, Frenchmen, but I do not know man in general" wrote the French conservative Joseph de Maistre.[33] Edmund Burke agreed; rights are a "metaphysical abstraction",[34] their "abstract perfection is their practical defect".[35] "What is the use of discussing a man's abstract right to food or medicine? The question is upon the method of procuring and administering them. In that deliberation I shall always advise to call in the aid of the farmer and the physician, rather than the professor of metaphysics".[36] Rights are not universal or absolute, they do not belong to abstract men but to particular people in concrete societies with their "infinite modification" of circumstances, tradition and legal entitlement.

Marx, at the other end of the political spectrum, agreed: "Man is in the most literal sense of the word *zoon politikon*, not only a social

---

[31] C.L.R. James describes an interesting incident during the session of the National Assembly which abolished slavery in 1794. A black woman who had regularly attended the Assembly fainted when the abolition vote was passed. On hearing this, a representative asked that she be admitted to the sitting. She was sat next to the speaker with tears in her eyes and was greeted with applause. *The Black Jacobins: Toussaint d'Ouverture and the San Domingo Revolution* (New York, Vintage, 1980) 140–1.

[32] Joan Scott, op. cit., supra n. 22, 11. See infra part iv for the treatment of foreigners in post-revolutionary France.

[33] Quoted in Claude Lefort, *The Political Forms of Modern Society* (Cambridge, Polity, 1986) 257.

[34] Edmund Burke, *Reflections on the Revolution in France* (J.G.A. Pockock ed.) (Indianapolis, Hackett, 1987), 85

[35] ibid., 105.

[36] ibid., 85.

animal, but an animal which can develop into an individual only in society".[37] Their agreement is only partial and follows Aristotle and Montesquieu, by emphasising the concrete action and historical provenance of rights. But the critique of the abstract "man" of rights is not simply an attack on their excessive rationalism or their metaphysical "speculativism". For Marx, the "man" of the rights, rather than being an empty vessel without determination, and therefore unreal, non existent, is too full of substance. The rights of the declarations, under the cloak of universality and abstraction, celebrate and enthrone the power of a concrete, too concrete man: the possessive individual, the market orientated white bourgeois male whose right to property is turned into the cornerstone of all other rights and underpins the economic power of capital and the political power of the capitalist class. For Burke and Marx, the subject of rights does not exist. It is either too abstract to be real or too concrete to be universal. In both cases, the subject is fake because its essence does not and cannot correspond with real people.

IV. RIGHTS CAN BE GUARANTEED ONLY BY NATIONAL LAW

All struggle against oppression, when successful, divides into the excitement of newly-found freedom and the urge for order. The eighteenth century revolutions and declarations were expressions of rebellion against the old destined to mature, first, into the passion and, then, into the boredom of the new. But history had to wait before the potential grew into the actual and natural rights mutated into human rights. In the meantime, as with most successful revolutions, the emphasis shifted from freedom to law and from nature to order. Natural rights link the promise of freedom to the discipline of law. The institution of rights was not unknown to the *ancien régime*. Private law rights and some protections against administrative abuse were recognised in civilian France, while the American colonists enjoyed many of the common law remedies and protections of the "free-born Englishman". What distinguished the revolutionary from earlier conceptions of right was the claim that a new type of state organisation was to be grounded on the recognition and protection of these rights.

---

[37] Karl Marx, *Grundrisse* in D. McLellan (ed.), *Selected Writings* (Oxford, Oxford University Press, 1975) 346.

But here we come across one more paradox. Human rights were declared inalienable because they were independent of governments, temporal and local factors and expressed in legal form the eternal rights of man. If all men share a common human nature, there is no need to invoke any power for their proclamation and no special legislation was necessary since all law-making power now emanated from the sovereign people. Yet, the French Declaration is quite categorical as to the real source of universal rights. Let us follow briefly its strict logic. Article 1 states that "men are born and remain free and equal of right", Article 2 that "the aim of any political association is to preserve the natural and inalienable rights of man" and Article 3 proceeds to define this association: "The principle of all Sovereignty lies essentially with the nation. No group, nor individual may exercise any authority that does not expressly proceed from it". Finally, according to Article 6, "The law is the expression of the general will; all citizens have the right to work towards its creation either in person or through their representatives".

Rights are declared on behalf of the universal "man", but the act of enunciation establishes the power of a particular type of political association, the nation and its state, to become the sovereign lawmaker and secondly, of a particular "man", the national citizen, to become the beneficiary of rights. First, national sovereignty. The declarations proclaim the universality of right but their immediate effect is to establish the boundless power of the state and its law. It was the enunciation of rights which established the right of the Constituent Assemblies to legislate. In a paradoxical fashion, these declarations of universal principle "perform" the foundation of local sovereignty. The progeny gave birth to its own progenitor and created him in his own image and likeness.

The metonymical relationship and the mirroring effect between the "sovereign" man of the declarations and the "sovereign" state is also apparent in international law and politics. The standard presentation of states in the international scene is of a unitary, free and willing actor who, like the individual, is autonomous and formally equal with others. International law is littered with analogies between man and state and its legitimacy is founded on them. Internally, the principle of popular (or in Britain parliamentary) sovereignty states that the will of all citizens becomes trans-substantiated, through elections, votes and law-making, into a singular general will which expresses the common interest of the nation and resembles, in all particulars, the free will of the individual. Internationally, this free and united will is confronted with similar actors and, as a result, all the main tropes of eighteenth century political philosophy come into play. The state of nature (absence of international law), the social contract (the treaty creating the United Nations) and the fearful and calculating attitude to others characterise also the nature and relations of these oversized individuals.

The key principle of territorial integrity and non-intervention, for example, is presented as the logical outcome of the negative freedom that states and individuals enjoy equally. In international law, "[n]ations are regarded as individual free persons living in a state of nature . . . Since by nature all nations are equal, since moreover all men are equal in a moral sense whose rights and obligations are the same; the rights and obligations of all nations are the same".[38] Every single trait of the natural man of the declarations has been displaced onto the state and, undoubtedly, the grand proclamations sound more realistic in relation to the autonomy and freedom of action of the state: "Sovereign man and sovereign states are defined not by connection or relationships but by autonomy in decision-making and freedom from the power of others. Security is understood in terms not of celebrating and sustaining life but as the capacity to indifferent to 'others' and, if necessary, to harm them".[39] Negative liberty and formal equality lead to the contractarianism of treaties and to reciprocal relations between mutually disinterested parties in which "I observe your territorial integrity (negative liberty) because in doing so I reinforce a system in which you are expected to observe mine".[40] International law presupposes a subject similar in all particulars to that of the declarations. The modern nation-state came to existence and acquired legitimacy by pronouncing the sovereignty of the subject and adopting all its characteristics. In this elaborate hall of mirrors, the fictions of the free individual and of the all-devouring Leviathan became intimately connected companions and determined the political trajectory of modernity. If the declarations ushered in the epoch of the individual, they also launched the age of the state, mirror of the individual. Human rights and national sovereignty, the two antithetical principles of international law were born together, their contradiction more apparent than real. But we are rushing. Let us return to the declarations and their effects.

[38] Quoted in Fiona Robinson, "The limits of a rights-based approach to international ethics", in Tony Evans (ed.), *Human Rights Fifty Years on: A reappraisal* (Manchester, Manchester University Press, 1998) 62.

[39] V. S. Peterson and A. Sisson Ryan, *Global Gender Issues* (Boulder, Westview Press, 1993) 34.

[40] ibid., 63.

It was not just the state-as-individual that was the other side of the coin of rights. The legislator of the proclaimed universal community of reason was none other than the historical legislator of the French or American nation. "The sovereignty of the nation had just been asserted at the expense of the privilege of a state or class. And it was impossible to leap beyond that point into the unfolding of history".[41] From that point, statehood, sovereignty and territory follow the principle of nationality. If the Declaration inaugurated modernity, it also started nationalism and all its consequences: genocides, ethnic and civil wars, ethnic cleansing, minorities, refugees, statelessness. Citizenship introduced a new type of privilege which was protected for some by excluding others. After the revolutions, nation–states are defined by territorial boundaries, which demarcate them from other states and exclude other people and nations. Citizenship shifted exclusion from class to nation, which became a disguised class barrier.

Thus, the universal legislator and the Kantian autonomous subject turn into a mirage, as soon as empirical characteristics are added to them. The principle of autonomy is created in the moulding together of the split self and the split community that modernity introduced against the horizon of an alleged universal community. This paradox was first acted out by the French revolutionaries. The National Assembly notionally split itself into two parts: a philosophical and a historical. The first legislated on behalf of "man" for the whole world, the second for the only territory and people it could, France and its dependencies. The gap between the two is also the distance between the universality of the law of reason (eventually of human rights) and the generality of state legislation. From that point onwards, it remains unknown:

> whether the law thereby declared is French or human, whether the war conducted in the name of rights is one of conquest or one of liberation, whether the violence exerted under the title of freedom is repressive or pedagogical (progressive), whether those nations which are not French ought to become French or become human by endowing themselves with Constitutions that conform to the Declaration.[42]

The French Assembly, of course, did not and could not legislate for the world; what it did was to attempt to make the discourse of

---

[41] Julia Kristeva, *Nations without Nationalism* (L. Roudiez trans.) (New York, Columbia University Press, 1993), 26.

[42] Lyotard, op.cit., supra n. 15, 147. This statement seems to represent also the post-Kosovo late modernity, if one substitutes American for French.

universal right part of the foundation myth of modern France. The universality of the claims was the reason why to many the French Revolution seemed to possess the characteristics of a religious uprising. As Toqueville put it, the revolution "seemed more interested in the regeneration of humankind than in the reform of France".[43]

And yet, by introducing the distinction between human being and citizen, the Declaration acknowledged the tension between the universal and the local and accepted its historical specificity. The performative contradiction between the declaration of rights for all humanity which created the power of the National Assembly to establish these rights only for the French introduced an element of exclusion and violence in constitutional politics. From now on political legitimacy derives from the fact that the legislator and the addressee of his commands (the legal subjects) are one and the same. The essence of political freedom is that the subjects who make law are also law's subjected. Democratic legislation is introduced on behalf of the citizens who, in the Rousseauan version of the social contract, participate in the creation of the general will. But the law of the state, despite its generality excludes from the community of its subjects all those who do not belong to the nation. There is a gap between the subject of the statement "we the people legislate norm x" and of its passive form "we the people ought to obey x". The first group consists of the legislators, the voters and those whose interests are represented in politics. The second includes additionally others, aliens, immigrants and refugees as well as internal aliens, the "enemy within", who are given notice that if they come in contact with the state, the authority of its law will be engaged. They are subjected to the law but they are not law's subjects. A necessary dissymmetry develops therefore between the addressees of the law (subjects, citizens, the nation) and those others, its secondary and potential addressees. As Kristeva puts it, "never has democracy been more explicit, for it excludes no-one – except foreigners".[44]

Immediately after the French Revolution, the National Assembly adopted a decree which allowed the naturalisation of most foreigners residing in France. Cosmopolitan clubs and newspapers were founded, foreigners joined the revolutionary army and, in 1792, a number of foreign radicals and writers were given the honorary title of French citizen, because they had been "allies of the French

---

[43] Alexis de Tocqueville, *L'ancien régime et la révolution* (Paris, Gallimard, 1967) 89.

[44] Julia Kristeva, *Strangers to Ourselves* (Leon Roudiez trans.) (Columbia University Press, 1991) 149.

people" and had attacked "the foundations of tyranny and prepared the way for liberty".[45] They included Priestley, Paine (who became a member of the National Assembly representing the Pas-de-Calais), Bentham, Wilberforce, Clarckson, Washington, Hamilton and Madison.[46] But the climate changed dramatically after the first defeats in the revolutionary wars and the victory of the Jacobins. By 1794, foreigners were forbidden to stay in Paris and other major cities and towns, they were excluded from public service, political rights and public bodies and the property of English and Spanish citizens was confiscated. Many revolutionary foreigners and cosmopolitan French were executed during the Terror. "The scaffold took care of the cosmopolitan's lot, while nationalism – perhaps 'regretfully' and 'reluctantly' – became paramount in both minds and laws".[47] Tom Paine was arrested in December 1793; he was lucky to avoid the guillotine and was released ten months later through the intercession of the American Ambassador who claimed that he was an American citizen.[48] "It should be noted", Kristeva dryly concludes "that those steps [against foreigners] were not as harsh as those taken during the war of 1914" and pale into insignificance when we reach the war of 1939.[49]

The elevation of the national law into the only upholder of rights and the resulting treatment of foreigners as lesser humans, indicates that the separation between man and citizen is a main characteristic of modern law. The nation-state comes into existence through the exclusion of other people and nations. The modern subject reaches her humanity by acquiring political rights of citizenship, which guarantee her admission to the universal human nature by excluding from that status others with no rights. The citizen has rights and duties to the extent that he belongs to the common will and to the state. The alien is not a citizen. He does not have rights because he is not part of the state and he is a lesser human being because he is not a citizen. One is a man to greater or lesser degree because one is a citizen to a greater or lesser degree. The alien is the gap between man and citizen. The modern subject is the citizen and citizenship guarantees the

[45] ibid., 156.

[46] Ehsan Naraghi, "The Republic's Citizens of Honour" in *1789: An Idea that Changed the World*, in *The UNESCO Courier*, June 1989, 13.

[47] ibid., 160.

[48] This fascinating story is narrated in Albert Mathiez, *La Révolution et les étrangers* (Paris, La Renaissance du Livre, 1928). For a concise history, on which the present account is based, see Kristeva, supra n. 44, 148–67.

[49] Kristeva, supra n. 44, 161.

minimum requirements necessary for being a man, a human being. We become human through citizenship and subjectivity is based on the gap, the difference between universal man and state citizen.

We can conclude that the "man" of the declarations is an abstraction, universal but unreal, an "unencumbered" entity stripped down of its characteristics. As the representative of Reason, he has no time or place. The citizen, on the other hand is always a Burkean "Englishman". (S)he has the rights and duties given to him by state laws and national tradition, (s)he must be subjected to the law in order to become law's subject. As Jay Bernstein puts it, "citizenship stands between and mediates the abstract particularity of personal identity and the abstract universality of human rights. Individuals only have rights in community".[50] For those who lack representation very little is left. The stateless, the refugees, the minorities of various types have no human rights. When liberal states claim that they abolish privileges and protect universal rights, they mean that privileges are now extended to a group called citizenry, still a small minority. Modern subjectivity is based on those others whose existence is evidence of the universality of human nature but whose exclusion is absolutely crucial for concrete personhood, in other words for citizenship.

It may be argued, therefore, that the Declaration of Human Rights is the precondition of sovereignty and is inescapably intertwined with legislation. The modern sovereign comes into its omnipotent life by proclaiming the rights of citizens. Looked from this perspective, human rights are attempts to build a protective principle against Leviathan, based on the recognition of desire and its erection as a counter principle to the desire of the state. If modern public law is the legalisation of politics, human rights are the legalisation of desire and their main components mirror closely the characteristics of Leviathan. The Hobbesian natural right finds its limit in the other and the absolute other is death. These two principles that appear to be contradictory, to speak to two totally different logics, are the two sides of the same coin. Their historical combination could only succeed in absolute apocalyptic moments, at which a revolutionary class grasps history and imposes a radical new logic. But this combination of law and revolutionary reason which can change the root of the ancient rivers of history is only feasible through apocalyptic violence;

---

[50] Jay Bernstein, "Rights, Revolution and Community: Marx's 'On the Jewish Question'" in Peter Osborne (ed.), *Socialism and the Limits of Liberalism* (London, Verso, 1991) 91–119, 114.

man became the principle of politics in a momentary eruption and its accompanying declarations in France and America. Once the contradictory logic was normalised and put into practice, the two limbs of the paradox, according to which man can have inalienable rights when he has no rights other than those granted to him by the sovereign, break up and determine two opposing trajectories. That of sovereignty, legal positivism and utilitarian intervention and, that of a self-creating desire which is potentially critical of the state and its law. Positivism is an attack on all principles of transcendence. The radical project of human rights, while accepting modernity's rejection of religious transcendence, insists on the importance of the principle of transcendence for the reconstruction of historical forms and inherits the classical task of imagining a political and legal order which is beyond the here and now.

6

The Triumph of Humanity: From 1789 to 1989 and from Natural to Human Rights

I. THE DECLINE OF NATURAL RIGHTS

It is a common historical lesson that victorious revolutionaries turned rulers can become as oppressive as their predecessors. It is no wonder, therefore, that the years following the publication of the great declarations saw a decline in the popularity of natural rights. The reasons were political and intellectual. Politically, the great monarchies of the nineteenth century treated natural rights as a dangerous, revolutionary doctrine which could be effectively utilised by the emerging democratic and socialist opposition movements. The dominant political forces and social classes of the nineteenth and early twentieth centuries were closely linked with the revolutions of the eighteenth. They had vivid memories of their own victories and appreciated fully the incendiary potential of naturalist ideas which had been successfully used against the old regimes in France and America. As Bentham insisted, these rights were not just nonsense and fallacies, they were also mischievous and anarchical.[1] Their use in political discourse, during that period, was extremely limited and they were almost unknown to law. The gradual evolution and eventual domination of a combination of limited democracy and unlimited legal positivism meant that the sovereign people (defined in an extremely restricted way) could do no wrong. All assertions of human rights by the groups and classes excluded from citizenship, women, blacks, workers or political and social reformers, were dismissed as selfish attacks against the common good and the democratic will. This was the era of state and empire-building, of utilitarianism and social engineering, the time of emergence of nationalism,

---

[1] Jeremy Bentham, *Anarchical Fallacies; being an examination of the Declaration of Rights issued during the French Revolution* in Jeremy Waldron (ed.), *Nonsense upon Stilts* (London, Methuen, 1987) 46–76.

racism and sexism. It was not that these ideas and practices were unknown before the nineteenth century but they now became theorised and respectable elements of European culture. Individual rights and the associated legal constraints were not part of the first phase of modernity.

The intellectual reasons for the decline were more complex. We will examine in the second part the devastating critiques of natural rights by some of the finest minds of the late eighteenth and nineteenth centuries.[2] Edmund Burke derided their abstraction and rationalism, Jeremy Bentham their obscurantism and indeterminacy, Karl Marx their close link with class interests which, despite the theory's apparent claims, made them antipathetic to human emancipation. They all contributed to the fatal undermining of the intellectual presuppositions of naturalism alongside many other factors at work. The most important intellectual force in law was positivism. The positivist approach and empiricism, its handmaiden, already dominant in the natural sciences and triumphant in technology with its many marvels, migrated to law and the emerging social sciences. As Hobbes had accurately predicted, the most important political consequence of the positivisation of natural rights was the emergence of the legislative Leviathan. The power of free will to shape the world according to its preferences was shadowed by the unlimited competence of the state to shape individuals according to the dictates of *raison d'état* and political expediency and, individual freedom was reflected in the legislative and administrative ability of the state to interfere with and regulate all aspects of social life. The free and willing individual finds no inherent restrictions to his world making power; similarly, the state finds no limits to the scope, reach and breadth of its sovereignty. The beginnings of all modern law, which is by definition posited law, can be traced in this mirroring: positivism, the claim that valid law is exclusively created by acts of state will, is the inescapable essence of legal modernity, the mirror image of the claim that the individual legislates the ends and aims of his action and arranges his life plan through sovereign acts of choice. One could argue, by paraphrasing Foucault, that the ideal of emancipation was shadowed by the technology of legislation and the aim of self-fulfilment by techniques of disciplining the subject and of shaping the body politic and the docile and productive individual body.

The process of positivisation united the major Western legal systems. In England, John Austin and A. V. Dicey removed all

---

[2] See Chapter 7.

remaining naturalist fallacies from jurisprudence and proclaimed the absolute primacy of state law. Dicey's classic *Introduction to the Law of the Constitution* arrogantly dismissed the ability of the French tradition with its Bills of Rights and special *droit administrative* to constrain public power. With us "the principles of private law have . . . been by the action of the Courts and Parliament so extended as to determine the position of the Crown and its servants . . . The constitution is the result of the ordinary law of the land . . . the law of the constitution is not the source but the consequence of the rights of the individuals".[3] Dicey's Victorian combination of English parochialism and imperial triumphalism expressed a wider turning away from moral principle and natural right, seen as metaphysical abstractions and myths, towards a more pragmatic appreciation of the great potential of state power left to its untrammelled resources. Burke's aggressive traditionalism had finally become the principle of the Constitution. In the United States, race relations were defined for a century by the apartheid principle of "separate but equal" which was set aside as late as 1954.[4] The free speech guarantee of the First Amendment, the most litigated right in the history of the American Constitution, would have to wait until 1919 for its first outing before the Supreme Court.[5] In continental Europe, Hannah Arendt noted that, before the Second World War, human rights "were invoked in a *perfunctory* way to defend individuals against the power of the state and to shield them from the social insecurity". Those jurists and philanthropists who tried to use human rights to protect minorities "showed an uncanny similarity in language and composition to that of societies for the prevention of cruelty to animals".[6] And the German legal theorist Otto Gierke, writing in 1934, as the Nazis were taking hold, lamented that in Germany, "natural right" and "humanity" "have now become almost incomprehensible . . . and have lost altogether their original life and colour".[7]

This process was facilitated and accelerated by the transformation of political philosophy and jurisprudence into political science, the

---

[3] A. V. Dicey, *Introduction to the Study of the Law of the Constitution* (London, 1885; 10th edn, 1959) with introduction by E.C.S. Wade, 198–9.

[4] *Brown v. Board of Education of Topeka* 347 U.S. 483 (1954). The judicial part of the struggle for desegregation is told in Richard Kluger, *Simple Justice* (London, Andre Deutsch, 1977).

[5] *Schenck v. United States*, 249 U.S. 47 (1919).

[6] Hannah Arendt, *The Origins of Totalitarianism* (San Diego, Harvest Books, 1979) 293, 292.

[7] Otto Gierke, *Natural Law and the Theory of Society* (translated with Introduction by Ernest Baker) (Cambridge, Cambridge University Press, 1934) 201–2.

turn of history into the philosophy of history and by the evolution of grand social theory. Hegel, Comte, Durkheim, Marx, Weber and Freud replaced the earlier interest in individual rights with an examination of the social processes and structures which shape subjectivity and action. As the creator of sociology, Auguste Comte put it, the spirit of the rights of man

> was useful in demolishing old feudal-military policy and in exploding the myth of divine rights by insisting on the rights of man. But it was totally incapable of projecting any positive conceptions to replace those it had destroyed; every so-called liberal principle was in fact only a "dogma" created by trying to erect some criticism of the theological into a positive doctrine, e.g., the dogma of liberty of conscience – mere abstract expression (like metaphysics), of the temporary state of unbounded liberty in which the human mind was left by the decay of the theological philosophy.[8]

In this intellectual climate the idea of society was invented, it was given priority over the individual and became the main object of scientific inquiry. Durkheim's collective conscience, Marx's primacy of the economic over the moral aspects of historical development and Weber's process of rationalisation delivered severe blows to the naturalist idea, which had placed individuals and their rights higher than societal claims or had asserted that society was the outcome of contractual agreements. Societies were no longer seen as the product of deliberate individual action nor was the protection of natural rights their main task. As historian Joan Scott put it, "by the end of the nineteenth century, the individual was defined by social theorists not in opposition to the social or society, but as its product".[9] For the emerging social theory, structure became politically and cognitively more important than agency, individuals had low epistemological value and were the targets of multiple external determinations and internalised constraints. The newly liberated individual soon became the object of disciplinary power and his putative sovereignty and right gave way to techniques of normalisation.[10]

An important effect of this theoretical turn, was the creation of the concept of ideology. Ideology was defined either as false conscious-

[8] *The Positive Philosophy of Auguste Comte* (Harriet Martineau ed. and trans.) (London, 3rd ed., 1893) Vol. 2, 51.

[9] Joan Scott, *Only Paradoxes to Offer: French Feminists and the Rights of Man* (Cambridge Mass., Harvard University Press, 1996), 10.

[10] Michel Foucault, *Discipline and Punish: The Birth of the Prison* (Harmondsworth, Penguin, 1979); Michel Foucault, *The History of Sexuality, Volume I: An Introduction* (Harmondsworth, Penguin, 1981).

ness, which could be corrected by science, or as a set of ideas representing narrow, sectional interests but claiming the dignity of the universal. Natural rights became a prime example of ideological illusion; against their absolutist pretensions, they were now seen as conventional and interested discourse of the most dubious character. Reinterpreted ideologically, natural rights turned from eternal into historically and geographically local inventions, from absolute into contextually determined, from inalienable into relative to cultural and legal contingencies. No longer the basis of society or the main purpose of its action, natural rights became disputed entities, objects of historical analysis and ideological debunking. The new morality was a morality of groups, classes, parties and nations, of social intervention, legal reform and utilitarian calculations. Natural rights were reduced to the scrapheap of ideas, their relevance exhausted with the end of the Napoleonic adventures. They placed no obstacle into the path of power and could be removed or restricted at will in order to promote state purposes and social engineering.

Hegel's philosophy of history, although antithetical to utilitarianism, further undermined natural rights. The historicist reaction to the French Revolution had insisted that all knowledge is situated and can be acquired only within clear historical constraints. The historical horizon cannot be transcended, because it forms the absolute presupposition of all understanding. Hegel radicalised historicism; while Burke had argued that the attempt to resolve fundamental philosophical problems from a transcendent perspective was absurd, Hegel turned this insight into the spirit of history. The claim that the rational, the actual and the real had finally coincided in the Hegelian system meant that the quest for wisdom had finally been transformed into wisdom itself and that the search for the "ideal polity" had come to an end.[11] When Hegel heard, from his study, the fury of the battle of Jena, he famously declared that he saw in Napoleon "reason on horseback". Napoleon's and "reason's" defeat led Hegel to diagnose the completion of the system closer to home and to identify it with the Prussian State. Either way, the spirit had been incarnated in history and reason had subjected power to the demands of right. Rights had triumphed in the *Rechtstaat* and there was no need to fight for their realisation any longer.

Natural rights passed away alongside the abstract man of the eighteenth century whose nature they had defined. When an idea or

---

[11] Leo Strauss, *Natural Law and History* (Chicago, University of Chicago Press, 1965) 33. But see Chapter 10 for a response to this criticism from a Hegelian position.

concept is entrusted in the hands of historians or sociologists, its vitality has been lost, its usefulness has migrated from history to historiography and its excitement displaced from political battles to academic disputes. Even more, when an ideal becomes law and a dissident movement governmental legitimation, it often turns into its opposite. As the great philosopher E. M. Cioran put it, "the man who proposes a new faith is persecuted, until it is his turn to become a persecutor: truths begin by a conflict with the police and end by calling them in; for each absurdity we have suffered for, degenerates into a legality, as every martyrdom ends in the paragraphs of the Law . . . An Angel protected by a policeman – that is how truths die, that is how enthusiasms expire".[12]

Radical natural law, on the other hand, from the Stoics to early modernity had used nature as the marker of the future in the present and had always suspected the reduction of right to the rational or the real. As Heidegger put it, from a different perspective, "higher than actuality stands possibility".[13] What is cannot be true or self-identical, because at the heart of the present lurks what is still to come. But the historicist rejection of natural right meant that

> all right is positive right, and this means that what is right is determined exclusively by the legislators and the courts of the various countries. Now it is obviously meaningful, and sometimes even necessary, to speak of "unjust" laws and "unjust" decisions. In passing such judgements we imply that there is a standard of right and wrong independent of positive right and higher than positive right: a standard with reference to which we are able to judge of positive right. Many people today hold the view that the standard in question is in the best case nothing but the ideal adopted by our society or our "civilisation" and embodied in its way of life or its institutions . . . If there is no standard higher than the ideal of our society, we are utterly unable to take a critical distance from that ideal.[14]

The loss of the critical ideal and the legal translation of the utopian perspective had catastrophic effects. The road between the demise of natural rights in the nineteenth and early twentieth centuries, and the recent pronunciations of the final triumph of human rights, passes through two world wars, a huge number of local wars and innumerable atrocities and humanitarian disasters. It is lit by the fires of the Holocaust.

[12] E. M. Cioran, *A Short History of Decay* (R. Howard trans.) (London, Quartet Books, 1990) 74.

[13] Martin Heidegger, *Being and Time* (New York, Harper and Row, 1962) 63.

[14] Strauss, op.cit., supra n. 11, 2–3.

II. THE IRRESISTIBLE RISE AND RESISTIBLE WEAKNESSES OF INTERNATIONAL HUMAN RIGHTS

Human rights entered the world scene after the Second World War. The history of their invention has been repeatedly and exhaustively told and will not be attempted here.[15] Its symbolic moments include the Nuremberg and Tokyo Trials, the signing of the Charter of the United Nations (1945) and the adoption of the Universal Declaration of Human Rights (1948). Following these foundational acts, the international community launched a long campaign of standard-setting. Hundreds of human rights conventions, treaties, declarations and agreements have been negotiated and adopted by the United Nations, by regional bodies, like the Council of Europe and the Organisation of African Unity, and by states.[16] Human rights diversified from "first generation" civil and political or "negative" rights, associated with liberalism, into second generation, economic, social and cultural or "positive" rights, associated with the socialist tradition and, finally, into "third generation" or group and national sovereignty rights, associated with the decolonisation process. The first generation or "blue" rights are symbolised by individual freedom, the second, or "red" rights by claims to equality and guarantees of a decent living standard, while the third or "green" rights by the right to self-determination and belatedly the protection of the environment. But what lies behind this apparently unstoppable proliferation of human rights?

The most obvious change in the transition from natural to human rights was the replacement of their philosophical ground and institutional sources. The belief that rights could be protected either through the automatic adjustment of the entitlements of human nature and the action of legal institutions, or through the legislative divinations of popular sovereignty, proved unrealistic. As Hannah Arendt put it "it is quite conceivable that one fine day a highly organised and mechanised humanity will conclude quite democratically –

---

[15] Amongst many, see the following theoretically minded introductions to the history and philosophy of human rights: Louis Henkin, *The Age of Rights* (New York, Columbia University Press, 1990); Norberto Bobbio, *The Age of Rights* (Cambridge, Polity, 1996); Jack Donnelly, *Universal Human Rights in Theory and Practice* (Ithaca, Cornell University Press, 1989).

[16] The most comprehensive compendium of the fast proliferating international law of human rights, see Ian Brownlie (ed.), *Basic Documents on Human Rights* (Oxford, Clarendon, 1994).

namely by majority decision – that for humanity as a whole it would be better to liquidate certain parts thereof".[17] Her statement, phrased as a prediction, has already become a terrible historical fact. The "market" of human dignity and equality did not conceal a "hidden hand" and people voted and still vote for regimes and parties determined to violate all human rights, as the examples of Hitler's Germany and Milocevic's Yugoslavia show. If the French Revolution and the first proclamation of rights were reactions against monarchic absolutism, the international law of human rights was a response to Hitler and Stalin, to the atrocities and barbarities of the War and to the Holocaust. In this latest mutation of naturalism, humanity or civilisation was substituted for human nature, the Frenchmen of the *Déclaration* were enlarged to include the whole humanity, international institutions and law-makers replaced the divine legislator or the social contract and international conventions and treaties became the Constitution above constitutions and the Law behind laws. An endless process of international and humanitarian law-making has been put into operation, aimed at protecting people from the putative assertions of their sovereignty. To paraphrase Nietzsche, if God, the source of natural law, is dead, he has been replaced by international law.

The higher status of human rights is seen as the result of their legal universalisation, of the triumph of the universality of humanity. The law addresses all states and all human persons *qua* human and declares their entitlements to be a part of the patrimony of humanity, which has replaced human nature as the rhetorical ground of rights. And yet human rights declarations have little value as a descriptive tool of society and its bond. The French and American revolutionaries were aware of the gap between their universal claims and their local jurisdiction and used it to legitimise their actions. International legislators have lost that historical awareness and discretion. Comparing their documents with those of the eighteenth century is like comparing a Jane Austen novel with its period costume adaptation for television. "It was clearly understood" said an American delegate to the San Francisco conference which drafted the UN Charter "that the phrase 'We the Peoples', meant that the peoples of the world were speaking through their governments at the Conference, and that it was because the peoples of the world are determined that those things shall be done which are stated in the preamble that the governments have

---

[17] Arendt, op.cit., supra n. 6, 299.

negotiated the instrument".[18] The rhetorical organisation of this passage is instructive because it represents admirably the logic of international human rights. What the "people" have determined is what the governments have expressed and negotiated and what has been put in the Charter. State power, public and private domination and oppression have been dissolved in this perfect chain of substitutions: peoples and states have finally merged and the governments or the international organisations speak for both, as there is no other way for that mythic beast, the "people of the world", to express itself.

Every state and power comes under the mantle of the international law of human rights, every government becomes civilised as the "law of the princes" has finally become the "universal" law of human dignity. But this is an empirical universality, based on the competitive solidarity of sovereign governments and on the pragmatic concerns and calculations of international politics. The variable universalism of classical natural law or the Kantian universalisation acted as regulative principles: they gave a perspective from which each particular action could be judged, in theory at least, in the name of the universal. The empirical universality of human rights, on the other hand, is not a normative principle. It is a matter of counting how many states have adopted how many and which treaties, or how many have introduced which reservations or derogations from treaty obligations. When normative universality becomes a calculable globalisation, it turns from a lofty, albeit impossible ideal, into the lowest common denominator of state interests and rivalries. The community of human rights is universal but imaginary; universal humanity does not exist empirically and cannot act as a transcendental principle philosophically.

Universal positivised rights close the gap between empirical reality and the ideal left open by the French split between man and citizen, despite its obvious problems. A state that signs and accepts human rights conventions and declarations can claim to be a human rights state. Human rights are then seen as an indeterminate discourse of state legitimation or as the empty rhetoric of rebellion; it can be easily co-opted by all kinds of opposition, minority or religious leaders, whose political project is not to humanise oppressive states but to replace them with their own equally murderous regimes.

---

[18] Leo Pasvolsky in Committee on Foreign Relations, *The Charter of the United Nations Hearings* quoted in Norman Lewis, "Human rights, law and democracy in an unfree world" in Tony Evans (ed.), *Human Rights Fifty Years on: A reappraisal* (Manchester, Manschester University Press, 1988) 88.

Let us now turn from foundations to institutions. The weaknesses and inadequacies of international law, particularly when faced with individuals, are well-known. Traditionally, the law of "civilised princes" had no interest and gave no *locus standi* to ordinary people. This has certainly changed since the adoption of the Universal Declaration, but the conceptual problems remain. First, human rights are still predominantly violated or protected at the local level. They were created as a superior or additional protection from the state, its military and police, its political and public authorities, its judges, businesses and media. These are still the culprits or – rarely – the angels. Irrespective of what international institutions say or how many treaties foreign secretaries sign, human rights are violated or upheld in the street, the workplace and the local police station. Their reality is Burkean not Kantian. Even at the formal level, the provisions of national constitutions and laws are much more important than international undertakings.

This leads to a related point. Human rights treaties and codes are a new type of positive law, the last and most safe haven of a *sui generis* positivism. Codification, from Justinian to the *Code Napoléon,* has always been the ultimate exercise of legislative sovereignty, the supreme expression of state power. We examined above, how the early declarations of rights helped bring into legitimate existence the sovereignty of the nation-state with its accompanying threats and risks for individual freedom. Something similar happened with the post-war expansion of international law into the human rights field. National sovereignty and non-intervention in the domestic affairs of states were the key principle on which the law was built, from the UN Charter to all important treaties. While the major powers fought tooth and nail over the definitions and priorities of human rights, they unanimously agreed that these rights could not be used to pierce the shield of national sovereignty. Human rights were a major tool for legitimising nationally and internationally the post-war order, at a point at which all principles of state and international organisation had emerged from the War seriously weakened. The contradictory principles of human rights and national sovereignty, schizophrenically both paramount in post-war international law, served two separate agendas of the great powers: the need to legitimise the new order through its commitment to rights, without exposing the victorious states to scrutiny and criticism about their own flagrant violations. As Lewis put it, "the debate about human rights and the upholding of human dignity, was in reality a process of re-legitimation of the principles of sovereignty and non-intervention in the domestic affairs of sovereign states. The most powerful states, through the human rights discourse, made their priorities the universal concern of others".[19] Once again human rights were a main way for underpinning the power of states.

Law-making in the huge business of human rights has been taken over by government representatives, diplomats, policy advisers, international civil servants and human rights experts. This is a group with little legitimacy. Governments are the enemy against whom human rights were conceived as a defence. Undoubtedly, the atrocities of this century shook and shocked some governments and politicians as much as ordinary people. But the business of government is to govern not to follow moral principles. Governmental actions in the international arena are dictated by national interest and political considerations and, morality enters the stage always late, when the principle invoked happens to condemn the actions of a political adversary. When human rights and national interest coincide, governments become their greatest champions. But this is the exception. The government-operated international human rights law is the best illustration of the poacher turned gamekeeper.[20]

Problems in law-making are confounded by difficulties in interpretation and implementation. The international mechanisms are rudimentary and can scarcely improve while national sovereignty remains the paramount principle in law. The main method is the drawing of periodic or *ad hoc* reports about human rights violations; the main weapon, adverse publicity and the doubtful force that shame carries in international relations. There are various types of

[19] Norman Lewis, ibid., 89. For the relationship between domestic policies and international attitudes, see P.G. Lauren, *Power and Prejudice: The Politics and Diplomacy of Racial Discrimination* (Oxford, Westview Press, 1996 (2nd edition)).

[20] An extreme illustration of this problem existed until 1998, in the most successful human rights machinery, the European Human Rights Convention. While the Convention provided for a semi and a fully judicial body (the Commission and the Court), the final decision in cases not referred to the Court was taken by the Committee of Ministers. As a result, many politically controversial cases were left to the Ministers who, often, rather than accept the decisions of the investigatory Commission put them on hold. The problem was compounded by the fact that the individual who had launched the complaint was not entitled to refer the case to the Court for final determination. This has changed with the implementation of the 11th Protocol to the Convention and the merging of Commission and Court. But the members of the new unified Court are still nominated by the governments and, from past experience, are reluctant to vote against perceived national interests. Indeed, many of the new appointees to the new Court are former diplomats or civil servant giving rise to serious doubts about their independence. It may sound impossible but, unless governments are removed from the running of human rights institutions, these will have little legitimacy.

reporting: monitoring, the most common, is carried out usually by volunteers and experts around the world under the auspices of the UN Human Rights Commission. "Special rapporteurs" appointed by the Commission draw up reports about specific areas of concern, like torture, or about individual countries with a poor human rights record. Under another model, states are invited to submit periodic reports about their compliance with certain treaty obligations, to committees created for that purpose (the most famous being the Human Rights Committee under the International Covenant for Civil and Political Rights).

Weak implementation mechanisms ensure that the shield of national sovereignty is not seriously pierced, unless the interest of the great powers dictates otherwise, as recent events in the Balkans have proved. The war crimes tribunal for the former Yugoslavia issued, early in its life, indictments against Karadjic and Mladic, the genocidal leaders of the Bosnian Serbs. But the International Force for Bosnia has not been allowed to take steps to arrest them. In a symbolic illustration of the status of human rights law, the Force has been authorised to arrest them, if they happen to come across them, but not to seek them out.[21] Finally, in a few instances international courts or commissions investigate complaints by victims of human rights abuses and conduct quasi-judicial proceedings against states. But the jurisprudence of human rights courts is extremely restricted and dubious and its rapid changes in direction confirm some of the worst fears of legal realism: barristers appearing before international bodies such as the European Court of Human Rights quickly learn that it is better preparation to research the political affiliations of the government-appointed judges than to read the Court's case-law. It is well-known that changes in the political orientation of the appointing governments are soon reflected in the personnel of international human rights courts and commissions.[22]

[21] A similar outcome followed the indictment of Milosevic during the Kosovo war. As President Clinton admitted after the end of the war, the NATO Kosovo force has not been authorised to arrest Milocevic and his arreignment is not imminent.

[22] Only the European system follows a fully-fledged judicial procedure and has a developed case-law. Even in Europe, however, for most of its existence the Strasbourg organs declared "admissible" and examined fewer that 3% of all the applications submitted to them. This percentage has slightly increased since the admission of the Eastern European states in the nineties. The jurisprudence of the European Commission and, even more of the Court, has followed the political views of the appointing governments which have ensured that their nominees are ideologically sympathetic to their views. For a considered view of the political priorities and methods of human rights courts and institutions, see Rolando Gaete, *Human Rights and the Limits of Critical Reason* (Aldershot, Dartmouth, 1993) Chapters 6,7 and 8.

In this light, the creation of a permanent war crimes tribunal acquired increased significance. A treaty setting up an International Criminal Court (ICC) was adopted in Rome by representatives of 120 countries, in July 1998. The Court will have jurisdiction over war crimes and crimes of aggression, crimes against humanity and genocide. It will replace *ad hoc* war crimes tribunals, like those of Nuremberg, Tokyo, Yugoslavia and Rwanda and will be in a better position to defend its actions from the standard criticism that international criminal liability amounts to a particularly vindictive case of "victors' justice". Undoubtedly, all measures which remove human rights and their administration from governments, the main villains of the piece, are welcome. Independent judges, sensitive to the plight of the oppressed and dominated of the world and appointed for long periods with security of tenure, are better qualified to judge war criminals than diplomats and *ad hoc* governmental representatives.

This is not the place to examine in detail the many criticisms of the use of criminal responsibility as a method of promoting human rights, nor of the specific shortcomings of the treaty of Rome.[23] A few general comments are, however, necessary. The symbolic value and the emotional force generated by war crime prosecutions are undoubtedly considerable, particularly for those on the "right" side of the conflict which led to the crimes. But as we know from domestic experience, the individualisation and criminalisation of politics has rarely ended political conflict. Similarly, one suspects that not many wars or atrocities were prevented because leaders feared for their fate, if defeated, and, not many dictators were deterred by Nuremberg or will be deterred by Pinochet's sojourn in Surrey. Criminal punishment, like all individualised legal procedures, is likely to have little effect on massive human rights violations, particularly if the minimal media coverage of the Yugoslav War Crimes Tribunal and the nonexistent of the Rwandan one are an indication of popular interest.

One incident in the process of setting up the ICC deserves mention. The United States was the greatest enthusiast for setting up the tribunals for Yugoslavia and Rwanda. When it came to negotiations for the criminal court, however, the American position was reversed. The Americans fought hard, using threats and rewards, to prevent the

[23] Henry Steiner and Philip Alston, *International Human Rights in Context* (Oxford, Clarendon, 1996) Chapter 15 review the debate leading to the establishment of the Court. For early criticisms of the Treaty of Rome, see Steve Tully, "A vain Conceit? The Rome Statute of the ICC and the Enforcement of Human Rights", 11 *Wig & Gavel* 1999, 16–20; Morten Bergsmo and David Tolbert, "Reflections on the Stature of the ICC", 11 *Wig & Gavel* 1999, 21–6.

universal jurisdiction of the court.[24] They claimed that the court would be used for politically motivated prosecutions against American soldiers when, as the world's last superpower with global interests, they invade or intervene on foreign soil. The Americans tried to restrict the court's jurisdiction to nationals of states which have ratified the treaty, something which would have undermined the premise behind the new court. David Scheffer, the American representative, stated that, if the conference approved universal jurisdiction for the court, the United States would "actively oppose" it from its inception.[25] The conference, anxious to include the major international military power in the treaty, seriously restricted the court's powers and weakened its independence, but did not give the absolute guarantee that no American soldier would ever be brought before the court. As a result, the United States was one of seven countries, which included Iraq, Libya and China (states which American foreign policy has often demonised), to vote against the final and much compromised version.

The United States usually promotes the universalism of rights. Its rejection of the world criminal court was a case of cultural relativism which took the form of an imperial escape clause. It was also an implicit admission that war crimes and atrocities are not the exclusive preserve of "rogue" regimes.[26] It should not surprise us. Universalism, domestically and internationally, comes with an opt out facility. This is not just a question of the hypocrisy of power; a claim to universality can be made, if one power at least is not covered by it and is able to define the parameters of the universal. This was France in the early modern order and the United States in the new world order.

III. HUMAN RIGHTS AND STATE HYPOCRISY

The history of human rights has been marked by ideological point-scoring and intense conflict between Western liberal and other

---

[24] "US troops will quit, allies warned", *The Guardian*, July 10, 1998, 3.

[25] "Self-interest brings court into contempt", *The Guardian*, July 14, 1999, 15.

[26] Recent historiography has shown that atrocities are a common occurrence in wars and have been committed by allied forces in both world wars and in Vietnam. See Joanna Bourke, *An Intimate History of Killing: Face to Face Killing in 20th Century Warfare* (London, Granta, 1999) Chapter 6. The concern was therefore to avoid having American soldiers tried for atrocities by an international body and try them, if necessary, under American military and criminal law, as in the case of Colonel Callan after the My Lai massacre.

conceptions of human dignity. Both problems were evident from the inception of the international human rights code. The ideological colours of the Universal Declaration were evidently Western and liberal. The members of the preparatory committee were Mrs Eleanor Roosevelt, a Lebanese Christian and a Chinese. John Humphrey, the Canadian Director of the UN Division of Human Rights, who was asked by the committee to prepare a first draft, recalls that the Chinese member suggested at a party that he should "put [his] other duties aside for six months and study Chinese philosophy, after which [he] might be able to prepare a text for the committee". Humphrey prepared the text, which was substantially adopted by the committee, but his response to the suggestion indicates the Western attitude which eventually became the universalist side of the debate in opposition to cultural relativism: "I didn't go to China nor did I study the writings of Confucius".[27] The *traveaux préparatoires* he used to prepare his draft came, with only two exceptions, from Western English language sources with the American Law Institute submission a main influence.[28] Only one of the seven principal drafters was not Christian and, as Stephen Marks remarks, "the level of the group [of drafters] as philosophers and moralists falls short of their eighteenth century predecessors".[29]

Humphrey thought that his draft "attempted to combine humanitarian liberalism with social democracy."[30] The social democratic component of the Declaration consisted in a number of economic, social and cultural rights which, according to Antonio Cassese, "considerably reduced the impact of Western ideas by securing approval for some fundamental postulates of the Marxist ideology."[31] That is not how the Soviet delegate saw it, for whom the Declaration was just "a collection of pious phrases". The Soviet bloc and Saudi Arabia abstained from the final vote in the General Assembly, while South Africa voted against. But the Soviet position was not unique. Similar sentiments have been expressed by the American representative to the United Nations during President Reagan's administration, who called the Declaration "a letter to Santa Claus" and, by US Ambassador Morris Abram, who addressing the UN Commission on

[27] John Humphrey, *Human Rights and the United Nations* (Epping Bowker, 1984) 29.
[28] ibid., 32.
[29] Marks, "From the 'Single Confused Page' to the 'Decalogue for Six Billion Persons': The Roots of the Universal Declaration of Human Rights in the French Revolution", 20 *Human Rights Quarterly* 490 (1998).
[30] Humphrey, op.cit., supra n. 27, 40.
[31] Antonio Cassese, *Human Rights in a Changing World* (Cambridge, Polity, 1990) 44.

Human Rights, dismissed the right to development as "dangerous incitement" and "little more than an empty vessel into which vague hopes and inchoate expectations can be poured".[32]

Following this inauspicious beginning, human rights became a main ideological weapon during the Cold War. The battlelines were drawn around the superiority of civil and political over economic and social rights. As a result, the attempt to produce an inclusive and binding Bill of Rights was abandoned and two separate covenants were drawn and eventually adopted, in 1966, some eighteen years later. Human rights, following Western priorities were hierarchised. The Civil and Political Rights Covenant creates a state duty "to respect and ensure to all" the listed rights (art. 2, ICCPR). The Economic and Social Rights Covenant is much more flexible and equivocal: member states undertake "to take steps, individually and through international assistance and co-operation . . . with a view to achieving progressively the full realisation" of the Covenant rights (art. 2, ICESCR). Still, while the Americans have taken a leading role in setting standards and use human rights violations to criticise other countries, it took twenty-six years for the United States to ratify the Civil and Political Rights Covenant, forty years for the Genocide Convention and twenty-eight for the Convention against racial discrimination. The State Department publishes annually huge country reports on human rights practices.[33] Congress has not ratified, however, the Economic and Social Rights Covenant, the Convention banning discrimination against women and, it is the only country, with Somalia, that has not ratified the Convention on the rights of children. In April 1999, human rights organisations led by Amnesty International launched an unprecedented appeal with the UN Human Rights Commission, asking it to take action against human rights abuses in the United States. "When we use international human rights standards, then clearly the US is failing the test daily" stated Amnesty Director Andre Sané launching the appeal. Human rights groups point to a consistent pattern of violations which include unchallenged police brutality, the treatment of asylum seekers, prison

[32] Quoted in Noam Chomsky, "A letter to Santa Claus", *The Times Higher Education Supplement*, 19 February 1999, 23; Noam Chomsky, *The Umbrella of US Power* (New York, Seven Stories, 1999).

[33] A much more modest British annual report on human rights was published for the first time by the Department for International Development, in April 1998. Part of new Labour's "ethical" foreign policy, it was compared "in style and format [to] a big public company announcing its results", with "upbeat" tone and "corporate and glossy" mood. *The Guardian*, April 22, 1998, 11.

conditions and the death sentence and explain that these and other violations "disproportionately affect racial minorities".[34]

But the United States does not have exclusive rights to hypocrisy. During the Cold War, any criticism of human rights abuses by the communist states was followed by a ritual Soviet denunciation of British policies in Northern Ireland and of American racism, and a similar approach has been adopted by many developing countries after the fall of communism. The Europeans and their Union have not fared much better. In 1997, the EU launched an initiative entitled a "Human Rights Agenda for the New Millennium". A committee of *sages* or "wise men" was asked to draw up a set of European human rights policies to mark the 50th anniversary of the Universal Declaration. A group of academics and human rights activists was convened, as part of this initiative, under the auspices of the European University Institute, to draw up detailed reports on various human rights concerns and advise the *sages*. At a meeting of the advisory group held in Florence, in October 1997, as part of the programme, a respectable researcher presented an early draft of the report he had been asked to prepare on the work of European "supervisory bodies". The rapporteur proposed to look into the European Convention of Human Rights, the European Convention against Torture and the reports of the European Commission against Racism and Intolerance and summarise problems identified by the respective organs. At that point, the European Commission representatives strongly objected to the inclusion of a report of this kind, although it would be based on official, published and widely available materials. The Brussels official funding the luxurious conference threatened to withdraw the funding, prompting a delegate to inquire whether she could wait until after lunch. It became clear, during heated exchanges, that the official political purpose behind the "agenda" was to present a rosy European picture, to link aid and trade to Western human rights priorities and to give European representatives in international bodies something to say, as one delegate put it, when Europe was (justifiably allegedly) criticising others for human rights violations and was (unjustifiably) attacked in return for applying double standards. The exercise was not about washing European

---

[34] "Amnesty urges curb on US 'human rights abuse' ", *The Guardian*, April 14, 1999. 9. It is noticeable that the European Court of Human Rights has ruled that the conditions of detention in American death rows amount to a violation of Article 3 of the Convention which prohibits torture, inhuman and degrading treatment. *Soering* v. *UK* (1989) 11 EHRR 439.

"dirty linen" in public but, about showing how seriously Europeans view human rights.

The respected researcher and a few academics found the position of the Brussels officials unpalatable. The metaphorical lunch was saved, however, through a rather strange compromise: the researcher would be allowed to present the report but, instead of cataloguing the violations under an alphabetical list of European states (which was thought unacceptably critical), he would present them thematically thus minimising the embarrassment of the culprits. After this incident, it was no surprise that the publication of the final report of the *sages* was accompanied by controversy. It was widely reported that European governments moved before publication to downgrade proposals that the European Union should set up a special department headed by a new commissioner to co-ordinate human rights work throughout Europe. References to the inhumane and degrading treatment of detainees and details of deaths of asylum-seekers in police custody in the initial report were deleted from the final version. But the report did conclude, despite the efforts of the Claret-pinching eurocrats, that Europe's "strong rhetoric on human rights is not matched by the reality".[35]

If ideological point-scoring is the symbolic prize behind human rights controversies, trade and market-penetration is often the real stake. An interesting example comes from the flourishing Sino-Western relations. These were allegedly seriously disrupted, after the Tiananmen square massacre of hundreds of protesting students in May 1989 and the widespread repression of dissidents which still takes place in China. But this cooling of relations lasted for a limited period and normal relations were soon resumed. It has been repeatedly reported that every time a Western leader visits Beijing, lists of well-known dissidents are handed to the Chinese authorities. "Cynical diplomats say it keeps the human rights lobby quiet at home. From time to time, China earns diplomatic credit by releasing a big name".[36] China has been particularly adept in using trade deals to avoid international opprobrium. As a result, no resolution criticising Chinese violations has been passed by the UN Human Rights Commission. Similarly, the British Government, despite its "ethical"

[35] "Europe's human rights rhetoric at odds with reality", *The Guardian*, October 10, 1988. The final report "Leading by example: A Human Rights Agenda for the European Union for the Year 2000" is published in Philip Alston, "The European Union and Human Rights" (Oxford University Press, 1999) appendix.

[36] "The price of dissent", *The Guardian*, May 31, 1999, G2.

foreign policy, went ahead, in 1997, with the deal to sell Hawk jets to the genocidal Indonesian regime of President Suharto during whose long and repressive reign half a million East Timorese were killed. As an opposition politician put it, "other governments will give Robin Cook pretty short shrift, if he goes around the world lecturing them about human rights when they know the British Government has issued eighty-six new export licenses [for arms] to Turkey and twenty-two to Indonesia [between May 1997 and April 1998]".[37] According to recent revelations, the United States trained the Indonesian military, including an elite anti-insurgency force involved in East Timor massacres until late 1998 despite the official suspension of the programme after earlier massacres in 1991. Britain too made a significant contribution to Indonesian military training which was suspended a few days before the UN peacekeeping force arrived in East Timor.[38]

The fashionable moral turn in the foreign policies of Western governments, which characterised the late nineties, indicates that the symbolic capital of human rights has increased in the West. Clinton, Blair and Shroeder, despite their differences, claim to be united in the pursuit of ethically informed international relations. But we have little evidence of such a turn, which is historically and theoretically improbable. American and British-led NATO was prepared to take military action against Iraq and against the Serbs over Kosovo, while little protest was heard about the killing of some 250,000 Kurds by Turkish forces over the last twenty-five years, the genocide of the people of East Timor by Indonesian forces for over thirty years, or the ethnic cleansing of Serbs from Croatia. Saddam Hussein and Slobodan Milocevic are old-time dictators steeped in Cold War anti-American rhetoric. Successive Turkish governments, on the other hand, whether military dictatorships or democracies supervised by the armed forces, have always been strongly pro-American and a valued ally in the sensitive eastern Mediterranean. Similarly, the Indonesian dictator Suharto had been a reliable Western ally and major anti-communist force in south-east Asia, until he was overthrown by the daily protests of people who took to the streets for months, despite being killed and maimed by the dictator's security forces.

These discrepancies give rise to criticisms of the hypocrisy or cynicism of the great powers. But these accusations would be valid, if

[37] "Robin Cook's tour of the global badlands", *The Guardian*, April 22, 1998, 6.

[38] "US aided butchers of Timor", *The Observer*, September 19, 1999. See also John Pilger, "Under the influence", *The Guardian*, September 21, 1999, 18.

one accepted, counterfactually, that foreign policy is guided by the consistency of Kantian moral principles. To paraphrase Richard Rorty, if that was possible, moral foreign policy, like ethnic cleansers, would wash the world clean of prejudice and oppression. But the moral claim is either fraudulent or naive. Experience tells otherwise: human rights, like arms sales, aid to the developing world and trade preferences or sanctions, are tools of international politics used, according to the classical Greek saying, to help friends and harm enemies. Every good diplomat boasts that principled consistency in foreign affairs is impossible in practice, undesirable in negotiations but indispensable in the public presentation of policy. Moral consistency requires the existence of a common international and transcultural morality which would underpin policy initiatives to the satisfaction of humanity's conscience. But none of these elements exists or can come about in inter-state relations. As Noam Chomsky put it, "the sophisticated understand that to appeal to legal obligations and moral principles is legitimate, but as a weapon against selected enemies".[39] The criticism of hypocrisy is valid, therefore, only in relation to governmental claims that foreign affairs can be guided by ethics or human rights. The foreign policy of governments is interest-led and as alien to ethical considerations as the investment choices of multinational corporations.

It is therefore unconvincing to present the *sui generis* positivism of government-legislated international codes, government-appointed commissions and politically motivated enforcement mechanisms as the remedy for the positivism of national law, its persistent inhumanity and its divorce from ethics and justice. People are still murdered, tortured and starved by national governments, laws and institutions. The greatest crimes by and against humanity have been carried out in the name of nation, order or the common good and there is no convincing evidence that this is likely to come to an end because humanity has been declared sacrosanct. The Rousseauan *droits de l'homme* and the Burkean "rights of the Englishman" were the legal facet of the enlightenment promise of emancipation. They have clearly proved insufficient and their international re-statement cannot be the sole answer to man's inhumanity to man.

---

[39] Chomsky, op.cit., supra n. 32, 24.

IV. HUMAN RIGHTS AND THE USE OF FORCE

These criticisms have acquired great urgency in the wake of the war over Kosovo, the first war officially conducted to protect human rights. According to Tony Blair, this was a just war, promoting the doctrine of intervention based on values, while Robin Cook declared that NATO was a "humanitarian alliance". The war gave us the opportunity to witness and evaluate these claims and the recent ethical turn in western foreign policy in full action.

Throughout history, people have gone to wars and sacrificed themselves at the altar of principles like nation, religion, empire or class. Secular and religious leaders know well the importance of adding a veneer of high principle to low ends and murderous campaigns. This is equally evident in Homer's Iliad, in Thucidides' chilling description of the Athenian atrocities in Melos and Mytilene, in the chronicles of the crusades and in Shakespeare's historical plays. In the most famous passage of the *Peloponnesian War*, the defeated Melians argued unsuccessfully that, if the Athenians slaughtered them after winning in battle, they would lose all claim to moral superiority and legitimacy amongst their allies and citizens. For the pragmatist Athenians, however, a limited genocide would give a clear lesson to their wavering allies and would be of great political value, unlike the moral and humanitarian position. The Athenians compared terror and moral principle according to their likely effect, chose the former and provided an early example of *realpolitik*. Stalin's turn to the Orthodox patriarch and his use of religious themes in the defence of the Soviet fatherland against the Nazi attack in 1941, despite decades of religious persecution, was a good illustration of the moral and metaphysical turn often taken by pragmatic or scared dictators. The theory of the "just war", on the other hand, developed in the Middle Ages, was an attempt by the Church to serve Caesar without abandoning fully its pledges to God.[40]

[40] The contemporary religious theory of just war has a number of components: force should be used to defend unjust aggression; there should be proportionality between harms inflicted through the use of force and ends hoped for; the targets chosen should be military; force should never be an end in itself. It is arguable that two elements of the definition of just war (the second and third) were missing in the Kosovo war. The churches, with some reservations, either supported the war or remained silent. After the end of the war, a report by the Church of England's Board of Social Responsibility stated that the "scale of the human tragedy has created the perception that NATO's action precipitated rather than prevented the human catastrophe". "Church of England questions air campaign", *The*

The cynicism of the powerful is well-known and has been treated with wry smiles by writers and poets. Shakespeare as much as Brecht was fascinated by the way in which the hawks of war put on the fleece of moralist and preacher, better to persuade soldiers and citizens about the value of dying and killing for the cause. The moralisation of war is relatively easy when the moralisers are victims of external aggression, but the crusaders, the empire builders, the colonialists and the Nazis were not lacking in moral high ground either. The ability to present most wars as just and the lack of a moral arbiter who could sift through conflicting rationalisations has made the just war one of the hardest moral mazes. The question of the justice of a war (or of a liberation struggle a.k.a. campaign of terror) has always presented an interesting paradox: for the warring parties there is nothing more certain than the morality of their cause, while for observers there is nothing more uncertain than the rightness of the combatants' conflicting moral claims. As C.H. Waddington put it, "the wars, tortures, forced migrations and other calculated brutalities which make up so much of recent history, have for the most part been carried out by men who earnestly believed that their actions were justified, and, indeed, demanded, by the application of certain basic principles in which they believed".[41] War is the clearest example of what Lyotard has called the "differend":

> As distinguished from a litigation, a differend would be that case of conflict, between (at least) two parties, that cannot be equitably resolved for lack of a rule of judgment applicable to both arguments. One side's legitimacy does not imply the other's lack of legitimacy. However, applying a single rule of judgment to both in order to settle their differend as though it were merely a litigation would wrong (at least) one of them (and both of them if neither side admits that rule).[42]

All this seems to have changed in the late twentieth century. We are told that the new world order is based on respect for human rights, that universal moral standards have been legislated and accepted by the international community and that legal tribunals and moral directorates have been set up to navigate through conflicting moral claims. One may be slightly suspicious of the moral probity of

Guardian, 13 July 1999, 14. Michael Walzer, *Just and Unjust Wars: A Moral Argument with Historical Illustrations* (London, Penguin, 1980) is the best introduction to the topic.

[41] C.H. Waddington, *The Ethical Animal* (London, Allen & Unwin, 1960) 187.

[42] Jean-François Lyotard, *The Differend* (G. Van den Abbeele trans.) (Manchester, Manchester University Press, 1989) xi.

the Security Council of the United Nations, which includes a state which only a few years ago slaughtered its own demonstrating students (China), or another which has ratified the smallest number of human rights treaties and has voted against setting up the new permanent War Crimes Tribunal (USA). These concerns become even more serious when one realises that the United States and Britain went ahead with the bombing of Iraq in 1998 and of Serbia in 1999 without the authorisation of the Security Council of the United Nations, the only body entitled to order military action in defence of international peace and security. The willingness of Western powers to use force for apparently moral purposes has become a central (and worrying) characteristic of the post-Cold War settlement. But Waddington's law still stands. The Serbian brutalities were carried out in the name of national sovereignty, territorial integrity and the defence of history and culture against terrorist and foreign aggression. Nations owe their legitimacy to myths of origin, narratives of victory and defeat, borders and imagined or real historical continuities but not to humanity. On the Western side, Waddington's "basic principles" have been re-defined as reason, emancipation and cosmopolitanism and have helped generate an "ethical impulse" in public opinion[43] which has put some pressure on Western governments. But who authorises the discourse of the universal? Will universal human rights overcome moral disagreement or are they one side of the conflict? Are they a "rule of judgment" which can reconcile the differends, in Lyotard's terms, or, are they one more differend in the conflict?

Three instances which stand out in the 1990s, can help us consider this question. First, the continuing sanctions against Iraq and the renewed bombing of that country since 1998. The economic embargo, imposed by the UN after the end of the Gulf War in order to force the regime to destroy its weapons of mass destruction, had already taken its toll by that time. The sanctions were slightly eased in 1996, under the "oil for food" programme, after the World Health Organisation found that most Iraqis had suffered from near starvation for years and 32 per cent of all children were seriously malnourished. Operation Desert Fox, which involved the blanket bombing of military and associated targets, was launched in December 1998, on the

---

[43] This was particularly evident in Britain during the Kosovo conflict, where consistently high majorities supported the war. The American reaction was more muted. A majority opposed the war when respondents were asked to contemplate more than fifty American casualties.

eve of the vote to impeach President Clinton by the American
Congress. The United Nations were not consulted before the presi-
dential decision to start the bombing, although the Security Council
was in session discussing the latest report of the United Nations
weapon inspectors when the decision was taken. The daily bombing
of Iraqi sites has continued relentlessly, after the end of that operation,
but has gone largely unreported.

The combined effects of ten years of sanctions, bombing and mismanagement of food and medical supplies by Saddam's regime have
brought the country to the brink of collapse. Repeated reports
describe how Iraqi urban society has been ruined and the social
fabric seriously degraded. According to a Western reporter, "the west
is conducting a monstrous social experiment with the people of Iraq.
A once prosperous nation is driven into the pre-industrial dark ages.
It will take years to fathom the harm being done to the lives of 21.7
million people by a policy intended . . . to bring Iraq back into the
international community of nations by toppling Saddam Hussein".[44]
Dennis Holloway, the UN humanitarian co-ordinator in Iraq,
resigned his post in the summer of 1998, stating that the sanctions had
killed one million Iraqis, half of whom were children. When this sta-
tistic was put to Madeleine Albright, in 1996, she responded: "I think
this is a very hard choice but the price – we think the price is worth
it".[45] Currently, according to UNESCO estimates, four to five thou-
sand children die every month because of poor water supplies, inadequate food and lack of medicines.

It is interesting to compare the willingness of the West to blockade
and bomb its erstwhile allies in Iraq with the response to the Rwandan
genocide. During a few long months, in 1994, one million people
were slaughtered, in what remains with Cambodia the greatest genocide of the twentieth or "human rights" century, after the Holocaust.
According to the minutes of informal Security Council meetings
which have recently emerged, the United Nations peacekeepers sent
detailed messages about the developing genocide, early in April 1994,
and warned that the situation would quickly worsen without the presence of United Nations officers. General Dallaire, the commander of
the UN peacekeeping force sent six messages to New York, the first
as early as January 11, warning of the impending crisis and requesting
permission to act but received a routine answer from the secretariat

---

[44] "Iraq is falling apart. We are ruined", *The Guardian*, April 24, 1999, 14.

[45] Quoted ibid. For a recent and moving presentation of the damage sanctions have
inflicted on the Iraqi people, see James Buchan, "Inside Iraq" 67 *Granta* (1999), 169–92.

ordering him not to act.[46] The first priority of the United States and Britain, was to withdraw the peacekeepers because any casualties would have a "negative impact on public opinion". According to the historian Linda Melvern, Karl Inderfurth, the American UN representative, stated that the peacekeeping force "was not appropriate now and never will be" and that the United States had "no stomach for leaving anything there".[47] Having spent 80 per cent of the time deciding whether to withdraw the peacekeepers and only "20 per cent trying to get a ceasefire", the Council finally voted, on April 24, to withdraw the peacekeepers, except for a token force of 270. Five days later, the Council President proposed a resolution declaring that a genocide was taking place and putting into effect the sanctions of the Genocide Convention. The western powers objected; the British representative did not want the word genocide used because it would make the Council "a laughing stock".[48] The lives of the few hundred western peacekeepers were clearly more important than the hundreds of thousands of Africans. General Quesnot, a French general who knew the Rwandan situation well, estimated that "2,000 to 2,500 'determined' soldiers would have sufficed to halt the slaughter".[49] As the Nigerian ambassador rhetorically asked, "has Africa dropped from the map of moral concern?".

Finally, Kosovo. Since the collapse of Yugoslavia, in 1991, the United States played a "curious poker game" with the Serb President Slobodan Milocevic, trying to isolate him, on the one hand, and treating him as the "deal cutting guarantor of its peace plans" on the other.[50] According to The Economist, at the end of 1998, American thinking was "if you can't bomb, at least support democracy", a policy of the "ballot box and the cruise missile", one could say. No help or support was given, however, to the Serbian opposition which for many months in 1996 and 1997 had mobilised huge crowds daily calling for democratic reforms. The preference for democracy came too late. A few weeks later, NATO warplanes started bombing targets in

---

[46] Alison des Forges, Leave None to tell the Story: Genocide in Rwanda (New York, Human Rights Watch, 1999) 172–7.

[47] Linda Melvern, "How the system failed to save Rwanda", The Guardian, December 7, 1998, 10.

[48] Alison des Forges, op.cit., 638–9. When the US was asked by various NGOs to jam RTLM, a radio station which was inciting genocide, the State Department, after receiving legal advice, responded that "the traditional American commitment to freedom of speech was more important than disrupting the voice of genocide", 641.

[49] The full story is chillingly told in Alison des Forges, "Ignoring Genocide", op.cit., 595–635 and 607.

[50] "Will Slobodan Milocevic fall?", The Economist, December 5, 1998, 51.

Kosovo, Serbia and Montenegro. Was there still time for negotiations and sanctions? Was further talking pointless, as NATO claimed? We will never know but Mary Robinson, the UN High Commissioner for Human Rights, has stated that Western attitudes in 1998 "represented a fundamental failure of the international community". Despite the efforts of her office to alert governments to the looming crisis "none was listening".[51]

A strict hierarchisation of the value of life was again evident during the conflict. The United Nations monitors were withdrawn, in March 1999, before the bombing campaign started. More importantly, every precaution was taken during the war to eliminate the likelihood of NATO casualties. The possibility of engaging ground troops was repeatedly and categorically denied by NATO spokesmen until late in the campaign. The bombers flew at extremely high altitudes (some 15,000 feet) which put them beyond the reach of anti-aircraft fire. The tactic was successful: NATO forces concluded their campaign without a single casualty. But there were serious side-effects too: first, total air domination without the willingness to engage in a ground war did not stop Serb atrocities. Evidence emerging after the war shows that the worst massacres occurred after the start of the bombing campaign. According to NATO sources, several hundred Albanians were killed by Serbs after March 1999 and the flight of Albanians was dramatically accelerated. It is reasonable to conclude that the declared war aim of "averting a humanitarian catastrophe" failed badly. Secondly, as a result of the high flight altitudes of the bombers, the likelihood of civilian "collateral damage" increased significantly. Civilians were killed in trains and buses, in TV stations and hospitals, in the Chinese Embassy and other residential areas. One of the most grotesque mistakes was the killing of some 75 Albanian refugees whose ragtag convoy was hit repeatedly, on April 14. Part of the explanation offered by a contrite NATO was that tractors and trailers cannot be easily distinguished from tanks and armoured personnel carriers at an altitude of 15,000 feet.

From Homer to this century, war introduces an element of uncertainty, the possibility that the mighty might lose or suffer casualties. Indeed, according to Hegel, the fear of death gives war its metaphysical value, by confronting the combatants with the negativity that encircles life and helping them rise from their daily mundane experi-

---

[51] Quoted in "Kosovo: the Untold Story", *The Observer*, 18 July 1999, 16.

ences towards the universal.[52] In this sense, the Kosovo campaign was not a war but a type of hunting: one side was totally protected while the other had no chance of effectively defending itself or counter-attacking. Many (retired) army and armchair generals argued during the campaign that it could not be won swiftly without ground troops. They were proved partly wrong. A war without casualties for your side, an electronic game type of war or Reagan's unbeatable "star wars", may be the dream of every military establishment. But a war in which a soldier's life is more valuable than that of many civilians cannot be moral or humanitarian. In valuing an allied life at many hundred Serbian lives, the declaration that all are equal in dignity and enjoy an equal right to life was comprehensively discredited.

Finally, as we learned after the end of the war, the total protection of Western aircrews meant that the success of bombing was extremely limited. Despite NATO's cautious triumphalism during the campaign, only thirteen Serbian tanks were hit in eleven weeks of intensive bombing and the vast majority of Serbian surface to air missiles survived. Civil targets were easier to identify and destroy. A few weeks after the start of the war, General Michael Short of the US Air Force told journalists that what was necessary for success was to hit civilian morale. His tactic was going to be "no power to your refrigerator. No gas to your stove, you can't get to work because the bridge is down – the bridge on which you held your rock concerts and all stood with targets on your heads. That needs to disappear".[53] According to first estimates, some fifty bridges were destroyed as well as a number of TV and radio stations, hospitals, schools and nurseries, cultural, economic and industrial sites, computer networks and electricity generating plants.[54] The targeting of the civilian infrastructure

[52] "In order not to let [people] become rooted and set in this isolation, thereby breaking up the whole and letting the community spirit evaporate, government has from time to time to shake them to their core by war. By this means the government upsets their established order, and violates their right to idnependence, while the individuals who, absorbed in their way of life, break loose from the whole and strive after the inviolable independence and security of the person, are made to feel by government in the task laid on them their lord and master, death." Hegel, *The Phenomenology of Spirit* (A.V. Miller trans.) (Oxford, Oxford University Press, 1977) 272–3. Jacques Derrida, *Glas* (Lincoln, University of Nebraska Press, 1986) comments: "So war would prevent people from rotting; war preserves 'the ethical health of peoples', as the wind agitating the seas purifies them, keeps them from decomposing, from the corruption, from the putrefaction with which a 'continual calm' and a 'perpetual peace' would infect health", 101 and 131–49.

[53] *The Observer*, 16 May, 1999, 15.

[54] Professor Ian Brownlie, the eminent human rights expert, in evidence to the International Court of Justice said, on May 10, 1999: "There is no general humanitarian purpose to the [bombings] . . . the pattern of targets indicates political purposes unrelated to

and the repeated mistakes led Mary Robinson to state, after four weeks of bombing, that the campaign had "lost its moral purpose".[55]

None of this explains or justifies the atrocities committed by Serbs and the systematic ethnic cleansing of the Kosovo Albanians. The actions of the Serbian police, paramilitaries and army will enter the annals of twentieth century barbarism alongside those of Hitler, Stalin, Saddam Hussein and Pol Pot. No moral arithmetic exists to allow us to compare the number of massacred Albanians with that of the maimed Serbs, or of the gassed Kurds with that of starving Iraqis. Nor would a few Texan or Scottish dead soldiers in Kosovo balance out the hundreds of killed civilians. To paraphrase the Holocaust survivor Emmanuel Levinas, in every person killed the whole humanity dies.

This could be the beginning of an answer to the universalism *versus* relativism debate. Serbs massacred in the name of threatened community, while the allies bombed in the name of threatened humanity. Both principles, when they become absolute essences and define the meaning and value of culture without remainder or exception, can find everything that resists them expendable. We can see why by briefly exploring their structure, as they move from the moral to the legal domain. The universalist claims that all cultural value and, in particular, moral norms are not historically and territorially bound but should pass a test of universal consistency. As a result, judgments which derive their force and legitimacy from local conditions are morally suspect. But as all life is situated, an "unencumbered" judgment based exclusively on the protocols of reason goes against the grain of human experience, unless of course universalism and its procedural demands have become the cultural tradition of some place. The US would be a prime candidate; but even die-hard liberal Americans cannot claim this for their country, as they die in the hands of their rightful gun-totting compatriots, a good example of the murderous nature of a cultural relativism which has turned the possession of guns into the most sacrosanct right and vivid expression of American parochialism. The counter-intuitive nature of universalism can lead its proponent, to extreme individualism: only myself as the real moral agent or as the ethical alliance or as the representative of the universal can understand what morality demands. Moral egotism

humanitarian reasons", *The Guardian*, May 11, 1999, 8. The Court declined the Serbian Government's application to declare the bombing illegal, although it expressed concerns about its effects on civilians.

[55] "Shift in bombing a warning to Serbs", *The Guardian*, May 29, 1999, 4.

easily leads into arrogance and universalism into imperialism: if there is one moral truth but many errors, it is incumbent upon its agents to impose it on others. What started as rebellion against the absurdities of localism ends up legitimising oppression and domination.

Cultural relativism is potentially even more murderous, because it has privileged access to community and neighbourhood, the places where people are killed and tortured. Relativists start from the obvious observation that values are context-bound and use it to justify atrocities against those who disagree with the oppressiveness of tradition. But the cultural embeddedness of self is an unhelpful sociological truism; the context, as history tradition and culture, is malleable, always under construction rather than given and unchanging. Kosovo is a good example of this process. It was only after Milocevic withdrew its autonomy in 1994 and declared that it would remain for ever in the Yugoslav state, as the cradle of the Serb nation, that Serb oppression started and the KLA, the Albanian Liberation Movement, became active. Between that point and 1999, a fratricidal nationalism took hold of the two communities but it was not the result of ancient enmities; it was created and fanned by the respective power-holders. This process was even more evident in Rwanda. The genocide there was not committed by monsters but by ordinary people who were coaxed, threatened and deceived by bureaucrats, the military, politicians, the media, intellectuals, academics and artists into believing that killing was necessary to avoid their own extermination in the hands of their victims. The tribal rivalry between Hutus and Tutsis was re-defined, fanned and exaggerated to such a point that the "action" became eventually inevitable.[56]

Too often respect for cultural differences, a necessary corrective for the arrogance of universalism, has turned into a shield protecting appaling local practices. When the Malaysian Prime Minister Mahathir Mohamad attacked the Universal Declaration because it "was formulated by the superpowers which did not understand the need of poor countries" adding that the West "would rather see people starve than allow for stable government. They would rather have their government chasing demonstrators in the street . . . there are other things in human rights other than mere individual freedom",[57] he was expressing not his cultural tradition but his dismay that human rights may be used in opposition to his regime, one of the most oppressive in the world. The same ambiguity is evident with

[56] See Alison des Forges, supra, n. 46, Chapter 2.
[57] Quoted in Marks, op. cit., supra n. 28, 461.

respect to minorities within minorities. Ethnic groups, like the French in Quebec, religious sects, like the scientologists, and political parties, like some Western communist parties, demand autonomy, human rights and respect for their practices only to use them to suppress smaller minorities in their body, the English speakers, heretics, traitors, those who do not conform. Again, the cause of the problem is not the truism that values are created in historical and cultural contexts but, an exclusionary construction of culture as immanent to belonging and the interpretation of majority values as the absolute truth; these traits mimic, at the local level, state disdain and oppression of all minorities. According to the French philosopher Jean-Luc Nancy, communitarian authoritarianism is catastrophic because "it assigns to community a *common being*, whereas community is a matter of something quite different, namely, of existence inasmuch as it is *in* common, but without letting itself be absorbed into a common substance".[58] The difference between a universalism premised on the essence of man and a relativism premised on the essence of community is small; in their common determination to see man and community as immanent, they form "the general horizon of our time, encompassing both democracies and their fragile juridical parapets".[59]

Both universal morality and cultural identity express different aspects of human experience. Their comparison in the abstract is futile, as the endless debates have shown, and usually proves, in a self-fulfilling fashion, the position from which the comparer started.[60] The universalism and relativism debate has replaced the old ideological confrontation between civil and political, and economic and social rights, and is conducted with the same rigour. Yet the differences between the two are not pronounced. When a state adopts "universal" human rights, it will interpret and apply them, if at all, according to local legal procedures and moral principles, making the universal the handmaiden of the particular. The reverse is also true: even those legal systems which jealously guard traditional rights and cultural practices against the encroachment of the universal are already contaminated by it. All rights and principles, even if parochial

[58] Jean-Luc Nancy, *The Inoperative Community* (P. Connor ed.) (Minneapolis, University of Minnesota Press, 1991) xxxviii. See chapter 8 below.

[59] ibid., 3.

[60] Hillary Lim and Kate Green, "What is this Thing about Female Circumcision", 7/3 *Social and Legal Studies* 365–87 (1998); Henry Steiner and Philip Alston, op.cit., supra n. 23, Chapter 4 gives an overview of the debate.

in their content, share the universalising impetus of their form. In this sense, rights carry the seed of dissolution of community and the only defence is to resist the idea of right altogether, something impossible in the global capitalist world. Developing states which import Hollywood films, Big Macs and the Internet, import also human rights willy nilly. As Prime Minister Mohamad's comments make clear, his ends and those of American foreign policy are identical, after all, even though the means may differ at times: "The people cannot do business, cannot work because of the so-called expression of the freedom of the individual".[61] The claims of universality and tradition, rather than standing opposed in mortal combat, have become uneasy allies, whose fragile liaison has been sanctioned by the World Bank.

One could conclude, that both positions can become aggressive and dangerous. When their respective apologists become convinced about their truth and the immorality of their demonised opponents, they can easily move from moral dispute to killing. At that point, all differences disappear. From the position of the victim, the bullet and the "smart" bomb kill equally, even if the former travels a few yards only from the gun of the ethnically proud soldier, while the latter covers a huge distance from the plane of the humanitarian bomber. Bauman comments that:

> while universal values offer a reasonable medicine against the oppressive obtrusiveness of parochial backwaters, and communal autonomy offers an emotionally gratifying tonic against the stand-offish callousness of the universalists, each drug when takes regularly turns into poison. Indeed, as long as the choice is merely between the two medicines, the chance of health must be meagre and remote.[62]

One could only add that the name of the common poison is self-satisfied essentialism: whether communal, state or universal it suffers from the same heterophobia, the extreme fear and demonisation of the other.

Are there any circumstances in which forceful intervention is justifiable? This author's answer is a highly qualified *yes*, in extreme cases and only to prevent genocide. The United Nations Security Council can and has authorised the use of force to prevent or stop threats to international peace and security, in other words, to prevent substantial risk to the interests of the intervening powers. There is no greater

---

[61] Quoted in Marks, op.cit., supra n. 29.
[62] Zygmunt Bauman, *Postmodern Ethics* (Oxford, Blackwell, 1993) 239.

threat to peace than genocide and no greater threat to the national interests of third states than the disintegration of a state with the resulting conflicts, mass migration and loss of markets. If the international community were to legitimise such "humanitarian" interventions on a permanent basis on something more than the contingent and often interested agreement of a few great powers, a new institutional framework is needed. The role of governments and governmental organisations, like NATO, should be minimised.[63] Even consistent liberals are weary of regional groupings, power blocs and less than universal alliances intervening as representatives of the universal. As Bauman argued, "with the universalism-promoting agencies well short of truly universal sovereignty, the horizon of 'actually existing' (or, rather, realistically intended) universality tends to stop at the state boundary . . . Consistently universalistic can be only a power bent on identifying the human kind as a whole with the population subjected to its present of prospective rule".[64] This typically French eighteenth century position perfectly encapsulates the current American mood, as shown in the opposition to the International Criminal Court.

Representatives of the victims and of non-governmental organisations operating in the area of intervention should be actively involved in decision-making. The aims and methods of the campaign should be removed from the power games of presidents, prime ministers and generals and focus on protecting individuals. The military should be in close contact with local democratic organisations and observers and should aim to enable them to protect civilians and help them overthrow the murderous regime. No person or community can gain their dignity or freedom through foreign intervention or a gift from above. The intervening powers can only help local people re-assert their rights against their government. Finally, a clear set of guidelines should regulate the conduct of the war and minimise casualties on all

---

[63] Kofi Annan, the UN Secretary-General, reminded the General Assembly of the organisation, after the approval of the East Timor peace-keeping force, of the inaction in Rwanda in 1994 and added: "The inability of the international community in the case of Kosovo to reconcile . . . universal legitimacy and effectiveness in defense of human rights can be viewed as a tragedy". "Annan pays tribute to swift action", *The Guardian*, September 21, 1999, 14. Annan's statement is a warning to the West: the universal has to be authorised by the global (the UN) or it will lose its persuasive force. But this is a demarcation and status dispute between UN and NATO, not one about the meaning of universals. If a normative universal exists, it makes no difference whether it is put forward by the whole world or a single soul. Conversely, if it does not, putting a strong majority behind it will make no difference to its status.

[64] Bauman, op.cit., supra n. 62, 41.

sides. Such a war aims to rescue the victims and prevent putting more people at risk and not to engage another government. None of these conditions exists today and it would be pious to expect that they will develop soon.

But the most important point is this: "humanitarian" war is a contradiction in terms. War and its consequences, bombing and maiming people can never be part of human rights and morality. Even if we were to accept that a large part of the motive for the Kosovo campaign was humanitarian, the war was not and could not be "moral". Bombing does not protect people and does not prevent atrocities. A destructive war, by definition a devastating negation of human rights, can be seen as humanitarian only because human rights have been hijacked by governments, politicians and diplomats and entrusted in the hands of those against whom they were invented. In a world in which humanity's dues are decided by the powerful, the inhumanity of dictators can only be confronted with the inhumanity of semi-"smart bombs" and civilian "collateral damage". But in these circumstances, the righteous commit the crime they set out to prevent.

V. THE "TRIUMPH" OF HUMANITY

It is arguable, therefore, that the grandiose claims about the importance of international human rights are a little exaggerated. These rights, by being presented as a description or statement about the state of law, present the legislator (humanity or its self-appointed representatives in New York, Geneva or Strasbourg) as co-extensive with the right-holders (all concrete people in the world). Writing in 1951, Hannah Arendt expressed with typical acuity this dilemma:

> Man of the twentieth century has become just as emancipated from nature as eighteenth century man was from history. History and nature have become equally alien to us, namely, in the sense that the essence of man can no longer be comprehended in terms of either category. On the other hand, humanity, which for the eighteenth century, in Kantian terminology, was no more than a regulative idea, has today become an inescapable fact. This new situation, in which "humanity" has in effect assumed the role formerly ascribed to nature or history, would mean in this context that the right to have rights, or the right of every individual to belong to humanity, should be guaranteed by humanity itself. It is by no means certain whether this is possible.[65]

[65] Arendt, op.cit. , supra n. 6, 298

This dilemma is best exemplified by the treatment of refugees and other populations fleeing natural or man-made disasters. This is the greatest human catastrophe of the twentieth century outside war and, in ethnic cleansing, it reaches the nadir of the many evils of nationalism. Refugees have replaced foreigners as the main category of otherness in our postmodern and globalised world. The foreigner was the political precondition of the nation-state and the other the ontological precondition of individual identity. When the roving foreigner arrives at the borders of the state, the assumptions of national and personal integrity come under severe pressure. For national law, the refugee is a threat to the principle of territorial jurisdiction. But she also represents the violence at the inception of the modern state, the exclusion of other peoples, nations and minorities necessary for the creation of territorial and legislative sovereignty. For the citizen of our globalised world, the refugee represents a threat to jobs and amenities, but also a deeper threat to the construction of national identity. As we saw, the modern subject reaches her humanity by acquiring political rights which guarantee her admission to the universal human nature, by excluding from that status those who do not have such rights. It is the law of the nation state which defines the alien as alien and the refugee as refugee. The alien is not a citizen. She does not have rights because she is not part of the state and she is a lesser human being because she is not a citizen. In the terms of the French Declaration, the alien is the gap between man and citizen, between human nature and political community lies the moving refugee. To have citizens we must have aliens, to have a home or a home country others must not share it, or they must be in movement or in transit, in perpetual flotation or in orbit, like those medieval mad people who were travelling the rivers of Europe in the ships of the fools.[66] Unable to speak our language, having left her community and with no community, the refugee is the absolute other. She represents in an extreme way the trauma that marks the genesis of state and self and puts to the test the claims of universalisation of human rights.

The absolute otherness of the refugee is evident in a number of ways. Hannah Arendt reviewing the great movement of refugees and stateless persons after the First World War, people who today would have been called "economic migrants", concludes that "they

---

[66] Refugees are commonly put "in orbit" under the "first safe country" rule which allows a state to send back a refugee to a state she comes from in which she does not have a fear of persecution.

were persecuted not because of what they had done or thought, but because of what they unchangeably were – born into the wrong kind of race or the wrong kind of class or drafted by the wrong kind of government".[67] People become refugees not for their criminal or revolutionary acts, but for who they are. Most of them have done nothing wrong, except to flee, to move across frontiers, to cross boundaries. Their rightlessness, the absence of legal personality, is not a consequence of severe punishment or the sign of extreme criminality but the accompaniment of utter innocence and of movement, of a sacrificial circulation. The refugee is defined not by what she has done or does – the defining characteristic of modern human nature – but for who she is, for her being rather than for her action and becoming. In this, she joins the other great dangerous beings of modernity, the mad, the homosexual, the Jew. But as her threat is on the move she also represents the great postmodern danger, the virus.

Refugee status is not the result of the lack or loss of this or that right but of the total loss of community and of the legal protections associated with it. Rightlessness accompanies the lack of community and the globalisation of national law and right. Refugees have been removed from their own community and are kept outside the bounds of all potential receiving ones. It is not so much that they are not equal before the law, but that there is no law for them. It is not that they are not persecuted, but that none wants to persecute them. "The world of barbarity thus comes to a head in a single world composed of states, in which only those people organised into national residences are entitled to have rights. The 'loss of residence', a 'loss of social framework' worsened by the 'impossibility to find one' are characteristics of this new barbarity issued from the vary core of the nation-state system" in a globalised world.[68] The rightlessness that accompanies removal from the community shows the deep truth of the critique of human rights by Edmund Burke and the communitarians who insist that only national law can create and effectively protect rights. In a globalised world, in which nothing is exempt from state sovereignty, and human rights have become posited and universal, the refugee is the representative of the non-representable, she has no state or law, no nation or party to put forward her claims. "Only in a completely organised humanity", comments Arendt,

[67] Arendt, supra n. 6, 294.
[68] Kristeva, *Strangers to Ourselves* (Leon Roudiez trans.) (Columbia University Press, 1991) 151.

"could the loss of home and political status become identical with expulsion of humanity altogether".[69] The refugee is the total other of civilisation, the zero degree of humanity. She represents the state of nature in all its stark nakedness and the world finds nothing sacred in the abstract nakedness of being human. But as Lyotard argued, "to banish a stranger is to banish the community, and you banish yourself from the community thereby".[70]

★★★

All this does not mean that human rights treaties and declarations are devoid of value. At this point in the development of international law, their value is mainly symbolic. Human rights are violated inside the state, the nation, the community, the group. Similarly, the struggle to uphold them belongs to the dissidents, the victims, those whose identity is denied or denigrated, the oppositions groups, all those who are the targets of repression and domination. Only people on the ground and local action can improve human rights; outsiders, including human rights organisations, can help by supporting them. From this perspective, international conventions are of use to human rights activists, by offering a standard for criticising their governments. When a state has adopted a particular set of rights, it will be harder, although by no means impossible, for its government, to deny committing obvious abuses. Similarly, external monitoring and reporting may raise awareness about a state's violations and the shaming that accompanies exposure may lead to improvements. But the successes of monitoring are limited and the adverse effects of publicity are intangible and take long in coming.

When Greece was forced to leave the Council of Europe in 1969, after the European Commission of Human Rights found that every article of the Convention was violated by the colonels, the response of the dictators was characteristic. They stated with great fanfare that the European Council and Commission were a conspiracy of homosexuals and communists against hellenic values and dramatically increased repression. Similarly, while Pinochet's Chile and the South Africa of apartheid were repeatedly condemned by UN human rights bodies and the General Assembly, the regimes attacked 'meddling foreigners' and survived for decades. Nigel Rodley, the United Nations special rapporteur on torture since 1993, saw the uses of his task as follows:

[69] Arendt, op.cit., supra n. 6, 297.

[70] Jean-Francois Lyotard, "The Other's rights", in *On Human Rights* (Stephen Shute and Susan Hurley eds), New York: Basic Books, 1993, 136.

The information gets to families that someone outside is investigating or appealing to the government. Occasionally the prisoner learns of this too. And I feel that somehow the drip, drip of external demands that a government do something or stop things like torture will have an effect . . . It's not the UN that can change things directly. It's groups in the country itself. International monitoring gives these forces, both non-governmental and within government, some support.[71]

If the victims of repression become recognised in the eyes of the international community as actors, the value of international human rights will increase for those who matter.

The tradition of human rights, from the classical invention of nature against convention to contemporary struggles for political liberation and human dignity against state law, has always expressed the perspective of the future or the "not yet". Human rights have become the cry of the oppressed, the exploited, the dispossessed, a kind of imaginary or exceptional law for those who have nothing else to fall back on. In this sense, human rights are not the product of legislation but precisely its opposite. They set limit to "force, declared laws and 'founded' rights (regardless of who has, or demands, or usurps the pre-rogative to found them authoritatively)".[72] Human rights, as the principle of hope, work in the gap between ideal nature and law, or real people and universal abstractions. The promise of a future in which, in Marx's memorable phrase, people are not "degraded, enslaved, abandoned, or despised" does not belong to governments and lawyers. It certainly does not belong to international organisations and diplomats. It does not even belong to the abstract human being of the declarations and conventions or of the traditional humanist philoso-phy, including the Kantian subject which, for Derrida, is "still too fra-ternal, subliminally virile, familial, ethnic, national etc".[73] The energy necessary for the protection, horizontal proliferation and vertical expansion of human rights comes from below, from those whose lives have been blighted by oppression or exploitation and who have not been offered or have not accepted the blandishments that accompany political apathy. In the meantime, we can leave the United Nations and their diplomats to their standard setting and their lunches and return to the state or the community, the only territory where human rights are violated or protected.

[71] "The world is watching: A survey of human rights law", *The Economist*, December 5, 1998, 6.
[72] Jacquas Derrida quoted in *La Liberation*, November 24, 1994, 8.
[73] Quoted in Bauman, *Postmodernity and its Discontents* (Cambridge, Polity, 1997) 33.

PART II

THE PHILOSOPHY OF
HUMAN RIGHTS

7

The Classical Critiques of Rights: Burke and Marx

I. BURKE AND THE HISTORICISM OF RIGHTS

If the eighteenth century declarations are the foundation of the discourse of rights, Burke's and Marx's reflections on the French Revolution are the foundational critiques of rights. Later critics have developed and expanded their main points in a number of directions but have not added much new. We examined briefly above, the objections of Burke and Marx to the abstract "man" of the declarations. Let us now take a closer look at the classics by emphasising the points of continuity between the early and contemporary critics.

First, Burke. Edmund Burke's essay "Reflections on the Revolution in France" was the first considered attack on the recently inaugurated theory of the rights of man.[1] Its commercial success and political influence cannot be overestimated. Published in November 1790, as an immediate and emotional response to events in Paris, it sold some 17,000 copies by the end of that year and went on to many editions in the following years. The exaggerated invective of the essay and many of its predictions sound obsolete today, a chapter in the history of reactionary thought, which finally exited the historical scene after the Second World War and the world-wide spread of mass democracies and human rights. The eulogies for the ancient constitution replete with deference towards the monarch and the aristocracy, the insistence that rights are antithetical to the English way of life, the proclamation of the natural superiority of English institutions and temperament, sound almost comically absurd to contemporary British ears. Devolution, the Human Rights Act 1998, the reform of the House of Lords and closer links with Europe have turned the 1990s into the decade of rights and constitution-making, and have

---

[1] Edmund Burke, *Reflections on the Revolution in France* (J.G.A. Pockock ed.) (London, Hackett, 1987).

condemned Burke's predictions and musings to the annals of a peculiarly insular English heritage put to rest by Brussels and Tony Blair.

But there is something of lasting relevance in Burke's attack on "the pretended rights of these theorists". Most critics of rights belong today to the political left and hardly know, let alone use, the jejune ideas and polemics of an eighteenth century arch-conservative. Yet many of Burke's comments about the difficulties faced by any consistent theorisation of human rights have not been proved wrong or improved by contemporary critics. Hannah Arendt agreed with Burke's emphasis on the local character of the protection of rights.[2] Michel Villey reminded us that Burke was no ordinary reactionary.[3] He fervently supported the American revolution and was scathing about the treatment of Indians and homosexuals by the English establishment of his day. Feminist and communitarian critics share Burke's critique of the abstract, indeterminate character of rights discourse, even though they despise his politics. Finally, postmodern approaches to law, influenced by the ethics of alterity associated with the philosophies of Levinas and Derrida, are critical of the rationalism of rights and emphasise their situated and embedded character. In this, they are not too removed from Burke's assertion that only individualised justice can protect freedom.[4] Let us return to Burke's attack on the revolution and its rights from a contemporary critical perspective. What are his main arguments and lines of attack?

1. Burke's main criticism is that rights discourse suffers from metaphysical idealism and rationalism. The proponents of rights follow a clumsy political metaphysics, they are metaphysical rationalists or, "speculatists", the worst insult in Burke's rich vocabulary of abuse.[5] Speculatism is the belief that political practice, the art of the possible, should be guided by theory, that the intricate web of political life and

---

[2] Hannah Arendt, *The Origins of Toralitarianism* (Harvest Book, 1979) 300.

[3] Michel Villey, "La philosophie du droit de Burke" in *Critique de la pensée juridique moderne* (Paris, Dalloz, 1975). Villey presents Burke as a true Aristotelian who has adjusted legal philosophy to the circumstance of his time. "He refuses to construct the law according to the idea of human essence or reason but, like classical natural lawyers, according to what exists in nature, positively", 178. For Villey, Burke is not against rights but against "abstract liberty which, like other abstractions, does not exist". Rights are, on the contrary, many and diverse, always relative to space and time, 171.

[4] C. Douzinas and R. Warrington, *Justice Miscarried* (Edinburgh, Edinburgh University Press, 1994) Chapter 4; "A Well-founded Fear of Justice" 11/2 Law and Critique 115, 1991; Marinos Diamantides, "Ethics in Law: Death Marks on a 'Still Life' ", VI/2 *Law and Critique*, 209, 1995; Mark Armstrong, "Face to Face with Child Abuse: Towards an Ethics of Listening", X/2 *Law and Critique*, 147, 1999.

[5] Reflections, op.cit., supra n. 1, 51.

the complex and ancient patrimony of legal duties and entitlements, should be re-arranged according to some plan conceived by human reason and carried out by radical action. The French Revolution was the first "complete revolution", led by philosophers, metaphysicians and men of letters, "not as subordinate instruments and trumpeters of sedition, but as the chief contrivers and managers".[6] These philosophers aimed to uproot the *ancien régime* in all its institutional and moral power and to re-draw the map of nation and state completely, following philosophical prescriptions and recipes. But this is the greatest folly. Political practice and practical wisdom or prudence, differ from theoretical speculation; the former is concerned with the particular and the changeable while theory with the universal and immutable. No aspect of politics can be conceived in the abstract.

The "science of government" deals with morality and the proper ends of government as they present themselves in the here and now. Similarly with the means of politics: no political method or tool is universally valid and applicable; trusted methods must often be set aside in deference to the twists and turns of chance or *fortuna*. Contingency, context and chance rather than theoretical speculation determine politics: "Circumstances (which with some gentlemen pass for nothing) give in reality to every political principle its distinguishing colour, and discriminating effect. The circumstances are what render every civil and political scheme beneficial or noxious to mankind".[7] Political or practical and theoretical judgments are therefore opposed: the former involve concrete cases and cannot wait for long, bound as they are to pressing needs and to deadlines. Practical judgments cannot be suspended until all the arguments have been canvassed and assessed; they must be satisfied therefore with a lower degree of certainty and clarity than theory. Theoretical judgments, on the other hand, are detached and impartial, cold and languid. Theory begins each time from the beginning and goes all the way; practice starts with precedent and convention and comes quickly to an end. Finally, theory rejects error and prejudice, while the statesman puts these to good use.[8]

For Burke, therefore, the standpoint of the absolute and universal blinds the politician to the realities of the particular and concrete and turns him into a metaphysician and prophet, full of rhetorical

[6] ibid., 53.

[7] ibid., 7.

[8] Leo Strauss, *Natural Right and History* (Chicago, University of Chicago Press, 1965) 310–1.

hyperbole (not unlike Burke's own) but unable to rule. Speculative politicians of the French variety, fascinated by mathematics and obsessed with *a priori* deductive reasoning, devise constitutions and bills of rights. But while this type of theoretical reason may be able to produce simple and clear ideas and patterns, it is totally unsuited to political affairs. Its proponents become "moral geometers" and use reason to construct "geometrical and arithmetical constitutions". But their simplicity and plainness cannot match the messiness of life and, as a result, when "these metaphysical rights enter into common life, like rays of light which pierce into a dense medium, are, by the laws of nature, refracted from their straight line".[9] Rights are not only cognitively wrong in their conception; they are also morally wrong in their application which tries to make life follow the orthopaedics of reason. Political prudence, on the contrary, computes, balances and works with compromises, calculations and exceptions; it requires delicate and subtle skills, a discernment honed through long experience and practice rather than through abstract thinking and the study of treatises.

The cognitive confusion and moral poverty of rationalist constitution makers and rights enthusiasts is compounded by their ignorance of history and human nature. They believe that human reason, unaided by history, tradition and practical wisdom, can create stable and legitimate institutions but they are hopelessly deluded. The constitutional tradition must be approached with humility because an element of mystique is necessary to give an aura to the living constitution. In the *Reflections* and his earlier essay on the *Beautiful and the Sublime*, Burke developed an aesthetic theory of politics which associates the sublime with language and verbal expression and the beautiful with vision and imagery.[10] The sublime is the feeling generated before ineffable, distant, terrifying power. People submit to the figure of God, King or Father because these male figures of power generate terror and pain, they are awesome.[11] They make us submit through an overwhelming force which cannot be fully comprehended. But this political aesthetic of sublimity must be protected from visualisation. An image or a painting gives a clear idea of its

---

[9] Reflections, op.cit., supra n. 1, 54.

[10] Edmund Burke, *A Philosophical Enquiry into the Origins of the Sublime and the Beautiful* (J.T. Boulton ed.) (Notre Dame, University of Notre Dame Press, 1958).

[11] Burke's patriarchal sublimity is echoed in Freud's totemic myth of the genesis of law and is a key theme in Pierre Legendre's theory of the "paternity of law". See Chapter 11 below.

object, leaves nothing to imagination and doubt and can be judged according to conventional criteria of aesthetic beauty. "A clear idea", Burke remarks pithily "is therefore another name for a little idea".[12] The sublime is obscure, it overawes but also creates intense pleasure in the attempt to comprehend what overwhelms the mind and defies reason.

Burke uses this analysis to reinterpret the Protestant iconoclastic tradition in a political direction. Invisibility, darkness and visual deprivation are the political signs of sublimity: "despotic governments, which are founded on the passions of man, and principally upon the passion of fear, keep their chief as much as may be from the public eye. The policy has been the same in many cases of religion. Almost all heathen temples are dark".[13] In Burke's hierarchy of the sublime, language comes before imagery and, unwritten law convention and custom before written positive law. Saxon customs "operate better than laws" and provided the basis for later laws and the constitution which only fashioned or finished what had been created by the ancient oral tradition. "All your sophisters cannot produce anything better adapted to preserve a rational and manly freedom than the course we have pursued, who have chosen our nature rather than our speculations, our breasts rather than our inventions, for the great conservatories and magazines of our rights and privileges" writes Burke.[14] A visible, written constitution, on the other hand, is "criminal".[15] The real constitution is an "organism, something like a human body, constituted as a community of senses with distinct powers and privileges, a mixed being of natural and conventional behaviour, a creature of biology and habit, pleasure and pain"[16] and preserved by immemorial custom.

The constitution should therefore cultivate emotional attachments and affections. Its symbolic forms and representations should be moving and beautiful. In an exquisite phrase, which reminds his arch-enemy but fellow stylist Rousseau, Burke posits the principle of constitutional politics thus: "to make us love our country, our

---

[12] *Sublime and Beautiful*, op.cit., supra n. 10, 63.

[13] ibid., 59.

[14] *Reflections*, op.cit., supra n. 1, 31.

[15] Edmund Burke, "Appeal from the New to the Old Whigs", quoted in W.J.T. Mitchell, *Iconology* (Chicago, University of Chicago Press, 1986), 141.

[16] ibid., 142. Burke's position on the English constitution was an important, although often unacknowledged, influence on 19th century constitutional writings from Bagehot to Dicey and still lurks behind contemporary debates on British parliamentary sovereignty, membership of the European Union and the introduction of a Bill of Rights.

country ought to be lovely". The conscious planning of the rational-ist constitution makers, on the other hand, eliminates the secret and sacred part of the constitution and leaves force only to underpin the power of the state:

> On the scheme of this barbarous philosophy . . . laws are to be sup-ported only by their own terrors, and by the concern, which each individual may find in them, from his own private speculations, or can spare to them from his own private interests. In the groves of their academy, at the end of every vista, you see nothing but the gallows. Nothing is left that engages the affections on the part of the com-monwealth. On the principles of this mechanic philosophy, our insti-tutions can never be embodied, if I may use an expression, in persons; so as to create in us love, veneration, admiration or attachment. But that sort of reason which banishes the affections is incapable of filling their place.[17]

Constitutions and human rights cannot replace this kind of attach-ment. On the contrary, they threaten the organic composition and constancy of the commonwealth by disconnecting it "into the dust and powder of individuality", and weakening its cement by the "unprincipled facility of changing the state as often, and as much, and in as many ways as there are floating fancies or fashions".

In these formulations, Burke has predated some of the main argu-ments of psychoanalytical jurisprudence by two hundred years.[18] "To avoid the evils of inconsistency and versatility . . . we have conse-crated the state that no man should approach to look into its defects or corruption but with due caution . . . ; that he should approach the wounds of the state as to the wounds of a father, with pious awe and trembling solitude".[19] Similarly, for Pierre Legendre, the state and the constitution represent the patriarchal principle which is necessary for both subject and the commonwealth.[20] Without reference and reverence for the principle of paternity, social reproduction, Legendre's principle of filiation, would be destroyed because, according to Burke, "no one generation could link with another. Men would become little better than flies of the summer".[21]

2. The rationalism of rights discourse makes their formulation so abstract and general as to render them unreal and unrealisable. This

---

[17] *Reflections*, op.cit., supra n. 1, 68.

[18] "On this scheme of things, a king is but a man, a queen is but a woman; a woman is but an animal, and an animal not of the highest order", ibid., 67.

[19] ibid., 85.

[20] See Chapter 11 below.

[21] *Reflections*, op.cit., supra n. 1, 83.

argument has two distinct strands. First, the abstraction of rights makes them inoperable and ends being their greatest practical defect. Abstraction is necessary of course, if the great plan of rights is to cohere in the face of all the great differences of people and place and circumstance. Indeed, the more metaphysically true and consistent their formulation is, the more formal and general they must appear to be and, as a result, the greater their political disutility and moral falseness. "What is the use of discussing a man's abstract right to food or medicine? The question is upon the method of procuring and administering them. In that deliberation I shall always advise to call in the aid of the farmer and the physician, rather than the professor of metaphysics".[22] What is the use of the abstract right to life or to free speech and press to the victims of famine and war or to people who are cannot read through lack of education facilities? What is the use of proclaiming the right to health care in a place like Haiti where one basic hospital covers more than two million people and AIDS patients are routinely turned away because they cannot be treated due to the lack of resources? Burke's comments, made some two hundred years ago, sound prophetic in light of the burdens placed on the developing world by huge debt and the mismanagement, corruption and inefficiency that has followed humanitarian aid.

Burke's attack focuses mainly on the metaphysical delusions of constitution designers and rights enthusiasts, but lawyers do not escape censure. They too can turn to "speculatism", when they assert that the law, replete with its abstractions and universals, can provide answers to political questions. Indeed, according to Strauss, Burke "questioned less the rights than the wisdom of exercising these rights . . . he tried to restore the genuinely political as against a legalistic approach".[23] There is no greater insult to the victims of natural or man made catastrophes, of famines and war, of earthquakes and ethnic cleansing, of epidemics and torture, there is no greater scorn and disregard than to be told that, according to the relevant international treaty, they have a right to food and peace, to a shelter and home or to medical care and an end to maltreatment. The contemporary professors of metaphysics and moral geometers are the diplomats and international lawyers, the government emissaries and the functionaries of international organisations. They construct codes of rights and entitlements which allow governments to appease their collective conscience in the most public of ways. Human rights have become

[22] ibid., 53.
[23] Strauss, op.cit., supra n. 8, 303.

the symbol of superiority of Western states, a kind of mantra, the repetition of which soothes the painful memory of past infamies and the guilt of present injustices. When this happens, Burke's fears are confirmed: human rights block the future.

Burke's second criticism addresses the abstract nature of the subject of human rights. The man without determination of the declarations is not only a non–existent person; he is also so indeterminate that his pale outline can provide very little protection. For Burke, human nature is socially determined and each society creates its own type of person. No general rights of man exist therefore, or, if they do, they have no value. The only effective rights are created by a particular history, tradition and culture. The common humanity advertised in the declarations of rights is imaginary; real humanity consist of "as it were so many different species of animals".[24] Both conservative and radical critics of rights agreed. The French Joseph de Maistre stated that "I have met Italians, Russians, Spaniards, Englishmen, Frenchmen, but I do not know man in general". Marx thought that only concrete individuals exist, historically and socially determined and shaped by their class position.[25] Another early critic, H.A. Taine found the French declaration as:

> nothing but abstract dogmas, metaphysical definitions, and more or less literary axioms, and therefore more or less false, sometimes vague, sometimes contradictory, susceptible to various interpretations . . . a kind of pompous sign-board, useless and heavy which . . . is in danger of falling on the passers-by and is every day shaken by violent hands.[26]

The ontological unreality of the abstract man of rights inexorably leads to their limited usefulness. Abstract rights are so removed from their place of application and the concrete circumstances of the persons who suffer and hurt that they are unable to match their real needs. [27]

Against those useless abstractions, Burke advertised the rights of the freeborn Englishman. These rights, inherited from their forefathers, have a long pedigree and ancient provenance "without any reference whatever to any other more general or prior right."

---

[24] *Reflections*, op.cit., supra n. 1, 166.

[25] Quoted in Claude Lefort, "Politics and Human Rights", in *The Political Forms of Modern Society* (Cambridge, Polity, 1986) 66.

[26] H.A. Taine, *Les Origines de la France Contemporaine. La Revolution, l' anarchie*, quoted in Norberto Bobbio, *The Age of Rights* (Polity, 1996) 86.

[27] This is the main criticism of communitarians against the universalism of rights.

Longevity, local provenance and organic evolution guarantee rights better than the rational plans of "sophisters, oeconomists, and calculators".[28] Rights exist and are violated in communities and only domestic law and local custom can protect them effectively, if they are disposed to do so. Burke assumed the benevolence and superiority of English law against the metaphysical grandeur of the French. But at the end of the twentieth century, this assumption cannot be easily entertained in relation to the British or any other domestic legal system. Indeed, the international law of human rights has emerged from the realisation that, if anything, people need to be protected most from their local custodians of legality.

3. The rationalism and abstraction of rights turn them into absolute moral principles, equally applicable against old and benevolent governments as well as the "most violent tyranny": "these admit no temperament, and no compromise: any thing withheld from their full demand is so much of fraud and injustice". This is the deep, political fear of Burke, the conservative politician. The rights of man may help import the French disease. In France, they have led to the greatest infamies, to regicide and the murder of aristocrats and judges. They are now put forward to the English people and are canvassed against English law and the constitution. This must be stopped, these rights are extreme, against them "no agreement is binding . . . no government [can] look for security in the length of its continuance, or in the justice and lenity of its administration". [29] Their propagation, rather than protect, will inevitably lead to tyranny: "Kings will be tyrants from policy when subjects are rebels from principle".[30] The close link between the rights of man and revolutionary terror colours the essay.

Such absolute rights forget that different societies lead to different institutional arrangements. Burke wants to vindicate the "*real* rights of man", presented in Aristotelian fashion as a "middle, incapable of definition, but not impossible to be discerned".[31] Until power and right coincide fully, these mean rights are what is practicably reasonable and can never be inconsistent with virtue and "the first of all virtues, prudence". In this sense, the wisdom of the ages with "its super-added ideas, furnished from the wardrobe of a moral imagination, which the heart owns, and the understanding ratifies, as necessary to cover the

---

[28] *Reflections*, op.cit., supra n. 1, 66.
[29] ibid., 51.
[30] ibid., 68.
[31] ibid., 54.

defects of our naked shivering nature, and to raise it to dignity" is more important than the machinations of reason or the science of constructing, renovating or reforming a commonwealth.[32] Constitutions that grow organically are much better than those made. No wise legislator can construct the best polity; that comes through the imitation of nature, "in a great length of time and by a great variety of accidents".[33]

These premises make Burke the founder of communitarianism. Like many contemporary communitarians, Burke combined a degree of relativism with a strong preference for a particular local tradition, that of the English constitution, the most perfect in the world. The constitution is not the outcome of conscious planning or of unity of design, but the gradual accretion and crystallisation, from time immemorial, of institutional patterns and legal remedies which are not directed to a particular purpose or aim but to the greatest variety of ends. This variety and the importance placed on "individual feeling and interest" indicates that the Aristotelian hierarchical teleology has been irretrievably lost and the continuous references to the Aristotelian themes of virtue, the middle or the organic community are remnants only of antiquity, fighting a rearguard action against the spirit of individualism. In the absence of classical teleology, which recognised the good in the purpose of each entity as it coheres with the whole, the Aristotelian mean becomes the outcome of balancing and compromises between good and evil or even between evil and evil. Despite Burke's longing looks to the past, politics has moved from its classical vocation and has turned into the science of calculation and computation of interests by means of "adding, subtracting, multiplying and dividing morally and not metaphysically or mathematically".[34]

This change is evident in all the key concepts of Burke. Natural law is no longer a standard for the theoretical construction of the best polity. It has become a natural process of selection, through which the force of law has been transferred from divine commands to the positive rules of the English constitution. Similarly, individual liberty, the highest goal of the polity, suffers if its implementation is entrusted to systematic planning and excessive reflection. The social order must be left to develop "naturally" to allow the free flourishing of individuality. But this is a very different sense of "natural" from that of

---

[32] ibid., 67.
[33] Strauss, op.cit., supra n. 8, 314.
[34] *Reflections*, op.cit., supra n. 1, 54.

the classics. The hidden hand of the market economy has moved to politics and the constitution and has found its perfect example in England.

If Burke discovered the importance of historical jurisprudence, as Strauss points out, historical for him meant the local and accidental. History is presented as a secularised and partly intelligible providence, in which the eternal has been temporalised. The English constitution, presented rather unrealistically as "the unintended outcome of accidental causation", is the best example of this process of almost natural selection. But how can this British superiority be established? Burke at times seems to invoke the idea of natural right, which preceded the immemorial constitution but was later fully embodied and protected by it; at others, he claims that the constitution does not have, or need any reference to, a prior right. But the contradiction is only apparent. His preference for the "real rights" of Englishmen against those contrived by reasoned designs has no need of external validation through naturalist justifications or otherwise. The constitution is the guarantee of its own goodness and "transcendent standards can be dispensed with if the standard is inherent in the process".[35] Burke's philosophy of "real rights" becomes a parochial eulogy, based on the claim that a latent or immanent wisdom of right is present in the English law and constitution, an empiricist preview of the Hegelian claim that the actual and the present coincide with the rational.

Burke's legacy is mixed, but it would not be inaccurate to say that all major critiques of rights share some aspect of his positions. Yet, despite his stylish, pertinent and unsurpassed invective against the metaphysical arrogance of the rights fanatics, he was the first writer to claim that ordinary law is the best depository and guarantor of rights. The recent triumphalism of rights has made the critique of their rationalism, abstraction and absolutism highly topical. But in another sense, liberal theorists are following in Burke's footsteps without his historical sensitivity. Contemporary liberals, who claim that rights are both immanent in Western legal systems and can act as a principle of critique of state activity, have adopted Burke's historicism and added to it the rationalism of rights he so eloquently denounced. In doing so, they are left with the combined problems of historicism and rationalism without the redeeming qualities of transcendence.

---

[35] Strauss, op.cit., supra n. 8, 319.

II. MARX ON THE RIGHTS OF MAN

The contribution of Marx and Marxism to the theory and critique of human rights has been fundamental. Understandably, for many, Marxism has been indissolubly associated with the Communist Bloc and its ideology, and is considered as a simplistic and brutal dismissal of human rights and their aspirations. If we take a closer look, however, at the huge *oeuvre* of Marx and his epigones, a more complex picture emerges. The early writings of Marx were an attempt to continue and radicalise the Hegelian dialectic, to "turn it on its head", by accepting the dialectical method but rejecting its idealist assumptions about reason's incarnation in history. In his later political writings, Marx became more interested, albeit still from a critical distance, in the potential of political and economic rights. But the impression remains, fortified by the record of the communist states, that Marx expressed a radical opposition towards human rights.

To understand Marx's detailed and nuanced approach to human rights, we must place it within the wider perspective of his thought. The best starting point is his commentary on the French Declaration, in the early essay *On the Jewish Question*.[36] Marx, following Hegel, argued that the revolution split the unified social space of feudalism into a political domain, which was confined to the state, and a predominantly economic one, civil society. As a result, individuals were released from the communal bonds of the *ancien régime*, became atomised and a distinction was drawn between the rights of man with their egotistic content and the emerging, unclear and still idealistic image of the citizen and his rights. Marx based the distinction between man and citizen or society and state on his fundamental claim that the French Revolution was bourgeois and political and would be superseded by another, universal and social. Hegel had famously claimed during his Yena years, that seeing Napoleon on horseback was like seeing the spirit become incarnate. Marx disagreed; the revolution, despite appearances, had not completed the historical process. The universal and the particular, humanity and the world stood still opposed to each other. While, in theory, the state was entrusted with the task of serving the universal good, in reality it promoted the narrow class interests of the bourgeoisie and its dominance over civil society. The French Revolution succeeded in eman-

---

[36] Karl Marx, "On the Jewish Question" in *Early Texts* (D. McLellan trans.) (Oxford, Blackwell, 1971), 85–114.

cipating the capitalist economy politically; what was necessary now
was a social revolution that would bring about full human emancipation.

The rights of man were the dominant ideology of the revolution.
These rights belong to the abstract universal man but they promote,
in practice, the interests of a very concrete person, the selfish and possessive individual of capitalism. From this perspective, Marx's critique
of human rights was total and constant. Rights idealise and support an
inhuman social order, underpinned by the abstract man of the declarations and, they help turn real people into abstract ciphers. The man
of human rights is abstract and empty:

> man frees himself from a constraint in a political way, through the state
> when he transcends his limitations, in contradiction with himself, and
> in an abstract, narrow and partial way. Furthermore, by emancipating
> himself politically, man emancipates himself in a devious way, through
> an intermediary, however necessary this intermediary may be.[37]

The subject of human rights loses her concrete identity, with its class,
gender and ethnic characteristics; all real human determinations are
sacrificed on the altar of the abstract man lacking history and context.
But at the same time, this abstract man stands in for a real person and
his rights support someone replete of substance. The emancipation of
the unreal man, subjects real people to a very concrete rule: "the
rights of man as distinct from the rights of the citizen are nothing but
the rights of the member of bourgeois society, i.e. egotistic man, man
separated from other man and the community".[38]

Again when Marx examined specific rights his criticisms were
scathing. The freedom they proclaim is negative, based on a society
of isolated monads who see each other as threat and hindrance to
their ends. The private property of the means of production separates
people from the tools of their labour and divides them into capitalists
and wage labouring slaves. The freedoms of opinion and expression
are the spiritual equivalent of private property, a position which may
have been slightly exaggerated at a time of political upheaval, when
Marx wrote, but which sounds more plausible in the era of Murdoch,
Turner and Gates. Formal equality promotes real unequality and
undermines real and direct relations amongst people:

> Right by its very nature can consist only in the application of an equal
> standard; but unequal individuals (and they would not be different

[37] ibid., 92.
[38] ibid., 102.

individuals if they were not unequal) are measurable only by an equal point of view, are taken from one definite side only . . . One worker is married, another not; one has more children than another and so on and so forth . . . To avoid all these defects, right instead of being equal would have to be unequal.[39]

As a result, only the right to security constructs links, albeit artificial, between fearful individuals and society. The ultimate social value is not the public good but the principle of the police, the "supreme concept of bourgeois society, the insurance for [bourgeois] egoism",[40] which is entrusted with keeping social peace and public order in a highly conflictual society.

In this bourgeois hall of mirrors, civil rights support selfishness while politics and the state replace religion and the Church and become a terrestrial quasi-heaven, in which social divisions are temporarily forgotten and the citizens participate equally in popular sovereignty:

> [Man] lives in the political community, where he regards himself as a communal being, and in civil society, where he acts simply as a private individual, treats other men as means, degrades himself to the role of a mere means, and becomes the plaything of alien powers. The political state, in relation to civil society, is just as spiritual as is heaven in relation to earth . . . In the state . . . where he is regarded as a species being, man is the imaginary member of an imaginary sovereignty, divested of his real, individual life, and infused with an unreal universality.[41]

Men thus live a double life: a social life of strife and private conflict during the working week and a second, which like a metaphorical Sabbath, is devoted to public political activity in pursuit of the common good, while private interests are allegedly temporarily abandoned. In reality, a clear hierarchy subordinates the political rights of the ethereal citizen to the concrete interests of bourgeois man presented as natural rights. Equality and liberty are ideological fictions which belong to the state, while the reality they sustain is of a society and daily existence of exploitation, oppression and individualism.

Marx was critical too of the rights of the citizen. But this was not because these rights are false and oppressive, but because they cannot deliver what they promise within the confines of bourgeois society.

---

[39] Karl Marx, "Critique of the Gotha Programme" in *Selected Writings* (David McLellan ed.) (Oxford, Oxford University Press, 1977) 569.

[40] W. Benjamin, "Critique of Violence", in *Reflections* (New York, Schocken Books, 1978) 104.

[41] ibid., 94.

"Political emancipation is of course a great progress. Although it is not the final form of human emancipation in general, it is nevertheless the final form of human emancipation inside the present world order".[42] Indeed, political rights are not rights of "an isolated monad withdrawn into himself . . . without regard for other men". These rights create a political community, in which man "counts as species being", is "valued as a communal being" and as "a moral person".[43] But while political rights prefigure the future community, the main innovation of the revolution and its declaration was to abstract politics from society and confine them into the separate domain of the state. Turning property and religion into social institutions, belonging to the private sphere and protected from state intervention through the operation of rights, makes them more effective and safeguards their dominance better than the medieval fusion of public and private power. In this dialectical formulation, the main aim of human rights was to remove politics from society and depoliticise the economy. The separation presents the state as (politically) dominant, while capitalist society is where real (economic) power lies. The bourgeois abandonment of the direct political power of feudal lords and kings, was the precondition for the ascendancy of bourgeois society and its capitalist principles.

The rights of man, like all rights, are not natural or inalienable but historical creations of state and law. Their emergence and dialectical operation is quite complex: while the separation between state and society was the outcome of economic changes in society, the state turned the conditions of existence of capitalism, which brought it to life, into legally recognised rights and consecrated them as natural and eternal. Human rights are therefore real and effective but they achieve much more and different from what is apparent. "Insofar as legal form is construed as the protection of natural right, the structural and historical conditions of civil society are suppressed".[44] A real revolution would be social and not just political and would abolish the rights of property and religion, which perpetuate the social inequality and class domination. Commenting on the Revolution of 1848, Marx spoke of a very different right which would represent the spirit of such a revolution: "The right to work is, in the bourgeois

---

[42] ibid., 95.
[43] ibid., 93, 94, 95.
[44] Jay Bernstein, "Right, Revolution and Community: Marx's 'On the Jewish Question' " in Peter Osborne (ed.), *Socialism and the Limits of Liberalism* (London, Verso, 1991) 109.

sense, nonsense, a wretched, pious wish. But behind the right to work stands power over capital. The appropriation of the means of production, their subjection to the associated working class. That is the abolition of wage labour, capital and the mutual relationship".[45]

The proletarian revolution will realise the aspirations of human rights by negating both their moralistic form and idealistic content, exemplified by the abstract and isolated man. The combined negation of content and form, in communism, will give fundamental rights their true meaning and will introduce real freedom and equality for a new socialised man. Freedom will stop being negative and defensive, a boundary and limit separating self from other, and will become a positive power of each in union with others. Equality will no longer mean the abstract comparison of private individuals but catholic and full participation in a strong community. Property will cease being the limitation of each to a portion of wealth to the exclusion of all others and will become common. Real freedom and equality look to the concrete person in community, abandon the various formal definitions of justice and social distribution and inscribe on their banners the principle "from each according to his ability, to each according to his needs". The French Revolution, on the contrary, consecrated the right to hold property and to practice religion and, in this way, the capitalist pre-conditions of exploitation and oppression were ideologically reversed in the discourse of rights and were fraudulently presented as freedoms.

The real rights of the citizen pertain to the spirit of the revolution and will be fully realised only when "the actual individual man takes the abstract citizen back into himself and, as an individual man in his empirical life, in his individual work and individual relationships becomes a species-being; man must recognise his own forces as social forces, organise them and thus no longer separate himself from this social power in the form of political power".[46] This realisation of rights in association with others will reconcile universality and human singularity and, as a result, state law, the effect and defender of the earlier gap between the two, will become obsolete and wither away. In communism, human qualities, aptitudes and interests will not be described as rights; they will be the attributes of individual existence, accepted and celebrated as integral elements of each person. Capitalism, which

[45] Karl Marx, "The Class Struggle in France: 1848 to 1850" quoted in Ferry and Renaut, "From the Rights of Man to the Republican Idea" (F. Philip trans.) (University of Chicago Press, 1992) op.cit., 88.
[46] *On the Jewish Question*, op.cit., supra n. 36, 108.

invented rights, cannot realise their promise and gives them an exclusively negative form. But when their real preconditions come into
being in socialism, they are no longer of use and disappear. It looks as
if human rights have little positive role in Marxism.

Undoubtedly many problems plague Marx's analysis, some contingent on the historical constraints of his period, others more structural and basic. The most important is the relative devaluation of the
social "superstructures" – of moral, legal and political institutions –
and the excessive privileging of the economic "base", which had
catastrophic effects for the analysis of human rights. These are well-
known criticisms and have been extensively commented upon. But
Marx was the first radical critic of rights who insisted on their historical character against the assertions of the natural rights ideologues.
After the critique of Marx, it became clear that while human rights
were presented as eternal, they are the creations of modernity; while
they passed for natural, they are social and legal constructs; while they
were presented as absolute, they are the limited and limiting instruments of law; while they were thought of as above politics, they are
the product of the politics of their time; finally, while they were
asserted as rational, they are the outcome of the reason of capital and
not of the public reason of society. All these reversals between phenomena and reality meant that, for Marx, human rights were the
prime example of ideology of their time.

But whatever his criticisms of historical rights, Marx expressed
forcefully sentiments, not dissimilar to those of radical natural law,
and based his attacks on capitalism on the principles of dignity and
equality, which only socialism could realise. In his critique of Hegel's
Philosophy of Right, Marx was unequivocal: "The critique of religion
ended with the doctrine that man is the highest being for man, and
thus with the categorical imperative to overthrow all relations in
which man is a degraded, enslaved, abandoned, or despised being".[47]
Marx sided with those who, despite the declarations, were neither
free nor equal. He may have despaired of the idealism and unreality
of human rights but not with their aim. As Ernst Bloch put it, "precisely with respect to the humiliated and degraded, Marxism inherits
some of this wealth of natural law . . . Socialism can raise the flag of
the ancient fundamental rights which has fallen elsewhere".[48] One

[47] Karl Marx, *Critique of Hegel's Philosophy of Right*, Introduction in *Early Texts*, op.cit.,
supra n. 36, 115–129, at 123.

[48] Ernst Bloch, *Natural Law and Human Dignity* (D. Schmidt trans.) (Cambridge Ma.,
MIT Press, 1988) 188.

could argue that Marx was critical of human rights, because they were not human enough and their entitlements were not equally shared. His exalted belief in the scientific character of his theory often derailed his moral vision, but Marx cannot be faulted for lack of passionate commitment to the end of human dignity and social well-being. [49]

★★★

Contemporary critiques of human rights follow the pattern of those early reactions to the declarations. The Burkean position emphasised the historical character of law and right and rejected the existence of transcendent or universal standards or their ability to criticise the concrete reality and power of legal institutions. Its contemporary "left wing" versions can be found in theories of communitarianism, legal pluralism and multi-culturalism. But Burke's appeal to the innate wisdom of the British constitution, which allegedly expresses the "nature" of the Englishman and prescribes its forms and rights without any reference to prior or higher right, have also led to conservative versions. In these, the state or the nation and its law are identified with tradition and endowed with a peculiar kind of timeless timeliness. The next, although not inevitable step, leads to the celebration of autocratic legalism or of an indigenous proceduralism: the past is right because it is the past or the law is just because it repeats ancient practice or custom and is accorded legitimacy and dignity because it is immersed in archaic formalities. Tradition becomes the guarantee of its own validity and goodness without reference to external criteria or principles. For right-wing Burkeans, the non-recognition or the violation of human rights is logically impossible; rights are the creations of state law and the judgment of right is internal to the history of the institution. This was often the – unspoken – premise of those who opposed the introduction of a Bill of Rights in Britain. Communitarians, on the other hand, reject the identification of community with state law and oppose the incursions of universal principles into the territory of community values.

Burke's theory was a critique of the political philosophy of transcendence, Marx's of the impossibility of transcendence. Burke insisted on the goodness of tradition and particularity against the claims of reason and universalism, whereas Marx saw in the emerg-

---

[49] Costas Douzinas and Ronnie Warrington, "Domination, exploitation and suffering: Marxism and the opening of closed systems of thought", 1986/4 *Journal of the American Bar Foundation*, 801–44.

ing new order sectional and class interests masquerading as universal. They are both right and wrong. Right can only be grounded on national and local laws, and traditions and the declarations of human rights remain a "nonsense on stilts" unless translated into the culture and law of a particular society. But unless the universalising idea of human rights retains a transcendent position and dignity towards local conditions, no valid or convincing critique of the law can be mounted. Rights are local but can only be criticised and redirected from the point of view of an unrealised and unrealisable universal. Right operates as a critical function only against a future horizon, that of the (impossible) ideal of an emancipated and self-constituting humanity.

Marx too was right in pointing the dissymmetry between the universal "man" of rights and the concrete capitalist whose image fills the frame of the abstraction. Contemporary feminist or critical race theories follow this path of critique of ideology: the "man" of human rights is literally a Western white middle-class man who, under the claims of non-discrimination and abstract equality, has stamped his image on law and human rights and has become the measure of all things and people. But Marx neglected the possibility that the groundlessness of the discourse of rights and the non-determination of the concept of man – admittedly more asserted than real in the eighteenth century – would install indeterminacy in the heart of human identity and undecidability in politics and thus create the conditions of future self-realisation. Concrete people can be recognised in their uniqueness and realise their potential if they are allowed to shape their identities freely outside the diktats of state, law or party. In this sense, the critique of the false abstraction of human nature finds its horizon, not in true abstraction, but in the proliferation of local and partial contents that will fill the empty "man" with a multitude of colours, shapes and characteristics.

III. WESTERN MARXISM AND THE POLITICS OF HUMAN RIGHTS

The Marxist critique of human rights was extensively mobilised by right-wing and liberal theorists during the Cold War to prove that the communist Gulags and lunatic asylums were logical extensions of Marxism's immanent totalitarian tendencies. The standard response of pro-Soviet Marxists was twofold: they argued that social and economic rights were superior to the classical liberal rights because material survival and decent conditions of life are more important than the right to vote or to form and join political parties. Furthermore, meeting basic economic and social needs was the indispensable precondition for the effective exercise of political rights. "The right to a free press is of no interest to a starving and illiterate peasant in an African village" ran the argument. These ideological arguments were seemingly strengthened by comparisons between Eastern and Western practices. The communist states guaranteed full employment, subsidised food prices and provided state care for their citizens from cradle to grave. Western governments, on the other hand, tolerated armies of unemployed in order to bring down labour costs and allowed people to starve and die if they could not afford private health care.

Liberal intellectuals and Western governments responded in kind. Civil and political rights have a clear priority over social and economic ones. Historically, they were the first to enter the world scene, and they are superior because of their negative and individualistic character. Their aim is to place limits around state activities, thus opening areas free of political and legal interference where individuals can exercise their initiative without prohibitions or excessive regulation. For early liberals, this negative conception of freedom, freedom as the absence of constraint or state impositions, is the heart of human autonomy and rights. Economic rights, on the other hand, are not proper legal rights. They are claimed by groups, not individuals; they are "positive" in their action, in other words, they call for extensive state intervention in economy and society, for heavy taxation and central planning, all necessary in order to deliver the levels of employment presupposed by the right to work or the welfare provision necessary for free health care or education. Finally, economic and social rights are not "justiciable": they cannot be guaranteed by legislation in a liberal state and, moreover, courts cannot enforce them. The appalling oppression of dissidents was seen as proof of the correctness of the Western arguments and the assertion that the market is the superior, if not the only, mechanism of distribution was recited as a mantra in response to the communist claims about capitalist squalor and unemployment.

This brief summary of arguments, conducted on the floor of the human rights bodies, in the United Nations and in numerous academic journals from the fifties to the eighties, indicates the fruitless and politically motivated character of the debate. In practice, however, these two diametrically opposed positions were being superseded. The welfare state had already created a safety net for the poorest in the West and large parts of the developing world had started adopting a cautious pluralism with the attending civil and political rights. In this climate, the collapse of the Soviet bloc and the American triumphalism that accompanied it, brought the human rights arguments to an end. After 1989, the Marxist and left-wing critiques of human rights seemed irrelevant at best, and disastrously wrong at worse. Socialist reservations about the all-conquering powers of the market and the centrality of the individual were undermined with such finality that soon one expected them to be totally purged from the annals of the history of ideas. This was the time of the "ends": of ideology, of history, of Utopia and of the beginning of the human rights millennium.

But this euphoric picture, penned in thousands of Western newspaper articles and promoted at all levels of international politics, had been shattered by the late nineties. The unprecedented humanitarian disasters of the decade and NATO's conduct of the war against Yugoslavia, the first war to be explicitly fought for the protection of human rights, brought the doubts, reservations and critiques of human rights back onto the political and theoretical agenda. The civil versus economic rights debate has been superseded by that between universalists and cultural relativists or communitarians, but human rights are here to stay and no argument can detract from their global appeal. But it is precisely because the early ideological and political confrontations which defined their discourse and practice have come to an end, that we can have, for the first time, a more detached examination of their problems. In this re-assessment of the function and problems of rights, the Marxist tradition occupies, historically and intellectually, a central place. Over the last twenty years, post-Marxist theorists have been trying hard to explore both the unexplored potential and the limitations of the Marxist critique.[50]

Indeed, respect for human rights and democracy was the main platform on which Western European communists in Italy, Spain, Greece and Great Britain broke away from their earlier unqualified adulation and defence of the Soviet Union, and moved towards the

[50] See amongst many, Nicos Poulantzas, *State, Power, Socialism* (London, New Left Books, 1978); Claude Lefort, *The Political Forms of Modern Society* (Cambridge, Polity, 1986); Ernesto Laclau and Chantal Mouffe, *Hegemony and Socialist Strategy* (London, Verso, 1985); Wendy Brown, "Rights and Identity in Modernity: Revisiting the 'Jewish Question' " in A. Sarat and T. Kearns (eds), *Identities, Politics and Rights* (Ann Arbor, University of Michigan Press, 1997) 85–130; Jay Bernstein, op.cit., supra n. 44.

strategy of a "democratic road to socialism". This fundamental re-evaluation was partly due to the appalling violations of all aspects of human dignity and equality suffered by the Spanish, Portuguese, Greek and Chilean people, and predominantly amongst them by leftist radicals, during the American-supported dictatorships in these countries and elsewhere in the last sixty years. The simple bipolar divides of the Cold War were not able to explain the wholesome violation of minimum political rights in many Western capitalist states which boasted for their civil and political freedoms or the woeful lack of many basic amenities in the communist countries which prided themselves for their universally guaranteed economic rights.

This process of re-assessment of old orthodoxies had important practical effects. One of the most obvious was the abandonment by Western communist parties of hard-line policies and symbols and their emergence as left of centre democratic socialist parties, most spactacularly in Italy. The Italian Communist Party had been excluded from government for some fifty years but became the natural and trusted party of government in the late nineties, after its re-branding as the party of the democratic left. These political developments were accompanied by parallel moves in theory. Ernst Bloch and many post-Marxists, like Nicos Poulantzas, Claude Lefort and Etienne Balibar, emphasised the centrality of rights for socialism. Beyond the ideological pyrotechnics of the Cold War and its demise, Marxist thought took on the challenge of human rights. But can Marxism make a contribution to the post-Cold War assessment of human rights?

One of the main tasks of post-Marxists was to explore the "ideological reversals" which, according to Marx, characterised human rights. Irrespective of the original accuracy of these insights, the reversals had been stabilised, human rights had been extended in content and scope, and had become a main expression of rebellion and protest against dominant political and social forces and of empowerment of the dispossessed. In the wake of Foucault and discourse theory, we learnt that "ideological" concepts are not false. To be sure, one Marxist school had consistently presented ideology as "false consciousness" and, in the work of the French philosopher Louis Althusser, had made the strong claim that Marxism as "science" emerged only when the later Marx abandoned the idealism and ideological misrecognitions of Hegel.[51] But for another post-Marxist

[51] Douzinas and Warrington, *Postmodern Jurisprudence* (London, Routledge, 1991) Chapter 6.

tradition, influenced by the Italian political leader and philosopher Antonio Gramsci, political ideas and concepts are neither true nor false but the tools through which we make sense of our world. In law and politics, therefore, the task is not so much to discard "wrong" ideological concepts, like human rights, but to re-define them against whatever conservative connotations they may have acquired, adjust them to the project of popular politics and build around them a "hegemonic" bloc. But the analysis, critique and re-assembly of the concept of human rights was only partially carried out. Marxist theoretical tools, even when reworked in a democratic direction, proved inadequate. A fuller critical understanding of human rights from the left would have to wait the re-discovery of Hegel and the use of the insights of psychoanalysis and postmodern ethics.

It would be a serious mistake, however, to jettison fully the Marxist tradition. Its contribution to our understanding of rights is still indispensable and has informed, quite often without attribution, many contemporary critical approaches to rights, such as critical legal studies, feminism and critical race theory. One point that unites many post-Marxist theorists is a renewed emphasis on the importance of political rights and action.[52] Marx believed, as we saw, that political emancipation and citizen rights were a limited improvement on the politically integrated society of feudalism where social belonging and political power were organically linked. The political state treats people as if they are free and equal and, as a result, the desire and struggle for real freedom and equality enters the historical agenda. But more importantly, political rights introduced for the first time the principle of publicity into politics and led people to abandon their private isolation and collaborate in common campaigns. These rights are exercised in association with others and reject, admittedly ineffectually for Marx, the individualistic character of the rights of man. Political rights are "exercised only in community with others. What constitutes their content is participation in community, in the political community or state. They come under the category of political freedom".[53] But the drift of the overall theory and the emphasis on the inadequacy of political emancipation meant that these insights remained marginal and incomplete.

---

[52] Jay Bernstein, Etienne Balibar and Wendy Brown emphasise the significance placed by Marx on the rights of citizenship. Claude Lefort, on the other hand, criticises Marx, the first debunker of ideological fictions, of falling a victim of ideology and taking the claims of the French Declaration at face value without realising their revolutionary democratic import.

[53] *On the Jewish Question*, op.cit., supra n. 36, 104.

The political nature and collaborative potential of human rights has been a main theme in the writings of three former leading marxists, Claude Lefort, Etienne Balibar and Jean-François Lyotard. They are part of a sustained re-assessment of the role of human rights in the history of ideas, which combines historical evidence with philosophical argumentation. Lefort has argued in a series of impressive essays that Marx misunderstood the character of the French revolution and, as a result, underestimated the nature and significance of human rights. According to Lefort and contra Marx, the main novelty and achievement of the revolution was its political character. Its success should be seen as an episode in the history of state and politics and not as the "superstructural" effect of economic developments. The monarchical state had introduced a limited rule of law through the secularisation of Christian value, well before the revolution. The role of Christ had been transferred to the king, who mediated between political and civil society and was subjected to legal principles, which had an almost religious aura and protected the subjects from administrative arbitrariness. But the king followed the law and enforced citizens' rights as part of his own nature or as an exercise of his freedom. While limited in principle, therefore, the king found no boundaries to his will in fact. In this sense, by ushering in the democratic state and human rights, the revolution continued the tradition which had separated power from right and knowledge but in a new direction. The abolition of monarchy detached the image of power, right and society from the king's body. The corporeal metaphor, which had symbolised and united law and justice, sovereignty and nation, secular concerns and spiritual forces, dissolved into a myriad of people now declared sovereign.

The essence of the democratic state is that, while power and right are not fully separated, power becomes the object of law and its legitimacy the subject of public disputation. In this new configuration of power and right, human rights are the best example of a sphere which is not controlled by and, indeed, is programmatically external to power. Marx in his zeal to attack the French Declaration presented its freedoms as negative and anchored them in an isolated individual limited only by the rights of others. But he failed to understand that the freedoms of opinion and expression instituted a new form of politics and of access to the public sphere. The atomising effects of human rights, if any, were confronted and reversed by the inauguration of the right to free speech,

> one of [man's] most precious rights, to step out of himself and to make contact with others, through speech, writing and thought . . . It is the independence of thought and opinion with regard to power, the sep-

aration between power and knowledge, that is at stake in the affirmation of the rights of man, and not only or not essentially the split between the bourgeois man and the citizen, between private property and politics.[54]

It was Marx's "refusal to think in political terms that prevented him" from recognising this new type of democratic politics.[55] When human rights become the ultimate reference of politics, all established right and justice are open to question and challenge. While in monarchical societies the person of the king united sovereignty and justice or power and knowledge and guaranteed the unity of society, in democratic societies the place of power becomes "empty". The social space can no longer be symbolised by any one body or concept, in other words, no foundation or other unitary principle can safeguard the polity's integrity or homogeneity. As a result, the old concept of unitary right, emanating from God or king, and radiating sun-like through the body politic, becomes fragmented: a multiplicity of rights develop, resisting the attempts of all power, "religious or mythical, monarchical or popular" to take hold of them. Thus, while the rule of law implies the possibility of opposing right to power, a human rights polity goes much further: it tests and accepts rights that have not yet been established, its logic extends into areas of activity the state cannot entirely master and its limits remain open to further contestation and expansion. "From the legal recognition of strikes or trade unions, to rights relative to work or to social security, there has developed on the basis of the rights of man a whole history that transgressed the boundaries within which the state claimed to define itself, a history that remains open".[56] What opposes the principle of human rights is the – psychoanalytically explained – desire of people for unity and security, their craving for the principle of the One, for a new unitary historical actor, be it nation, class or party, or a new foundational principle or law which will breathe consistency and coherence into the dismembered body of the social and the fragmented and heterogeneous struggles for human rights.

Similarly, the Marxist philosopher, Etienne Balibar, has argued that the French Revolution turned the pre-modern subject into the modern citizen, replaced monarchical with popular sovereignty and opened a political space for argument and critique based on citizen

---

[54] Lefort, "The Political Forms of Modern Society", op.cit., n. 50, 250–1.
[55] ibid., 254.
[56] ibid., 258.

equality as a pre-requisite of freedom.[57] Balibar, like Lefort, criticises Marx for placing too much emphasis on the separation between public and private and between citizen and man and misunderstanding, as a result, the political novelty of the French Declaration: rather than separating, it identified man and citizen, it brought together for the first time freedom and equality and created a universal right to political participation. Balibar argues that while equality and freedom are not the same, the conditions for their successful application and expansion are identical. The proof is negative: under no conditions is equality suppressed while freedom survives and vice versa. Capitalism denies equality and destroys freedom, as evidenced in infant mortality, the shortened life expectation and the ruined lives of the Western underclass and the poor in the south. Communism denied political rights and ended up with a society of huge disparities amongst citizens and almost feudal privileges for the party cadre and state officials. "There are no examples of restrictions or suppressions of freedoms without social inequalities, nor of inequalities without restrictions or suppressions of freedoms".[58] The equation of equality and freedom, their indissoluble link, means that all rights-claims are politicised: they express a demand for an extension of the meaning of citizenship or for a further expansion of freedom and equality and inscribe indeterminacy or "negative universality" at the heart of the polity:

> In this indefinite opening come to be inscribed – and attempts to do this can be seen beginning with the revolutionary period – the rights-claims of salaried workers or dependants, as well as those of women or slaves, and later of the colonised. Such a right would later be formulated as follows: *the emancipation of the oppressed can only be their own work*, which emphasises its immediately ethical signification.[59]

The task of humanity is self-emancipation through collective political action. This means, logically, that there can be no liberty without equality, ontologically, that the main characteristic of human beings is their collective construction of individual freedom and, politically, that emancipation cannot be a gift but must be achieved in community and common action with others. "The humanity of man is identified not with a given or an essence, be it natural or supra-natural, but with a practice and a task: the task of self-emancipation from every

---

[57] See Chapter 8 below.

[58] Balibar, " 'The Rights of the Man' and the 'Rights of the Citizen' ", in *Masses, Classes, Ideas* (Cambridge, Polity, 1994) 49.

[59] ibid.

domination and subjection by means of a collective and universal access to politics".[60] Human rights are the legal title and institutional guarantee of the indeterminate. For Balibar, the subjection to social superiors, God or king, which characterised the pre-modern world came to an end with the identification of subject and citizen in the French Revolution. But, in his attempt to redeem human rights for radical politics, Balibar exaggerates the egalitarian effects of the French Revolution and its Declaration. It is true that the democratic politics of modernity established a public space in which political equality could help minimise the real inequalities of the private sphere. This is the equality of citizenship created through the exercise by citizens of identical political freedoms. But the citizenry remained severely restricted in its composition by racial, ethnic, legal and gender exclusions for more than a century, and citizenship still follows often arbitrary territorial boundaries, as the collapse of Yugoslavia clearly showed. The hoped for extension of political rights to the whole population and their expansion into social economic and cultural rights can be explained, from Balibar's perspective, as the transfer of the logic of equal political freedom to areas previously considered as part of the private or social domain with its "acceptable" inequalities. The fight for workers and union rights, for example, politicised the place of work and, when successful, expanded citizenship by making inequalities and differences in treatment at the workplace as illegitimate as the denial of the right to vote or of free expression in the public domain.[61]

From a different perspective, Jean-François Lyotard emphasises the way in which human rights construct people and political structures in a manner that makes the other always present.[62] Using linguistic philosophy, Lyotard argues that the basic human trait is communication. The structure of interlocution organises relations between speakers on the basis of their similarities and differences and helps arrange temporality. The speaker's "I" always addresses a "you" now and, will in turn become "you" to the interlocutor's "I" in the future. Identity and community, the "I" and the "we", are effects of this alternating conversation and, the other as trace, as an actual or potential interlocutor, remains embedded in both. This ontological and

[60] Balibar, "Subjection and Subjectivation", in Joan Copjec (ed.), *Supposing the Subject* (London, Verso, 1994) 12.
[61] For an analysis along these lines, see Ernesto Laclau and Chantal Mouffe, *Hegemony and Socialist Strategy*, op.cit., supra n. 50, Chapter 5.
[62] Jean-François Lyotard, "The Other's Rights", in *On Human Rights* (Stephen Shute and Susan Hurley eds) (New York, Basic Books, 1993) 135–47.

linguistic structure demands that freedom of expression, the institu-
tionalisation of the humanising capacity of speech, becomes the fundamental human right. But like humanity, this right remains under
constant threat. The ultimate horror and the strongest abjection is felt
when the right and capacity to speak are taken away. This is what
happened to the Holocaust victims, who were denied the right to
speak and be addressed by others. As a result, they were removed
from humanity; "neither *I* nor *you*, the deportee is present in the language of his lords and in that of the deportees themselves only as a
third person, who is to be eliminated".[63] In this approach, every
question or address to another presupposes a request not to be abandoned to the abjection of speechlessness and to be allowed into
community. Lyotard, like Lefort and Balibar, argues that modernity,
by introducing a right to speak, has legitimised the human condition.
But he is also more cautious: the total and non-speaking Other, God,
death or unconscious abjection, is both a threat and the desire of the
subject. It lurks in the background and, as a result, the project of individual or group integrity is never complete or safe.

The political turn of the post-Marxists is a welcome corrective to
the earlier economic reductionism and has contributed to our understanding of human rights much more than the many tired and trite
repetitions of liberal rights theorists. The post-Marxist refutations of
the classical critique emphasise the political character of rights which
arguably weakens their atomising effects. Lefort and Balibar offer a
paradigmatic image of the postmodern political condition, in which
freedom has been freed from the formalism of liberalism in an existential direction and, equality accompanies freedom as its indispensable partner. But the excessive politicisation of rights carries its own
problems. Emphasising their political character, in other words their
equalising potential, is not always useful. Right-claims organised
around gender and sexuality, for instance, prioritise difference and
identity rather than equality and participation and their theoretical
tools can scarcely emerge from the re-worked Marxist repertory.
Indeed, one of the characteristics of contemporary popular human
rights campaigns is the side-stepping of formal political institutions in
favour of direct action and single issue initiatives. These however
challenge the Marxist claim that only politics can bring together the
many and disparate social conflicts and unite fragmented struggles to
a common cause.

[63] ibid.,145.

The excessive valorisation of human rights is one instance of a wider tendency amongst post-Marxists which lowers the critical threshold when faced with law and legal history. In their justified concern to rescue human rights from vulgar Marxism and to emphasise the importance of the French Revolution against revisionist historians, they underestimate the often counter-productive role of legalism in the history of rights.[64] The juridification and internationalisation of human rights has led to attempts to impose a logic of closure and planned extension which invalidates the messy and open practice of rights, so well presented by the French theorists. Power and right may have been partly separated, as Lefort insists, and the citizens may have been declared sovereign, according to Balibar. But legal rights remain a state language and power can shape them in its own image. Through their formal equality and less than universal citizenship, rights emerged as a highly paradoxical institution: both an instrument of emancipation and a means for empowering bourgeois dominance. Their history has been equally ambiguous; they have been used to protect from arbitrary power but they have also helped secure and naturalise dominant social powers and their class, gender, race, and ethnic exclusions. "Not only did bourgeois rights discourse mask, by depoliticising, the social power of institutions such as private property or the family, they also organised mass populations for exploitation and regulation, thus functioning as a modality of what Foucault termed 'bio-power' ".[65] As a result of taking law at face value, the critical purchase of the French philosophers is seriously undermined.

IV. HUMAN RIGHTS AND UTOPIA

Lefort and Balibar, the postmodern and post-Marxist theorists of politics, have paradigmatically deconstructed the universal pretensions of human rights but have left the universalist claims of legal reason intact. In an attempt to rescue radical politics from the political excesses and theoretical weaknesses of communism, they have neglected the paradoxical nature of rights and forgotten the often reactionary and violent role of law. But human rights are Janus-like, they carry the dual ability to emancipate and dominate, to protect and discipline. The Marxist philosopher who first emphasised their

[64] See Chapter 9 below.
[65] Brown, op.cit., supra n. 50, 89.

paradoxical action was Ernst Bloch.[66] His grandiose and eloquent utopianism, steeped in central European Jewish culture and German romantic values remains unsurpassed although, after the collapse of communism, it is no longer fashionable or "politically correct". Bloch represents a genuine advance on Marx; he retains the main elements of his critique of rights but discovers in the tradition of natural law and right the historically variable but eternal human trait to resist domination and oppression and to imagine and fight for a society in which "man will walk upright". There can be no real foundation of human rights without an end to exploitation and no real end to exploitation without the establishment of human rights.

According to Bloch, from the Sophists and the Stoics to the moderns, nature was constituted in different ways as a category which confronted existing social relations as "a fetish against social defaults".[67] But the struggle between this ever-changing nature and the sedimented world of positive law was always lost until modernity invented democracy and socialism in the work of Rousseau and Marx respectively. Rousseau resolved the problem of how to protect individual freedom, by establishing an immediate relationship between the citizens and the general will thus turning natural law from a philosophical or religious construct into a historical institution. Natural law became the law legislated by popular sovereignty and the general should ensure that the principle of individual freedom could only exist in a human rights community. In this sense, politics and rights were indissolubly connected and guaranteed the achievements of the revolution by subjecting the government to the constant control of citizens. Natural law was no longer deduced from the abstract rule of reason and axiomatic propositions about human nature, but became the outcome of the concrete reason of people. For the first time in history, right or *jus* became synonymous with the rights of the people, politics adopted the idea of equality for all, and the triptych of liberty, equality and fraternity acquired normative weight. But property counted as one of the inalienable rights and, as a result, equality was restricted to politics and even there to white males; the potential of rights was not allowed to materialise. "This was the high

---

[66] Bloch's combination of utopianism, interest in natural law and qualified support for the socialist regimes, meant that he did not feature in the pantheon of Western Marxists, despite his great interest and affinity with Walter Benjamin and the Frankfurt School. The only offerings in English are, Vincent Geoghegan, *Ernst Bloch* (London, Routledge, 1996) and J. O. Daniel and T. Moylan (eds), *Not Yet: reconsidering Ernst Bloch* (London, Verso, 1997).

[67] *Natural Law and Human Dignity*, op.cit., supra n. 48, 192.

point of natural law, but the epoch in which it flourished was an illusion, for out of the *citoyen* there came the bourgeois; it was a foreshadowing, for the bourgeois was judged by the *citoyen*".[68] Expanding Marx's distinction between man and citizen, Bloch saw the latter as a prefiguration of the future socialised freedom. Although the idea of citizenship had been damaged by its bourgeois misuse, it did not represent "a barrier to freedom as it does in the egotism of the *droits de l'homme* . . . indeed, as Holderlin pointed out, it always possessed the capacity of self-purification".[69]

The foreshadowing, the prophesying of a future not yet and not ever present helps in the self-purification of moral ideas contaminated by the powerful. The triptych of the French Revolution shows this strategy at work. Freedom as ethical and political, as personal and public, as freedom of choice and of action, is the ability to "act *contra fatum*, thus in a perspective of a still *open* world, one not *yet determined all the way to the end*".[70] Oppression and domination are obvious violations of freedom, because they turn political power and economic conditions into inescapable destinies. But freedom is also irreconcilable with a fully determined and closed world, in which the only possible personal intervention is a judicious adjustment to dominant ideas and the exploitation of given and inescapable structures to the subject's advantage; an advantage whose contours have been well demarcated and boundaries are strictly policed. In this sense, freedom is enhanced by the ability of rights to extend the limits of the social and to expand and re-define self and group identities. It operates only if as yet unclosed possibilities remain in the world and is extinguished when the double determination of the subject as free and subjected moves towards the pole of subjection. But in a regulated world, in which little margin of play is allowed outside the parameters of global capitalism and authoritarian order, freedom might come to mean resistance to the "freedom" to own and control ever more objects as the ultimate sign of self-expression or to the "freedom" to define and shape life according to a closed list of rights defined by "moral experts". Freedom cannot be defined in advance, except as the "human comportment in the face of objective real possibility".[71] Its every exercise opens in turn a new vista which, if petrified, becomes

---

[68] ibid., 65.
[69] ibid., 177.
[70] ibid., 162.
[71] ibid., 163.

itself an external limitation that must be overcome again. Freedom is an ambiguous concept, that starts from past determinations and crystallisations and continuously defies them in the name of an ever elusive and deferred future.

The openness of the concept of freedom has allowed its co-optation by ideologies and movements hostile to its essence, like those of de-regulated market capitalism or of neo-liberal law and economics. This cannot happen with equality, freedom's twin concept. Its meaning may be restricted to equality before the law or obscured as the equality of souls in God's plan of salvation, but its obvious and gross violations cannot be concealed. The huge gap between north and south, between rich and poor or, in its postmodern version, between the satisfied middle classes and the disenfranchised underclass, cannot be falsified. The life threatening consequences of poverty exemplify the fact, well-known for over a hundred years, that there can be no freedom without economic equality. The first task of freedom as liberation from oppressive determinations, is therefore to eliminate economic deprivation. Freedom not linked to equality is a chimera. Equality's work to this day, some one hundred and fifty years after the first socialists identified its internal link with freedom, is about giving a minimum of freedom to the great majority of people in the world. While their action differs, the aim of equality and freedom coincide: they are both inclined towards "the *human identity* that has yet to arrive; namely, that identity which always threatens, always glimmers like the harmony of men with the image they have of the *humanum*".[72]

This identity that is "not yet" draws its inspiration from the past and the best traditions of radical natural law. Bloch's humanism presents Marxism as the heir of rebels and reformers, who replaced faith to gods and loyalty to kings with human dignity and equality. But as reality is always incomplete and the present pregnant with future possibilities, all realism has utopia at its core. Utopia is the name for the great power of imagination which finds the future latent in every cultural product and preserves the kernel of radical enthusiasm in every ideology it criticises. Natural law, despite its many religious and reactionary formulations, emerges from this revisionist history as the unwavering passion to save the dignity of the *humanum*. While Bloch's criticisms of the illusions of "bourgeois natural law" are devastating, he concludes that "men were in agreement in the intention

[72] ibid., 167.

of freeing themselves from oppression and installing human dignity, at least since the time of the Greeks. But only this will is immutable, and not . . . 'man' and his so-called eternal right".[73]

Natural law was perfectly complemented by the great social utopias of the nineteenth century. The two share many characteristics, but they have important differences as well. More, Campanella, Bacon, Owen, Fourier and St Simon wrote their utopias casting an eye to natural law ideas. But while the natural lawyers derived their schemes of rights from axiomatic principles about human nature in a way resembling mathematical deductions and scientific proofs, the utopian imagination used narratives, images and allegories to project the future society. Natural law draws its power from the great thinkers of the past while utopias are imaginary projections of the future. More importantly, natural law aims to abolish degradation and uphold human dignity while social utopias aim to reduce suffering and promote human happiness, to bring about the *eu zein* or living well of the Greeks. Admittedly, many of these utopias were unrealistic displays of philanthropy and had no possibility of success. Bloch's principle of utopia does not coincide with the various grand places and schemes of that name. His magnum opus *The Principle of Hope* is not restricted to formal plans but encompasses under the utopian moment day-dreams and private reveries of ordinary everyday life, the apocalyptic vistas of religion and mysticism, the sublime tableaux of literature, music and art but also the fairy-tales, folk songs, carnivals and pagan traditions of popular culture. "A free-flowing utopian energy" is pursued in high and low history, "channelled into a multiplicity of forms, some reactionary, some progressive; utopianism is therefore not confined to 'the Utopia' ".[74] Utopianism is a dream of the future, fuelled by the past and immanent in the present.

Happiness and dignity have marched separately during the ages (and, we are repeatedly told, that their definite separation is also the greatest achievement of liberalism). But "there can be no human dignity without the end of misery and need, but also no human happiness without the end of old and new forms of servitude".[75] This dialectical relationship between dignity and happiness or between rights and utopia permeates the edifice of both *Principle of Hope* and *Natural Law and Human Dignity,* although the priorities seem to change, as Bloch became increasingly aware of the abuses of com-

---

[73] ibid., 191.
[74] Geoghegan, op.cit., supra n. 66, 145–6.
[75] *Natural Law and Human Dignity,* op.cit., supra n. 48, 208.

munism and a sense of melancholy started permeating his texts. But the main argument throughout his work is that the Enlightenment promise remains unfulfilled: "We are concerned with a peculiar heritage. Its best remains in abeyance and is still to be appended. What is past does not return, especially not in an out-of-date way but it can be taken at its word. It is just as urgent *suo modo* to raise the problem of a heritage of classical natural law as it is to speak of the heritage of social utopias".[76] Bloch's narrative did not involve a simple appropriation or repetition of the past. The radical impetus of natural law had been implicit, from the Stoics until early modernity, and the task, started but still incomplete, is to redeem a past not fully present to itself and re-activate moments that "remained dormant in the margins of illusionary excess".[77] For the utopianist, tradition does not follow linear time and is not a direct descent from the past. It is rather a restrospective recreation of the past reminiscent of the psychoanalytical interpretation of a contemporary symptom as the effect of an unknown but active unconscious cause. And as this past is put in the service of an undetermined future, utopia can be defined as the remembrance of the future. In this, we are reminded of the theses on history of Walter Benjamin, the other great messianic Marxist, for whom all hope lies in a memory of past defeats and resistances: "The danger affects both the content of the tradition and its receivers. The same threat hangs over both: that of becoming a tool of the ruling classes. In every era the attempt must be made anew to wrest tradition away from a conformism that is about to overpower it".[78] It is precisely this conformism which threatens human rights when they become a tool of states, governments and international organisations.

Bloch, despite his criticisms of the authoritarian tendencies of communism, remained too closely connected with the regime and did not fully appreciate how this combination of the "best traditions of natural law and social utopia" came to violate all his basic principles and hopes. But in his later work, natural law and human rights are given priority over utopia. While state law which supports oppression and domination has no place in the society of the future, human rights will be at the heart of socialism and will ensure that the "pathos of the free individual seems like a warning against any con-

---

[76] *Natural Law and Human Dignity*, op.cit., supra n. 48, xxix.

[77] David Kaufmann, "Thanks for the Memory: Bloch, Benjamin, and the Philosophy of History", in Daniel and Moylan, op.cit., supra n. 66, 41.

[78] Walter Benjamin, "Theses on the Philosophy of History", in *Illuminations* (H. Zohn trans.) (New York, Schocken, 1969) 255.

fusion or mixing up of collectivity with the herd or herd character".[79] For Bloch, the "stipend" of human rights takes the concrete
utopian form of a promise which anticipates a real humanity still to
come. "Freedom, equality, fraternity, the orthopaideia of the upright
carriage, of human pride, and of human dignity point far beyond the
horizon of the bourgeois world".[80] This "principle of hope", according to which all relations in which man is a "degraded, enslaved,
abandoned or, despised being" should be overthrown, remains as
valid today as it has even been and forms the best justification and
most effective end for human rights. But its success is not guaranteed
and the recent rhetorical triumph of human rights may be one more
instance of co-optation of natural law by the powerful for the purposes of conformist conservatism, similar to earlier theological
attempts. As the new millennium opens with a promise of satisfied
uniformity for some and oppressive domination for many, a state of
affairs not dissimilar to that of all previous temporal landmarks,
utopian hope is one of the few principles left.

[79] Ernst Bloch, *The Principle of Hope* (N. and S. Plaice and P. Knight trans.) (Oxford, Blackwell, 1986) 547.
[80] *Natural Law and Human Dignity*, op.cit., supra n. 48, 174.

8

Subjectum and Subjectus: The Free and Subjected Subject

Whether we deal with the subject in philosophy, the person in law, the agent in sociology or the self in psychology, the constitution, meaning and action of the subject is a defining characteristic of our modernity. Indeed, according to a philosophical tradition which stretches from Descartes to Kant and Heidegger, modernity is the epoch in which the world was "subjectified". Despite the indifference of jurisprudence to these matters, there can be no legal system without a legal subject, no human rights without the "human" and no morality without a responsible self and agent of choice. But there is more. If the subject is the engine and symbol of modernity, the tangible contours of its figure appeared first in legal and moral discourses. The modern subject started its journey in the annals and operations of law, as the legal subject of rights. It could not be otherwise; the subject comes to existence before the law, subjected to its norms and held responsible at its bar. Law and subject are intimately related and human rights are the paradigmatic place in which humanity, subject and the law come together. In a sense, all modern moral and legal philosophy is a long meditation on the meaning of the (legal) subject.

This Chapter turns to the question of the subject. After a brief historical introduction to the idea of humanity, we will examine, first, the philosophy of Immanuel Kant, the most advanced and still unsurpassed early defence of the centrality of the subject and of the normativity of humanity. We will then turn to three critiques of the subjective turn of modernity: first, the friendly critique of existentialism which emphasises the groundlessness of freedom and the "nothingness" of humanity. Secondly, Heidegger's ontological critique, according to which, modernity's forgetfulness of Being turns the force of humanity's endless quest for mastery and control against humanity itself. Finally, in a more political and historical direction, we will examine how the freedom of the subject, celebrated or threatening, has another side: the subject is philosophically hailed into existence as a willing and autonomous entity but its genealogy is one of subjection to law and domination by power.

I. THE AUTONOMOUS SUBJECT: KANT AND SARTRE

a. Humans and humanity

What entities are the legitimate bearers of rights? The answer appears obvious: humans, rights exist for the sake of humanity, they are the acme of humanism. And yet, if we question the self-evidence of common sense, the intellectual reasons for creating human rights instead of rights for all living beings are not clear. The idea of *humanitas* or of the human being is not self-defining or self-determining. Classical natural law and early modern definitions of rights drew their normative force from claims about what counts as characteristically human and derived their prescriptions from the nature and needs of "humanness". But their definitions of the "human" differed widely according to age, place and school of thought and, similarly, the position of humanity in the world and its relation to other beings has varied enormously in all ages. Human slaves have been excluded from humanity throughout history; in the Middle Ages, on the other hand, pigs, rats, leeches and insects accused of various crimes were formally summoned to courts of law, tried with all the pomp of due process and acquitted or convicted and punished.[1] Legal recognition has rarely followed the modern understanding of humanity and, as a result, human rights give rise to a number of difficult conceptual and ontological questions.

Can we have a concept of rights without having a definition of who or what is human? And even if we were to assume that we can answer the question of humanity, when does the existence of a human being and the associated rights begin and when does it end? What about children, the mentally or terminally ill, prisoners?[2] Are

---

[1] Jean Vartier, *Les procès des animaux du Moyen Age à nos jours* (Paris, Hachette, 1970); Luc Ferry, *The New Ecological Order* (Carol Volk trans.) (University of Chicago Press, 1992) ix–xvi.

[2] "At common law, it used to be the case that prisoners, if convicted of felonies, lost all their civil rights and liberties. They even lost the right to bring legal proceedings, so that they became, in legal terms, non-people." David Feldman, *Civil Liberties and Human Rights in England and Wales* (Oxford, Oxford University Press, 1993) 276. In a slow process, greatly

they fully human, entitled to all the rights that belong to humanity or, are they only partially human since their rights are severely restricted? Do they enjoy fewer rights because they are lesser humans or on account of some other quality? What about animals? The animal rights movement, from deep ecology and anti-vivisection militancy to its gentler green versions, has placed the legal differentiation between human and animal firmly on the political agenda and has drafted a number of Bills of animal entitlements. Important philosophical and ontological questions are involved here. At one end of the debate, rights are being promoted for those animals, like the great apes, who are genetically closest to humans.[3] The dividing line between humanity and animality is maintained but moved along. At the other deep end, the divide itself is challenged and humans are seen as one, non-privileged species in the organic continuum of the cosmos.

Companies and other non-human legal persons have been given legal rights, of course, for centuries. Christopher Stone, an American law professor, has argued that trees, parks and other natural objects too should be given rights,[4] and a French author has called for turning greenbelt zones into legal subjects with the power to go to court, through representatives, to protect their ecosystem from intrusion.[5] It appears, therefore, that legal subjectivity has not been exclusively bestowed on humans; its use as an economic strategy indicates that the distinction between humanity and its others is not strict or unchangeable. The meaning of humanity was not conclusively settled when we abandoned classical thought or settled for a weak sense of natural law *ala* Hart.[6] As Leo Strauss argued, the question of human nature has continued to "haunt modern thought and has

facilitated by decisions of the European Court of Human Rights in the seventies and eighties, prisoners have been admitted to a second class humanity. See Stephen Livingstone and Tim Owen, *Prison Law* (Oxford, Oxford University Press, 1993) particularly Chapters 3, 6 and 10.

[3] The Great Ape project, a group of scientists, philosophers and lawyers which includes among others Douglas Adams, Richard Dawkins, Jane Goodall and Peter Singer, has drawn up a list of rights for large primates and argues that chimpanzees, orang-utans and gorillas should be given rights to life, liberty and freedom from torture. Peter Singer, "Rights for chimps", *The Guardian*, 29 July 1999, 9; Peter Singer and Paola Cavalieri (eds), *The Great Ape Project: Equality before Humanity* (London, Fourth Estate, 1993).

[4] Christopher Stone, "Should Trees have Standing? Towards Legal Rights for Natural Objects", 1972 *Southern California Law Review*.

[5] Marie-Angèle Hermitte, "Le concept de diversité biologique et la création d'un status de la nature" in *L'homme, la nature, le droit* (Paris, Bourgeois, 1988).

[6] H.L.A. Hart, *The Concept of Law* (Oxford, Clarendon) 189–94.

become more complicated as a result of the contradictions engendered by positive science and historicism".[7] But how did we arrive at the modern concept of human nature and humanity?

Premodern societies did not develop ideas of freedom or individuality. Both Athens and Rome had citizens but not "men", in the sense of members of the human species. The *societas generi humani* was absent from the *agora* and the *forum*. Free men were Athenians or Spartans, Romans or Carthaginians but not persons; they were Greeks or barbarians but not humans. The word *humanitas* appeared for the first time in the Roman Republic. It was a translation of *paideia*, the Greek word for education and cultivation, *eruditio et institutio in bona artes* (scholarship and training in good conduct). The Romans inherited the idea of humanity from Hellenistic philosophy, in particular Stoicism, and used it to distinguish between the *homo humanus*, the educated Roman and *homo barbarus*. The first humanism was the result of the encounter between Greek and Roman civilisation and the early modern humanism of the Italian Renaissance retained these characteristics. It was presented as a return to Greek and Roman prototypes and was aimed at the barbarism of medieval scholasticism and the gothic north.

A different conception of *humanitas* emerged in Christian theology, superbly captured in the Pauline assertion, that there is no Greek or Jew, free man or slave. All men are equally part of spiritual humanity which was subjected and juxtaposed to deity. They can all be saved through God's plan of salvation and enjoy eternal life in the true city of heaven. If for classical humanism, man is a *zoon logon echon* or *animal rationale*, for Christian metaphysics, man is the vessel of the soul. Only humans, not animals, trees or spirits, possess an immortal soul, only humans can be saved in Christ. To be sure, this spiritual universalism was accompanied by a strict political and social hierarchy. During the Middle Ages, the only subject was the king, God's representative on earth. But the religious grounding of humanity was undermined by the liberal political philosophies of early modernity. The foundation of humanity was transferred from God to (human) nature and equality was re-defined as political, in a process which strengthened the intellectual trend and the popular determination to recognise the centrality of individuality. This was the most dramatic effect of the Enlightenment. By the end of the eighteenth century, the concept of "man" had become the absolute and inalienable value

[7] Claude Lefort, *The Political Forms of Modern Society* (John Thompson ed.) (Cambridge, Polity, 1986) 240.

around which the whole world revolved. Humanity, man as species existence, entered the historical stage as the peculiar combination of classical and Christian metaphysics.

Humanism believes that there is a universal essence of man and that this essence belongs and is the attribute of each individual who is the real, empirical subject.[8] As species existence, man appears without differentiation or distinction in his nakedness and simplicity, united with all others in an empty nature deprived of substantive characteristics. This is the man of the rights of man, an abstraction that has as little humanity as possible, since he has jettisoned all those traits and qualities that build human identity. A minimum of humanity is what allows man to claim autonomy, moral responsibility and legal subjectivity. Man enters the historical scene by philosophically severing his ties with family, community, kinship and nature and by turning his creativity and wrath against tradition and prejudice, all that created, nourished and protected him in the past. The universal man of the declarations is an unencumbered man, human, all too human. His soul unites with all others in Christ and his ontological minimalism links him to humanity philosophically. As species existence, all men are equal, because they share equally soul and reason, the *differentia specifica* between humans and others. But, as we saw, this equality, the most radical element of the declarations, applied only to the abstract man of species existence and his institutional foil, the legal subject. It had limited value for non-proper men (that is men of no property) even less for women and was denied altogether to those defined as non-humans (slaves, colonials and foreigners).

By the middle of the nineteenth century and after the abolition of slavery, humanity reached its final modern formulation in juxtaposition to the non-human world of animals and objects. But the "non-human vermin" of the concentration camps, the potential of world annihilation of nuclear weapons and recent developments in genetic technology and robotics, indicate that even this most banal and obvious of definitions is not definite and conclusive. Humanity's mastery, like God's omnipotence, includes the ability to re-define who or what counts as human and even to destroy itself. From Aristotle's slaves to cyborgs and Blade Runner, the boundaries of humanity have

[8] "If the essence of man is to be a universal attribute, it is essential that *concrete subjects* exist as absolute givens; this implies an empiricism of the subject. If these empirical individuals are to be men, it is essential that each carries in himself the whole human essence, if not in fact, at least in principle; this implies an idealism of the *essence*. So empiricism of the subject implies idealism of the essence and vice versa." Louis Althusser, *For Marx* (B. Brewster trans.) (London, Allen Lane, 1969) 228.

been shifting. These shifts can be traced in the history of the legal institution. What history has taught us is that there is nothing sacred about any definition of humanity and nothing eternal about its scope. Humanity cannot act as an *a priori* normative principle and is mute in the matter of legal and moral rules. Its function lies not in a philosophical essence but in its non-essence, in the endless process of re-definition and the continuous but impossible attempt to escape fate and external determination.

b. Kant and the autonomous modern subject

Critics and defenders of modernity agree that the modern age is one of endless dynamism and ceaseless innovation, of continuous leaps of imagination, triumphs of science and technological breakthroughs. No limits seem to restrain humanity's ability to assert its power over nature and continuously rewrite the boundaries of the world. Genetic technology promises to deliver us from illness, adversity and even death. The vicarious, metaphorical immortality of physical and intellectual procreation is about to be overtaken, we are told, by the literal eternity of cloning and cryonics. According to the prophets of the new millennium, our civilisation which placed its greatest premium on production and consumption seems on the verge of overcoming scarcity and the associated economic, generational, ethnic and political conflicts. What lies behind this endless expansion of human creativity and the attendant and ceaseless extension of domination over the world? The transition to modernity, in philosophy, ethics and aesthetics was long and tortuous.[9] But what were the philosophical presuppositions of the subjective turn of modernity and of the rights revolution? What is the essence of modern man or, in Kantian terms, "what is man"?

This is a preliminary issue to our main concern, the question of the legal subject. We will follow the birth of the subject in the critical philosophy of Kant, starting with the faculty of theoretical reason. In the premodern world, truth was given in divine revelation or it consisted in the adequation between a thing and its man-made image.

9 Ernst Cassirer, *The Philosophy of the Enlightenment* (F.C.A. Koelln and J.P. Pettegrove trans.) (Princeton NJ, Princeton University Press, 1968); Martin Heidegger, *Being and Time* (New York, Harper and Row, 1962); Costas Douzinas and Ronnie Warrington with Shaun McVeigh, *Postmodern Jurisprudence: The Law of Text in the Texts of Law* (Edinburgh, Edinburgh University Press, 1991) Chapters 1 and 2; Richard Kearny, *The Wake of Imagination* (London, Hutchinson, 1988); Agnes Heller, *Beyond Justice* (Oxford, Blackwell, 1987).

Descartes was the first to argue that the phenomenal world should be approached on the analogy of the subject's self-understanding. Thinking not only established the certainty and centrality of the subject, but also turned the world into an object, set before the subject as target of representation, cognition and intervention. After Descartes, philosophy became a meditation on the subject and its relationship with its opposite, the object. My relation to the world is based on my understanding of myself over time. The world was thus reduced to its representation, in Heidegger's phrase, it became a "world picture" and man the centre of everything that is.

But it was Kant's theoretical anthropology which finally reversed the relationship between nature and humanity. Kant's first contribution was to systematise the Cartesian revolution and make experience and theory prerogatives of the subject. The subject is the "thinking thing", that which thinks in its capacity of thinking, and in its thinking relation with the object of thought. According to Kant's principle of apperception, the manifold sensations and representations that bombard us can be synthesised and make the world appear, insofar as they belong to a subject. The thinking "I" lies behind and organises these otherwise chaotic perceptions and, in doing so, it becomes conscious of itself. I, the subject, am the being who can both organise and doubt the perceptions of the outside world and, insofar as I have doubts, it cannot be doubted that I exist. The subject possesses consciousness, conscience and language and is present and transparent to itself. Intentionality, self-understanding and freedom are all attributes of the coincidence of self with itself. In Cartesian terms, behind every *cogito* there is an *ego*, "the apodictically certain and last basis of judgment upon which all radical philosophy must be grounded".[10]

After Kant's epistemological revolution, the real follows the laws of rationality and a perfect correspondence is declared to exist between the principles governing the human mind and the world. Truth expresses a new certainty conquered through the examination of the contents of human consciousness and knowledge. All truth originates and exists in man and, as a result of this cognitive revolution, the complete understanding and mastery of the world becomes possible. Leibniz claimed that *nihil est sine ratione,* that the principle of reason, this most human of faculties, applies fully and animates the world. This claim was ontologised and radicalised by Hegel who, by identifying the ideal and rational with reality, proposed a principle of

---

[10] Edmund Husserl, *The Paris Lectures* (The Hague, Nijhoff, 1964) 7.

radical unity between the two. But the necessary precondition was the discovery of subjectivity and its elevation to cosmic principle. Hegel used to shout excitedly to his students that modern philosophy arrived only when man was conceived as subject.

Classical thought made nature a critical principle independent of man's will and superior to his institutions and customs. Now nature was reduced to inert matter, deprived of values, a meaningless and purposeless chaos which man can conquer and control by discovering in it regularities, patterns and laws. Subject and object, freedom and necessity, will and proscription are the twin outcomes of the same process which turned the human being into subject and ground of being and the world into an object and picture for the subject. Their history from that point is irrevocably both separated and linked. The link is man's *ratio*, which in clear and concise ideas, numbers, concepts and categories, describes and orders the world. Man and the world no longer exist side-by-side in a wider universe. The idea of nature as standard is lost but, as compensation, man can now treat nature, including social and human nature, as artefacts and impose order and change on them. Torn from the natural habitat of the premodern world, deprived of the limited certainties of existence, humanity embarks in an endless quest for fulfilment, its essence the continuous invention of new worlds.

But the subject is not just a rational entity, it is also a being of will. Its relation to the world is both cognitive and active. Modern will is always directed towards an outside; action projects the sovereign self in its orientation towards others and in its work, which bestows value on nature. The power of will is unique; it is no longer slotted in the natural world, it springs neither from emotions nor from pure intelligence but follows the subject's desires and interests. Descartes described it as the same in us as it is in God. Modern will knows no theoretical but only empirical limits. It is the absolute power of choice, an indivisible sovereignty of the self. This power finds its perfect expression in decision. In making a decision, the self becomes agent, an autonomous and responsible subject, whose mark is found in his external manifestations, those actions that can be imputed on him. Without free will, there can be no self or subject and, without an agent, there can be no free action. "There can be no agent without this power that links the action to the subject who decides upon it and thereby assumes full responsibility for it".[11]

[11] J.P. Vernant and P. Vidal-Naquet, *Myth and Tragedy in Ancient Greece* (New York, Zone Books, 1990) 50.

In the classical period, the good and justice coincided as did moral judgment and political action.[12] In these conditions, ethical conflict inevitably took tragic dimensions and created Antigones. But with freedom the main aspiration and achievement of modernity and subjectivity its ontological corollary, the modern subject becomes free to decide what is good for himself and, his actions cannot be restricted to the unquestioning application of norms and rules. Modern conscience and will become legislative: subjects can now examine the rules themselves and can reject and replace them. And while the classical link between society and citizen remains, its content changes radically: legislative will can no longer refer to a consensual horizon of shared purposes and must, for the first time, construct the "good" almost *ex nihilo* on two conditions: it must be acceptable to the newly emancipated bourgeois but additionally it must have the ability to shape the virtuous citizen of the modern state. Freedom, reason and morality must be combined against a background of a polyphony of values. Theoretical anthropology must be supplemented with a practical side.

The conundrum of a freed will that must find its limitation in itself found its almost perfect solution in the practical philosophy of Kant, who brought together subject and object under the reign of reason. Kant's *Critique of Practical Reason* is the foundation of modern jurisprudence.[13] Kant set out to deduce the (moral) law in the same way that he arrived at the principles of knowledge in the first *Critique*. His starting point was the experience of personal, social and intellectual fragmentation of early modernity and his interest was both philosophical and political. He wanted to show how freedom and reason are inseparable in their common concern to enlighten man and release him from his self-incurred tutelage, his "inability to make use of his understanding without direction from another".[14] Reason accordingly has two forms. In the theoretical domain the subject acquires knowledge by using *a priori* forms of intuition (space and time) and categories of understanding (identity/difference, cause/effect, necessity/contingency, substance/accident) to construct the manifold data of experience as coherent and unified. Practical reason, on the other hand, helps unite the personality by subjecting conflicting inclinations and desires to an *a priori* moral law. In this sense, reason acts as the principle that unites the subject and the world.

[12] Douzinas and Warrington, *Justice Miscarried* (Edinburgh University Press, 1994) Chapter 4.
[13] Immanuel Kant, *Critique of Practical Reason* (London, Macmillan, 1956).
[14] ibid., 3.

But moral reason is fundamentally different from its theoretical version. The theoretical meta-language of science – the principles of causality and non-contradiction – is the same with that used for first-order observation (a scientist uses the same form of language for experimentation, for example, and for expressing axioms and hypotheses). With the moral law, however, no simple homology exists. A defining dissymmetry separates prescriptive from constative statements. In ethics, the language of facts, commands and proscriptions ("You must X") and the meta-language of norms and rules ("It is decreed that in circumstances Y, persons of type Z should X") are not isomorphic. As a result, knowledge cannot be the basis of moral judgments and action nor can principles of law be extracted from the examination of particular commands. Furthermore, as the good is no longer given and cannot be derived from experience, moral judgments are not emotional reactions to perceptions and empirical properties. Moral law does not follow causality; on the contrary, morality is the cause of acts. What is moral law's status then? In a move that resembles the operations of aesthetics in the *Critique of Judgment*, Kant deduces the law by analogy, *as if* it were a fact of nature amenable to reason, as if it were a "universal law of nature". The law exists but cannot be derived from other sources or statements. It is a "fact of reason" and not of experience, and freedom is the result of its operation.

These ideas give Kantian practical philosophy its revolutionary character. Morality is no longer grounded in a pre-existing idea of the good nor does it derive from an external source. Classical philosophy made the mistake, Kant believed, of positing first good and evil and then fashioning the moral law accordingly. "The ancients openly revealed this error by devoting their ethical investigation entirely to the definition of the concept of the highest good and thus posited an object which they intend subsequently to make the determining ground of the will in the moral law".[15] But in so doing "their fundamental principle was always heteronomy, and they came inevitably to empirical conditions for a moral law".[16] Kant reversed the procedure; it is not the concept of the good that posits the law but the moral law which defines good and evil. The universal preconditions of moral action are discovered in the free and rational action of the autonomous agent, who follows the law of the categorical imperative without any incentive, except for a pure sense of duty and respect:

[15] ibid., 66–7.
[16] ibid., 66.

"Act in such a way that the maxim of your will can always be valid as the principle establishing universal law",[17] in other words, whenever you face a moral choice, act according to a principle which is universally applicable without contradiction to all similar situations. Its Christian debt is apparent in another of its many formulations: "act so that you treat humanity, whether in your person or in that of an other, always as an end".[18]

This law is rather strange: it is imperative (act in such a way . . .) but its command is to follow a pure form, that of legality (the principle of the action should be always valid, in the form of a universal norm). The categorical imperative asks me to act as if the maxim of my will can become a principle of universal legislation. The law commands to follow a pure form, that of universality, declared to be the essence of practical reason. But while the law forces and obligates the will, it emanates from it. The moral will is free because it finds all its determinations in itself; the subject becomes the willing legislator of its own subjection. But the moral law hurts; following its injunction to universalise means abandoning individual feelings, passions and desires and acting totally disinterestedly, out of a pure sense of duty. Kantian autonomy makes modern man the law's *subject* in a double sense: he is the legislator, the subject who gives the law and the legal subject, subjected to the law on condition that he has participated in its legislation. And again as a quasi-law of nature, the moral law appears as both regularity, the universal interconnection of things, and as a purposeful order in the tradition of natural law.

The recognition of will's involvement in action is a typically modern move and distinguishes pure from practical reason. Furthermore, the pronouncement of self as both law-giver and subject marks the inauguration of the modern conception of autonomy or self-determination, the other side of will's enthronement. The moral law gives the subject his freedom. The moral subject is autonomous while the non-moral, including the legal subject, by taking its law from outside, is heteronomous. Freedom as autonomy is the gift of subjectivity and the essence of man is to be a subject both *de jure* (as the addressee and representative of the moral law) and *de facto* (as its legislator).

When Kant turns to the theory of state, he sees the social contract not as a historical covenant but as the cause and effect of pure reason. All previous versions of the contract had included references to those

---

[17] ibid., 30.
[18] ibid., 47.

characteristics and drives the theorist considered as natural and from which reason drew its principles. For Kant, all such empirical impurities must be removed as methodologically unacceptable and morally wrong. As a result, the contract becomes a regulative fiction, according to which the state should be treated as if it were its product. Its presiding principle is that "justice is the limitation of the freedom of each person in such a way that it accords with that of everyone else, insofar as this is possible according to a universal law; and public law is the aggregate of the external laws that make possible such a thoroughgoing agreement".[19] Justice commands the legislator to introduce laws, as if they had been legislated by the people and to determine their content under the principle of universality. But the logical principles of necessity and non-contradiction can support any content whatsoever, as Hegel forcefully argued *contra* Kant. The logical necessity of a proposition says nothing about its empirical substance or moral worth.

Autonomous morality and heteronomous legality were initially strictly separated. But the division was soon weakened as both were made to follow pure reason and were similarly unconcerned about the empirical characteristics of the people they are supposed to guide. A strong sense of duty and respect for the law became equally important for both morality and legality; moral action follows the universal law of reason, legality is obedience to the laws of the state. But only those maxims, rules and norms that meet the criteria of universality are morally binding, since all others are contradictory. Nature, the concept which since classical Greece acted as a standard of critique, dissolved into reason and its formal commands, and into state law and its sanctions. But a moral will, which was totally disassociated from passions and bodily desires, could not motivate even the pious burghers of Kant's Prussia and its rigour was perforce displaced onto legality. The laws of the autocratic Prussian State, Kant argued, meet the formal criteria of legality, while the right to pardon is the most obscene of all laws because "if legal justice perishes, then it is no longer worthwhile for men to live on earth".[20] In this way, absolute moral autonomy became the mask of total heteronomy and the free will of the subject was underpinned by the gallows.[21] Formality, as

---

[19] Kant, *Works* (12 vols) (Frankfurt am Main, Suhrkamp, 1977) VI, 332.

[20] Kant, ibid. VII, 150.

[21] "Even if a civil society were to dissolve itself by common agreement of all its members . . . the last murderer remaining in prison must first be executed, so that everyone will come to know what his actions are worth and so that the blood guilt of those actions will

rule formalism or as proceduralism, will become from now on the moral component of positive law. All the main oppositions of the jurisprudence of modernity were inaugurated by Kant: legality and morality, form and substance, validity and value, norm and fact.

The Kantian revolution transferred the foundation of meaning and the ground of law from the divine and transcendent to the human and social. Moral law is granted to us before we can start questioning its nature or operation and binds us immediately and absolutely. But this radical first step comes to an end in the assertion that we live in a totalisable community of reason. The command to follow principles that would be acceptable and willed by all rational people assumes that the desires and actions of the self are compatible and coherent with those of all others. Kantian practical philosophy brings together reason, freedom and the law on the body of the modern subject; but morality has become exclusively obedience to the law, and the exclusion of passions and desires from rule-following makes the reconciliation too perfect philosophically and totally unrealistic practically. The (moral) law appeals for its operation to the horizon of a universal community which should act as a regulative principle. But such community does not exist empirically and its excessive formalism cannot make it a normative value either. The limited usefulness of the concept has become apparent in the international human rights law, where it acts as a rationalising and legitimising device for state laws largely devoid of ethical content.

We can conclude that the essence of subjectivity is free will. Kant's re-interpretation of the Cartesian "I think" as the moral "I want" and his insistence on autonomy as self-legislation provided the philosophical and moral basis for the ascendancy of rights and the public recognition of individual desire. At the same time, the enthronement of the subject prepared the ground for the infinite manipulation of the natural, social and psychic worlds. Before modernity, will was subordinated to the ends it was supposed to pursue within the teleological scheme of the world. In Kant, practical reason wills itself as freedom; reason as pure will is the completion of the being of will which, unconditioned and absolute, became a will to will.

---

not be fixed upon the people because they failed to insist on carrying out the punishment; for if they fail to do so, they may be regarded as accomplishes of this public violation of legal justice". Ibid., 151.

c. The nothingness of human nature

The philosophical invention of nature in Greece was an act of rebellion against religion, customs and the tradition of the ancestors. Classical philosophy defined the nature of an entity as both its essence and its end and, in this sense, nature was a "thick" concept. It placed the entity on a clear life trajectory and determined what steps were necessary for maturing into a perfect specimen of its kind. Human nature, too, was teleologically determined and multiform; it differed from person to person across social hierarchies and roles and slotted people into distinct positions which endowed them with highly differentiated characteristics: free men and women, slaves, foreigners and *metoikoi*, philosophers, soldiers and cobblers all had different aims, duties and virtues. Early modern natural law, influenced by Stoicism and Christian spiritual universalism, amended this highly differentiated ontology and developed the idea of species existence, of a common human nature that unites all people, irrespective of their individual characteristics and cultural or social determinations. For Hobbes or Locke, Descartes or Voltaire, men share a common humanity which gives all empirical men the same essential needs and characteristics, even though their specific content differs according to the theorist. Each person is an individual application of the universal man; human essence comes before existence.

The displacement of traditional ontology from manifold ends and natures to a common humanity was challenged and developed early on by a nascent philosophical approach, which characterised modernity by the priority of freedom over nature and of law over fact and, in this sense, was a radical version of Kantian morality. Rousseau, for example, believed that after the withdrawal of classical teleology, the emerging new man was defined by the tendency to perfectibility and by his groundless freedom, the capacity to tear himself away from natural and historical determinations, to migrate and leave behind hearth, home or *patria*, and to discard the call of nature. As the closed universe of the ancients retreated before the open world of the moderns, man lost his assigned place and function and his nature could no longer dictate his mission. At that point, freedom was enthroned as the master and tormentor of the moderns. Rousseau found freedom at its most imperious, when it acted against nature and instinct:

> [The beast] chooses or rejects by instinct and [man] by an act of freedom, so that a beast cannot deviate from the rule that is prescribed to

it even when it would be advantageous for it to do so, and a man devi-
ates from it often to his detriment. A pigeon would die of hunger near
a basin filled with the best meats. And a cat upon heaps of fruits or
grain, although each could very well nourish itself on the food it dis-
dains if it made up its mind to try some. Thus dissolute men abandon
themselves to excesses which cause them fever and death, because the
mind depraves the senses and because the will still speaks when the
nature is silent.[22]

Moral anti-naturalism has been a persistent undercurrent of modern philosophy. For Kant, moral attitudes and actions are disinterested. While I can act in conformity with heteronomous state law out
of interest, out of fear of sanctions for example, moral action is motivated exclusively by respect for the moral law which demands that
needs, passions and interests are set aside. Good will is moral will and
virtue is not the perfection of natural talents but a struggle against natural inclinations and sensual interests. Freud, too, argued that civilisation is an attempt to negate sexual desires and drives and both he
and his follower Lacan found in Kant's sadistic renunciation of the
flesh a typical expression of modernity.[23] Finally, in the Jewish tradition, it is the law that sustains the community, often against the
demands of nature or reason. To be just, the Jew must obey the law
without any reason or justification. For Martin Buber, Jews act in
order to understand, while Emmanuel Levinas denounces the Greek
or Western "temptation of temptation", the demand to subordinate
action to knowledge and thus overcome the "purity" of obedience
to the law.[24] As a liberal philosopher put it, man is "indetermination
par excellence: he is so oblivious to nature it can cost him his life.
Man is free enough to die of freedom . . . *Optima videre, deteriora
sequor*. Seeing the best, he can choose the worst: this is the motto of
the antinatural creature . . . His *humanitas* resides in his freedom, in
the fact that he is undefined, that his nature is . . . to possess the capacity to distance himself from any code within which one may seek to
imprison him".[25]

---

[22] Jean-Jacques Rousseau, *The First and Second Discourse* (R. and J. Masters trans.) (New York, St. Martin's Press, 1964) 5.

[23] Jacques Lacan, "Kant avec Sade", 51 *October* (Winter 1989), 55–75; Costas Douzinas, "Law's Birth Antigone's Death: on Ontological and Psychoanalytical Ethics", 16 *Cardozo Law Review*, 1325–62, 1995; Douzinas, "Deathbound Legality" in D. Manderson (ed.), *Courting Death* (London, Pluto, 1999).

[24] Douzinas and Warrington, Justice Miscarried, supra n. 12, Chapter 4.

[25] Luc Ferry, *The New Ecological Order* (C. Volk trans.) (Chicago, University of Chicago Press, 1992) 5.

From a different perspective, Nietzsche declared that the superior man is his own creator; he finds in himself the source of all meaning, truth and responsibility. Authentic creativity is achieved by leaving behind social constraints and moral determinations and by creating a new law for oneself that derives from the impulse to obey, not God or any other authority but, the highest commandment of self-affirming will positing its own laws. But the most striking contemporary presentation of existential freedom is found in the early work of Jean-Paul Sartre. Sartre identified humanism with existentialism, in a famous article, and throughout his oeuvre reversed the philosophical priority of essence over existence.[26] Existence precedes essence; a human person starts as nothing, a degree zero, and constructs himself through his choices and actions. Man first exists and acts on the world and only in a second stage defines himself and his nature. Against ontological essentialism, Sartre argued that the main characteristic of human nature is not its historical, cultural or social determinations, but its ability to break away from any given codes, traditions and other social burdens. The nature of humans is to have no intrinsic nature, other than what they make of themselves; human essence is nothingness, the absence of all essence.

This radical emptiness means that no *a priori* values or conceptions of the good can be found in history, religion or tradition. When Dostoievsky wrote, in *Notes from the Underground,* that "if God did not exist, everything would be permitted", he predicted the value system of existentialism.[27] But according to Sartre, self-legislation, although deprived of the unworkable Kantian self-discipline, does not lead to nihilism. Man must choose his own values, he is the legislator of his own morality and, in this sense, his responsibility is extreme. Neither past values nor hopes of the future can explain or excuse our actions: "We are left alone, without excuse. That is what I mean when I say that man is condemned to be free. Condemned, because he did not create himself, yet is nevertheless at liberty, and from the moment that he is thrown in this world he is responsible for everything he does".[28] No moral rule can guide this choice and no laws can replace the responsibility of decision which is at the same time an invention of self. The ultimate criterion is whether one's judgments and actions promote freedom of choice and responsibility

---

[26] Jean-Paul Sartre, *Existentialism and Humanism* (P. Mairet trans.) (London, Methuen, 1980).

[27] ibid., 33.

[28] ibid., 34

for oneself and for others. Man is always "outside of himself: it is in projecting and losing himself beyond himself that he makes man exist; and, on the other hand, it is by pursuing transcendent aims that he himself is able to exist. Since man is thus self-surpassing, and can grasp objects only in relation to his self-surpassing, he is himself the heart and centre of his transcendence".[29] This transcendence, which constitutes identity through its self-overtaking, is what Sartre calls "existential humanism". In the Heideggerian idiom, existence comes from ek-sistence, it is the ability to break away, to "wrench oneself free of codes".[30]

If existential freedom is the main human characteristic, human nature cannot be reduced to its biological, psychological and social determinations. Undoubtedly, environmental conditions and limitations cannot be totally discarded and existential will cannot overturn or abolish them. But while such limitations may be objectively given and unavoidable, they have also a subjective aspect: determinations survive in people's lives and fate dictates only if not challenged. Oedipus could have chosen not to search for the murderer of Laius, but once he chose to do so, he defined himself freely according to destiny. To put it differently, while many environmental factors define our existence, our own choice decides whether to live through them or reject them. But certain choices are inauthentic because they deny existential freedom. This is the case when a partial characteristic, such as race, nation, gender or tribe, is defined as the essence of belonging to humanity and privileges those who possess it against others who do not. In this sense, while one can choose to be racist, sexist, nationalist or tribal, by doing so he prioritises − a false − essence over existence and naturalises belonging over freedom.

This absolute freedom of self-creation should not lead to individualism and selfishness. Sartre argued, against Descartes and Kant, that the person who recognises herself in the *cogito*, discovers in the same act that all others are the necessary precondition of her existence. The other is a freedom confronting me and it is only through this encounter that I achieve my own subjectivity and self-knowledge. We open to the world of freedom by finding ourselves in the company of others and the realm of the universal. But this universal is not the categorical law or catholic reason but the freedom of nothingness,

[29] ibid., 55.
[30] Luc Ferry and Alain Renaut, *Heidegger and Modernity* (F. Philip trans.) (Chicago, University of Chicago Press, 1990) 4.

the *differentia specifica*, which enables humanity to break free from conditions and limitations. The only universal experience is the act of departing from the known and constricting and, as such, it can be communicated across cultural and historical divides. Existential freedom denies, resists and, only when defeated, accommodates environmental limitations and constraints. While these constraints differ in time and place, the force and violence of external determinations is universally understood and breaking free from them universally valued. In this sense, universality is not something given as fact or law, but is continuously made, in the act of choosing oneself and of understanding others. The universality of nothingness ceaselessly destroys the customary and traditional and opens new horizons and vistas in communication with others. Breaking away, the ability to fashion oneself freely and to understand the other as equal freedom are the two aspects of the universal.

Existentialism as a philosophical tradition lies behind Hegel's dialectics and Heidegger's ontology. Its emphasis on radical freedom sounds at times naive and at others anarchic, and this has not endeared it to legal theorists and jurists. Yet, existentialism could help us re-situate the appeal to human nature and universal principles of human rights without losing the valuable critiques of the Kantian abstractions, by the likes of Burke and Marx. Existential freedom is the ability of modern man to transcend the constraints of nature and of second nature: those historical and cultural determinations which often ossify into nature-like external impositions. The groundless freedom of the declarations points in the same direction, in which the shaping of self and the world has priority over any essential, past or established characteristics. Existentialism seems to capture an aspect of the human rights declarations forgotten by liberal philosophy after its political victory. It retains the critical uses of human nature against authority, but totally empties it of any essential determination except for its groundless but potent freedom. Human rights declarations represent this power of nothingness, of a nature *contra* nature and a universalism of detachment from historical constraints and cultural encumbrances. In this sense, human rights belong to the radical tradition of natural law, for which nature represented the rebellion against law and tradition. As Ferry puts it, "if we did not have the ability to detach ourselves from the traditional culture that is imposed upon us like a second nature, we would continue, like all animals, *to be governed by natural codes* . . . Tradition, reduced to the pure and simple transmission of the past, would be merely the *instinct* peculiar to the human species, just as programmatic as it is in the other animal species".[31]

We can conclude, that the man without determination is a fiction, a philosophical trope, justly attacked, by Burke and Marx, when it first entered the world. Existential self-creation was not part of the rich philosophical language of the eighteenth century. While we can use it today to explain partially the project of self-foundation of modernity, existentialism's enthusiasms underestimate the social constraints, historical determinations and conscious and unconscious structures which have succeeded classical *fortuna* in shaping modern subjectivity. But the negative universality of the "degree-zero" man carries a powerful sense of reform and rebellion, almost totally lost in the anaemic version of the abstract "man" of liberal philosophy. One of the tangible effects of the human rights declarations was to place openness at the heart of politics and to shatter the corporeal symbolisation of society. "The rights of man reduce right to a basis which, despite its name, is without shape, is given as interior to itself and, for this reason, eludes all power which would claim to take hold of it".[32] No formulation given to human rights, universal or particular, Kantian or Burkean can become definitive and unquestionable. But this universalism has no relation with that of liberal enthusiasts for Western principles and european "human" values. Its defiance of tradition and its negation of reified constraints applies equally to the local cultures of relativists and to the universal laws of the arrogant orthodoxy of globalised humanity. The escape from either may be impossible perhaps; Icarus may be deluded or doomed. But it is only in planning a line of flight and dreaming of the beauty of the sun that he can understand the beastliness of the Minotaur.

II. THE HOMELESS SUBJECT: HEIDEGGER'S ONTOLOGICAL CRITIQUE

Martin Heidegger, one of the most powerful existential interpreters of modernity, accepted the accuracy of the Kantian description. Ours is the epoch of the autonomous subject, of the self emancipated from the medieval order to remake the world in its own image. Modernity is marked by ceaseless and even aimless self-assertion, its project is to increase infinitely the power of the subject. Man becomes the

[31] Ferry, op.cit., *The New Ecological Order*, fn. 25, 11.
[32] Lefort, op.cit., supra n. 7, 258.

grounding principle, master of the world and measure of all things both in theory and in practical life.[33] But this is not cause for celebration because the will to will of modern man is not authentic. It conceals a deep existential insecurity, a desire to master Being as a whole and make it permanently and definitely present. The subjective turn of modernity gives Heidegger the opportunity to reflect on the way in which metaphysical thought has waylaid humanity from its primordial destiny of "caring for Being". Modern megalomania is the sign of a new epoch in the history of metaphysics. But what is metaphysics?

Metaphysics – *meta ta physica* or beyond nature – is a way of thinking about what lies beyond the sensible and immediate experience of things. Metaphysics believes in the existence of an ideal, transcendent world over against which everyday reality must measure itself. In our ordinary lives, we are immersed in streams of unrelated, incoherent, criss-crossing streams of people, events and emotions which invade our world in unpredictable and uncontrollable ways. Behind metaphysics lies a simple and urgent desire: to make sense of the disorder that surrounds us, to master finitude. The foundation of metaphysics was laid in classical Greece. The great philosophers, from Anaximander to Plato, claimed that the world of the senses was an external only appearance, while the other world, which could be reached only through the mind, was the true one. Plato completed the reversal between the sensible and the intelligible: the phenomenal world is only a series of shadows on the dark wall of a cave, while the world of ideas and forms is the sunlit empire of true reality. The supra-sensible domain, unlike chaotic nature, is united, harmonious and coherent. Phenomena and appearances are many, but the truth is one and can be approached through reason or *logos*, truth's cause and effect. Reason is the origin of causation and, metaphysics the knowledge of first causes and the exploration of essences. The philosopher's task, therefore, is to guide us to this ideal world, in which the reason of things that "rule the world" resides (Anaxagoras). The metaphysical urge creates ideal, unified and logically harmonious worlds and calls them reality.

Properly metaphysical concepts do not have immediate purchase upon the phenomenal world. The main characteristic of metaphysical systems, of materialism or idealism, being or nothingness, the finite and the infinite, is that they follow their own internal logic and

---

[33] Ferry and Renaut, op.cit., supra n. 30, 42–3.

build their propositions from the pure and necessary interconnections between their founding axioms. Consider, for example, the Kantian critical revolution in ethics and the philosophy of right. Kant abandoned the attempts of earlier natural lawyers to derive right from some empirically given datum, like the need for security (Hobbes), the urge to sociability (Grotius) or individual freedom (Rousseau). For Kant, human nature and freedom are not empirical realities but pure concepts, constructions of an empirically uncontaminated thought and, only as such can they become the basis for the derivation of right. This way the social contract loses its rather precarious claim to historical reality and becomes a regulative concept. Everything that happens in the state happens, as if the state was based on a social contract and as if the legislator acted as the representative of all citizens. But while this regulative principle may be sufficient for inward-looking morality, legality needs an added external idea to arbitrate over the vacuity of the imperative. This is provided by the principle of co-existence under which the freedom of each is to be limited so as to provide the same freedom to everyone else, according to universal law. This purely formal imperative, even when coupled with the principle of non-contradiction, cannot give content to law. A metaphysical philosophy of right as much as ethics is empty of any substance and its norms are purely formal propositions.

According to Heidegger, the main metaphysical urge is to ask "what" questions: what is an entity, what is its essence, what it means for a being to be such. Once this type of question has become the leading concern of philosophy, its strategy is to offer a number of determinations or theses about the meaning and truth of Being or of the being of an entity, to pronounce a series of "words for being". The metaphysical operation thinks through principles, asserts the primacy of a value or origin, and then proceeds to arrange all entities and experiences, according to their distance from that *arche*. The principle is assumed to exist beyond language and signification, to be immediate and immediately present to consciousness. This way, unity is privileged over plurality and sameness over difference. Aristotle, an early metaphysician, called this ground *hypokeimenon*, "that which lies under": it is the substance or essence of which all other entities are predicated but which is itself not predicated of anything else.[34] The Latin *subjectum* or substratum translated the Greek

---

[34] Simon Critchley, "Prolegomena to any Post-Deconstrucive Subjectivity" and Ute Guzzoni, "Do we still want to be Subjects?" in S. Critchley and P. Dews (eds), *Deconstructive Subjectivities* (New York, S.U.N.Y. Press, 1996) 13–46 and 201–16.

hypokeimenon and became the word for the foundation, the ground-ing principle.[35] The subjectum is the subject of predication, that which is thrown under and persists through time, the matter or con-tent upon which form imposes type and change. It has the qualities of stance and stability, of permanent presence and of an unchanging relation with itself. Many names have been given to this origin and ultimate value in the history of metaphysics: essence, substance, the good, God, belatedly Man, reason, truth. They are the epochal names for Being, intangible ideas and bloodless principles, seen as always present in beings. Metaphysics has developed by inventing and sys-tematising these metaphors for presence and order. In this process, Being is reduced to a word or meaning while temporal becoming turns into atemporal but intangible presence. These characteristics make metaphysics a type of knowledge obsessed with mastery and control. Positing an ideal meta-being and measuring everything against its transcendent principles is an attempt to manipulate the world.

The modern epoch was announced by Descartes whose *cogito ergo sum* removed the metaphysical foundation or underlying ground from (Aristotelian) substance (Platonic) form or (Christian) God and placed it on humanity understood as subject. Metaphysics was always attached to the *subjectum*, the ultimate foundation or Being of beings. According to Heidegger, it was Descartes who turned classical meta-physics into anthropology, by finally identifying the *subjectum* with the human subject, "the first and only true *subjectum*", the original and final point of reference. The subject in its various forms and guises, as self-identical, as ego or consciousness, as the *res cogitans,* the being behind thinking or thinking thing, is now the ultimate ground of all that exists.

After the subjective turn, metaphysics became obsessed with the relationship between the empirical individual and the universal tran-scendental ground or principle which endows humans with identity, reason and morality. Kant's philosophical anthropology was of such great significance precisely because his enthronement of man, as the ground of thought, action and history, did not privilege either the individual as the agent of willed change, or humanity as the represen-tative of the universal. Its radical innovation was to present man as the subject and therefore replace the fundamental pre-modern equation between God and Being with that between subject and the essence of

[35] Aristotle, *Metaphysics*, 1028b33–1029a33.

man. "The essence of humanity, of being (a) human, which should be present both in the universality of the species and in the singularity of the individual, both as a reality and as a norm or a possibility, is *subjectivity*".[36] This equation gave the solution to all questions of essence, by inscribing the normative form of the universal in the empirical singularity of the individual. This was the basis of modern humanism. When the Being of being human is exclusively presented in terms of the conscious subject, who sets the world forth and understands it through the reduction of being to (self)-representation, "man becomes the relational centre of that which is as such".[37]

In Heidegger's interpretation, the enlightenment quest for human emancipation and happiness has gone terribly wrong through a combination of arrogance and forgetfulness of Being. After the destruction of classical teleology, reason became instrumental, a means to ends set elsewhere.[38] This malady of modern rationalism was both unmasked and perpetuated by Nietzsche. Nietzsche's "will to power" succeeded in revealing the self-seeking action of modern will but Nietzsche's will too is self-perpetuating. It is a will that aims at nothing beyond itself, a will to will which glorified will's mastery. An unconditioned will no longer has any given aims. It becomes a quest of mastery for its own sake and realises the Cartesian project of absolute ownership and control by turning humanity itself into an object standing against the subject like all other objects. The metaphysics of subjectivity keeps "objectifying whatever is" by "a setting before, a representation that aims at bringing every particular being before it in such a way that man who calculates can be sure of that being".[39] The will to mastery through truth has reached its most extreme and self-destructive stage in modern science and technology, the latest turn in the metaphysical quest to name and interpret the meaning of Being and impose its law on the real. But this recent development was already present in the Cartesian project of "subjectification" of the world and its Kantian completion.

[36] Etienne Balibar, "Subjection and Subjectivation", in Joan Copjec (ed.), *Supposing the Subject* (London, Verso, 1994) 4.
[37] Martin Heidegger, "The Age of the World Picture" in *The Question Concerning Technology and Other Essays* (W. Lovitt trans.) (New York, Harper and Row, 1977) 133.
[38] The attacks on "instrumental reason" and technology link Heidegger with the left-wing Frankfurt critical school of Adorno, Horkheimer and Marcuse. Theodor Adorno and Max Horkheimer, *Dialectics of Enlightenment* (J. Cumming trans.) (London, Verso, 1979); Theodor Adorno, *Negative Dialectics* (E.B. Ashton trans.) (London, Routledge: 1990); Herbert Marcuse, *Eros and Civilisation* (Boston, Beacon Press, 1966).
[39] Heidegger, supra n. 37, 127.

For Heidegger, the determination of humanity as subject, cogito, Spirit, transcendental ego or Man, is the culmination of the closure of metaphysics and its forgetfulness of Being. Forgetfulness takes two forms: the failure to ask the question of being of being human, and the accompanying designation of the human as subject or consciousness, as an ever-present essence that determines the world. Man's essence, on the contrary, is to guard the truth of Being in order for beings to appear in the light of Being as what they are. The various beings and entities, gods, heroes, animals or nature came to presence and departed without man's intervention or decision. Their advent is the destiny of Being, they are ways in which Being discloses itself. Being is something other than the totality of beings; it gives itself to beings and the human way of being is ecstatic: man is "thrown out of a past and 'projects' himself toward a future by way of the present".[40] The Being of humanity is therefore its historical existence or *Dasein* (being there). Metaphysical humanity, on the other hand, posits its essence as a perpetual presence which has freed itself from the past and cleansed all traces of the future as it stands falsely self-contained and satisfied.

Man's responsibility is to find in himself what befits the destiny of guarding the truth of Being because, unlike objects, "man is the shepherd of Being".[41] Being is nearer to man than to any other being, yet metaphysics keeps it farthest away. Man's forgetfulness, aggravated in modernity, makes him cling to things and think only of beings and not of Being and leads humanity to objectification and homelessness. The only glimpses of Being remain in language. We are given to language, particularly poetic language which is the house of Being. In language, man ek-sists in the proximity of Being. Ek-sistence, like ek-stasis, is a key term: it signifies a subject that stands or moves out of itself in an existence of becoming, in which humanity achieves its destiny by always leaving the familiar for the unknown, by being itself in the act of departing from certainty and stability. In this perspective, the essence of man is to be more than mere human, if human means *animal rationale*. This "more" is what Heidegger calls, "dwelling in the nearness of Being", man's historical essence and the only real humanism.

Different names were given to Being in various epochs: the Greeks saw the world as *physis*, as Being that arises and opens itself in the

[40] Martin Heidegger, "Letter on Humanism", in *Basic Writings* (D.F. Krell ed.) (Harper, San Francisco, 1977) 204.

[41] ibid., 221.

manifold of beings; the medievals, as *ens creatum*, as divine creation; for the moderns, the world has withdrawn and has become a picture, something that can be set forth, represented and grasped as a whole by man. The withdrawal of the world is the precondition of its becoming a picture. The world is emptied of meaning, humanity loses its organic place in it and becomes its homeless master, for whom Being is the objectivity and truth the certainty of representation. "Subjectification" is therefore the specifically modern type of forgetfulness; it turns everything into a representation for the subject and affects humanity as much as the world. Man in his narcissism forgets that Being is something other than the totality of beings and that he is thrown by Being in a position of special responsibility of caring for it.

The value system is a good example of this subjectifying attitude which paradoxically transforms every being into an object. Turning an entity or activity into value, for example defining a person as someone with human dignity or, turning someone's acting towards another into a case of moral rule-following or, presenting a work as an artistic object, deprives those beings of their intrinsic worth and temporality and turns them into objects of valuation and assessment. Valuing reifies beings and validates them only as objects of its activity, their value whatever worth they get as a result of their quality assessment. It does not let beings be, valuable in their own being as authentic disclosures of Being, but values them only because they have been evaluated by the subject. Arguing against values, however, does not mean that what is interpreted as value, be it culture, art, dignity, or God, is valueless. It is to insist that a thing in its being is not exhausted by being a – valuable – object. To call God the highest value, for example, is to degrade God's essence, as negative theology well understood. Thinking in values, concludes Heidegger, is the greatest blasphemy against Being. By rejecting such thinking beings are not devalued but are allowed "to bring the lighting of the truth of Being before thinking, as against subjectivising beings into mere objects".[42]

This is not the place to discuss Heidegger's ontology in detail. His diagnosis is that, as a result of the forgetfulness of Being, a totally misleading and catastrophic idea about the centrality of the subject is propagated while, at the same time, this apparent humanism creates the necessary preconditions for turning man, the proclaimed centre

---

[42] ibid., 228.

and foundation of the world, into the final object of his objectifying gaze. Indeed, the essence of contemporary metaphysics is technology. But technology is not an instrument or means, its aims, purposes and methods are not set outside itself in public debate and moral argument, as the apologists of scientific reason claim. From this perspective, technology is not the tool of science or politics, its "essence" is not technological. Technology is the culmination of the modern "will to power" which, once it turns upon itself, becomes an infinite and aimless will to will.

In late modernity, self-assertion takes a further step into an abyss from which humanity may not be able to exit again. In Heidegger's difficult ontological terms, contemporary humanity "comes to the very brink of a precipitous fall". Man

> comes to the point where he himself will have to be taken as standing-reserve. Meanwhile man, precisely as the one so threatened, exalts himself to the posture of the lord of the earth. In this way the impression comes to prevail that everything man encounters exists only insofar as it is his construct. This illusion gives rise in turn to one final delusion: It seems as though man everywhere and always only encounters himself. In truth, however, precisely nowhere does man today any longer encounter himself, i.e. his essence.[43]

Both humanity and the world are now "standing-reserve": they are regulated and ordered to stand by, to be at hand, prepared for further regulating and ordering. The world no longer stands opposite humanity as its object, but is placed next to us. When humanity as much as the world submits to an inescapable regime of ordering and regulation, and the subject accepts its fate as the most important raw material, the endless objectification of modernity reaches an end. Metaphysics finally triumphs: it establishes a completely secure and unchangeable ground and proclaims man's freedom from finitude. A completely humanised world is in fact "techno-nihilistic", "a world driven by the demand for increased power and orderability", in which global cycles of production and consumption "fix" man as a labouring and consuming animal. Max Weber's process of disenchantment with a meaning-less world comes to its logical conclusion, as technology follows the ceaseless demands of systematisation and unification without end or purpose. "Making humans fit for technological treatment was an effect of the total 'technological revolution'

---

[43] Martin Heidegger, "The Question Concerning Technology", in *Basic Writings*, supra n. 40, 308.

in positing and handling 'nature', but the latter would not be possible were the 'human resources' not liberated first for use in the massive-scale, concentrated efforts to churn out the excess of resources, tools and instruments feverishly searching for ends they may serve".[44] The evidence of man's destructive mastery over nature and of his own reification is everywhere and there is no need to detail it. Metaphysical humanism lies at the heart of an unprecedented colonisation of nature in its various meanings, as territory and physical landscape, as human or animal nature or, as the nature of the "naturals", the indigenous people. But aren't human rights a defensive shield against the self-destructive horrors of metaphysical arrogance?

A non-metaphysical humanism?

The morality of technology is value-less, nihilistic. As Louis Dumont put it, "this world devoid of values, to which values are superadded by human choice, is a subhuman world, a world of objects, of things . . . It is a world without man, a world from which man has deliberately removed himself and on which he is thus able to impose his will".[45] The only values left are technology's inexorable process and aggrandisement and man's desires. Humanity's highly disciplined and ordered desires become the latest transient defining characteristic of human nature and inescapably push to be recognised as legal rights. The significance of this critique for (legal) humanism cannot be overestimated. Heidegger identified the metaphysics of the subject with humanism and claimed that we must abandon humanism in order to respect the human:

> The highest determinations of the essence of man in humanism still do not realise the proper dignity of man. To that extent the thinking in *Being and Time* is against humanism. But this opposition does not mean that such thinking aligns itself against the humane and advocates the inhuman, that it promotes the inhumane and deprecates the dignity of man. Humanism is opposed because it does not set the *humanitas* of man high enough. Of course the essential worth of man does not consist in his being the substance of beings, as the "Subject" among them, so that as the tyrant of Being he may deign to release the beingness of beings into an all too loudly bruited "objectivity".[46]

[44] Zygmunt Bauman, *Postmodern Ethics* (Oxford, Blackwell, 1993) 193.

[45] Louis Dumont, *Essays on Individualism: Modern Ideology in Anthropological Perspective* (Chicago, University of Chicago Press, 1986) 262.

[46] Heidegger, "Letter on Humanism", supra n. 40, 210.

These statements appear in an essay attacking humanism, in particular Sartre's existentialist humanism.[47] They could be accused as paradoxical, if not hypocritical. Heidegger's collaboration with the Nazis in the early thirties, and his persistent silence on the Holocaust, make his pronouncements on humanism highly problematic and have sparked one of the most vociferous debates about the politics of philosophy.[48] This is not the place to review this conflict which has addressed important political and theoretical issues. Yet, Heidegger's critique of humanism must be placed within his wider philosophy which, despite his odious politics, has profoundly influenced all major schools of continental thought. His conclusions on the predicament of contemporary culture are shared by most critical thought of the second half of the century. The central indictment is that humanism, by defining the essence of man once and for all, turns human existence from "open possibility" into a solidified value which follows the prescriptions of the metaphysicians. This "degrading" question "lies at the root of all metaphysical attempts to 'jump over our own shadows' and delimit humanity from a God's eye perspective. Metaphysical humanism presumes that existence must be redeemed by essence; that the world has value only in relation to this essence; and that human inessentiality is equal to nihilism".[49]

Heidegger did not deal extensively with normative questions and, in the "Letter on Humanism", he famously refused to develop an ethics to complement ontology. For Heidegger, ethics does not equate

---

[47] Heidegger accuses Sartre that he reverses only the metaphysical priority of essence over existence but leaves the structure intact. Sartre had argued that after the death of God, only human beings and their freedom exist. The non metaphysical position would be that "we are precisely in a situation where principally there is Being", ibid., 214.

[48] The most recent round of the Heidegger affair started with the publication of Victor Farias, *Heidegger and Nazism* (J. Margolis and T. Rockmore eds) (Philadelphia, Temple University Press, 1989) which detailed Heidegger's engagement with the Nazis. All main European philosophers have contributed to the debate thus proving the central influence of Heidegger's thought. Some of the most important contributions to the debate include Philippe Lacoue-Labarthe, *Heidegger, Art and Politics* (C. Turner trans.) (Oxford, Blackwell, 1990); Jean-François Lyotard, *Heidegger and the "Jews"* (A. Michel and M. Roberts trans.) (Minneapolis, University of Minnesota Press, 1990); Jacques Derrida, *Of Spirit: Heidegger and the Question* (G. Bennington and R. Bowlby trans.) (Chicago, University of Chicago Press, 1989); Fred Dallmayr, *The Other Heidegger* (Ithaca, Cornell University Press, 1993). If a tentative conclusion can be drawn is that one should not stop reading Heidegger but start demythologising him. On the critical side, see John Caputo, *Demythologising Heidegger* (Bloomington, Indiana University Press, 1993), Luc Ferry and Alain Renaut, *Heidegger and Modernity*, op.cit., supra n. 30.

[49] Dana Villa, *Arendt and Heidegger: The Fate of the Political* (Princeton NJ, Princeton University Press, 1996) 183.

with morality and has nothing to do with codes and commands. Ethics should be defined according to the original Greek meaning of *ethos*, as the thinking about the "abode of man" and as proximity to the "truth of Being as the primordial element of man, as one who eksists".[50] This primordial ethics is an integral part of ontology and has nothing to do with the circumlocutions of moral philosophy. It is possible, however, to use the attack on metaphysical humanism to develop a critique of its legal variety. Humanism, the self-referential concern that man becomes free for his humanity and finds his worth exclusively in it, means that "the *humanitas* of *homo humanus* is determined with regard to an already established interpretation of nature, history, world, and the ground of the world, that is, of beings as a whole".[51] By dealing with "beings as a whole", humanism forgets the difference between Being and its appearance in beings, takes the transient and historically determined subjectification of the world as eternal and stable, and proclaims its own definition of humanity as unquestionably true. Furthermore, this metaphysical closure is accompanied often by the exclusion of those who do not meet the requirements of the human essence. Classical humanism, to which all modern versions return, juxtaposed, as we saw, the *humanum* to the *barbarum*. As Joanna Hodge put it, all versions of humanism are followed by a "double marking, of a return to half-understood Greek ideals and a gesture of setting oneself apart from some perceived barbarism".[52]

The humanism of rights, like all humanism, is similarly based on the definition of the essence of humanity and a desire to go back to the classical sources of the *humanum*, evident in the extravagant claims of early modern legal humanists and their contemporary followers that Greece and Rome developed first the institution of rights. Again, legal humanism was a discourse of exclusion, not just of foreign barbarians but also of women and people of colour. To be sure, the various political and legal philosophies differ in their definitions of the human essence. For liberals, legal humanism protects freedom and dignity, for left liberals and socialists, it promotes equality and liberty while, for multi-culturalists, it safeguards a multiplicity of values and life-plans determined in each community by local conditions and historical traditions. In all cases, however, individual and collective human possibilities are demarcated and defined in advance, through

---

[50] Heidegger, "Letter on Humanism", supra n. 40, 235. See also Douzinas, "Deathbound Legality", supra n. 23.

[51] Heidegger ibid., 201–2.

[52] Joanna Hodge, *Heidegger and Ethics* (London, Routledge, 1995) 90.

the axiomatic determination of what it is to be human and the dogmatic exclusion of other possibilities.

These criticisms are equally applicable to the concepts of humanity that underpin the most heated debate in human rights, that between universalism and cultural relativism. Both positions exemplify, perhaps in different ways, the contemporary metaphysical urge: each side has made an axiomatic decision as to what constitutes the essence of humanity and follows it, like all metaphysical determinations, with a stubborn disregard of opposing strategies or arguments. They both claim to have the answer to the question "what is human value" and to its premise "what is (a) human", and take their answers to be absolute and irrefutable. But in this mood both universalism and localism are extensions of the metaphysics of subjectivity. The former has become, as we have seen throughout, an aggressive essentialism which has globalised nationalism and has turned the assertiveness of nations into a world system. Community, on the other hand, is the condition of human existence but communitarianism has become even more stifling than universalism.

The individualism of universal principles forgets that every person is a world and comes into existence in common with others, that we are all in community. Being in common is an integral part of being self: self is exposed to the other, it is posed in exteriority, the other is part of the intimacy of self. My face is "always exposed to others, always turned toward an other and faced by him or her never facing myself".[53] But being in community with others is the opposite of common being or of belonging to an essential community. Most communitarians, on the other hand, define community through the commonality of tradition, history and culture, the various past crystallisations whose inescapable weight determines present possibilities. The essence of the communitarian community is often to compel or "allow" people to find their "essence", its success is measured by its contribution to the accomplishment of a common "humanity". But this immanence of self to itself is nothing other than the pressure to be what the spirit of the nation or of the people or the leader demands or, to follow traditional values and habits and exclude what is alien and other. This type of communitarianism destroys community in a delirium of incarnated communion. The solid and unforgiving essence of nations, classes or communities turns the "subjectivity of man into totality. It completes subjectivity's self assertion, which

---

[55] Jean-Luc Nancy, *The Inoperative Community* (Minneapolis, University of Minnesota Press, 1991) xxxviii.

refuses to yield".[54] Community as communion accepts human rights only to the extent that they help submerge the I into the We, all the way till death, the point of "absolute communion" with dead tradition.

The community of being together, on the other hand, "is what takes place always through others and for others. It is not the space of the egos – subjects and substances that are at bottom immortal – but of the Is, who are always others (or else nothing) . . . Community therefore occupies a singular place: it assumes the impossibility of its own immanence. The impossibility of a communitarian being in the form of a subject".[55] In this sense, community represents transcendence without a sacred meaning and resistance to immanence, "to the communion of everyone or to the exclusive passion of one or several: to all forms and all violences of subjectivity".[56] The modern creation of society, as a space of competing atoms, forces and signs, has been commonly seen as the outcome of community's destruction. But according to Jean-Luc Nancy, the historical sequence is different: society emerged not out of disappearing communities but out of disintegrating empires and tribes, which were as unrelated to community as is postmodern society. It is only after the disappearance of the society of atomistic subjects that the non-immanent community of singular beings-in-common will have a historical chance. The community of non-metaphysical humanity is still to come.

The continuing pathos of the universalism/relativism debate, coupled with its repetitive and rather banal nature, indicates that the stakes are high. Postmodern mass societies and the globalisation of economics, politics and communications increase existential anxiety, and create unprecedented uncertainty and insecurity about life prospects. In this climate, the desire for simple life instructions and legal and moral codes with clearly defined rights and duties becomes paramount. Codification transfers the responsibility of deciding ethically to national or international legislators or to resurgent religious and national fundamentalisms, to false prophets and fake tribes. In an over-legalised world, rules and norms discourage people from thinking independently and discovering their own relation to themselves, to others, to language and history. The proliferation of human rights treaties and the mushrooming of legal regulation are part of the same process, which aims to relieve the burden of ethical life and the

[54] Heidegger, "Letter on Humanism", supra n. 40, 221.
[55] Jean-Luc Nancy, op.cit., supra n. 55, 15.
[56] ibid., 35.

anxiety or, in Heidegger's terms, the "homelessness" of postmodern humanity. International human rights law promises to set all that is valuably human on paper and hold it before us in triumph: the moral world picture of humanity will have been finally drawn and everyone will be free to follow his essence as defined by world governments and realised by technologies of dismembering and re-assembling the prosthetic human.

But are human rights not the value or principle which resists these tendencies and raises human life and dignity into the end of civilisation? If this is the case, they have not been successful in resisting the endless objectification of humanity. It is arguable that human rights may participate rather than oppose the dismembering and re-assembling operations of technology and law.[57] If technological objectification is the metaphysical urge of modernity, it could not be otherwise. But another aspect of their action becomes important in the context of modern value nihilism. If the satisfaction of endlessly proliferating desire is the only morality left in a disenchanted world, rights become the last human value. Human rights are the values of a valueless world, but their action is not ethical in the Greek sense or moral in the Kantian. When they move from their original aim of resistance to oppression and rebellion against domination, to the contemporary end of total definition and organisation of self, community and the world, according to the dictates of endless desire, they become the effect rather than the resistance to nihilism. As Bauman puts it "when the job of fragmentation is done, what is left are diverse wants, each to be quelled by requisition of goods and services; and diverse internal or external constraints, each to be overcome in turn, one-constraint-at-a-time – so that this or that unhappiness now and then can be turned down or removed" or turned into the next human rights campaign.[58]

Nietszche, who taught the meaning of nihilism to Heidegger, had realised the metaphysical link between the modern individual and the operation of rights. "In fact it was Christianity that first invited the individual to play the judge of everything and everyone; megalomania almost became duty: one has to enforce eternal rights against everything temporal and conditioned".[59] Individualism and egalitarianism, the two apparently opposed grounds of human rights, are in

---

[57] See Chapter 12 below.

[58] Bauman, op.cit., supra n. 44, 197.

[59] F. Nietzsche, *The Will to Power* (W. Kaufmann and R.J. Hollingdale trans.) (New York, Vintage, 1968) 765, III, 401.

reality allies, according to Nietzsche, in a world where the individual is the only (valueless) value left. "The modern European is characterised by two apparently opposite traits: individualism and equal rights; that I have at last come to understand".[60] While individualism claims to promote difference and uniqueness, it is only a form of egalitarianism which makes people, fearful of an existence without meaning and values, to demand that everyone should count as their equal, in other words the same, in an endless quest for personal gratification. But when individual desire is turned into the ultimate principle, its protective value is devalued. The individual is an extremely vulnerable piece of vanity, predicted Nietzsche. His prophesy has become the bitter truth of our century.

But how would a non-metaphysical approach to human rights look? Such predictions cannot escape the metaphysical horizon and, from a strict Heideggerian position, the concept of rights may be irredeemably associated with metaphysical humanism. But by way of the *vita negativa*, we could hazard some guesses about how it would not look. It would reject the attempt to interpret "all beings as a whole", as if some common essential denominator lies under the historical differences and the myriad of groups and individuals. A key claim of liberalism is that it does not impose a conception of the good life, but allows people to develop and carry out their own life-plans, through the use of rights. And yet this is denied by the urge to set forth the "essence" of humanity in a code or mirror, which can only capture and freeze the features of its legislators and holders or, to define this essence as the fearful competition of antagonistic interests. A non-metaphysical humanism would not treat people as synthetic entities for which the prosthetic operation of fragmentary rights satisfies disconnected wants. Community would not be constructed by the following of the past or obedience to tradition but by the exposure to the other person, whose trace creates self. Finally, it would reverse the arrogance of subjectivity and assign rights, if at all, because, as humans, we have been destined to be near Being and to care for the human as well as the other entities in which Being discloses itself. Some human rights may be consistent with non-metaphysical humanism. But the overall form of the social bond would change from rights and principles to being-in-common, to the public recognition and protection of the becoming-human with others, a dynamic process which resists all attempts to hold humanity to an

---

[60] ibid., 783, III, 410.

essence decided by the representatives of power. To coin a term, this would be a process of "righting" and not a series of rights and, like writing, it would open Being to the new and unknown as a condition of its humanity. At the centre of critique, in this as in many other philosophies we will encounter in our journey, lies a utopian hope (or despair) for a future that may never come.

III. THE SUBJECTED SUBJECT: POWER, LAW AND THE SUBJECT

It is often said that, in Britain, we have "subjects but not citizens". In this context, the subject is seen as the victim of the "democratic deficit" of our constitution. The British subject has no rights, she is not part of the sovereign body but only the Queen's subject, submitted to arcane constitutional and legal procedures. On the other hand, the supporters of the new Human Rights Act tell us that it will turn us into citizens and subjects of rights, enjoying all the legal protections and guarantees of our American cousins and European partners. It looks as if the word "subject" suffers from schizophrenia, from an intrinsic ambiguity, captured in the double genitive "law's subject". The subject of law or *subjectum* is the holder of rights and the bearer of duties and responsibilities. But at the same time, the subject as *subjectus* is subjected to law, brought to life by law's protocols, shaped by law's demands and rewards and called to account before law's bar. The paradoxical double determination of creator and created, free and compelled, active and passive, animates and permeates the life of the legal subject.

It is remarkable that philosophy and language have developed the concept of the subject around the playful contrast and paradoxical combination of *subjectum* and *subjectus*, two etymologically related but semantically opposed terms. The Latin word *subjectum* translated, as we saw, the Greek *hypokeimenon*, the permanent substance or substratum beneath a being's individual properties, the underlying essence of a thing. When this *subjectum* or ground assumed the form of the modern subject, it became the vehicle of freedom and the agent of morality. This process was facilitated, according to Heidegger, by the subjective turn of Descartes and Kant. According to Kant and the neo-Kantians, personal autonomy is achieved through the disinterested obedience to the moral law and, in this sense, the subject is the necessary support of moral commands. The subject is by definition autonomous: by following the moral law, which she both finds in herself and legislates, she makes choices opposed to her emotions and immediate interests and becomes free. The non-moral person, on the other hand, is heteronomous, not fully a subject: he submits to instincts, passions and inclinations, to the brute facts of nature and of state law rather than to freely legislated morality. The essence of the subject is to be autonomous; calling a subject autonomous is therefore pleonastic, while a heteronomous subject is a contradiction in terms.

Subjectus, on the other hand, refers to subjection and submission. It is a political and legal term signifying that someone is subjected to the power or command of a superior, a ruler or sovereign. The commanding power may have different origins and take many forms but, in all cases, the *subjectus* implies hierarchy and domination, violently imposed through war and conquest or voluntarily accepted and legitimate. The philosophical and linguistic paradox is striking: modern philosophy uses the same term to signify Heidegger's originary ground of being as well as subordination, submission and voluntary or otherwise limitation of freedom. Can we explain this strange paradox and its implications for law?

The French philosopher Etienne Balibar has argued, in a number of essays, that the political history of the *subjectus* should take priority over the philosophical trajectory of *subjectum*.[61] Balibar takes issue with Heidegger's argument that the metaphysics of subjectivity started with Descartes.[62] This cannot be the case, argues Balibar, because Descartes never referred to the subject as autonomous self-consciousness or as the reflexive centre of the world. On the contrary, Descartes used the term in a profoundly historical and political sense, totally missed or underestimated by Heidegger. The *subjectus* of Descartes is a synonym for the *subditus* of medieval political theology: it refers to the person submitted to the *ditio* or command of the sovereign king, "an authority expressed in his orders and itself legitimated by the Word of another Sovereign (the Lord God)".[63] The subject becomes *subjectum* or ground of metaphysics much later, in the work of Kant, who projected his transcendental subject back onto

---

[61] Etienne Balibar, "Citizen Subject" in E. Cadava, P. Connor and J.L. Nancy (eds) *Who Comes after the Subject* (New York, Routledge, 1991) 33–57; "Subjection and Subjectivation", supra n. 36, 1–14; " 'The Rights of Man' and the 'Rights of the Citizen' " in *Masses, Classes, Ideas* (Cambridge, Polity, 1994) 39–59.

[62] "Citizen Subject", supra n. 63, 33–40.

[63] ibid., 41.

the Cartesian text. It was Kant's *Critiques* which raised the subject into the common ground of consciousness and conscience and turned it into the foundation and measure of philosophy.

Balibar's remarks alert us to the fact that the subject, this centre of knowledge and free will, appears first on the historical stage as *subjectus*, as someone subjected or submitted to external power. From a political perspective, the question of the subject was always involved with the conditions of subjection and brought together the person submitted to power and the entity exercising it. The juridical figure of the *subjectus* unites Western history from Rome to the present. The Greeks had no concept or word for the subject or for rights. The term *subjectus* appeared first in Rome. The *subjecti*, the non-Romans who benefited from the *jus gentium*, did not become a collectivity however because they had no strong links to connect them. As with many political and philosophical concepts, it was Christianity that redefined the subject and gave it substance. The *subjectus* was turned into *subditus*, someone who exists in and through a relation of obedience to a power originating in God. This relationship of obedience connected a "*sublimus*, 'chosen' to command, and *subditi*, who turn towards him to hear the law".[64] The feudal hierarchical chain, organised in a pyramidal fashion, linked its elements through the cement of obedience, which starting from the bottom was turned upwards and was eventually directed towards its transcendent apex. The *subjectus* willed his obedience, partly as secular loyalty to the king and partly as religious faith to God and his representative on earth. In obeying the king, he obeyed God, from whom all power emanated and followed a law that came from beyond the temporary law-giver. Spiritual and temporal laws were hierarchically organised and issued from God, the ultimate *causa causans*. This pyramidal inter-dependence turned, for the first time, the *subditi* into a coherent body politic, united through their immortal soul which linked them with God.

The classical method of subjection was based on a strict ontological hierarchy, which graded dignity and honour and entitled some to participate in political life while others, women, children, foreigners or slaves, were always subjugated to those above them on the social

---

[64] "Citizen Subject", supra n. 41. For a general discussion, see Walter Ullman, *The Individual and Society in the Middle Ages* (Baltimore, The Johns Hopkins University Press, 1966) and *A History of Political Thought: The Middle Ages* (London, Penguin, 1965). For an English perspective, see John Figgis, *The Divine Right of Kings* (Bristol, Thoemmes Press, 1994) (original ed. 1914).

ladder. Christianity created a new and unified category of subjection: a willing obedience which came from inside. In the interstices of the confessional and the assizes, the body became attached to a soul and a plan of salvation and, a new inner *subjectus* emerged. In this economy, "the surface – the body – must be penetrated to get at its soul" in order to generate "belief, obedience, loyalty, and love, all of which require the active movement and consequent involvement of the soul".[65] The soul, this prison of the body became the addressee and vessel of the law, a juridical construct which, by subjecting the body, led to the genesis of the modern subject. The law which commanded the subject was both transcendent, spoke to him directly and called him to account for his infractions and, temporal, a law of strict rules and harsh judgments issuing from secular authorities. This terrifying power or Big Other, in Lacanian terms, who called the subject to account oscillated between visible and invisible, individual and universal, empirical and metaphysical: lord or sovereign, God or the subject's own conscience, the voice that shouts from outside or murmurs incessantly from within at the dead of the night took the same form, that of the legal commandment. The mechanism of subjection of the

> inner voice . . . that of a transcendent authority which everyone is bound to obey, or which always already compels everyone to obey, including the rebels (they certainly do not escape the voice of the Law, even if they do not surrender to it) – because the foundation of authority is not located outside the individual, in some natural inequality or dependency, but within him, in his very being as creature of the verb, and as faithful to it[66]

was always accompanied by the external voice and force of king, lord or judge and the two together, in stereophonic harmony, brought the subject to life.

This new type of subjection had certain advantages for its subjects. The subject whose soul obeys cannot become a slave or an object of the king's whims. The obedient soul inserted the subject into the divine order and created for the king responsibilities as well as powers and rights.[67] But the rights and liberties of the subject did not precede or override the power of the sovereign. Instead, they were

---

[65] W. T. Murphy, *The Oldest Social Science? Configurations of Law and Modernity* (Oxford, Oxford University Press, 1997) 11.

[66] "Subjection and Subjectivation", supra n. 63, 10.

[67] The *subditus* "is submitted as a member of an order or a body that is recognised as having certain rights and that confers a certain status, a field of initiative on him", "Citizen Subject", supra n. 63, 43.

presented as his unilateral grants, even when they were the outcome of social conflict and monarchic compromise or defeat. Without royal magnanimity and concessions, the subjects had no rights whatsoever. This combination of loyalty and faith unified the subjects in obedience to the law, but the result was intrinsically unstable, open to potential conflicts and splits between its spiritual and temporal components. The same fragile economy characterised the king, whose body was split between a physical and a mystical part and, whose right was both a grant of God and the prerogative of his nature.

Absolutism was the period of the king's and subject's double existence *par excellence*. The absolute kings pushed the aspirations for a total, coherent and illimitable form of self-founding power to its extreme and, in doing so, they led the whole edifice to its downfall. The king claimed to be the incarnation of the good and the true; as a result, the subjects had no need or reason to understand what was prescribed to them. The rights respected by the monarch were said both to derive from a long history and tradition and to be the outcome of a limited pact between sovereign and subjects. Similarly, while God was the ultimate source of right, these rights were said to constitute the essence of kingdom and, in respecting them, the king simply honoured his own nature. Thus, while the king appeared juridically bound, his actual power was unlimited. By exaggerating inner tensions, concentrating power, dissolving intermediate centres of influence and emphasising the unity of state, absolutism weakened the dual concept of obedience and subjection. Many of its theorists presented the *subjecti* as free citizens, but a fault-line had started developing in the idea of a free and legally protected *subjectus*. When king and the absolute state ceased being the representatives of the divine order, the belief that a subject dependent on the absolute power of another could at the same time be free was fatally undermined. At this point, the revolution entered history and ushered in modernity.

The split between man and citizen, which can be seen as a development of the *subjectus/subjectum* dyad, characterised the French Declaration and its politics and became the target of the two early critiques of human rights by Burke and Marx. But according to the neo-Marxist Balibar, the most revolutionary consequence of the Declaration was to reverse the monarchical sovereignty of absolutism and create the concept of citizen sovereignty. The indivisible and omnipotent *volonté générale* replaced the unitary and illimitable sovereignty of Leviathan in all its particulars.[68] But this new legislative sovereign, despite the appearance of indivisibility was a composite: it consisted of the sum total of the wills of citizens. In this sense, popular sovereignty was both a revolutionary and a highly artificial idea. Monarchical sovereignty was hierarchical, with the king, as God's disciple and servant at its apex, receiving the freely-given and commanded obedience of the subjects. The sovereignty ushered in by the French Revolution, on the other hand, was based on the unprecedented principle of citizen equality and freedom.

The citizen now becomes a free man. He enjoys his natural rights, as an equal with all others (except of course for women and non-whites).[69] But, the principle of equality, even in its limited form, is highly paradoxical. "[E]galitarian sovereignty [is] practically a contradiction in terms, but the only way radically to expel all transcendence and to inscribe the political and social order in the element of immanence, the auto-constitution of the people".[70] According to Balibar, the novelty of the idea was so great, logically and historically, that it led to a second equally hyperbolic innovation: the claim that all men are born free, a palpably untrue statement, which was used to justify retrospectively the revolutionary assertion that all citizens are equal. In this way, the *subjectus* became citizen and started his journey towards becoming the free and autonomous modern subject. As Balibar puts it, "the idea of the rights of the citizen, at the very moment of its emergence, thus institutes an historical figure that is no longer the *subjectus*, and not yet *subjectum*. But from the beginning, in the way it is formulated and put into practice, this figure exceeds its own institution".[71] After this brief moment of combined freedom and subjection, equality and liberty became the defining characteristic of modern democracies and politics and the element of subjection receded.

Claude Lefort, another former Marxist philosopher, adopts a similar position. The idea of a body politic, of an organic entity symbolised by the body of the king, was undermined by the revolution, which led to the

---

[68] Marcel Gauchet, *La Révolution des droits de l'homme* (Paris, Gallimard, 1989) argues that in order to justify democratic representation, the French Revolution inaugurated a concept of absolute national sovereignty which was the mimetic inversion of the absolutist sovereignty of the ancien regime.

[69] See above, Chapter 5.

[70] " 'The Rights of Man' and the 'Rights of the Citizen' ", supra n. 63, 43.

[71] "Citizen Subject", supra n. 63, 46.

phenomenon of disincorporation of power and disincorporation of right which accompanies the disappearance of "the king's body", in which community was embodied and justice mediated; and, by the same token, it signifies a phenomenon of disincorporation of society whose identity, though already figured in the nation, has not yet been separated from the person of the monarch.[72]

After the revolution, the concept of right was deprived of its fixed point of reference in God or king. Power was separated from right; indeed, power became the object of a juridical discourse which placed human rights, with the fragile concept of man, at its centre and according to which power must now justify its exercise.

The immediate aim of Balibar and Lefort is to defend the revolution against revisionist historians by emphasising the political nature of human rights. Balibar, in particular, has shown how philosophical concepts and political and legal constructions sometimes develop in parallel and others in intertwined trajectories. Without the help of the juridical *subjectus*, the free subject, the metaphysical ground of modernity would not have come into existence. Similarly, freedom, responsibility and equality, the key aspects of modern subjectivity, grew out of subjection, obedience and the shared soul of the Christian subject. Uniting subjection and freedom stands the law: as external, religious, royal or democratic or as internal, conscience, the categorical imperative or the superego, the law brings the subjected and free subject to life.

But have human rights installed the free and equal citizen at the centre of the constitution? Has the citizen superseded the subject? If we turn to Jean-Jacques Rousseau's classic *Social Contract*, the bible of French republicanism and a main source behind radical democratic politics, we find a much more sceptical approach to the possibility of forging links between citizens, legislators and the sovereign. According to this foundational text, people agreed, in a contract with themselves, to surrender their person, powers and possession to a common power. As compensation, they received a place in the body politic and became indivisible parts of the sovereign. As members of the sovereign, they are the ultimate lawmakers; as recipients of the sovereign's commands, they are its subjects. In addressing themselves, in the initial contract or in their position as law's subjects, a metaphorical split takes place and the people are divided in two. The law and the social bond are based on this radical split, which divides

72 Lefort, op.cit., supra n. 7, 255

individuals and the collective body into subjects and subjected. These two sides, like the lips of a wound come together in citizenship, which precariously stitches them and promises to heal the split. The line which divides self makes him also part of the indivisible sovereign. In this sense, the social contract manages to create, rhetorically at least, a new ground for authority, while safeguarding the autonomy of the subject. "The Sovereign, by virtue of what it is, is always what it ought to be".[73] But Rousseau fully appreciated that the splitting and suturing which allowed the contract and the sovereign to come into existence are fictional and their promise false:

> For a people to appreciate the sound maxims of politics and to follow the fundamental rules of political reason, effect should become cause, and the social spirit the institutions are to produce should preside over their elaboration. Men should be prior to laws, what they are to become through them.[74]

Unlike his modern followers, Rousseau recognised that citizen freedom and equality, upon which the whole contractual and constitutional edifice is based, may be impossible. Indeed, a large part of the textual organisation of the *Social Contract* can be understood as a response to the failure of its promise. The sovereign is always right, if it speaks through general laws, "valid for all alike". But how will the general will express itself? In *Of the Civil State*, entry into the contract produces "a remarkable change in the individual . . . turn[ing] him from a limited and stupid animal into an intelligent being and Man".[75] In *Of the Laws*, however, the general will seems strangely muted and the citizens are presented as an ignorant crowd: "How could a blind mob, which often does not know what it wants because it rarely knows its own good, carry out by itself as huge and difficult an enterprise as the promulgation of a system of laws?"[76] To resolve the difficulty Rousseau repeats the split which established the sovereign in the contract: those subject to the law must also be its authors. The original division is now reproduced, in the person of the legislator, but is equally deceitful.

---

[73] J.-J. Rousseau, *The Social Contract* in *Political Writings* (F. Watkins ed.) (London, Nelson, 1953) 18.

[74] ibid., 44. For an analysis of this passage, see Douzinas and Warrington, "Posting the Law: Social Contracts and the Postal Rule's Grammatology", IV/11 *International Journal of the Semiotics of Law* 115 (1991).

[75] ibid., 20.

[76] ibid., 40.

The legislator must be a genius. He need be, if he is to preside over the extraordinary temporal and causal reversals noted above: he must make sure that men should be prior to laws what they are to become through them. But this is such an improbable trick that the legislator must attribute his laws to the gods. "The legislator, by putting into the mouths of the immortals that sublime reasoning which is far beyond the reach of poor mankind, will, under the banner of divine authority, lead those to whom mere mortal prudence would ever be a stumbling block".[77] Thus, the contract is organised along a series of splits and reversals: the subjects are the sovereign; the law-takers should be the law-makers; people should be before the law what they are to become through its operation; the law performing all these tricks should come from a human legislator who should be presented however as divine. Rousseau eventually admitted that the legislator is an impostor. "Though the philosopher's pride, or blind party spirit, considers them to be no more than lucky impostors, the true student of politics admires in their institutions that great and powerful genius which presides over all durable institutions".[78]

Citizen sovereignty and equality display the same structure of splitting and suturing which we observed in the extraordinary *subjectum/subjectus* couple. The citizens are equal members of the sovereign law-maker but, it is the legislator and his commands which will make them what they ought to become. Rousseau, who theorised first the democratic revolution, was much more realistic about its egalitarian prospects than his contemporary followers. His rhetorical reversals and tricks are a recognition of the fact that citizen sovereignty, even in Rousseau's direct democracy, is an improbable proposition. The concentration of economic and political power, the disciplining role of the parties and the directive influence of the media, last but not least the globalisation of culture and information, make the idea totally incredible in a contemporary representative capitalist democracy, despite the human rights rhetoric. If anything, for the majority of humanity, the pole of subjection represents daily experience much more than that of freedom.

★★★

In conclusion, the subject's subjection refers to a dual, temporal and religious, concept of power. This power appoints the subject to his place and endows him with certain rights and protections in return

---

[77] *International Journal of the Semiotics of Law* 115 (1991) 44–5.
[78] ibid., 45.

for his obedience. The subject is the end point of these two processes, which invested the body with limited powers and the soul with infinite hope and meaning and ascribed to the person a position within the hierarchised space of the political body. The subject's obedience, both extracted and freely given, was crucial for the constitution of the individual. His unity depended on bringing together the two registers, body and soul, matter and spirit or temporal and divine and subjecting the first to the second, a process which also subjected the person to the power of the state. As Peter Goodrich put it, "the unity of the divinity – the uniqueness of the one God, and the correlative singularity of the sovereign – was mirrored by the unitary identity of the subjects of law".[79] In this sense, the original concept of the subject was as much theological as political and legal and his nature subjected and obedient as well as free and self-governing. The revolution brought together the historical and philosophical conceptions of subjectivity: the *subjectus* of the pre-modern subjects subjected to God, sovereign or the law and, the *subjectum* of metaphysics, the ground and foundation of all being and concept, re-defined by Kant as the free and autonomous person endowed with consciousness and conscience. But is this not the outline and structure also of the contemporary subject? One could argue that political theology may have lost its empire, but its creations persist in the democratic subject of modernity.

The paradoxical tension at the heart of the subject, recognised by Rousseau and emphasised by Balibar, retains all its force in the modern institutional subject. The subject underpins all contemporary institutions. Mass democracy could not come into existence without political subjects, "free" electors who choose amongst competing parties, policies and platforms and who, through the exercise of their rights, link individual interests, class position and the concept of the public good in a process which underwrites democracy but also stitches the political subject together and guarantees his existence. The form of the subject is the necessary prerequisite too for the operation of the markets. Capitalist economies need atomised subjects, who treat their labour power as a commodity to be freely exchanged in the labour market for the consideration of wages. Marx brilliantly exposed the underlining dynamic of these forms and insisted on the discrepancy between free choice and individual self-determination which underpin rights-discourse and, the exploitation, suffering and

[79] Peter Goodrich, "Social Science and the Displacement of Law", 32/2 *Law and Society Review* 473 (1998), 476.

injustice brought about by the economic system which created these concepts and institutions. Psychoanalysis again, a theory and practice obsessed with the subject, attributes its genesis to the infant's introduction to the symbolic order, in other words, to its subjection to language and law. We think of the subject as the exclusive vehicle of freedom, perhaps because the split is no longer fully apparent as it was in pre-revolutionary Europe; the *subjectum/subjectus* dyad has been fully internalised and the law, self-given and externally imposed, already inhabits and conceals itself in the recesses of the self.

In the composite term human rights, humanity represents the groundlessness of freedom, the potential of the future in the present, freedom not only as will and choice but as the ability to wrench away from legal and historical determinations and open to the unknown or, in Heidegger's terms, care for Being. But the legal element of rights returns us to subjection, external determination and constraint. The legal person argues Pierre Legendre, "literally derives from *persona* – which initially means an actor's mask – and authorises me to translate the formula *de jure personarum* by 'of the law of the masks'. In all institutional systems the political subject is reproduced through masks".[80] Behind all *personas* or masks of the subject, law's operation remains central: the historical provenance of the subjected but free subject is legal and moral more than philosophical. The modern subject is the moral ground of autonomy and freedom but, he is also subjected and it is only through subjection to the law that he can acquire his autonomy as Kant, Kafka, Althusser and Lacan recognised. The subject is born to the law and belongs to law.

Modernity is the epoch of a legally induced subjectivity and, to this extent, the excessive legalisation, liberals complain so much about, is perhaps the consequence of an inescapable metaphysical urge. Similarly, the centrality of the subject in philosophy, morality and aesthetics and the nomocentric organisation of modern society are not unrelated. As Althusser argued, "the category of the subject . . . appears . . . above all with the rise of legal ideology . . . which borrowed the category of the 'subject in law' to make an ideological notion: man is by nature subject".[81] The subject came to such prominence perhaps because of the metaphysical significance of legality, which could not function without an active centre and addressee,

---

[80] Pierre Legendre, *Le Désir politique de Dieu: Etudes sur les montages de l'Etat et du Droit* (Paris, Fayard, 1988) 225–6.

[81] Louis Althusser, "Ideology and Ideological State Apparatuses" in *Lenin and Philosophy and other Essays* (B. Brewster trans.) (London, Verso, 1971) 127–188, 160.

without a (legal) subject. Nothing escapes the empire of law which, in order to carry out its tasks, needs vehicles to endow with entitlements and duties, competencies and liabilities. As the creation and creator of law, the subject is law's indispensable partner and servant. Its historical continuity and institutional permanence indicate that the law is not just the creation of popular sovereignty; it is also the carrier of the dictates of social reproduction, the begetter of subjects and the vehicle of violence. Subjects and subjected, exalted and humbled, free and determined, we take our marching orders under the banners of the law.

9

Law's Subjects: Rights and Legal Humanism

During the bicentenary celebrations of the French Revolution and *Déclaration* in 1989, Mrs Thatcher stated, to the great annoyance of President Mitterand, that as far as the protection of freedom and individual rights were concerned, the British had nothing to learn from the French. The claim that the common law is radically different from civil law and much better at protecting freedom is an old rhetorical trope.[1] Mrs Thatcher may have intended the remark as an insult to the French, but she was undoubtedly on solid historical ground. She was repeating, at the end of the twentieth century, the claims we encountered in the writings of Burke, at the end of the eighteenth and of Dicey, at the end of the nineteenth, albeit in a less eloquent manner. Legal exceptionalism has followed village cricket and warm beer as a major symbol of English identity. Max Weber, Franz Neumann and Jurgen Habermas amongst others have felt that the differences were serious enough to require commentary.[2] One of the standard explanations on offer is that the common law did not adopt the conceptual logic of rights of Roman law and the Code Napoleon. English judges concentrated, on the contrary, on solid remedies and strict procedures and were not seduced by the abstract normative logic of the civilians. Rights in this country, if one wants to use the term, refer to expectations and entitlements created interstitially at the margins of court orders and at the interface of legal procedures. Before the entry to the European Union, many textbooks bluntly repeated that English lawyers do not understand the foreign

---

[1] Peter Goodrich, *Languages of Law* (London, Weidenfeld and Nicolson, 1993); *Oedipus Lex* (Berkeley, University of California Press, 1995).

[2] Max Weber discussed English "exceptionalism" in *Economy and Society: An outline of Interpretative Sociology* (G. Roth and C. Wittich eds) (Berkeley, University of California Press, 1978) 890 ff.; Franz Neumann, "The Concept of Political Freedom" in *The Rule of Law Under Siege* (W. Scheuerman ed.) (Berkeley, University of California Press, 1996) 195–230; Otto Kirchheimer, "The *Rechsstaat* as Magic Wall" ibid., 243–64. For a commentary, see W. T. Murphy, *The Second Oldest Profession* (Oxford, Oxford University Press, 1998) Chapter 3, 51–6.

idea of rights and shadowed the parochialism of the intellectual tradition, entreated famously by Edward Thompson to keep French
theory, like the rabies, out of England.

All that changed with the introduction of the Human Rights Act
1998, which incorporated into the common law the European
Convention of Human Rights. The Act has led to a field-day for publications on human rights.[3] The human rights record of Britain over
the last twenty years has been so undistinguished that only a small but
vociferous number of people dusted the old argument about the
exceptionalism of English law and constitution, and insisted that the
new rights mentality would give less protection to individuals than the
hallowed procedures, remedies and principles of the common law issuing, like mother's milk, from the bosom of its judges.[4] But the many
treatises on the new Act are not interested in discussing the theory or
history of rights and have turned human rights, this most philosophical and political of discourses, into a haven for doctrinal exegesis and
positivism. One particularly glaring omission is the total neglect of the
role of the subject, the person or individual whose rights and interests
the new law is supposed to protect. The (legal) subject, associated as it
is with French metaphysics, has not entered legal scholarship. For
mainstream scholarship, the nature of the individual is so clear and his
position in underpinning the law so basic and well-understood that
there is no need to address it. More socially aware scholars are worried
that a discussion of the subject may lead to extreme subjectivism,
romanticism and the associated ills. Martin Loughlin has argued, for
instance, that the realisation of the close link between facts and values,
in the post-realist world, has led some legal theorists to move violently
from dogmatic objectivism to radical subjectivism. On this occasion,
the home of the new malady is not France: "The recent attachment to

---

[3] Amongst many, see Keir Starmer, *European Human Rights Law* (London, LAG, 1999);
J. Coppell, *The Human Rights Act 1998* (London, John Wiley & Sons, 1999); Anthony Lester
and David Pannick, *Human Rights Law and Practice* (London, Butterworths, 1999).

[4] Lord Jowitt, the Lord Chancellor at the time of the signing of the European
Convention of Human Rights, denounced it as "some half-baked scheme to be administered
by some unknown court" and "so vague and woolly that it may mean almost anything",
quoted in William Wade, "The United Kingdom's Bill of Rights" in *Constitutional Reform in
the United Kingdom*, Cambridge Centre for Public Law, 1998, 61. For Lord Denning in 1985
the perils from a Bill of Rights came from litigants not judges: "You are going to have a myriad of cases by a lot of crackpots and they will have to be turned out sooner or later", 468
H.L.Deb. col.172 (10 December 1985), quoted in Geoffrey Marshall, "Patriating Rights –
With Reservations", ibid., 74. The argument about the un-English character of the European
system of human rights was rediscovered and brought out, in the late eighties and early
nineties, whenever the UK was found by the European Court in breach of the Convention.

the cult of subjectivity has been much stronger in the United States, where they tend not to do things by half". But its perpetrators and victims are again the contemporary heirs of the radical traditions against which the English establishment set its "exceptionalist" store: "[Radical subjectivism] has been a prominent strand in the self-styled Critical Legal Studies movement [in America] where, through the method of 'trashing', it forms a distinctive jurisprudence of drag".[5] We may be importing the un-English rights dragging our feet but all thought on the subject must be firmly kept out of the country.

The combination of intellectual isolationism, parochialism and dread of metaphysics has meant that this all-important foundation of modern law, civil, common and now international, has been scarcely discussed in Anglo-American jurisprudence and has been only partially addressed by critics.[6] But the question of law's subjects cannot go away. This Chapter will attempt to redress the omission. We will examine the nature of the subject or person presupposed by the liberal theory of rights. What is the relationship between legal subjects and real people? Is the modern subject, the pivot of the cognitive, normative and aesthetic faculties, related to the legal subject? Is there a link between the "subjectification" of the world and the introduction of rights as the main building block of modern law?

I. RULES, RIGHTS AND SUBJECTS

According to jurisprudence, rights are deontic concepts, they belong to the universe of norms and are couched in the language of rules. The existence of a right presumes the operation of a normative system, of a posited collection of legal rules or a set of moral or other norms which guide action. Positivism, in particular, defines law as a

---

[5] Martin Loughlin, *Public Law and Political Theory* (Oxford University Press, 1992) 33–4.

[6] See, Bernard Edelman, *The Ownership of the* Image (E. Kingdom trans.) (London, Routledge and Kegan Paul 1979); Paul Hirst, *Law and Ideology* (London, Macmillan, 1985); Peter Goodrich, *Languages of Law* (London, Weidenfeld and Nicolson, 1990); Alan Norrie, *Crime, Reason and History*, Alan Norrie, *Crime, Reason and History* (London, Weidenfeld and Nicolson, 1993); Rolando Gaete, *Human Rights and the Limits of Critical Reason* (Aldershot, Dartmouth, 1993); Costas Douzinas, "Human Rights at the End of History", 4/1 *Angelaki*, 99 (1999); Pierre Schlag, "The problem of the Subject", 69 *Texas Law Review*, 1627 (1991); W. T. Murphy, *The Oldest Social Science? Configurations of Law and Modernity* (Oxford, Oxford University Press, 1997). For recent efforts, inspired mostly by psychoanalysis, see Peter Goodrich, *Oedipus Lex*, supra n. 1; Jeanne Shroeder and David Carslon, "The Subject is Nothing", 5 *Law and Critique*, 93 (1994); David Carlson, "Duellism in American Jurisprudence", *Cardozo Law Review*, forthcoming 2000.

ensemble of rules, norms or normative statements which aim to regulate human conduct and derives all rights from those rules. For positivist jurisprudence, in its various guises, the law presupposes and promotes individual rights; conversely, legal rights presuppose and depend on an objective system of rules. We will follow the weak outline of the legal subject in this imbrication of rules and rights.

Within the broad positivist framework, the provenance of rights has been attributed to a number of ideas or theories. Under the contract theory, a right exists when a duty-bearer owes an obligation to the right-holder because of a prior promise. Under the so-called power theories, the right-holder has a right, if a rule makes his choice or will dominant over the actions or wills of others. Typically, a right exists if the right-holder has been given by law the power to demand that another person performs an obligation or abstains from certain activities, thus enabling the exercise of the right. Finally, under the interests theory, a right is an interest protected by a rule of law, which creates the necessary conditions for the enjoyment of that interest. Common to all these approaches is the claim that rights are personal capacities sanctioned by law in order to promote approved individual interests and to serve socially determined policy objectives. Rights are ways of pursuing social choices by recognising individual wants and assigning them to people.

In most instances, the exercise of a right depends on the provision of certain material preconditions and to that extent its effective implementation is context-dependent. The Abortion Act 1967, for example, created a legal right to abortion in certain circumstances. But the ability of women to carry out a termination within the terms of the Act depends largely on the provision and organisation of medical and other support services, on the availability of the necessary financial resources, finally, on women's awareness of existing facilities. Having a right in the abstract does not mean much, as Burke and Marx noted a long time ago, if the necessary material, institutional and emotional resources for its realisation are not available.

Contemporary rights theories recognise the context-dependence of the effective implementation of rights and, to that extent, they are a clear improvement on earlier normative versions. These were satisfied to declare the deontic nature and logical necessity of rights but remained totally uninterested in their conditions of implementation, insisting on the sterile distinction between "validity" and "effectiveness". But the "ontology" of rights remains fully wedded to the intrinsic connection between the concepts of rule or norm, occasionally expanded to include "principles" and institutionally sanctioned moral expectations, and that of right. Rights are analytically tied to rule-governed behaviour; rules create rights and rights belong to people, they exist only with the support of a subject.

This internal link has a number of implications. First, the relationship between law and the subject is circular. The law presupposes the existence of subjects and its rules define their capacities, powers, immunities and duties; without subjects rules would make no sense. A legal subject, whether a human being or an artificial entity (a company or association, the state or a municipality), exists if the law recognises its ability to bear rights and duties. The subject is a creation of the law, an artificial entity which serves as the logical support of legal relations.[7] Right and subject come into life together.[8] But on the other hand, the law operates effectively because legal subjects accept its legitimacy and recognise its power to create rights. There is no subject and right without the law, but the law cannot operate without assuming legal subjects. To be more precise, the relationship is triangular. Rule, subject and right come together and presuppose one another: the legal subject is the subject of rights through the operation of a legal norm which assigns rights and duties to subjects.

This is the approach of the greatest positivist jurist, Hans Kelsen. To purify "legal science" fully and turn it into a materially uncontaminated science of norms and concepts, Kelsen had to deconstruct the grandiose claims of legal humanism. For Kelsen, the legal subject, rather than being the centre of law, is a secondary legal construct, a logical space or *point de capeton* which helps bring together and combine a number of norms and rules of behaviour. The subject is the carrier of rights and duties, a personification of norms. As Kelsen put it, the "legal person is not a human being, but the personalised combination of legal rules which impose obligations and give entitlements to one and the same person. It is not a natural entity but a legal construct created by the science of law, an ancillary concept for the description and creation of the elements of law".[9] In this sense, the

---

[7] This approach was first emphasised by the French jurist Leon Duguit at the beginning of the century. See *Traité de Droit Constitutionnel*, Paris 1921, Vol. 1, 200, 319–326, 361ff. See also A. Manitakis, *The Subject of Constitutional Rights* (Athens, 1981) 42–46.

[8] G. de la Pradelle, *L"Homme Juridique* (Paris, Maspero, 1979), writes that "le sujet de droit est l'être quelconque à qui les normes juridiques s'adressent et qui est, par conséquent, titulaire des prérogatives que ces normes instituent en déterminant, par cela seul, sa personnalité au sens strict", 75–6.

[9] Hans Kelsen, *General Theory of Law and State* (Cambridge Mass., Harvard University Press, 1949) 93.

natural legal person is more artificial than a corporation, because its status as a human being obscures what is perfectly visible in the company: the fact that they are both creations of the law.

The legal subject is therefore a constructed *subjectus,* a legal creation or fiction. Its first manifestations were organised, according to "the scriptural definitions of king and subject, majesty and subjection . . . the fundamental substrate of the social order was a body of [religious and legal] texts, and in consequence the subject belonged first and most directly to a textual order. It was the text, in other words, that defined subjection, both the identity and the duty of the subject, and it was within the text that this legal fiction of a person had its being".[10] As we saw, these early limited protections assumed that human beings were obedient and dutiful souls. But when modern law made rights its building blocks, human beings were re-defined as creatures of will and desire. "The starting point of the science of law is Man, as soon as man is constituted into a legal subject. The point of arrival of bourgeois legal science is man. This science does not move, it starts with man and ends up rediscovering the subject".[11]

All human beings are legal subjects, constituted by the ensemble of legal recognitions and juridical relations. An infant is born to his mother and, for a second time, to the law. From birth, and in some instances from conception, the human being becomes more or less of a legal subject. The newly-born is an almost empty ground, a largely undifferentiated substratum or vessel which, as life passes, will be gradually invested with rights and duties, privileges and obligations until death. This would change radically, if a federal Bill before the US Congress in the summer of 1999 were to become law. It recognises the foetus as a separate legal entity from its future mother and makes it a crime for anyone, including the mother, to harm it in any way. This is a draconian anti-abortion measure; whether it enters the statute book or not, it is further evidence of the argument of this book that (legal) subjectivity, like humanity, is an elastic category that can be extended and contracted without great difficulty and that, in doing so, the law exercises its anthropogenetic power. The legal subject is a metaphorical place where the various capacities and powers assigned by law converge, a canvas upon which the different legal states and statuses will be painted giving the person her broad contour and definition. Legal rules do not address themselves to real

---

[10] Peter Goodrich, "Social Science and the Displacement of Law", 32/2 *Law and Society Review* 473 (1998), at 477.

[11] B. Edelman, *Le Droit saisi par la photographie* (Paris, Maspero, 1973) 102.

people, but to the juridical personality created by the law to represent the human person. As Tim Murphy puts it, "the legal subject
presents 'itself' to the law as a face, or a sur-face, which is to say a
screen on to which various projections will be effected".[12]

II. THE SUBJECT OF HUMAN RIGHTS

One notable exception to the jurisprudential abstinence on the subject of the subject is Carlos Nino, the Argentinean political philosopher, who attempted to reconstruct the philosophy and ethics of
human rights in order to refute the critics of liberalism.[13] Nino put
forward an impressive theory on the subject of human rights which,
he claims, while endowed with a large number of characteristics, has
nonetheless a consistent and clear constitution.

According to Nino, the uniting characteristic of legal subjects is
that they are "not tied to any end, they are an originating source of
valid claims, and they are responsible for their ends".[14] In this important formulation, we find the main elements of legal subjectivity. The
subject is the product of the destruction of the teleological view of
the world. Pre-modern virtue and the duties accompanying it have
been replaced by unencumbered people and free choices. The idea
of the naturally right is replaced by many rights, that of the good by
many incommensurable values and principles held and defined by
individuals, the classical concept of justice by freedom as autonomy,
in which self (*autos*) gives itself the law (*nomos*). Freedom defined as a
will freed to "choose ends, adopt interests, form desires" is the ultimate value in a valueless world. The subject "originates" his interests
and desires in God-like fashion and this election makes him responsible. The ability to choose is the most important characteristic and
"the person constituted by it, is prior to any end, interest and desire.
This implies, that when we refer to an interest or desire, we presuppose a subject, and that the identity of that subject, the moral person,
does not change with its ends, interests, or desires".[15]

---

[12] W. T. Murphy, supra n. 6, 196.
[13] Carlos Nino, *The Ethics of Human Rights* (Oxford, Clarendon, 1993). Interestingly,
Nino, unlike his Anglo-American colleagues, was actively involved in the legal rights movement against the Argentinean hunta and was a leading adviser of the first democratically
elected President. See his *The Radical Evil on Trial* (New Haven, Yale University Press, 1996).
[14] ibid., 110.
[15] ibid.

Nino has synthesised in these formulations the main classical civil-ian positions on the subject. Individual rights, the French *droit subjec-tive*, have been defined by Jellinek, "as that interest protected by the recognition of the human power to will".[16] Freedom of will, the will to will, to quote Heidegger, is the underlying and permanent force that constitutes the subject. It gives the subject its unity and identity over time; in classical metaphysical terms the (moral, legal) subject is the substratum presupposed and constituted by free will. A right raises an individual will into general will, in the sense that the state recog-nises and enforces it, thus giving it "objective" existence.[17] Rights legalise individual will and materialise individual desire. According to a leading Romanist, "man is the subject of rights because every pos-sibility of determining himself is accorded him, because he has a will".[18] For Hart too, rights give to people a kind of "sovereignty" over their world and entitle them to impose duties on others.[19] Values and laws not freely adopted by the subject have no validity. They are the legal form of individualism, in the same way that the market is its economic and perspectivism its artistic forms. As Bloch put it, "the person who is too free says that all that pleases is permit-ted. Juridically speaking the same view appears, not as limited, but as belonging to the capacity to will".[20]

The separation between the willing subject and his predicates or choices (ends, interests, desires) which can be realised outside of the subject, pits the subject against the world, which is revealed in its objectivity ready for objectification and mastery. The real is the rei-fied matter from which the subject will carve out the objects of his desires and interests. But the reification of the world leads to the impoverishment of the subject. The legal is the thinnest of the "thin conceptions of the person". It represents a state of personhood which not just divides the subject from its determinations, but also separates people into isolated monads. "Moral persons are also separate from each other . . . collectivities are not moral persons". This thin con-ception of the subject is "necessarily assumed when we participate in

---

[16] Jellinek quoted in Ernst Bloch, *Natural Law and Human Dignity* (D. J. Schmidt trans.) (Cambridge, Mass., MIT Press, 1988) 210.

[17] The so-called "will theory" is one of the most prominent and permanent theories of rights, according to which, someone has a right if he is in a position to determine how another person shall act. H.L.A Hart, "Are There Any Natural Rights?", 64 *Philosophical Review*, 175–91, 178, 181 (1955).

[18] Quoted in Bloch., supra n. 16, 217

[19] Hart, op.cit., fn. 17.

[20] Bloch, op.cit., supra n. 16, 210.

the practice of moral discourse" and is due to the "joint operation of the formal features of generality and universality of moral principles".[21] Finally it is "metaphysical in the sense of being obtained through some sort of 'transcendental' method".[22] We should add that it is metaphysical in a much deeper sense. It turns the subject into the measure of all that exists by attributing to him an infinite and unreal freedom to will and, turns the world into inert matter available to the subject for the realisation of his interests and desires.

Let us have a closer look at the "thin" fictional subject and compare it with a real "fat" person. People belong to the world of facts and contingency, emotions and passion, conscious desires and unconscious urges, voluntary actions, unknown motives and unforeseen consequences. The subject, on the other hand, belongs to the law, his personality constructed and regulated by legal rules. Rules follow logic and precedent, the methods of legal reasoning and the protocols of legal validity. As a result, a degree of simplicity and rigour characterises the legal subject that reminds of the submissive hero of Von Masoch's *Venus in Furs*.[23] There is a big difference between the real person and the legal subject representing her, a gap not dissimilar to that between a richly coloured and finely detailed portrait and an outline drawing of the same person. The legal subject is the caricature of the real person, a cartoon-like figure which, as all caricature, exaggerates certain features and characteristics and totally misses others. As Vining argues, legal individualism "has nothing to do with the concern for the dignity, happiness or importance of the individual. It defines rather a particular way of populating our thought with living units of reference, no more universal or basic than the various personifications of wind or water which have lost their vivid meaning".[24]

The gap between a real person and her legal persona takes the form of both excess and lack, and becomes fully visible when people start legal proceedings. Excess: the law ascribes to the subject a surplus of reason, an extreme rationalism, which portrays him as a calculating machine. The legal subject as much as the "economic" or "rational" man of neo-liberalism are "abstractions from real people emphasising one side of human life – the ability to reason and calculate – at the

[21] Nino op.cit., supra n. 13, 112, 113.

[22] ibid., 115.

[23] For the contractual basis of masochism and the constitutional of sadism, see Gilles Deleuze, "Coldness and Cruelty" in *Masochism* (J. McNeil trans.) (New York, Zone Books, 1989).

[24] J. Vining, *Legal Identity* (New Haven, Yale University Press, 1978) 2.

expense of every social circumstance that actually brings individuals to reason and calculate in particular ways".[25] This is the reason why the "reasonable man" is such a key figure in legal reasoning. When feminists or critical scholars attack the gender or racial constitution of this construct, they miss the basic point of the "Clapham omnibus". The reasonable man is not a conspiracy by conservative judges, but a cipher or symbol of the legal subject who cannot go cruising in Clapham, since anything to do with the body or the senses is not part of the realm of reason and must be bracketed or excluded. The legal subject is not just thin but ethereal, while real people are always "fat", full of weaknesses, inadequacies and uncertainties.

Indeed, the relationship between subject and person is mainly defined by what the former lacks, the absence of those characteristics which create human identity. In existential terms, the subject of legal and contractual rights and agreements stands at the centre of the universe and asks the law to enforce his entitlements without great concern for ethical considerations and without empathy for the other. If the legal person is an isolated and narcissistic subject that perceives the world as a hostile place to be either used or fended against through the medium of rights and contracts, she is also disembodied, genderless, a strangely mutilated person. As Schlag puts it, "this emancipation of the self from its contexts . . . is what enables it to be emancipated from all forces and influences other than law itself".[26] In the legal universe, both I and the other, as legal subjects, are rational beings with rights, entitlements and duties. We expect to be treated equally with the other and reciprocity of entitlement and obligation is placed at the basis of the legal mentality. But this equality is only formal: it necessarily ignores the specific history, motive and need the litigant brings to the law in order to administer the calculation of the rule and the application of the measure. The abstract juridical subject is a "metaphysical or calculating, self-interested being, conceived in an asocial way in a world whose sociality was no more than the coming together of individuals in a social contract . . . the law knew no real individuals, only their mystical abstractions".[27] Between lack and excess, the legal subject becomes a malleable vehicle:

> By addressing the consumer as an empty subject, liberal justification seduces or shames her into assuming this more noble and more ethically appealing version of herself, further causing her to put aside her

[25] Alan Norrie, op.cit., supra n. 6, 23.
[26] Pierre Schlag, *The Enchantment of Reason* (Durham, Duke University Press, 1998) 127.
[27] ibid., 31.

own particular tastes, references, idiosyncrasies, and other concrete aspects. By addressing the consumer as a full subject, liberal justification uses greed and fear to convince the consumer that it is in her own interest – within her own particular tastes, preferences, and idiosyncrasies as a full subject – to acquiesce in the rules laid down by the empty subject.[28]

We have examined elsewhere the strange amorality of legal mentality, which promises to replace ethical responsibility with the mechanical application of predetermined and morally neutral rules and justice with the administration of justice.[29] Analytical moral philosophy with its unbridled rationalism needs and creates the "generalised other". The law, on the other hand, sharing the preoccupation to abstract and universalise, turns concrete people into generalised legal subjects. The difference between the fictional agents of moral philosophy and those of the law, is that the legal subject is a persona or mask put on real people who, unlike the abstractions of moral philosophy, hurt, feel pain and suffer.

Let us examine, finally and briefly, some instances of this suffering, cases where the legal subject undermines the real person. One instructive instance is the division between intention and motive in criminal law. Motive refers to need, desire, purpose, individual and social history, conscious and unconscious urges to action, in other words, to what makes people real. Intention, on the other hand, is an artificial construction referring to fault, the ascription of responsibility irrespective of reasons or motives for action. And yet intention is the main concept in criminal law, while motive is totally ignored in the determination of guilt and is introduced in a peripheral way at the stage of sentencing or in certain exceptional defences, like duress. According to Alan Norrie, the law "neglects [motive] a normal mental element in human conduct" and does not go "beyond the standpoint of the small child".[30] As Anatole France put it, the law in its majesty punishes equally rich and poor for stealing bread or sleeping under bridges. Norrie and other Marxist theorists find this state of affairs irrational, the result of law's political bias. This may be partly true, but the real reason for the choice lies elsewhere: the legal person is the main cipher and metaphysical companion of the subject of

[28] Pierre Schlag, "The Empty Circles of Liberal Justification", 96 *Michigan Law Review* 1 (1997), 37.

[29] Douzinas and Warrington, *Justice Miscarried* (Edinburgh, Edinburgh University Press, 1994) Chapter 4.

[30] ibid., Chapter 3 and at 37.

modernity. Our whole anthropocentric universe has been built on the assumption that the subject is morally responsible for his freedom and legally liable for his actions. The law must disregard motives and circumstances, which introduce external determinations, in order to support the foundation stone of our epoch, the claim that free will is the dominant principle and the subject the master of his fate and the world. If motive were to replace intention in the determination of culpability, the centrality of subjectivity would come to an end. This does not appear to be on the historical agenda at the moment.

The same structure is evident in the operation of legally sanctioned freedoms. It is the freedom to accede to the available repertoire of legal forms and rights, the freedom to be what the law has ordained, accompanied by the threat that opting out is not permitted, that disobedience to a legal norm is disobedience to the rule of law *tout court* and that life outside the legal form ceases. Contract provides the example here; while the contracting parties are usually unequal and the consumer or worker has no alternative but to enter the agreement with the retailer, the utilities provider or the employer, the law assumes that the deal has been agreed after free negotiations between broadly equal partners. Again the facade is more important than the content, the principle than the facts, the logical neatness than the empirical experience or moral rightness. The legal subject, the key concept without which rights cannot exist, is by definition highly abstract, a frame or skeleton that will be filled in with the weak flesh of duties and the discoloured blood of rights. Legal metaphysics has no time for the pain of real people.

III. LEGAL HUMANISM AND HUMAN RIGHTS

Carlos Nino, who did not shy away from the philosophical tradition, shows clearly how the ontology of (human) rights follows the Cartesian and Kantian attitude towards subject and nature. Man has been expelled from nature which becomes estranged and alien, and the subject as an isolated monad with a solitary consciousness turns on himself to create programmes of legislation and life-plans. For the legal mentality, the being of being human is present in the willing unrestrained and solitary legal subject. The world is set against the subject, as object of representation and intervention; it takes its official designation in the objective definitions of the legal system and acquires its meaning and value by means of the subject's legal choices.

The turning of the human being into a legal subject goes hand in hand with the creation of an objective legal universe posited over against it. The jurisprudence of rights is the necessary and inevitable dancing partner of legal positivism; there can be no positivised law without the concept of the subject as the bearer of rights and there can be no conception of rights without a positive set of laws and institutions that bring the subject into existence and endow it with his patrimony of rights.

It can be argued therefore that the concept of rights is both the foundation and culmination of the philosophical, legal and moral world view of modernity. It encompasses all aspects of the organisation of self, community, state and the international world. It is the building block of law, the moral universe and freedom. A rights-based legal system, places the subject at the centre and reflects and enforces his powers, faculties or desires. Right is a public capacity given to the individual to allow him to attain his privates objects of desire. These subjective capacities have no inherent limitation and it is only when they come across the same rights of others that boundaries are erected. As a result, a social order based on rights comprises the sum total of legal subjects and has little organic existence or structural organisation; its moral and social principles are the outcome of acts of will, its judgments of calculations aided by legal reason. Legal rights, these *droits subjectives*, have an internal link with the metaphysics of subjectivity, they are its legal validation. The two entered the historical scene at the same time and complement each other perfectly.

Classical right or *jus* was a limitation on individual excess; modern rights have no inherent limit in them: they are the legalisation of desire and as such the sanctification of individual limitlessness. Rights do not derive from objective nature but from individual desire, they follow Burke's "catechism of passions". Subjectivity founds rights, "subjective rights express certain possibilities that are inherent in the *individual subject*".[31] The law translates desire into right and turns it into the cornerstone of the social bond. Desires are posited by individual wills, rights are their formal recognition and pre-conditions of humanity: the more rights an individual has, the more human he is. As Strauss put it, "rights express, and are meant to express, something that everyone desires anyway; they hallow everyone's self-interest as

---

[31] Luc Ferry and Alain Renault, *From the Rights of Man to the Republican Idea* (Franklin Philip trans.) (Chicago, University of Chicago Press, 1992) 40.

everyone can be brought to see it".[32] If a new object of desire gets couched in legal terms, if a new claim crosses the threshold of popular acceptability, its full legal recognition is a matter of time and legal recognition turns it into another "essential" human characteristic. At the limit, all desires will become legalised, all interests will give rise to enforceable claims and full humanity will be achieved, a state which, Villey, Strauss and Legendre believe, will lead to the total dissolution of the social bond and will not be far removed from total inhumanity.

We see this happening already in international relations after the collapse of the communist empires. Every minority, tribe or group which insistently claims to possess ethnic identity and cultural tradition eventually becomes an independent state or entity and proceeds to oppress smaller minorities in it, as the treatment of Russians in newly independent post-Soviet states and of Serbs in post-war Kosovo shows. When international politics are dominated by the rhetoric of rights, no moral argument can resist the desire of even small groups to acquire autonomy and statehood. But this defiance of history by desire has inevitably led to greater conflict and misery. A world map in the form of a mosaic of statelets will be a natural extension of the aggressive logic of rights but at a huge distance from the cosmopolitan peace which Kant hoped rights would lead to.

At the peak of the political and legal pyramid, the Sovereign power, itself constructed as a legal subject, is similarly endowed with powers and freedoms. Natural and human rights acquired special importance in early modernity because they promised to remove or limit some of these legislative or administrative powers thus preventing absolutism. But the endless extension of rights to match ever-expanding desire threatens their protective role. In Strauss' terms "if the ultimate criterion of justice becomes the general will, i.e. the will of a free society, cannibalism is as just as its opposite. Every institution hallowed by a folk-mind has to be regarded as sacred".[33] What started as the modern standard of critique of the real dissolves when rights follow factual agreements or impositions of power and no distinction is left between the real and the ideal. A right that belongs exclusively to the real is not far removed, indeed it is synonymous with the legal positivist conception of law-created rights; such rights can scarcely act as the standard of critique of what (legally) exists.

[32] Leo Strauss, *Natural Law and History* (Chicago, University of Chicago Press, 1965) 182–3.
[33] Leo Strauss, *What Is Political Philosophy* (Chicago, University of Chicago Press, 1959) 51.

Legal humanism posited man as the author and end of law and culminated in the idea of human rights. But when human rights undermine the distinction between the real and the ideal, they become the foundation of modern historicism. Rather than being a defence against the state and legal positivism, they end up the bedfellows of positivism, unable to provide a standard of critique and totally inadequate in their proclaimed task of defending the lonely individual against the demands of the all-powerful Sovereign, itself presented in the guise of a super-individual entity with its desires, rights and powers. Legal humanism, writes Villey, is the "tendency to posit man as the principle and end of everything . . . for nearly all modern thinkers about law man in the author of law".[34] This is no aberration of civilian metaphysicians, unknown to the pragmatism of common law. Reason and will, the two facets of legal humanism and rationalism and voluntarism, their two deformations, are perfectly encapsulated in the perennial conundrum of British constitutionalism: the contradiction between the rule of law and parliamentary sovereignty which, the Human Rights Act, loyal to tradition, retained in all its majesty.

The subject of law, as the double genitive indicates, is both what authors the law and what is subjected by it. Every posited rule presupposes an author, a legislative subject: Parliament for primary legislation, a minister for delegated rules, judges for the common law. But this superior legislative subject is also the product of rules, the addressee of norms defining its composition, procedures, and competence. The constitution of modernity, which started with the humanist premise of supporting the natural freedom of the individual, ends up covered by a hyper-inflation of norms: subjects breathe where rules speak, there can be no rule without subject and no subject without a rule. Our age suffers from what could be called "legal techno-nihilism": the more law we have the freer we are supposed to be, the more legal-technical relations define humanity, the more we should be able to order and control our lives. Like technocratic nihilism, metaphysical legalism turns against humanity in the name of freedom. But the protests of liberals against the over-legalisation of late modernity are as misguided as those of the orthodox Marxists.[35]

[34] Michel Villey, "L'Humanisme et le droit", in *Seize essais de philosophie du droit* (Paris, Dalloz, 1969) 60.

[35] The critique of over-legalisation and (particularly American) litigiousness is as old as Tocqueville. It has been joined recently by neo-liberals worried about over-regulation, communitarians worried about the corrosive effects of law on local communities and traditions and, interestingly, a number of Law Professors worried about the effects of too much

The proliferation of rules and the regulatory obsession is not an aberration of late modernity but the logical end of its strict operation,
which potentially will translate all human relations into legal rights.
For legal humanism, a fully legalised world is a human, all too human
world. There is an obvious continuity between metaphysics and historicism and legal humanism is part of the same process. One must
often attack legal humanism in order to defend humans against the
demands of (legalised) power.

But human rights hail also from another tradition, that of critique
of power convention and law and, they have developed in two directions. Bloch argued that there are two sources and types of rights.
The first is associated with possession and property as *dominium*, legal
dominance over things and people.[36] Its early formal development
aimed to protect the creditor from the debtor in cases of non pay-
ment of loans. The concept of human rights emerged from this earlier right to property but was "adopted in a quite different way by the
exploited and oppressed, the humiliated and degraded. It is precisely
this that appears in its incomparable second sense as the subjective
catchword of the revolutionary struggle and actively as the subjective
factor of this struggle".[37]

This statement remains true today. Rights are the building blocks
of modern law and are the legal expression of humanism and subjectivity. Human rights were initially law's critique and must be distinguished. With the extensive positivisation of human rights, however,
the external division between legal and human rights has been repli-
cated in the body of human rights themselves. When opposed to the
state and its laws, they act as a standard of critique, dissent and rebellion. When conceived solely as the never-ending legalisations of
desire and the grants of legislative largesse, they join the metaphysics
of subjectivity and are twinned with legal positivism.

We can see this bifurcation in the history of human rights. The
absolute protection of property led to the impoverishment of the
majority and the introduction of the second generation, and for

success on the soul of the profession. Mary Ann Glendon, *Rights Talk: The Impoverishment of
Political Discourse* (New York, Free Press, 1991); Michael Waltzer, *What it Means to be an
American* (New York, Marsillio, 1992); Solm Linowitz with Martin Mayer, *The Betrayed
Profession* (Baltimore, Johns Hopkins University Press, 1994); Paul Campos, *Jurismania: The
Madness of American Law* (Oxford, Oxford University Press, 1998).

[36] Richard Tuck too argues, in his influential *Natural Rights Theories* (Cambridge,
Cambridge University Press, 1979) Chapter 1, that the first conception of subjective right
developed out of the idea of *dominium* over property.

[37] Bloch, op.cit., supra n. 16, 217.

liberals second-rate, social and economic rights. The rights of man led to the belated introduction of children's and women's rights which, in turn, led to calls for greater parents' rights and fears of "male emasculation".[38] The limitless freedom of action led to mastery over the world and control of nature and to the call for new rights protecting animals and the environment. Boundless free speech led to the right to privacy and the obsession with pornography. Freedom of movement and establishment across Europe for its citizens, led to draconian restrictions of movement for immigrants and refugees. The often heard claim that the exercise of freedom carries responsibilities is a piece of unrealistic moralism. Freedom and rights carry no inherent limitations or moral duties; the only defence against their side-effects is to create even more rights and legal protections, increasing legalisation endlessly and making conflict the endemic and inescapable condition of the social bond. When rights justify every claim and sanctify every desire nothing has much value any longer.

Despite the problems, however, human rights are also the main tools we have against the cannibalism of public and private power and the narcissism of rights. Human rights are the utopian element behind legal rights. Rights are the building block of a liberal legal system. Human rights are its claim to justice and as such impossible and future looking. Human rights are parasites on the body of rights, judging the host. There is a poetry in human rights that defies the rationalism of law: when a burnt child runs from the scene of an atrocity in Vietnam, when a young man stands in front of a tank in Beijing, when an emaciated body and dulled eyes face the camera from behind the barbed wire of a concentration camp in Bosnia, a tragic sense erupts and places me, the onlooker, face to face with my responsibility, a responsibility that does not come from codes, conventions or rules but from a sense of personal guilt for the suffering in the world, of obligation to save humanity in the face of the victim.

IV. A HUMAN RIGHTS CULTURE?

Rights have recently acquired an unrivalled prominence in legal philosophy and political practice. After the collapse of communism, human rights have become the ultimate expression of the morality of

---

[38] Thomas Taylor, a precursor of the men's movement published his *Vindication of the Rights of Brutes* in 1792 arguing for full animal equality, as a lampooning response to Mary Wollstonecraft's defence of women's equality. Every right creates fears and anti-rights.

law, governmental policy and international relations. We live in a human rights culture. And as our epoch is the age of the end (of modernity, of ideology, of history, of utopia), rights are the ideology of the end. But this end-ism does not mean that the need and search for the foundation of rights has been forgotten, despite the claims of pragmatists, like Richard Rorty, that rights foundationalism is "outmoded".[39] The universalising urge has increased, in our globalised world, and the search for moral certainty and existential security has become even more grandiose after the exhaustion of grand theories. Admittedly, the old grounds, the good, God, transcendental man or abstract humanity, no longer command wide acceptance. The postmodern condition seeks foundations that do not look foundational.

Two such grounds have been used by contemporary jurisprudence. The first is a weak naturalist theory, under which a few minimal truisms about human nature have an almost universal validity and can therefore explain the permanent features of legal systems, including rights.[40] But the weakest of naturalisms is not persuasive against the pragmatist claim that human nature is malleable, the product of historically contingent cultural factors and cannot provide any morally relevant knowledge. The last resort of the modest foundationalist is an institutional moral intuitionism. When faced with a contested right, the most common jurisprudential method of argumentation and justification is to examine the deep values, underlying principles and institutional commitments of society in an attempt to show that they already include the contested right or that logic and morality demand its incorporation. In this approach, moral beliefs, values and rights are part of the universe we inhabit, a universe created through a process of institutional and cultural accretion over a period of time. Rights are not "objective" and have no independent external source. Similarly, they are not "subjective", arbitrary inventions of creative philosophers or crafty lawyers, but explicit or implicit long-term community commitments.

We may call this approach, the principle of "structural immanence" of morality and rights. Rights are creations of the imaginative interpretation of a particular political, legal and moral history. They exhibit coherence in style, consistency in principle and stability over time, and they are endowed with a certain intellectual force or "gravitational pull". They act as if they are the underlying grammar of the

[39] Richard Rorty, "Human Rights, Rationality and Sentimentality" in Stephen Shute and Susan Hurley (eds), *On Human Rights* (New York, Basic Books, 1993) 116.

[40] H.L.A. Hart, *The Concept of Law* (Oxford, Clarendon, 1979) Chapter IX.

sentences of law and, like all grammar, they enjoy a degree of oblig-
atoriness. This deep structure of principles and values is said to exist
both in the constitutional, legal and moral commitments of a particular society and in its wider cultural, literary and aesthetic values,
meanings and understandings. To say that Britain ought to recognise
a right to privacy means, for example, that our judges should
acknowledge the deep commitments of our legal, moral and political
system to principles such as freedom, autonomy and the protection
of private spheres of action, and extract from those the already immanent right to privacy. Our society and law should publicly admit
being what they already are.[41]

Dworkin's theory of rights is a good example.[42] He argues that
rights and principles are as much part of the law as rules and that the
institutional duty of judges is to present the law in its best possible
light. New decisions must further institutional history and present it
as a coherent whole, to which the addition falls naturally, like a new
chapter in a multi-authored novel. The "best" interpretation of legal
materials and the right(s) answer to a "hard case" must show the public standards of the community to be a single and coherent scheme,
animated by the principles of respect and concern. Principles and

---

[41] The most concise presentation of this view and cogent defence of liberal rights against
their critics is found in Jeremy Waldron, "Nonsense upon Stilts? – a reply" in J. Waldron
(ed.), *Nonsense upon Stilts: Bentham, Burke and Marx on the Rights of Man* (London, Methuen,
1987) 151–209. A variation of the immanent structure argument more evident in analytical
moral philosophy than jurisprudence, argues that human rights are normatively necessary
because "every agent logically must hold or accept that he and all other agents have these
rights because their Objects are the necessary conditions of human action", Alan Gewirth,
Human Rights (Chicago, University of Chicago Press, 1982) 20. Gewirth calls his method
"dialectically necessary": "it begins from statements presented as being made or accepted by
an agent; it proceeds from within his first-person conative standpoint, and it examines what
his statements logically imply within this standpoint . . . the statements logically must be
made or accepted by every agent because they derive from the generic features of purposive
action". This method is a "rational necessity" and rejecting its principle leads to "logical
inconsistensy", 210–6. The self-assuredness of contemporary neo-Kantianism is in astound-
ingly reverse proportion to the moral and political uncertainty that clouds the field of human
rights and can only be compared, in tone, with the arguments from "self-evidence" evident
in the writings of John Finnis. Most orthodox jurisprudence seems to hold to a combination
of the "immanent structure" and the "immanent moral and logical necessity" arguments for
rights. But even within the terms of analytical philosophy, the argument is unconvincing. As
Phaedra, Socrates, Kierkegaard, McIntyre and Nagel, amongst others acknowledged, even
the perfect moral theory has no guarantee that moral action will follow its prescriptions. I
know of many reasons why the powerful violate human rights but I know of no case where
violations stopped because the culprit felt that he was morally self-contradictory.

[42] Ronald Dworkin, *Taking Rights Seriously* (London, Duckworth, 1977); "Law as
Interpretation", in W.J.T. Mitchell (ed.) *The Politics of Interpretation* (Chicago, University of
Chicago Press, 1983); *Law's Empire* (London, Fontana, 1986).

rights are part of the law, both because they fit past legal choices and decisions, and because they justify them from the point of view of substantive political morality. If I object therefore to an act as a violation of human rights although it has not been legally recognised as such, I must use a type of argument which explains that the challenged act is inconsistent with deep commitments or principles our legal and political system values highly. If I succeed in linking the deep structure with the contested case, my interlocutor will have to accept the conclusion out of moral and/or intellectual honesty: morally, because he himself, values the same principles and beliefs of our society and therefore values also, *malgré lui*, the contested right or, because, unless he accepts that the contested right is a real one, a large number of positive commitments, principles and rights in our community would make no sense. More generally, political philosophers who follow this approach, conclude at the end of their deliberations that Western societies are committed to the principles of free will and autonomy, to formal equality and limited material equality. They discover, in other words, at the end of their quest the liberal principles they started with.

There are a number of obvious problems with all such "immanent structure" theories. The first and most serious takes us back to the discussion of the (Kantian) autonomous subject of rights. Autonomy was the result of the operation of moral reason: the subject becomes free by following the moral law he finds in himself. Moral philosophy hoped to "cleanse the worlds of prejudice and superstition. This cleansing would permit us to rise above our animality by becoming, for the first time, fully rational and thus fully human".[43] State law, on the other hand, is a heteronomous set of rules imposed on the subject from outside; morality and legality were initially strictly separate. But "immanent structure" theories have overcome the divide between law and ethics. The rationality of law was never in doubt for its apologists; now law has become fully moral too. In one sense, the immanence of rights is nothing more than the acknowledgement of the circular relationship between positive law and rights. But in the hands of "anti-positivist" rights theorists, like Dworkin, it becomes much more. The integration of law and rights means that law has been fully moralised, that all the resources for critique must be sought inside its body and that the radical aspect of human rights has been pushed out.

[43] Rorty, op.cit., supra n. 39, 112–3.

Edmund Burke argued that English law needed no transcendent principle of justification, because a latent or immanent wisdom of right was present in it. There were many reasons for this outburst of parochial megalomania, as we saw. They included the conservative fear of the French Revolution and of the radical, even revolutionary potential of the proclaimed rights. Natural rights were "an act of war against tyrants".[44] Burke believed that the British constitution was the perfect weapon against tyranny, and his denunciation of human rights and other principles of critique was a logical conclusion. English political and legal theory following his lead became preoccupied with the actual, with the creations of legal practice, and abandoned the quest for the ideal. The reality, which disqualifies or co-opts the ideal, may take an empiricist and positivist guise or, assume the form of idealised actuality. The first approach is that of legal positivism, the second, of the various rights theorists. Both claim that what is is what ought to be and both are equally hostile to critics who use external standards. Ronald Dworkin, for example, claims that law's empire must be defended from its enemies, external scepticism which does not use "arguments of the sort the enterprise requires"[45] and critical lawyers, the enemies within "in the service of undisclosed political goals".[46] In the passage from Burke to Dworkin, a certain loss of style and lowering of vision has occurred, but the sentiments expressed and the targets attacked are the same.

Immanent structure theories turn history into historicism. "The ideal (or, the rational identified with the true and the good) is not opposed to the real, but is realised by itself".[47] As a result, nothing escapes the empire of the existent. The fact/value distinction disappears, rights theories become exclusively "historical [and] unable to grasp anything eternal", a fake antidote to legal positivism.[48] Despite protestations to the contrary, the self-satisfied certainty of these theories is evidence of their metaphysical nature. The identification of rationality with the moral law was the early metaphysical move *par excellence*. State law has now become part of the equation and the form of legality, the ultimate principle of late modernity.

Metaphysics remains the plaything of the powerful and law, the will to eternalise momentary relations of power. For those who

---

[44] See Chapter 5, above.
[45] Dworkin, 1986, 303.
[46] Dworkin, 275
[47] Ferry and Renaut, op.cit., supra n. 31, 30.
[48] Leo Strauss, *Natural Right and History*, 12.

remain faithful to radical natural law and the aspiration and struggle for justice, on the other hand, acts of power cannot be successfully criticised through other acts of power. The record of liberal legal systems, when it comes to protecting real equality and existential freedom, is at best mixed. To that extent, human rights are in part the negation of the system of legal rights and cannot be grounded (if a ground is needed at all) in past decisions and commitments many of which are the cause of the problem or become fully legislated. Human rights are the utopian futural aspect of law. In their field, immanence trumps transcendence and history prevents the thought of the future.

Insipid historicism is not the only problem with "immanent structure" theories of rights. Their excessive dependence on contingent institutional choices, past preferences and historical commitments means that a right prevails only if the value attached to it by the relevant professional or wider community is relatively high. When opinion changes, nothing guarantees this right. Dworkin claims that rights demand opportunities or resources to be given even against the political and policy preferences of the moment. Rights are restraints on social policies and political choices, they have a "threshold weight" in relation to collective goods against which they act as "trumps". But their immersion in the history of the community means that their ability to restrict power is itself restricted. The history of anti-terrorism legislation in this country is a good example. Time and again governments legislated drastic restrictions on long-established civil liberties in the aftermath of terrorist outrages by exploiting the widespread revulsion against the perpetrators. The trumpeted "trump-card" of rights is of little value in situations where the alleged immanent structure of rights comes into direct conflict with strong surface illiberal emotion. These are the instances where the protective value of human rights is at the highest but their effectiveness at the lowest.

Similar problems exist when we move from the normative to the cognitive aspects of immanent structure theories. A main intellectual attraction of rights discourse is its ability to describe complex social and political situations, and especially conflicts, in simple normative terms. But this is also its most serious shortcoming. The claim that a set of solid, generally acceptable and non-controversial principles lies behind the complex and contradictory beliefs, value systems and emotions of a contemporary society or legal system, is empirically unprovable and theoretically absurd. It assumes that societies have somehow accepted liberal priorities and are on the way to a cultural and moral homogeneity. But sociologists, economists and cultural historians tell us that societies are becoming more diverse, open and conflictual. The politics of identity and cultural diversity of the eighties and nineties have, if anything, increased fragmentation and polyphony. The belief in underlying common values comes totally unstuck in cases of political conflict, where rights seem to evaporate and to transform into interests, will and power. But even within the more serene confines of private law, the claim that rights extend into new areas through the combination of the inexorable logic of underlying principles with consistency and good faith sounds extravagant. Dworkin implicitly recognises the empirical improbability of his theory, when he presents his ideal judge as a latter day Hercules and places demands on him which, in their difficulty, are not unlike Herculean labours.

A domestic conflict such as the miners' strike in the mid-eighties, could be described as a conflict between the right of striking miners to withhold their labour and the right to work of working miners. But such a description would not help us understand the background, issues and interests involved. Even worse, the presentation of conflict in terms of rights does not help and could even retard its resolution. Conflicting groups and interests in situations of acute struggle share few values and beliefs. The conflict itself is evidence of the absence or collapse of any immanent or shared value structure. In the absence of a meta-principle external to the conflict which could act as an arbiter, the importation of rights discourse is likely to strengthen the resolve of the parties and make them less amenable to negotiation or compromise, as it removes the fight from the terrain of warring interests into that of allegedly absolute truths and uncompromising entitlements. In these instances, rights–claims appear to be at their most compelling, but the justificatory power of "immanent structure" theories is at its least convincing. The use of rights discourse to describe normatively a conflict or a set of claims is a limited way of narrativising the situation. It is cognitively inaccurate and morally impoverished: inaccurate because it presents a limited view of the world as complete, as if one of Cézanne's drawings of the *Montaigne Sainte Victoire* was the definite representation of the mount. Impoverished, because it assumes that the various claims, interests and specificities of the parties can be translated into one common language.

Immanent value structures assume too much, both in terms of their theory of argumentation and of the society they try to represent.

They demand an unrealistic consistency of principle in argument and they presuppose their conclusions, namely that the whole society and its underlying principles are committed liberals. These problems are further exarcebated by the formalistic and indeterminate language of rights. It is arguable that the contemporary appeal of rights discourse is partly due to its language, which has become so wide, abstract and all-encompassing, that it may be used in all kinds of political and social conflicts to provide moral legitimacy to every interest and claim, from the most serious to the most trivial. This proliferation of claims and the inflation of language, risks making the discourse meaningless: in potentially justifying everything, human rights end up justifying nothing. But there is more: it is one thing to accept that a particular right exists or ought to be recognised and a totally different to determine what that means in practice, what concrete measures, including legal ones, should be taken to protect it. Arguing rights in the abstract is the prerogative of legal and moral philosophers, Burke's "metaphysical doctors". But their practical value is variable and context-dependent because they are applied locally and address concrete situations and singular problems. While the language of liberal jurisprudence is abstract and formalistic, the application of human rights depends on considerations, factors and circumstances unrelated to the grammar of rights. The individuation of a right moves from abstract and indeterminate language to the specifics of the situation and is so elongated, complex and context-specific that identical premises may justify totally opposed outcomes. The same provision of the American Constitution, for example, the Fourteenth Amendment equal protection of laws clause, established the principle of colour segregation and apartheid in *Plessey* v. *Fergusson* and the principle of desegregation and equality in *Brown* v. *Board of Education of Topeka*.[49]

The second consequence of the context-dependence of rights is that general statements about the state of rights are usually meaningless. We cannot say, for instance, that free speech is generally protected or violated in America. What we can say with a degree of confidence is that the rights of anarcho-syndicalists and socialists were violated in the twenties, the rights of communists in the fifties and

---

[49] Under the *Plessey* v. *Fergusson* "separate but equal" doctrine, equality of treatment is accorded when the races are provided substantially equal facilities, even though these facilities be separate, 163 U.S. 537 (1896). In *Brown* the Supreme Court reversed, stating that "in the field of public education the doctine of 'separate but equal' has no place. Separate educational facilities are inherently unequal", 347 U.S. 483 (1954).

those of anti-Vietnam war protesters in the sixties. Similarly, using the same term (freedom of expression) to describe such diverse situations as pornography, the Salman Rushdie affair and the marches of National Front supporters through ethnic minority communities, helps only obscure the totally different considerations and conflicts involved in each instance under the formally identical but meaninglessly vague term.

Finally, do we live in a human rights culture? Richard Rorty claims that we do and that, if we were to forget the metaphysical urge to find unitary grounds, we would better serve their ends. The task of good liberals should be to educate the sentiments and emotions of people so that they respond with sympathy to human misery and suffering. Rorty argues correctly, I believe, that reason alone can neither give universal answers to moral questions nor can it move people to act against their moral instincts. Sentimental education is obviously an important tool in the struggle for human rights. But his argument against foundational moralisms which are based on unprovable "claims to knowledge about the nature of human beings",[50] depends on the arrogant assertion that our "Eurocentric human rights culture" is obviously superior to that of others, and our task of directing their sentiments towards Western moral intuitions is self-evidently right. The experience of the last century tells us, however, that when the human rights phenomenon becomes a "fact of the world", as Rorty claims,[51] sympathy for the suffering other may lose the edge it had when it was a cry of protest and rebellion. If that is the case, we may have become a rights culture but, against Rorty's hopes, we have weakened the passion for human rights.

V. THE FLOATING SIGNIFIER: THE SEMIOTICS OF HUMAN RIGHTS

a. Linguistic tricks

Rorty's warning against the liberal metaphysics of the subject and reason is extremely timely. Despite reservations about his "anti-theory" theory and uncritical celebration of political liberalism, Rorty invites us to treat rights in a non-metaphysical way: as symbolic strategies of linguistic and legal communication with important political effects.

[50] Rorty, op.cit., supra n. 39, 117.
[51] ibid., 134.

We will discuss later how an ethical understanding of rights invests them perhaps with a "transcendence in immanence", which can be used as a corrective against their dominant voluntarism and historicism. Similarly, some of the concepts used in this part, such as the struggle for recognition and the psychoanalytical understanding of desire, will be discussed fully in Chapters 10 and 11. Our present task is more limited and technical. Accepting that rights are part of our legal and moral universe and participate in the construction of legal subjects, we will try to understand the semiotic, political and rhetorical strategies involved in the use and extension of rights to new claimants and areas of entitlement.

From a semiotic perspective, rights are highly artificial constructs, a historical accident of European intellectual and political history, which was taken up, simplified and moralised in America and, in its new form, bequeathed to the world in the 1940s as the mainstay of political morality. The concept of rights is flexible rather than stable, fragmented rather than unitary and fuzzy rather than determinant. It belongs to the symbolic order of language and law which determines the scope and reach of rights with scant regard for ontologically solid categories. As symbolic constructs, rights do not refer to things or other material entities in the world. Rights are pure combinations of legal and linguistic signs, and they refer to more signs, words and images, symbols and fantasies. No person, thing or relation is in principle closed to the logic of rights, since their semiotic organisation has no solid referent in the world. Any entity open to semiotic substitution can become the subject or object of rights, any right can be extended to new areas and persons or conversely withdrawn from existing ones. Nothing in the ontology of potential subjects or in the nature of objects inherently stops them from entering the hallowed space of rights. The rhetorical elasticity of language finds no fixed boundaries to its creativity and ability to colonise the world. The only limits to the expansion or contraction of rights are conventional: the success or otherwise of political struggles, or the effects of the limited and limiting logic of the law. The ceaseless expansion of rights is the main characteristic of their history: civil and political rights have been extended to social and economic rights and then to rights in culture and the environment. Individual rights have been supplemented by group, national or animal rights. The right to free speech or to annual holidays can be accompanied by the right to love, to good food or to have back episodes of *Star Trek* shown daily. Indeed, the statements "I have a right to x" or "this is my right" express the postmodern politics of identity. "I have a right" is used as synonymous to "I want" or "I demand" and if enough pressure is put behind the demand, it becomes a legal right. The abandoned lover, the raver who demands the right to party and the sacked worker are all united in asking for public recognition of their private desire. In semiotic terms, the right to work cannot be distinguished easily from the right to party. If something can be put into language, it may acquire rights and can certainly become the object of rights. But what processes are involved in this endless proliferation of rights?

We argued above, that the main characteristic of the "man" of the *droits de l'homme* is the total lack of determination of his substance beyond the declaration – itself empty of content – of his free will. Similarly, humanity, "man's" successor, is an ever-present but undifferentiated attribute of human identity that awaits to be assigned predication, characteristics, a time and a place. Using the terminology of semiotics, one can argue that the "man" of the rights of man or, the "human" of human rights, functions as a floating signifier. As a **signifier**, it is just a word, a discursive element that is not automatically or necessarily linked to any particular signified or concept. On the contrary, the word "human" is empty of meaning and can be attached to an infinite number of signifieds. As a result, it cannot be fully and finally pinned down to any particular conception, because it transcends and overdetermines them all.[52] But the "humanity" of human rights is not just an empty signifier; it carries an enormous symbolic capital, a surplus of value and dignity endowed by the revolutions and the declarations and augmented by every new struggle for the recognition and protection of human rights. This symbolic excess turns the signifier "human" into a **floating** signifier, into something that combatants in political, social and legal struggles want to co-opt to their cause in order to benefit from its symbolic capital.

To have human rights, which in modernity is synonymous to being human, you must claim them. A new right is recognised, if it succeeds in fixing a – temporary or partial – determination on the word "human", if it manages to arrest its flight. This process is carried out in political, ideological and institutional struggles. Typically, diverse groups, campaigns and individuals fight in a number of political, cultural and legal arenas and through divergent and interlocking practices, such as public protest, lobbying, party politics or test-cases,

---

[52] For a use of the psychoanalytical concept of "overdetermination" in political theory, see Ernesto Laclau and Chantal Mouffe, *Hegemony and Socialist Strategy* (London, Verso, 1985).

to have an existing right extended or a new type of right accepted. These occasionally disparate efforts are linked to each other through the symbolic and linguistic nature of the right claimed. The creative potential of language and of rhetoric allows the original rights of "man" to break up and proliferate into the rights of various types of subject, e.g. the rights of workers, women, children, refugees or the rights of a people to self-determination, or animal and environmental rights.

The mechanism of extension is usually the following: the claimants assert both their similarity and difference with groups whose claims have already been admitted. First, similarity. The affinity between human nature in general and the nature of the claimants grounds their claim of equivalence and their demand for equality of treatment. Equality despite the assertions of declarations and constitutions is not given or obvious. It is the outcome of political struggles and a social construct, as Hegel and Marx argued, typically expressed through the law, as Kant saw. In this sense, equality before the law acquires its concrete meaning: it has nothing "natural" about it. If anything, the main claim of the liberal-democratic tradition is that it can transcend social differences and accidents of birth and construct equality *contra* nature. New right-claims have therefore two aspects: an appeal to the universal but undetermined character of human nature and, secondly, the assertion that the similarity between the claimants and human nature *tout court* admits them to the surplus value of the floating signifier and grounds their claim to be treated on an equal footing with those already admitted.

Secondly, difference. The distance between abstract human nature and the concrete characteristics of the claimants justifies their demand for differential treatment which respects their specific identity. Concrete identities are constructed in psychological, social and political contexts, they are, in psychoanalytical terms, the outcome of a situated desire of the other. In this sense, all claims to differentiation are initially constructed outside of the law and its equalising abilities. If equivalence and equality result from political and legal action against abstract nature, the claim to difference reintroduces the particularity of concrete nature, situated, localised and context-dependent. Human rights-claims involve a paradoxical dialectic between an impossible demand for universal equality, historically identified with the characteristics of Western man and, an equally unrealisable claim to absolute difference. Because the nature of Western, white, affluent man cannot subsume under its universal aspirations the characteristics and desires of workers, women, racial or ethnic groups, etc., the claim to specific workers, women or ethnic rights arises. Thus, universality becomes a continuously receding horizon resulting from the expansion of an indefinite chain of particular demands.[53]

The assertion of similarity and difference between two terms is the typical operation of rhetoric. Claiming that two entities are similar or different does not follow their "natural" properties. Saying, for example, that "women are (not) like men" has little meaning in the abstract. This kind of essentialism has plagued feminist discussions on rights. Women have been invisible to human rights for too long, either through a denial of their similarity with the ground symbolic concept or through a denial of their specificity and difference from it. The admission of women to the status of humanity (the action of similarity) without responding to the demands of difference is equally problematic. It assumes that the bestowal of the rights of the representatives of humanity (white well-off males) on women would automatically enhance their freedom, equality and dignity. But as the feminism of difference has cogently argued, the universality of rights necessarily neglects the specific needs and experiences of women.[54] Domestic and international law has had great problems in accepting, for example, the special nature of domestic rape or of rape and sexual abuse during war. In the rhetorical game of rights, similarity and difference on their own can be used to promote the most contradictory objectives. A claim to difference without similarity, can establish the uniqueness of a particular group and justify its demands for special treatment but, it can also rationalise its social or political inferiority. Aristotle wrote that "some men are free by nature and some are slaves . . . From their birth some are marked out for subjection and others for rule".[55] A Greek or Roman slave was seen as an *animal vocale*, a worker in the nineteenth century was treated as a "cog in the machine" or disposable merchandise, a wife until relatively recently was the husband's chattel. In all these cases, empirical difference established and justified domination. More generally, the appearance of linguistic, racial, gender and other differences without an accompanying claim to similarity

---

[53] Ernesto Laclau, *Emancipation(s)* (London, Verso, 1996) Chapter 2

[54] Luce Irigaray, *Thinking the Difference* (K. Montin trans.) (New York, Routledge, 1994); *An Ethics of Sexual Difference* (Carolyn Burke and Gillian Gill trans.) (London, Athlone 1993); *I love to you* (Alison Martin trans.) (New York, Routledge 1996). For an excellent presentation of the various positions in feminism, see Nicola Lacey, *Unspeakable Subjects* (Oxford, Hart, 1998) passim and Chapter 7.

[55] Aristotle, *Politics* (H. Rakham trans.) (Cambridge Mass., Loeb, 1990) I. I, 6.

has been used in most cases to establish hierarchies and legitimise power imbalances.

The question therefore is when, how and in relation to what attributes are "women (not) like men"? Most human rights struggles take the form of this type of timely, historical and specific comparison. Their aim is to re-define the dominant way of understanding the relations amongst classes, groups and individuals and, to this effect, rhetorical tactics and discursive arguments are one of their main weapons. The cultural aim of anti-slavery, workers' and women's struggles was to re-articulate the relations between the free, the property owners or men (usually the three predicates coincided in the same person) and the slaves, the workers or women. The old hegemonic position claimed that the first groups related to the second on the basis of natural differences, that inequalities were the logical and necessary outcome of dissimilarities. The rebels and protesters, on the other hand, construed the relationship as not one of difference but of inequality and illegitimate domination, of an immoral denial of similarities, which turns neutral differences into social hierarchies.

Human rights struggles are symbolic and political: their immediate battleground is the meaning of words, such as difference, equality or similarity and freedom, but, if successful, they have ontological consequences, they change radically the constitution of the legal subject and affect peoples' lives. The imaginative use of rhetorical and, specifically, metaphorical and metonymical transfers of meaning, furthers the campaign. Metaphor operates when a new group has established in law and fact its claims to equality and difference and has appropriated the symbolic value of the "floating signifier". It then becomes itself the "ground" group for further proliferation of right-claims and for novel assertions of similarity and difference. After the recognition of a general right to equality for gays and lesbians,[56] for example, more concrete rights will be claimed: equal age of consent to sexual intercourse, the right of gay and lesbian couples to marry, to adopt children and to enjoy the same tax and social benefits as heterosexuals etc. The rhetorical operation of metonymy, on the other hand, allows the transfer of the presumed dignity of human nature to entities which, although not strictly analogous to people, are contiguous or in some other way related to them. The rights of the environment, of animals or the putative rights of the foetus are examples of such "metonymical" rights. It should be added that for the

---

[56] This basic recognition typically happens when homosexual relations are decriminalised. See *Dudgeon* v. *United Kingdom* 4 E.H.R.R. 149 (1981).

Western philosophical tradition, animality has been consistently opposed to humanity and the claims to animal liberation or rights cannot be based on any ontological similarity.[57] But the rhetorical character of rights discourse allows the crossing of one of the greatest metaphysical divides and permits what is "proper" to humans to be claimed for animals or the inanimate.

The common aim of human rights campaigns is to link the floating and symbolic signifier to a particular signified, to arrest its constitutive indeterminacy and to achieve the – partial – bonding of human nature with a regional conception of humanity which will bestow upon the latter the symbolic value of the core concept, turning it into a valid instance of human nature. In doing so, characteristics of humanity, like equality and freedom, are transferred to the group that achieves recognition. But at the same time, this partial linking gives content to the empty signifier and makes concrete the abstract and formal claims to equality and freedom. Every successful fixing of a partial signified to the floating signifier works therefore in two ways: it endows the new claim or claimants with the symbolic dignity of human nature and right but, secondly, it arrests temporarily the flight of meaning by filling abstract right with empirical determinations and historical predicates.

b. The ontology of rights

These battles over meaning have important ontological effects. The successful mobilisation of human nature for the claims of women, gays or children or its metonymic extension to animals or the unborn, is an important component in the construction of the identity of woman, child or the foetus. If we accept the psychoanalytical insight that people have no essential identities outside of those constructed in symbolic discourses and practices, a key aim of politics and of law is to fix meanings and to close identities by making the contingent, historical linkings between signifiers and signifieds permanent and necessary.[58] But such attempts can only succeed partially because identities are always open to new symbolic appropriations and articulations within different discourses and practices, and every

---

[57] Jacques Derrida, "Eating Well" in E. Cadava, P. Connor and J.L. Nancy (eds), *Who Comes After the Subject* (Routledge, 1993) 111–16.

[58] See Ernesto Laclau, *New Reflections on the Revolution of our Time* (London, Verso 1990) 3–85.

– partially – fixed identity is always overdetermined by the surplus value of the floating signifier.

If we now turn from the operation of language to law, rights act to formalise identities by recognising and enforcing one type of reciprocal recognition. The law uses the technical category of the legal subject and its repertory of remedies, procedures and rights to mediate between the abstract and indeterminate concepts of humanity and right and the concrete people who claim its protection. The legal subject is the middle point between abstract human nature and concrete selves. The legal validation of a contested category of rights, for instance women's rights, acts as the partial recognition of a particular type of identity linked to the relevant rights. Conversely, a person recognised as legal subject in relation to women's rights is acknowledged as the bearer of certain attributes and the beneficiary of certain activities, but at the same time as a person of a particular identity which partakes amongst others of the dignity of abstract human nature. It should be added immediately that the identity of a particular woman is not exhausted in her identification as a subject of women's rights or in her recognition as the beneficiary of the equality and freedom of human nature.[59] She will also have political rights as a citizen, others that emanate from her position in the economy (rights of workers and social rights) or as the inhabitant of a particular environment, etc. The legal subject acts as the organising, mediating and unifying concept and technique, through which the law assigns categories, fixes identities and tries to stabilise the proliferation of social meaning. An individual is a human being, a citizen, a woman, a worker etc. to the extent that she is recognised as the legal subject of the respective rights; her legal identity is the sum total of her bunch of rights. If to be outside the law you must be honest, you must be in the law to be human. In modernity, we know only what we can make; the legalisation of desire means that we can now "make" ourselves by investing desire with legal significance. We are potentially entitled to become legally all we want to be.

Legal personality is therefore a key strategy of individuation. Men and women are no longer the material vessels of the soul or, the external forms of a universal *psyche*. As sentient beings, they acquire their public persona through their recognised legal attributes which allow them to carry out significant acts to others. Legal subjectivity paradoxically represents both the principle of universalism and the

[59] This was the main aim behind the first phase of the legal struggles for women's rights and of every other social movement.

process through which individuation is carried out in modernity. In this sense, rights do not just belong to humans; rather, they make human by both recognising their legislative, right-making ability and free will, and by endowing them with the concrete powers and capacities through which they can realise their free will. This is the reason why a full definition of rights is impossible, why they are open to continuous expansion and proliferation. Human rights can never reach a state of definite acceptance or final triumph because the logic of rights cannot be constrained to any particular field or type of subject. Human rights law is caught in yet another paradox: as law, it acts as an agent of stabilisation of identity and of rationalisation of state power; as human rights it introduces into the state and into (legal) personality the openness of social and cultural indeterminacy. The abstract concept of human nature which underpinned the revolutionary declarations has been replaced in postmodern societies by the proliferating claims to new and specialist rights. As a result, desire itself replaces human nature as the ground concept and becomes the empty and floating signifier which can be attached either to the logic of power and the state or to the logic of justice and openness.

We can conclude that the common complaint about the excessive legalisation of the world is the inevitable outcome of the legalisation of desire. Desire became the formal expression of the subject's relationship with others and the polity and was given, initially limited, legal recognition, throughout the Western world by the turn of this century. Once that basic fact was established, the multiplication of right-holders, the proliferation of claims and the endless mutation of the objects of right was a matter of time, of letting language, politics and desire do their work. Rights are therefore extremely powerful fictions whose effect upon people and things is profound: they make people sacrifice their life or liberty, they lead people to kill or maim in their name, they inspire people to protest and rebel and change the world. Rights are linguistic fictions that work and recognitions of a desire that never ends.

10

Hegel's Law: Rights and Recognition

Hegel was unceremoniously excised from the annals of radical philosophy in 1969. He was re-discovered in 1989. In 1969, Louis Althusser published the influential *For Marx*, in which the French philosopher, a prominent representative of the then dominant structuralist school of thought, announced that the Marxist "epistemological revolution" started only after Marx jettisoned the idealistic influence of Hegel, which had marked his early writings.[1] But the burial was premature. After the collapse of communism and the attendant and often unfair blame placed on Marx for its ills, Hegel returned like a ghost and "dialectics without historicism" became a major source of inspiration for those who did not accept the linear logic of triumphant capitalism.

In a different sense, however, Hegel never left the philosophical scene. The colonialising powers of his system are such that almost all philosophical positions can be presented as a partial account of the spirit's progress to self-consciousness and every historical event can be easily co-opted into the monumental edifice. According to Jacques Derrida, modern philosophy is obsessed with the Hegelian system and, in the wake of Hegel's announcement of philosophy's closure, is unsure about its ends.[2] Yet, the inexorable post-War rise and eventual domination of structuralism in the humanities and social sciences and of political liberalism, meant that the historicism of Hegel's

---

[1] Louis Althusser, *For Marx* (B. Brewster trans.) (London, Allen Lane, 1969). In two seminal essays in that volume, "On the Young Marx" and "Marxism and Humanism", Althusser claimed that Marx broke away from humanism and defined humanism as ideology, in 1845, 227–231. This allowed him to create a non-humanist science of history which joined the other great scientific discoveries, Louis Althusser, "Marx's Relation to Hegel", in *Politics and History* (B. Brewster trans.) (London, New Left Books, 1972) 163–86.

[2] This is a main point of Jacques Derrida's, *Glas* (J. Leavy and R. Rand trans.) (Lincoln, University of Nebraska Press, 1986) which opens its left column, dedicated to Hegel, as follows: "what after all, of the remain(s), today, for us, here, of a Hegel? For us, here, now: from now on that is what one will not have been able to think without him. For us, here, now: these words are citations, already, always, we will have learned from him", at 1.

system and its quest for totalisation fell out of favour. For generations, radical intellectuals filtered the study of Hegel through the attacks of young Marx on his philosophical mentor. It was after the fall of communism, an event whose historical significance will take a long time to comprehend fully, that philosophers returned to Hegel *sans* Marx. The vastness and ambition of the Hegelian oeuvre has made newcomers look for a guide or foil, Soren Kierkegaard, Derrida himself or the French psychoanalyst Jacques Lacan, to help them enter the immense system. A minor Hegelian studies industry has been created and recently its operations have been extended to law.[3]

This is a welcome and long overdue return. Hegel's dialectical method can be used to explain the operation of liberal rights but also to criticise and transcend the limitations of rights theory. Hegel used law and legal forms extensively both as necessary steps in the historical process and as illustrations of the dialectic, the engine room of his system. Unlike most modern philosophers, he was still part of a tradition which turned to law and ethics as the determinants and perfect illustrations of the social bond. From Plato to Kant and Hegel, the study of law in its social setting was, if not the royal road, at least a main route to the understanding of the world. Jurisprudence, the prudence or wisdom of law *jus*, has always been both the consciousness, the study and understanding of law, and its conscience, the moral compass of legal and by extension political and social operations and arrangements. This moral dimension of legal studies was lost with the rise of positivism and its obsession with a pure science of law. Not only did positivism abandon any attempt to construct or imagine the ethical ends of law, it also downgraded the significance of jurisprudence as contemplation on the social bond and as a moral enterprise. Classical philosophy accepted, to paraphrase a maxim, that *ubi philosophia ibi jurisprudentia*. Positivism freed philosophers from the duty or need to know the law and turned jurisprudence into a parochial concern with the minutiae of legal technique.

According to rational natural law, human rights aim to acknowledge and protect the central and immutable characteristics of human nature. These differ from philosopher to philosopher, from the need and desire of self-preservation in Hobbes, to rational freedom and

---

[3] Michel Rosenfeld, "Hegel and the Dialectics of Contract", 10 *Cardozo Law Review* 1199 (1989); Drucilla Cornell, Michel Rosenfeld and David Carlson, *Hegel and Legal Theory* (New York, Routledge, 1991); Margaret Jane Radin, *Reinterpreting Property* (Chicago, University of Chicago Press, 1993); Alan Brudner, *The Unity of the Common Law: Studies in Hegelian Jurisprudence* (Berkeley, University of California Press, 1995); Jeanne Shroeder, *The Vestal and the Fasces* (Berkeley, University of California Press, 1998).

moral responsibility in Kant. The allegedly uniform and absolute character of these attributes makes them universal, establishes their priority over duties and determines the content of rights. In this sense, Hobbes and Kant were the philosophical founders of human rights. But contemporary conceptions of subjectivity and rights owe more to Hegel's critique of the Kantian conception of morality and of the person with their separation from others and the world. This Chapter will present the main Hegelian themes on rights and subjectivity. It starts with a concise introduction to some Hegelian themes of legal significance. It then turns to two recent attempts to reconstruct Hegelian theory, Alex Honneth's sociological Hegelianism and Jeanne Shroeder's psychoanalytical theory of property, in an attempt to develop a contemporary Hegelian theory of human rights.

I. HEGEL'S LEGAL JOURNEY

Kant's *Critiques* gave philosophical expression to the modern obsession with the separation between subject and object and between self and the world. Hegel's main task was to heal this rift and to reclaim the unity of existence. The early German Romantics had tried to overcome the separation by successively prioritising one or the other pole. Hegel's answer was more radical: the split was internalised and historicised and the fragmentation of modernity was seen not as a catastrophe but as a necessary stage in the odyssey of spirit or reason towards its own self-consciousness. For Hegel, thought, consciousness and the spirit are active forces, caught in a continuous struggle, in which the spirit fights its own alienation in the external world, recognises objectified existence as its own partial realisation, and returns to itself through its negation, acknowledging history as the process of its gradual realisation.

People, institutions, art, work, morals, religion and all aspects of social existence follow a similar trajectory. The struggle between principles, forces and forms of life moves history forward. Its dialectical character means that in each of its concentric stages, a force or institution and its underlying principle is "sublated", both negated and retained by its opponent. The institution of family, for example, and its central value of care for its members treated as unique individuals, is transcended – both preserved and overcome – by that of civil society with its emphasis on formal relations amongst legal persons treated as abstract right-holders. The dialectical absorption and overcoming moves the historical process in a spiral-like fashion towards the final stage, the state of ethical life or *Sittlichkeit*. The key oppositions of modernity are not catastrophic conflicts, therefore, but dynamic expressions of the ongoing struggle which defines existence, determines human consciousness and makes history the process in which the spirit (or reason) realises itself as history's underlying principle. From the perspective of the final stage, of the end of history, the spirit looks back and sees history, not as a random sequence of events, but as the unfolding of a progressive trajectory leading to the overcoming of conflict. Philosophy follows a parallel trajectory, eventually merging with the first, which gradually comes to recognise history as the incarnation of reason.

When Hegel turns to the normative field, he argues, against Kant's moral and legal formalism and his separation of morality from legality, that freedom and ethical life are intrinsically linked. In ethical life, the final stage which entered the historical scene with the modern state, morality and legality are finally re-united into an organic whole and become the state's institutional manifestation. All previous normative systems, from the Greek city-states, with its inequalities, to the absolute monarchy, with its limited legal protections, were partial stations on the road to the final reconciliation of ethical life. Subjectivity too, Hegel believed, is created through a struggle amongst people for the reciprocal recognition of their identity. This struggle led to social divisions and hierarchies, which culminated in the creation of a class of masters and slaves and, only with the modern overcoming of the master/slave relationship does the complete human person come to life. The dialectical evolution of the normative domain and of personality, are crucial for the development of a Hegelian critique of rights and deserve some detailed examination.

Hegel's *Philosophy of Right*[4] presents the movement to the absolute spirit or to reason's historical incarnation as a tripartite progress which assumes explicitly legal form. Abstract, formal right gives way to the morality of Kantianism (*Moralitat*), which is finally transcended by ethical life. In the first stage, rights have formal existence but no determinate content and, legal personality, the key organising concept, exists only in the abstract. Law and morality express the immediate and undifferentiated unity of universal principles and, as a result, human will is free but, its only action is to relate self to itself and thus create a person who lacks concrete characteristics and does not relate

---

[4] G. W.F. Hegel, *Philosophy of Right* (T.M. Knox trans.) (Oxford, Oxford University Press, 1967).

to others. This abstraction is the legal subject, a pure logical cipher, whose only role is to be the abstract support of universal norms and only quality, to possess legal rights and duties. Like the loving members of a family whose dealings with each other are beyond legal rules, the legal subject presupposed by formal right never comes into contact with the real world. State law does not address fictions nor are abstractions involved in conflicts. While legal personality is indispensable for the operation of the categories of property, contract and crime, it cannot create a fully recognised concrete individual on its own. This first moment of the spirit's legal progression is exclusively determined by the categories of Roman law.[5] Man is a legal subject but the kernel only of an embodied human being.

The passage from formal right to morality involves the incomplete differentiation and concretisation of the abstract subject. At this stage, the person stands before the world and becomes aware of his freedom and, gradually, the bare universality of legal personality and formal right develop into individual subjectivity. The person now realises that not only is he free to act on the world through his rights but, that freedom is his essence. This recognition emerges when, in relating to himself as the bearer of universalisable rights, he discovers an inner space of freedom and moral responsibility. Not just external actions but intentions and purposes have moral significance and are judged according to the principles of universal morality, the modern form of the good. But the good, the universal end of ethics, cannot remain internal to conscience; it must be realised in the world. Kantian moralism however does not allow the inner life of good intentions and the world to communicate.

The moral conscience, with its universalism and cruel disregard for human emotions and needs and, universal freedom, the authentic form of the good, face each other as two alien and unconnected forces. Man must act according to universal maxims but the categorical imperative creates an abstract morality which has no content and cannot provide concrete guidance. Its command is to follow and apply the empty form of the universal. But, as the young Hegel showed, any maxim can be universalised without contradiction and anything can be justified in the abstract.[6] Universality is part of the absolute spirit which unfolds in history but, in Kantian morality, it has

---

[5] ibid. 37–40.
[6] G.W.F. Hegel, *"System of Ethical Life" (1802–3) and "First Philosophy of Spirit" (1805–6)* (H. S. Harris and T. M. Knox trans.) (Albany, S.U.N.Y. Press, 1977) and *Natural Law* (T. M. Knox trans.) (Philadelphia, University of Pennsylvania Press, 1975).

not yet become an integral part of the personality. Similarly, abstract legal relations may create the conditions of equality under the law, but they do not recognise or respect the needs, desires or history of the concrete person. Formal law treats the individual as an abstract universal, who is respected for his moral responsibility and freedom but who is insufficiently individuated. If the abstract legal person is the kernel of the concrete human, the Kantian subject is its external only shell. To move from that to the unique individual, the "concrete universal", legal mentality must be complemented with emotional care. Without it, Kantian autonomy follows purely formal criteria and leads to internal moral arbitrariness, almost to a sadism according to Lacan,[7] and to a continuously expanding external-legal coercion.

Formal right and abstract morality are finally absorbed, cancelled and transcended in the third moment of *Sittlichkeit*. The abstract good and human conscience, which were kept apart from the world by morality, now come together and are realised in the actions of concrete individuals. Unlike the coercive law of Kantian freedom, ethical life is the living good practiced and experienced by each citizen. This living law constrains "subjective opinion and caprice"[8] with minimum need for external sanctions and makes virtue "reflected in the individual character".[9] Autonomy becomes real only when it is embodied in political institutions and universal laws which give content to reason, shape our personality and give substance to our moral duties. Unlike the abstract universality of right and the formal subjectivity of morality, in ethical life "right and duty coalesce, and by being in the ethical order a man has rights in so far as he has duties, and duties in so far as he has rights".[10] The universality of the historically incarnate spirit is a far cry from the formal order of legalism and the alien order of natural objects which "conceal their rationality under the cloak of contingency and exhibit it only in their utterly external and singularised or disconnected way".[11] In this final stage, laws and institutions are not the necessary supplements of a cruel and ineffective conscience, but the concrete embodiments of living morality. "This Spirit can be called the human law, because it is essentially in the form of a reality that is conscious of itself. In the

[7] Jacques Lacan, "Kant avec Sade", 51 *October* (Winter 1989), 55–75; Costas Douzinas, "Antigone's Death and Law's Birth: on Ontological and Psychoanalytical Ethics", (1995) 16 *Cardozo Law Review* 3–4, 1325.

[8] *Philosophy of Right*, op.cit., supra n. 4, 105

[9] ibid, 107,109.

[10] ibid., 109.

[11] ibid., 106.

form of universality it is the *known* law, and the prevailing custom".[12] The Greek city-states, the historical prefigurations of ethical life, were at home in their world and understood the particular, but did not see themselves as representatives of the universal. Ethical life, on the other hand, integrates the universal and the particular, makes freedom concrete, unites subject and object, is and ought, content and form. This is then the movement of the spirit in history: from right to morality to ethical life in the domain of morals and from family to civil society to state in institutions. The progress is full of internal and external contradictions, of conflicts, turns and tribulations, which are gradually absorbed in the inexorable march of the spirit towards its own self-consciousness.

Hegel followed a similar approach when he turned to the nature of the subject. His aim was to reconstruct the philosophical presuppositions and the necessary historical stages through which modern subjectivity and its historical and philosophical consciousness came to life. The dialectical movement is backwards: what happens today is explained through its necessity in a long and evolving history:

> The necessity of the dialectic is retrospective rather than prospective – it looks backward rather than forward. The retroactivity of the dialectic is reflected in Hegel's famous metaphor in his preface to *The Philosophy of Right*: "when philosophy paints its grey in grey, a shape of life has grown old and cannot be rejuvenated, but only recognised, by the grey in grey of philosophy; the owl of Minerva begins its flight only with the onset of dusk".[13]

Descartes and Kant had emphasised the solitary consciousness but, Hegel's *Phenomenology of Spirit* and the dialectic more generally insist on the reflexive constitution of self and its radical dependence on others. The starting point is that the ego as self-consciousness is a creature of desire. Simple consciousness discovers, through sense-perception and speech, the external world which exists outside the subject and is independent of her knowledge. For the ego to rise, however, this passive contemplation of the world must be complemented with desire. Desire belongs to a subject, it is exclusively and radically subjective, it is my desire which makes me aware of myself and of my difference from the object, the not-I. Desire reveals and creates self-consciousness in an attempt to negate and cancel the

[12] G.W.F. Hegel, *Phenomenology of Spirit* (A.V. Miller trans.) (Oxford, Oxford University Press, 1977) 267–8.

[13] Jeanne Schroeder, *The Vestal and the Fasces: Psychoanalytical and Philosophical Perspectives on the Feminine and Property* (Berkeley, University of California Press, 1998) 13–4.

otherness of the object. The desire for food, for example, negates the
otherness of the foodstuff and cancels its being, as self devours it to
satiate its hunger. Self assimilates and transforms the object in order
to survive but, at the same time, negates the object's independence
and givenness in an attempt to heal the split between subject and
object. Desire reveals a fundamental lack in the subject, an emptiness
in the self that must be filled through the overcoming of external
objects.

But this devouring negation abolishes the object and throws the
subject back, his hunger and desire temporarily met, to his illusory
self-identity which does not differentiate humans from animals. Man
must negate the object without abolishing it, because the abolition of
the world would lead to humanity's elimination. The fully human
desire is not addressed therefore towards an object or a being, but
towards a non-object, towards another self-consciousness. It is the
other's recognition and desire that gives rise to self, who sees himself
reflected in another, whose foreignness must be negated to give rise
to the ego but, whose existence and otherness survive.

> In recognition, the self ceases to be this individual. It exists by right in
> recognition, that is no longer in its immediate existence. The one
> who is recognised is recognised as immediately counting as such,
> through his *being* -but this being is itself generated from the concept.
> Man is necessarily recognised and necessarily gives recognition . . . As
> recognising, man is himself this movement, and this movement itself
> is what supersedes his natural state: he is recognition.[14]

Behind all types of desire a deep dialectic is at work: embodied
human life depends for survival on the external world and, as a result,
part of the self is always outside itself and the otherness of objecthood
is already launched in self. The aim of spirit's historical march is precisely to overcome this alienation and to unite man and the world,
the finite and the infinite, freedom and fate. Human history and
action move towards a "total integrity",[15] in which the opposition
between self and other will have been overcome and the external
reality, which determines us, will contain nothing alien or hostile.
Integrity will be achieved only when our dependence on the external world is dialectically negated, in other words, when humanity is
at home in its environment. But liberal philosophy, in its attempt to

---

[14] *Hegel and the Human Spirit: A Translation of the Jena Lectures on the Philosophy of the Spirit
(1805–6) with Commentary* (L. Rauch trans.) (Detroit, Wayne State University Press, 1983)
116.

[15] Charles Taylor, *Hegel* (Cambridge University Press, 1977) 148–50.

glorify the individual, denies our dependence on the world and, with arrogant self-certainty, artificially erases the traces of otherness and imagines self as identical with itself.

> Man achieves the illusion of self-identity by defining himself as an inner spiritual being, by fooling himself that he coincides with himself as a mind or spirit . . . the error expressed here being precisely the belief in simple self-coincidence . . . the subject is necessarily a being who incorporates his other (his embodiment) and "returns to himself" through this other . . . to achieve self-coincidence as spiritual beings is thus ontologically impossible . . . its achievements would be the abolition of the subject.[16]

This type of unreflective certainty, apparent in religious beliefs and in liberal ontologies, is both extremely vain and utterly futile. The delusion of self-identity is a palliative only for the painful but inescapable recognition that we depend on the other and are determined by the outside world. Self-consciousness, on the other hand, is the "unity of oneself in one's other-being" and is achieved by seeing oneself in the other and accepting self as the "identity of identity and non-identity".[17] The self-conscious subject, created through the other's desire, retains the separation from the other as one part of his identity, and recognises himself both in the other and in his difference from her. In this sense, self-consciousness both negates the split between self and other and preserves it. As a result, the subject can never be self-identical: he is an amalgam of self and otherness, of sameness and difference. As Zizek puts it "the picture of the Hegelian system as a closed whole which assigns its proper place to every partial moment is therefore deeply misleading. Every partial moment is, so to speak, 'truncated from within', it cannot ever become fully 'itself', it cannot ever reach 'its own place', it is marked with an inherent impediment, and it is this impediment which 'sets in motion' the dialectical development".[18]

Recognition works if it is mutual. I must be recognised by someone I recognise as human, I must reciprocally know myself in another. I can only become a certain type of person, if I recognise in the other the characteristics of that type, which are then reflected back onto me in her desire. But this full and mutual recognition is achieved only when humanity reaches its final universal purpose.

[16] ibid., 150.
[17] *Phenomenology*, supra n. 12, 140.
[18] Slavoj Zizek, *For they know not what they do: Enjoyment as a Political Factor* (London, Verso, 1991) 68–9.

Before the stage of ethical life, recognition was not complete and reciprocal and when self desired a thing, it did not do so for its own sake but in order to make another self recognise his right to that thing and therefore his existence and superiority. But as a multiplicity of desires desired to be so recognised, their action became a war of all against all and the universal struggle for recognition had to stop, before it led to global annihilation. For that to happen, Hegel assumes that one of the combatants must be prepared to fight to the end and risk his life. At that point, the other accepts his superiority and surrenders. He who risks his life for prestige becomes the master, the other his slave. The slave has subordinated his desire for recognition to that for survival.

The master's superiority will be realised in the slave's work, which transforms nature in the service of his master; in return, the master depends for his existence on slave labour. Hegel believed that the master-slave relationship is a necessary stage in humanity's ascent to its self-recognition as the universal value. This final transcendence is triggered by the fear of death and the knowledge created by labour. Preoccupied with daily mundane tasks, treated as objects at the mercy of the master, the slaves live a life of particularity separated from the universal. But death, their "lord and master",[19] puts them in touch with the universal and eventually frees them to negate their negation and to flee from the life of particularity towards freedom. The experience of work contributes also to the transcendence of slavery. The farmer, the builder and the labourer fight daily to transform nature in order to create value for their master. But nature resists their efforts; to tame it the slaves draw plans, develop technologies, invent work methods and soon realise that their work has humanised the environment. They gradually realise the power of thought which, through the creation of universal concepts and the application of the logic of the intellect, can master the world. When this realisation enters politics, the masters and slaves are finally transcended and replaced by the universal citizen. At this point, the spirit becomes conscious of itself and recognises human history as the process of gradual realisation of reason.

Hegelian philosophy sees history as an unfolding totality in which knowledge, social relations and the structure of subjectivity are, logically if not empirically, determined by the struggle between desiring selves, by its inevitable corollary in the master and slave dialectic and

---

[19] Hegel, *Phenomenology*, supra n. 12, 273.

by its eventual transcendence in the ethical state. History started when men opposed one another and will end when the struggle finishes in the realisation that the humanity is the universal principle and reason, its embodiment, animates the world and underpins the living value system of the ethical state. When the opposition between humanity and the world is transcended history ends. Master and slave are dialectically overcome, sublated in a final synthesis "that is the whole Man, the Citizen of the universal and homogeneous State". [20] For Hegel, the Prussian State had reached this stage; for Marx and the Left Hegelians, the universal will have to wait the future utopia.

After the defeat of communism, such grandiose claims are made only on behalf of liberal capitalism. For Francis Fukuyama, the "universal history of mankind" moved in the direction of liberal democracy. It has now been completed and "the struggle for recognition, the willingness to risk one's life for a purely abstract goal, the worldwide ideological struggle that called forth daring, courage, imagination, and idealism will be replaced by economic calculation, the endless solving of technical problems, environmental concerns and the satisfaction of sophisticated consumer demands".[21] For the prophet of the end, "we have trouble imagining a world that is radically better than our own, or a future that is not essentially democratic and capitalist . . . we cannot picture to ourselves a world that is essentially different from the present one, and at the same time better".[22]

II. LEGAL RECOGNITION AND SOCIAL DEMOCRACY

Jean-François Lyotard has famously defined the postmodern condition, as the exhaustion and incredulity towards grand narratives, of which the Hegelian historical narrative is the grandest of all.[23] But the Fukuyama debate indicates that the "world-wide liberal revolution" has claimed the mantle of the universal and announced a utopia light, illuminated by neon lights, publicised by Saatchi & Saatchi and available on the Internet. Is the new world order, Hegel's ethical state?

[20] Alexandre Kojève, *Introduction to the Reading of Hegel* (A. H. Nichols trans.) (Ithaca, Cornell University Press, 1989) 44.

[21] Francis Fukuyama, *Have we reached the End of History?* (Santa Monica, Ca., Rand Corporation, 1989) 22–3.

[22] Francis Fukuyama, *The End of History and the Last Man* (London, Penguin, 1992) 46.

[23] Jean-François Lyotard, *The Postmodern Condition: An Essay on Knowledge* (Manchester, Manchester University Press, 1984).

Was liberal capitalism the destiny of history? We will not attempt an answer here, except to say that when Hegelianism becomes a kind of philosophical journalism, it develops a rather bad taste. A more modest version of Hegelian theory can be used, however, as a corrective for the monological conception of rights and the self-identical personality of the liberal tradition.

From a Hegelian perspective, the main function of rights is to help establish the recognition necessary for the constitution of a full personality. Subjectivity passes through the mutual recognition by the other and rights are a necessary intermediary, an indispensable tool in this process. But if rights help constitute the subject through other-recognition, instead of being attributes of an atomic and isolated existence, they are deeply intersubjective. A second consequence is that rights, whether civil, economic or cultural, are deeply political: they presuppose logically and construct politically a community. Rights are not eternal, inalienable or natural. Their function is to bestow social identity and community membership on their bearers.[24] Let us examine this idea, as expressed recently by one of the heirs of Habermas, Alex Honneth.

Honneth argues that the struggle for recognition is the key ethical relationship or the main form of practical intersubjectivity, when the Hegelian system is viewed from a normative perspective. Moral conflicts, personal disputes and social antagonisms are partial expressions of this struggle which creates the agreements and reciprocity necessary for the socialisation and the individuation of the subject. My identity is the result of the recognition of my characteristics by another. This acknowledgement of the other's vital contribution to the constitution of self exposes self to the action of the universal and reconciles him with the world. At the same time, the identity created and underpinned through the other's recognition makes me aware of my specificity and difference from all others. This consciousness of uniqueness turns the subject against the world and re-kindles the antagonism with the other.

> Since, within the framework of an ethically established relationship of mutual recognition, subjects are always learning something more about their particular identity, and since, in each case, it is a new dimension to their selves that they see confirmed thereby, they must once again leave, by means of conflict, the ethical stage they have reached, in order to achieve the recognition of a more demanding

[24] Axel Honneth, *The Struggle for Recognition* (J. Anderson trans.) (Cambridge, Polity, 1995) 38.

form of their individuality . . . the movement of recognition that forms the basis of an ethical relationship between subjects consists in a process of alternating stages of both reconciliation and conflict.[25]

But what is the contribution of law and rights to the struggle for recognition and to personality formation? Following the usual trinitarian dialectic, Honneth presents legal recognition as one of the three main forms of mutual acknowledgement, the middle stage between love and solidarity. All three are ethical ways of recognising the other and creating self; they help constitute different types of identity. First, love. Its primary terrain is the family. Family members and lovers are in a state of mutual dependency and affection and recognise each other as a concrete person with unique needs and desires. The lover identifies himself through his loved one's particularities and develops a sense of independence supported by care. But this combination of autonomy and community can be sustained only amongst the members of small and closely-knit units.

Legal recognition could not be more different. It is the effect of the operation of a legal system which enforces equally the universalisable interests of all. To understand ourselves as right-holders with enforceable claims, in other words, to recognise ourselves as legal subjects, a system of general norms must exist which places on us the duties necessary for the recognition of others as bearers of rights. The reciprocal recognition of legal rights involves the adoption of the position of the generalised other. From that perspective, we learn to respect others as much as ourselves as right-holders, whose claims will be met.

[M]an is recognised and treated as a *rational* being, as free, as a person; and the individual, on his side, makes himself worthy of this recognition by overcoming the natural state of his self-consciousness and obeying a universal, the will that is in essence actuality will, the *law*; he behaves, therefore, towards others in a manner that is universally valid, recognising them − as he wishes others to recognise him − as free, as persons.[26]

Mutual recognition through law has three components not dissimilar to those identified by Kant. Legal relations presuppose a universalistic morality which forms the backdrop of law and ensures that persons are treated as ends and not means. Secondly, the recognition of the other as legal person is the effect of the fact that he enjoys

---

[25] ibid., 17.
[26] Hegel in *Encyclopaedia* quoted in Honneth ibid., 108.

moral autonomy and responsibility and possesses legal rights. This
type of recognition is typically called respect (f)or human dignity.
Finally, legal recognition leads to self-respect. Self-respect is the outcome of the realisation that I too am capable of moral action and that,
like others, I am an end in myself. Human dignity, self-respect and
respect for others are synonymous with the ability to make moral
decisions and to raise legal claims. "Indeed respect for persons . . .
may simply be respect for their rights, or that there cannot be the one
without the other. And what is called 'human dignity' may simply be
the recognisable capacity to assert claims".[27] Having rights is nothing
more than the symbolic expression that one is equal in his freedom
with everyone else or, what amounts to the same thing, that one is a
legal subject.[28] If according to Bob Dylan, to be outside the law you
must be honest, according to Hegel, to be in the law, to be a subject,
you must have rights.

Recognition through legal rights is identical with the middle stage
of the legal form, identified by Hegel as that of Kantian morality. But
what moves the law from abstract right to morality and eventually to
the ethical state and solidarity? Hegel's answer is extraordinary: the
legal dimension of social relations moves forward through the internal combustion engine of crime.[29] Legal dealings make property
owners reciprocally recognise each other and contractual exchanges
establish the minimum element of universality necessary for the full
and mutual recognition of identity. But the generalised person which
lies behind property and contractual deals is too abstract and formal
an identity for many and legal recognition, an insufficient acknowl-

[27] Joel Feinberg, *Rights, Justice and the Value of Liberty* (Princeton NJ, Princeton University
Press, 1980) 151.

[28] From a naturalist perspective, Jacques Maritain comes to a similar conclusion: "The
dignity of the human person? The expression means nothing if it does not signify that, by
virtue of natural law, the human person has the rights to be respected, is the subject of rights,
possesses rights", *The Rights of Man and Natural Law* (D. Anson trans.) (New York, Charles
Scribner's Sons, 1951) 65.

[29] Karl Marx in his wonderfully ironic style both endorsed and lampooned Hegel: "A
philosopher produces ideas, a poet poems, a clergyman sermons, a professor compendia and
so on. A criminal produces crimes . . . the criminal moreover produces the whole of the
police and of criminal justice, constables, judges, hangmen, juries, etc.; and all these different lines of business, which form just as many categories of the social division of labour,
develop different capacities of the human mind, create new needs and new ways of satisfy-
ing them. Torture alone has given rise to the most ingenious mechanical inventions, and
employed many honourable craftsmen in the production of instruments . . . would locks
have ever reached their present degree of excellence had there been no thieves? Would the
making of banknotes have reached its present perfection had there been no forgers?" *Theories
of Surplus Value* (J. Cohen trans.) (London, Lawrence and Wishart, 1972).

edgement of their concrete humanity. The inadequacy of the respect generated by law leads to crime. Let us examine the respective positions of the two protagonists, the criminal and the victim.

> The inner source of crime is the coercive force of the law . . . crime as such is directed against the person as such and his knowledge of it for the criminal is intelligence. His inner justification is the coercion, the opposition to his individual will to power, to counting as something, to be recognised. Like Herostratus, he wants to be something, not exactly famous, but that he exercises his will in defiance of the universal will.[30]

A thief may be stealing to meet unfulfilled material needs. But in the game of recognition, crime represents a much bigger stake. The "universal will" (the legal system with its abstract legal relations and rights) coerces the "individual will to power" (the particularity and concreteness of the individual) who uses the crime to bring forth those parts of his personality not yet recognised by the established order and by legal rights and duties. There are many ways, in which the law fails to consider the uniqueness of the individual. Some may be offended and turn to crime by the abstraction of the legal rule and the disinterested uniformity in its application. To paraphrase Anatol France, the law in its majesty punishes equally rich and poor for stealing bread and sleeping under bridges but the poor are likely to feel the greater urge to break it. Insult may also be the result of the equality of rights, which is however purely formal when the material conditions for their realisation are not provided. It may be fine to fight for the universal right to free speech and press, but for an illiterate and starving farmer in a developing country the right to read *The Times* or to express freely his views is not likely to be considered central to his family's well-being. The essence of crime is the criminal's demand to be recognised and to be respected as a concrete and unique individual against the uniform coercion of the legal system.

On the side of the victim, legal rights have two kinds of concentric effects. Generally speaking, rights create first a valid claim to a particular object, benefit or position but, at the same time, they present the right-holder to the world as a subject with certain characteristics (as a man of property, substance and propriety) which deserve and demand the corresponding recognition. The property owner as owner is a legal subject and like all subjects enjoys moral responsibility and freedom, deserves respect in his dignity and, as a corollary, is

---

[30] *Jena Lectures on the Philosophy of the Spirit*, op.cit., supra n. 14, 130.

entitled to claim protection and have his rights enforced. The theft denies his specific legal entitlement to his property but also negates the recognition given to him through his legal personality. If the victim defends himself against the thief, their conflict involves two different claims: the damage or loss inflicted on the property-owner affects in part his specific attributes and in part his whole personality. The thief's desire for recognition, on the other hand, makes him negate legal relations altogether.

According to Honneth, this conflict teaches the parties important moral lessons which help the law move forwards. The first type of disrespect, which derives from law's abstraction and formalism, calls for greater sensitivity to individual context, need and desire in the application of the law. The second, which stems from law's privileging of the formal over the material conditions of existence, asks the law to move towards greater substantive equality. At the same time, the criminal's attack on legal relations and on the recognition they support alerts people to their dependence on the community and its institutions. Crime and the response to it help the personality develop a type of recognition which should lead both to greater autonomy and to the more harmonious socialisation required by the final historical stage, that of ethical life. Here abstract legal relations are overtaken by a type of recognition in which individuals understand themselves as fully dependent on one another and at the same time as fully unique and concrete persons. In Honneth's narrative, law's formalism becomes the ontological motive for its negation by the criminal, but in turn crime contributes to the dialectical overcoming of formal legalism.

> Since the law represents a relation of mutual recognition through which every person, as bearer of the same claims experiences equal respect, it precisely cannot serve as a medium for the respect of every individual's particular life-history. Instead, this (to a certain extent) individualised form of recognition presupposes, in addition to cognitive achievement, an element of emotional concern, which makes it possible to experience the life of the other as a risky attempt at individual self-realisation.[31]

Against Honneth's expectations, however, Hegel did not take this route. Although he commended the ethical state as a big advance on legal Kantianism, he did not present its legal relations as less abstract in their content or less formal in their application than those of the Prussian State. The formalism of legal recognition remained unmiti-

---

[31] Honneth, op.cit., supra n. 24, 56–7.

gated and, if anything, the relationship between state and citizen became even more imbalanced. The state, the historical embodiment of the spirit in *Sittlichkeit*, mediates the relations amongst legal subjects in a necessarily asymmetrical manner. Legal recognition and personality do not seem to develop towards synthesising the characteristics of legal universalism and individual uniqueness. Honneth believes that the reason for this failure was methodological: from the *Phenomenology* onwards Hegel abandoned his earlier "recognition-theoretical" structure in favour of a more philosophically rigorous "consciousness-theoretical" one which, driven by the dialectic between whole and parts or between the spirit and its manifestations, became inevitably more hierarchical and state orientated.

But this is not convincing. The ethical approach to legal recognition seems to fail at its most crucial moment, precisely when the expectation has been created that the earlier partial and formal conceptions of law and rights would be transcended by a more inclusive ethic of care. Without that move, legal relations and rights remain at their Kantian stage and formulation and are open to Hegel's devastating critique.[32] Honneth admits as much: Hegel "construes the transition to a state-based legal system quite schematically, as Kant had already done in his *Rechtslehre*".[33] To redress this problem, Honneth supplements Hegel by introducing a third type of recognition, which he calls solidarity. A personality based on solidarity has all the elements of legal recognition, but it additionally enjoys social esteem, a recognition of its particular characteristics and qualities developed within its group and community. A society based on solidarity introduces economic and social rights into law and attempts to mitigate legal formalism by addressing real social needs and life-histories.

Honneth attempts to "save" Hegel by turning the huge edifice into a rather meek prefiguration of the Habermasian ethics of communication. Those aspects of the dialectical progress which do not match the ethical drift of the argument are read out or forgotten. Legal transgression, this all-important concept for Hegel, has been turned into a pedagogic moral conflict, the centrality of death in the struggle for recognition is neglected[34] and the specifics of legal

---

[32] Margaret Jane Radin reaches the same conclusion in relation to Hegel's approach to the person, which is "the same as Kant's – simply an abstract autonomous entity capable of holding rights, a device for abstracting universal principles, and by definition, devoid of individuating characteristics", in *Reinterpreting Property*, op.cit., supra n. 3, 44.

[33] Honneth, op.cit., supra n. 24, 55.

[34] ibid., 61–2.

recognition are left unexplored. Hegel left the analysis of rights largely at its Kantian stage. Did he think that rights would wither away in the ethical state, like Marx, or that no further development in the legal form was possible? Honneth's underlying argument is that while the Prussian State was misdiagnosed by Hegel as the embodiment of the spirit, the contemporary social-democratic state is much closer to the stage of "ethical life" and can achieve the final and complete recognition of personality. Social-democratic hegelianism turns out to be a rather tame affair which moves the equation of rational and real forward, from the nineteenth to the late twentieth century. But the idea of new Labour as the end point of history is not convincing. For a more legally aware and radical exploration of Hegelian philosophy for rights, we must look elsewhere.

III. RECOGNITION AND PROPERTY

Jeanne Shroeder's *The Vestal and the Fasces*,[35] is an imaginative attempt to develop a legal theory which takes seriously Hegelian philosophy and combines it with the insights of Lacanian psychoanalysis. Shroeder, unlike Honneth, addresses explicitly law and legal concepts and develops an approach to legal recognition in which property is the key category. Subjectivity is created through the struggle for recognition and property is an indispensable moment in it. The possession and enjoyment of property enables the abstract personality to acquire specific characteristics, to objectify itself.

> The self as abstract will claims to be essential reality, but the existence of external things, that is, objects, and our dependence on external reality contradicts this. The self, therefore, needs to appropriate external objects – it must own property. The self becomes particularised and concrete, rather than abstract, through ownership. Potentiality becomes actuality.[36]

The main aim of property therefore is to constitute "subjectivity as intersubjectivity through the mediation of objectivity". Property is indispensable for the construction of identity and in a good Hegelian move the author claims that, if property is inescapable, it cannot be anything but "alive and well, despite the efforts to deconstruct it and present it as a myth . . . it is coherent as a concept and logically nec-

---

[35] Shroeder, op.cit., supra n. 13.
[36] ibid., 34.

essary".[37] The trouble with property is not in its operation but in its theorising which is beset with two problems: an avoidable misunderstanding and an inevitable but understandable misrecognition. Property theory has not understood that the key function of property is to construct the (legal) subject. Subjectivity is achieved in a dialectical process in which an individual is recognised by someone she recognises as legal subject.[38] Property is a necessary moment in this struggle for recognition because the desire for objects is one aspect of the desire for others. The possession and enjoyment of property identifies subject and object for another subject, while alienation, the third element, actualises the free will of the abstract person and turns her into a concrete individual through the recognition of another already recognised as subject.

The property contract symbolises the birth of the subject. In conveyancing, the contractors not only exchange objects, but they also recognise each other as separate and free and as possessors of rights and duties – in and through the contract they constitute one another as subjects. We desire objects not for their own sake but as means to the desire of other persons. Subjectivity is therefore constructed symbolically and the property contract has a little bit of magic. The contractors get their object of desire but on top they receive something more than they bargained for: they become recognised, they achieve their true desire of the other. Thus, the law by recognising rights gives the person dignity and by upholding contracts makes her free. The lover, too, is like a property speculator: he sees in his love object more than she is, and that makes her give in exchange what she does not have. Legal theorists have misunderstood this role of property and present it either as exclusively possession and enjoyment over things (as a bundle of sticks or fasces) or as a relationship between subjects (as unbound separate sticks to be passed on). As a result, property's contribution to the constitution of the subject is forgotten or is exclusively associated with a masculine phallic metaphor.

Shroeder's main claim is that property belongs to the symbolic domain: its possession helps endow the abstract person with recognisable characteristics, thus turning the indeterminate free will, with which Hegel starts, into a concrete person. Its alienation is the necessary additional prerequisite which realises the other's recognition. For Hegel, the coming together of the abstract subject with external objects is necessary because the abstract subject is defined in the

[37] ibid., 11.
[38] ibid., 23.

rather ascetic Kantian terms: he has free will, legal capacity and is an
end in itself, qualities which will not take a real person far. But the
objects that must be combined to create the real person do not refer
exclusively to property. The object is everything that is not a subject
or a free will, but gives the subject its substance. Objects include tangible and intangible possessions and everything that is not a free and
abstract personality. Every characteristic or trait, such as "intellectual
accomplishments, sciences, arts, even religious observances (such as
sermons, masses, prayers, and blessings at consecrations) inventions,
and the like" which, while not a part of the abstract person, are super-
added onto it and turn it into a concrete and singular individual,
belong to the object world.[39] Property over objects and the associated legal relations are not therefore an indispensable aspect of the
logically necessary process of objectification of the abstract person.
What is necessary is that the initial free will becomes concretised
through properties which attach to the person and give it empirical
solidity. Real property may have been an important aspect of this
process in Hegel's time and in contemporary America, but there is
nothing inevitable or exclusive about its humanising abilities.

Indeed, Shroeder's approach to property and her celebration of its
creative, subject-making character has a missionary tone. "Property
is healthy and functioning . . . all legal rights must be reinterpreted in
terms of property".[40] The sound of triumphalism is audible. With the
collapse of communism, the era of proper recognition and of eroti-
cisation of property has dawned on the world stage. We may not have
fully reached the "end of history" but we are pretty close to raising
property to its universal status. But this is both logically unnecessary
and historically misconceived. What we need for the legal recognition of others and of ourselves through their eyes is not property but
properties. We want to be recognised as a person of such and such
talents, skills, characteristics and achievements and not just as the
owner of a Porsche or a Rolex, or indeed of nothing but our ragged
clothes, like the Rwandan or Kosovo refugees.[41] The Hegelian re-

---

[39] Hegel quoted in Shroeder, supra n. 13, 36.

[40] ibid., 11.

[41] Shroeder makes a similar point in her critique of Radin's approval of personal property,
which includes those objects which establish social status in (capitalist) America, notably "the
(big) house, the (fast) car, the (flashy) ring" 282. But Shroeder's insistence on property law
as the model of all human recognition makes her place an even more exaggerated emphasis
on all property and not just personal objects. This is clear in her grudging acceptance of the
possibility of collective property and of limitations on property rights: "Limitations on property for the sake of community may become appropriate . . . We protect property rights

conceptualisation of rights which explains and emphasises their central role in the construction of subjectivity is an important corrective of liberal theory. But turning all rights into property does not help, because most contemporary types of property divide and atomise people. On the contrary, property should be weakened and become one aspect only of rights, associated with the equality the universalism of rights introduces.

The reasons for this are historically obvious. We know of a particular object and contract which has the "magic" qualities attributed to property in general. The exchange of this commodity yields more to the buyer than he bargained for. It is the labour power and the employment contract. Commodities are exchanged in the market for a price that broadly represents the cost of their reproduction. But labour power, when bought and put to work, generates the wages necessary for the survival and reproduction of the worker, but it also creates something more. Marx called this more the surplus value, the extra that accrues to the buyer of the labour power as a bonus and ensures the economic, social and political domination of capitalists over the working class and of globalised corporate capital over the poor of the world. People misrecognise the function of this exchange, they think that the worker gets a fair wage for a fair day's work. In good Hegelian fashion, Marx argues that this is both true and false: workers receive both the right value (normally wages are a fair exchange for the work) and less than the right value (since the surplus value added on the product is kept by the employer). Again, individual workers enter the labour contract freely and may change employment, but the working class as a whole has no freedom not to work for the capitalists and avoid being exploited. Free contract and exchange, rather than upholding, destroy freedom. The great insight of Marx was to understand that the presumed freedom of contract was based on the inescapable "slavery" of workers and the formal equality of the contractors on the huge inequality and dependence of the poor on the rich. In good dialectical fashion, freedom and equality through their operation turn into their opposite. Misrecognition is a prerequisite for the success of the exchange relationship. If it was not there, the capitalist economy would not work.

The legalisation of the Hegelian-Lacanian concept of desire raises the mediating object into centre stage. It is the ownership of the object which allows the subject to constitute itself in its relation with

because they are necessary for the existence of the individual and the state . . . Property is necessary for human freedom and intersubjectivity", 283, 284.

another desiring subject. This is Hegel for late twentieth century America and Lacan for property lawyers. Shroeder's dialectic, as she repeats throughout, is strictly logical and scarcely historical. The various stages mentioned, that of the abstract person, of its objectification into external objects and of property rights, may be the logical presuppositions of capitalist America, but no hint is given as to the historical stages embodying their concept. What are the motives that lead each of the types of recognition and personality to move onto the next? We are not told. What other types of recognition are there except from the legal recognition based on property? Has contemporary America reached the stage of the ethical state? There are hints in this direction and the logic of the argument certainly supports it. If this is the dialectic, it is the dialectic of logic and not of history.

Historical "progress" was, as we saw, much more brutal. The desire for the other through the object leads to competition and the fear of death, the "absolute Master", and the catastrophic consequences could be stopped through the creation of masters and slaves.[42] Property crime is the necessary means for the conflictual development and concretisation of legal recognition and the legal subject was a station only on the way to the complete personality. Masters, slaves and theft do not sound particularly wholesome today, so we are left with the struggle for property without its consequences – the literal slaves or the "slaves" of capitalist society, from the disenfranchised workers of early capitalism to the urban underclass of contemporary America – in other words, we are left with law without desire. The American version tells us that owning, controlling and alienating objects answers the problem of subjectification. But as Hegel, Marx and Lacan insisted, property is both the cause of division and hatred and one moment only in the struggle for mutual recognition and acceptance. As Bloch put it "if, in the four ancient basic rights a new meaning is given to property – that is, instead of freedom to attain it, it is defined as freedom from attaining it – then, and only then, do liberty and security come to life".[43]

Approaching rights as tools of intersubjective recognition is a major improvement on the atomism of rights discourse. But conflict is not just ethical and property is not exclusively benign. Despite the sophistication, Honneth and Shroeder miss the power imbalances

---

[42] Lacan also understands the desire for recognition as leading to imaginary violence that must be sublimated through speech and the law. See Chapters 11 and 12 below.

[43] Ernst Bloch, *Natural Law and Human Dignity* (D. J. Schmidt trans.) (Cambridge, Mass., MIT Press, 1988) 65.

which conflicts presuppose and property creates. Power is the cause and effect of conflict; to understand its implications on rights-based recognition, we need to abandon the idealised world of ethical communication and property rights. Otherwise, the neo-Hegelians are condemned to repeat the critique of Kantianism, while accepting both the neo-Kantian concept and the recent triumphalism of human rights.

IV. RIGHTS, DOMINATION AND OPPRESSION

We examined above recent attempts to salvage human rights for Marxism.[44] Let us turn briefly to the quasi-Hegelian Marxism of Jay Bernstein, who makes citizenship the focus of his analysis. Citizenship is defined as the exercise of political rights and active membership in community activities and is created through "the mutual recognition of each member by every other member *as* citizen".[45] The idea of recognition is crucial here and indicates a return of Marxist scholarship to a number of Hegelian themes. Recognition as citizen makes politics central and introduces community at the heart of subjectivity. It is from this perspective, that Bernstein claims, rather counterfactually, that "nothing in Marxist analysis speaks against rights".[46] Marx predicted, according to Bernstein, that socialism would overcome the separation between state and civil society and not that it would destroy rights. In this society of the future, the individual will absorb the abstract human, the attributes of universality and of the common good will be extended from the state to the whole of society, and human rights will be re-defined as the rights of participation by everyone into all aspects of social activity. In socialism, all relations will be political. It is indeed true that Marx did not dismiss the possibility of a socialist society that respects certain types of rights and, after the collapse of communism, this is the type of society that socialists believe in. But the adoption of part of the Hegelian logic of recognition and part of Marxist economics, does not help us understand the contemporary operation of rights.

---

[44] See above, Chapter 7.

[45] Jay Bernstein, "Right, Revolution and Community: Marx's 'On the Jewish Question' " in Peter Osborne (ed.), *Socialism and the Limits of Liberalism* (London, Verso, 1991) 102. See Chapter 7, part III above.

[46] ibid., 109.

There is much we can learn however by combining Berstein's Marx *avec* Hegel strategy with Honneth's emphasis on the struggle for recognition and Shroeder's perspectives on property as the object of desire. First, the old debate about the priority of individual or community in relation to rights can be concluded. Do rights belong to persons as a recognition and protection of their innate characteristics, their consciousness, freedom, rationality or whatever, or, are they contingent creations of law and tradition subject to state utilisation and manipulation? The Hegelian-Marxist answer is clear: human rights may be presented as natural and eternal but they are highly historical and contingent. They may be asserted as above politics but they are the construction of political relations and of the ongoing struggle for (group, individual) recognition. Finally, they may be proclaimed as rational but they are partly the outcome of an all-powerful desire that defies legal and logical limits in its ceaseless attempt to attract the love of the Other.

Shroeder argues that the subject is created through her desire for recognition by the other, mediated by the object of property. If we adopt the wide definition of the object as every trait, characteristic or possession which is combined with the abstract person to turn it into a concrete individual, we can argue that rights are such "objective" intermediaries, which are necessary for the establishment of intersubjective recognition. In this approach, to "have" or exercise a right means to claim a particular type of recognition from others, to ask to be treated as a concrete type of person. To be recognised, for example, as someone who can not only speak and communicate, but can also express a particular controversial view generally disapproved of or, as someone who is not only recognised in his sexual orientation, but who can also organise his family and professional life around a same-sex relationship.

For Hegel, legal recognition operates under certain preconditions and has a number of effects: it presupposes a universalistic legal system under which people extend respect to one another because they are legal subjects aware of the laws and other norms which create and protect rights. Additionally, legal relations promote self-respect: the recognition that self is morally autonomous and has the ability to acquire the same rights and duties as all others. These presuppositions and effects of legal recognition or of right-holding exist only in a community which has legislated for all. In the matter of rights, there is no conflict between individual and community. Human rights, as a special type of the struggle for recognition, come into existence and can be exercised only in common with others. This is the case, in the obvious sense that the effective exercise of rights involves correlative duties by others or the action of the law. But the logic of recognition goes much further. Rights do not find their limit in others and community, as liberal theory claims. On the contrary, if the function of rights is to give rise to reciprocal recognitions, they presuppose the existence of others and of community, and they express the identity-forming contribution of others. A right is a particular way of being in common. A demand for recognition of an aspect of the claimant's identity couched in rights terms is always addressed at another and is validated through the other's acknowledgement. The role of legal institutions, on the other hand, is to guarantee that the other's recognition is not left to his arbitrary whim and that, if withheld, it will be publicly supported and enforced.

But the recognition implied in human rights goes much further than the respect and self-respect involved in ordinary legal rights. "Civil rights . . . are the legal-juridical expression of the mutual recognitions that constitute individuals as citizens of a political state . . . Community is formed through mutual recognitions, recognitions that typically take the form of the conferment on an individual of a social identity expressive of membership".[47] Community is both the background and the effect of recognitions. New rights create new ways of being in common and push the boundaries of community. Political rights in particular express the mutual recognition of citizens as citizens, they recognise the constitutive role of recognition itself. If political community is the presupposition of rights, participation exhausts their scope.[48] In this sense, all rights can be seen as political rights, as an extension of the logic of participation to areas of activity not hitherto public.

Human rights do not just confirm or enforce therefore certain universal personality traits. The fact that rights are always extended to new groups and expanded to novel areas of activity, indicates their deeply agonistic character. The recognition bestowed by human rights does not extend just to external objects, such as property and contractual entitlements. It goes to the heart of existence, addresses the fundamental other-appreciation and self-esteem of the individual beyond respect, and touches the foundations of her identity. This

[47] ibid., 102.

[48] The psychoanalytical approach accepts the subject forming role of the other and of rights but is much more sceptical about the contribution of rights to the creation and expansion of community. See below Chapters 11 and 12.

type of concrete recognition cannot be based on the universal characteristics of law, but on a continuous struggle for the other's unique desire and concrete recognition. Human rights, like desire, are a battlefield with an ethical dimension. Social conflict may be occasionally destructive of the social bond, but it is not necessarily so. It is also one step in the development of political and ethical forms of community. Every form of human antagonism involves claims for recognition and, if that is understood, catastrophic forms of conflict can be prevented. According to this approach, all conflict, even the Hobbesian war of all against all, involves mutual claims for recognition amongst the parties and presupposes an already active, albeit elementary, form of intersubjectivity. People enter the social contract not exclusively out of a concern for self-preservation but because the atomised and polemical relations of the state of nature give inadequate recognition to the various aspects of their identity, unlike the civil state and its rights. Similarly, war involves claims for recognition by states, nations or ideologies. The best way of avoiding war therefore is for both rivals to show respect for the fragile or disputed aspects of the other's identity.

Let us examine, finally, how the logic of recognition can help us understand the operation of human rights. We start with the classics. A main consequence of the early declarations was that they opened, at least in theory, political decision-making to the equal participation of citizens against a background of serious power imbalances. Citizens were recognised as equal, not only in formal legal relations, but also as regards political power, in Balibar's and Lefort's terms, they became equal members of the new "disicorporated" sovereign. The mutual recognition enjoyed by those endowed with civil and political rights entails two characteristics that abstract legal subjects do not possess. Their participation in decision-making about matters of public interest reduces, and potentially should eliminate, their dependence on others and on alien institutional powers which dictate large parts of their life. Political rights acknowledge and sanction other-dependence as mutual recognition and, consequently, reduce citizens' other-dependence as **domination**. Positively, they introduce a claim to self-determination, initially restricted, as to subject, to white male property owners and, as to scope, to public political life. Secondly, equality in participation entitles citizens to use their collective political and legislative power to reduce, and in theory eliminate, the institutional, social or economic constraints underpinning or contributing to their **oppression** and introduce, positively, a claim to unhindered self-development. Following Iris Marion Young's definition, oppression as a denial of self-development takes various forms: the most obvious are economic exploitation, social marginalisation, cultural worthlessness and violence.[49] The mutual recognition of citizens as self-determining agents results from free participation in democratic decision-making and its extension from politics to other areas of social life. Self-development, on the other hand, is the opposite of oppression: it requires the expansion of the principle of equality, from legal decision-making to an ever-increasing number of areas of social life, such as the work-place, domestic life, the environment, etc, and its transformation from a formal to a substantive principle. Domination calls for greater participation, oppression for greater equality; the former attaches to the enlightenment principle of emancipation, the latter to that of self-fulfilment.

We can pursue this analysis in relation to all important institutional and individual developments in human rights. The struggles for political rights and for the introduction of the universal franchise aimed at eliminating the domination of various groups, such as the poor, women or ethnic minorities, who were denied political self-determination. These struggles were formally, if not substantively, concluded when political rights and self-determination were extended, in the second half of the twentieth century, to the whole adult population with few exceptions. Similarly, the right to self-governance which characterised the decolonisation process of the 1950s and 1960s and prefaced the main human rights documents of the period,[50] extended collective political recognition from the excluded groups of the metropolis to whole nations and ethnicities in the developing world. In these instances, the groups of subjects enjoying political rights and claiming the corresponding recognition were significantly enlarged.

In other cases, it was the scope of the application of rights that was expanded to new areas. Workers' rights extended the principle of participation to the shop floor and to some aspects of industrial management. Privacy rights introduced the principle of autonomy into areas and activities associated with sexuality and with the control of

---

[49] Iris Marion Young, *Justice and the Politics of Difference* (Princeton, Princeton University Press, 1990) 56.

[50] "All people have the right of self-determination. By virtue of that right they freely determine their political status and freely pursue their economic, social and cultural development." This is the first article of both the Civil and Political Rights and the Economic, Social and Cultural Rights Covenants adopted by the United Nations in 1966.

one's body and domestic environment, such as abortion and contraception. Consumers' rights enlarged the decision-making bodies in education, health and other public utilities. The principle behind these rights is that people should be allowed to participate in public discussion and the decision-making of institutions to which they contribute or whose activities affect their lives. Each extension enlarges either the number of people entitled to decide issues of public concern or the issues open to the logic of public deliberation and decision and, to that extent, subjection to institutional domination is reduced and autonomy increased. In terms of recognition, the holders of these extended political rights are given the formally equal chance to determine important aspects of their life.

The continuous extension of political rights-holders and the expansion of the logic of public and political participation to hitherto private areas and activities, helps us understand the relationship between citizenship and universality. Every extension (or reduction) of political rights enlarges (or diminishes) the institutional definition of a particular polity; it literally moves the boundaries of society forwards or backwards. The idea of a body politic, of an incorporated social space symbolised by God, king, sovereign or law, is shattered every time a larger or smaller than before group is admitted to new rights and new participatory procedures. In the area of political rights, citizenship is the expression of universality: political rights are the result of the destruction of traditional communities and of the undermining of the pre-modern body politic and, these rights, in turn, accelerated the process. Mutual recognition has moved from the relations of mastership love and care which predominantly characterised the pre-modern world to legal recognition, the construction of identities through rights. If citizenship is the essence of universality, if community participation turns the abstract legal subject into a socially recognised person, its essence is negative. The universality of political rights is the point of excess or transcendence of political community which already exists within the community, both inside its boundaries and pointing to the outside. It negates the closing down of the political space and "sustains the moment of disembodiment, the groundlessness and the dislocation of power constitutive of democratic practice".[51] The logic of political rights is that of indeterminacy: rights are within and without the social space. They draw their power from their institutional declaration but their performa-

---

[51] Bernstein, op.cit., supra n. 45, 113.

tive force denies the institution every time their scope is extended to new areas or subjects. And as Marx insisted, political community and citizenship are both the recognition of the universality of rights and of their denial, since rights support and are supported in turn by the inequalities of economy and culture.

Using Young's terminology, we can argue that the negative universality of political rights addresses the problem of domination but not of oppression. Oppression is not just economic, although the exploitation and degradation of material deprivation is its main form. Oppression denies people's ability to decide what is the best life-plan for them and deprives them of the necessary means to carry it out. It does not allow its victims to live according to their desires and develop their potential, it prevents the fulfilment of their aspirations and capacities.[52] Economic exploitation of the metropolitan poor through unemployment, breadline wages, poor health and casual work, or of the developing world through unequal trade and crippling debt, undermines and eventually destroys the possibility of self-development. When daily survival is the order of the day, all aspirations for social improvement or cultural expression are extinguished. The profit-led national and international division of labour creates the structural and institutional preconditions for material deprivation and that in turn leads to oppressed lives. The oppressed cannot enjoy or even aspire to the Aristotelian *eu zein*, the good and complete life that allows their personality to flourish.

The recognition denied by oppression is not that of mutual respect or of political participation. Oppression denies the much more specific recognition enjoyed by a person in his uniqueness and integrity, the acknowledgement of his specific capacities and aspirations, and of his singular needs and desires. This type of recognition would bind the split between the (extendible) political community and its rights and civil society with its inequalities. Participation would be extended from public life to every aspect of social life, and the indeterminacy of society would change from being just a horizon into the reality of everydayness. In this postmodern Hegelian ethical life, the formality of dignity would merge with the warmth of personal love and communal care. This utopian project does not just negate the present; it negates all dominated and oppressed individual presents, in the name of an openness which takes hold of both society and identity. One could not improve much its organising principle from the maxim

---

[52] See generally, Alan Gewirth, *Self-Fulfilment* (Princeton NJ, Princeton University Press, 1998).

"from each according to ability to each according to needs". As a soteriological promise, it joins the other historical end games, such as Hegel's Prussian State, Marx's communism and Fukuyama's liberal capitalism. But all utopias, when they arrive, turn out to be the negation of their promise. Utopia's vocation is never to become a *topos* but to act as a negative prefiguration of the future which helps understand and judge the infamies of the present. In this sense, human rights as utopian principle can help identify and fight the denials of identity and lack of recognition created by domination and oppression.

We can develop for this purpose Hegel's insight that crime indicates the failings of a particular type of legal recognition and expresses the political and moral struggle to move law and identity to a higher and more nuanced plane. For Hegel, as we saw, crime is a reaction of the individual against the abstract and formal character of law. "[Crimes] are tied to the social preconditions of legal relations, in the sense that they stem directly from the indeterminacy of a form of individual freedom that is merely legal. In a criminal act, subjects make destructive use of the fact, that as the bearer of rights to liberty, they are integrated only negatively into the life of society",[53] in other words, their individuality is restricted to rejecting contractual offers and their freedom to saying no to the advances of others. Crime and the reaction to it are social struggles which, although deviant, help the law develop towards a more advanced stage and the people towards a more positive and concrete identity. In Honneth's interpretation, the collective effect of crime is to disrupt and negate old and inadequate forms of mutual recognition and help the development of new. If we jettison the teleological character of the dialectic retained by Honneth, this approach can be profitably used to understand the human rights trajectory.

Oppression and domination are the crimes of public or private power. The criminal here is often the state, its officials and the law. But the other aspects of the Hegelian analysis remain valid: recognition or its denial is the stake behind human rights struggles and their (un)successful conclusion moves the community towards new identities. Every new right-claim is a fighting response to dominant social and legal relations, at a particular place and time, a struggle against the injuries and harm they inflict; it aims to negate inadequate forms of recognition for individuals and groups and to create more complete and nuanced types. Human rights claims are, negatively, a reaction to

---

[53] Honneth, op.cit., supra n. 24, 20.

the multiple offences and insults of power to an individual's or group's sense of identity and, positively, an attempt to have as many aspects of that identity as possible recognised by others and the community. The negative principle is stronger, however, the sense of injustice much more tangible than the appeal to perfect justice. In this, human rights struggles share a common characteristic with many utopias: they negate the existent, they criticise present injustices and infamies in the name of an unknown and, even impossible, future. Because we have known hell we dream of paradise.

Examining the harm that a violation inflicts often gives us the best insight about the ends of human rights. The torture of political prisoners can illustrate the point. During the Greek dictatorship of 1967–74, many opponents of the regime were subjected to extreme physical and mental torture. The most dreaded place was the headquarters of the military police in Athens. Its officers became notorious for their cruelty and inventiveness. In many instances, however, the extreme pain inflicted did not aim at extracting from the victims secrets about the resistance. The beatings, fake executions and rapes were often used to make the prisoners describe acts or reveal names already known to the police. As the limbs were split apart and the flesh electrocuted and burned, the questions were of little practical value to the torturers and the regime. This redundant interrogation was often accompanied by the demand that prisoners sign a document, declaring that they had seen the wrong of their ways and accepting fully the legitimacy of the colonels' hunta.

The apparent futility of these demands indicates the nature of the torturers' enterprise. The torturers whip or the *falanga* aimed at the flesh of the victim as the outer shell of the soul. The useless confession, the already known activities, the naming of names was the way of destroying the victim's sense of identity. The evil of torture is not restricted to the wanton violence inflicted on the body. Many types of extreme pain and physical suffering in war, religious martyrdom or disease are endured with dignity and patience. The evil of torture lies elsewhere: it denies its victim the minimum recognition offered by a liberal social and legal system and, in doing so, it destroys the respect people routinely expect from others. More importantly, torture aims to undermine the way the victim relates to his own self, his self-respect, and thus to dissolve the mainsprings of his personality.

As Elaine Scarry puts it:

> the relation between body and voice that for the prisoner begins in opposition (the pain is so real that the question is unreal, insignificant)

and that goes on to become an identification (the question, like the pain, is a way of wounding; the pain, like the question, is a vehicle of self-betrayal) ultimately ends up in opposition once more. For what the process of torture does is to split the human being in two, to make emphatic the ever present but, except in the extremity of sickness or death, only latent distinction between a self and a body, between a "me" and "my body". The "self" or "me" which is experienced on the one hand as more private, more essentially at the centre, and on the other hand as participating across the bridge of the body in the world, is "embodied" in the voice, in language. The goal of the torturer is to make the one, the body, emphatically and crushingly *present* by destroying it, and to make the other, the voice, *absent* by destroying it.[54]

Slavery subjects the whole person to the domination of the other; torture rejects the unity of body and self. It disassociates the person's identity from the body and, by crushing the body, in ever new and imaginative ways, it denies the victim's sense of integrity and self-control. The phenomenological embeddedness of self in body is torn apart and the dismembering of limbs becomes a tool for the disassembly of the person's identity. The futility of the interrogation, always accompanied by more ferocious beatings, can thus be explained. The useless "betrayal" is a further denial of the victim's identity; it unravels his relation to self, a relation that passes through the mutual recognition of the other members of the group and the pride enjoyed in the solidarity of the common cause. The torture withdraws from the victim his self-respect as an autonomous moral agent, and the information or the signing of the declaration destroys his self-esteem as a valued member of a community of common goals and a world of shared values. It is no surprise, therefore, that after the fall of dictatorial regimes, the desire of political belonging, the participation in group activities with a strong identity, increases spectacularly.

A similar operation of identity-denial characterises extreme racial or homophobic hate speech. As critical race theorists have argued, verbal racial attacks intend to provoke the victim to question her identity and to acknowledge herself as inferior to the attacker.[55] In hate speech, one characteristic of the person, her colour, race or sex-

---

[54] Elaine Scarry, *The Body in Pain* (Oxford, Oxford University Press, 1985) 48–9.
[55] Mari Matsuda, Charles Lawrence III, Richard Delgado and Kimberley Crenshaw (eds), *Words that Wound: Critical Race Theory, Assaultive Speech and the First Amendment* (Boulder, Westview Press 1993).

ual orientation, is picked, presented as determining the person's overall value and denigrated. Racist or sexist speech, like torture, emphasises one particular trait of the person and denies her integrity. Furthermore, by devaluing an element or characteristic which is central to the identity of a group, it aims to withhold recognition and respect from the whole group and from each of its members, without concern for the individual's other capacities and desires. The terrain of the racist is identity and his weapons are, first, the withdrawal of moral recognition and legal equality and, secondly, the withholding of esteem from the whole group. The first denies the recognition of dignity and equal respect, the second aims at undermining esteem and respect amongst members of the group and at destroying the positive evaluation of its shared character and history. A similar analysis helps explain why critical race theorists have distanced themselves from the critique of rights associated with the American critical legal movement.[56] Racist oppression and domination denies the minimum legal recognition of a liberal legal system, something taken for granted by the successful members of the legal academy. For the historically oppressed person of colour, having rights and scrupulously following legal procedures offers much more than the actual contents of these rights; it offers the respect of others and the self-respect that legal recognition ensures but which has been systematically withheld. Being admitted to right-holding is a symbolic admission to the dignity of humanity and a very real introduction to the legal recognition of (formal) equality. This is the indispensable precondition of critique. Kant must be in place before we move to Hegel or Marx.

We can conclude that, from a Hegelian perspective, human rights are expressions of the struggle for recognition amongst citizens which presupposes and constructs the political community. The idea of mutual recognition has not been entertained in rights theory, but it is implicit in the operation of rights and in new rights-claims. Many aspects of recognition take the form of rights and all rights are in this sense political: they extend the logic of public access and decision-making to ever-increasing parts of social life. Human rights are not the trump cards against collective goals, as liberal theory has it, but signs of a communal acknowledgement of the openness of society and identity, the place where care, love and law meet. Similarly, rights to self-determination in international law are an expression of

---

[56] Rights are "a symbol too deeply enmeshed in the psyche of the oppressed to lose without trauma and much resistance", Patricia Williams, *The Alchemy of Race and Rights* (Cambridge Ma., Harvard University Press, 1991) 165.

the mutual recognition of societies and nations emerging from colonisation. Thus rights protect the ability of people to participate in the life of the community as a whole, and the struggle for new rights is a struggle for changing the meaning of equal participation and extending it from political life to the workplace, to the environment and to the private domain. If the life of law is not books but experience, the life of rights is not in the isolated individual but in the recognition of being with others.

11

Psychoanalysis becomes the Law: Rights and Desire

Psychoanalysis, the recent bonanza in social thought, is predominantly a theory of subjectivity and legality. The law is the foundation of the subject and the cement of sociality and, as both Jacques Lacan and his heretical follower Pierre Legendre insist, individuals and societies cannot escape its empire with impunity. If the classical maxim claimed that *ubi societas ibi jus*, the psychoanalytical version reverses it: *ubi jus, ibi subjectum et societas*. Psychoanalysis is a legal theory or at least a theory in which law plays a formative role. For psychoanalysis the subject, rather than being a pre-given substance or a fully constructed entity, is reflectively and intersubjectively constituted. But this is not just Hegelianism with therapy. The unconscious and desire both create and disrupt consciousness and subjectivity and, as a result, human experience, action and meaning involves always "another scene" and demands a "deep" interpretation of the causes and effects of "free will".

Psychoanalysis and in particular its Lacanian revision are fast becoming the latest great frontier for jurisprudence too.[1] The work of Pierre Legendre,[2] Peter Goodrich,[3] David Caudill, Jeanne

---

[1] Recent explorations of the relationship between law and psychoanalysis include David Caudill, *Lacan and the Subject of Law: Toward a Psychoanalytic Critical Legal Theory* (Atlantic, N.J., Humanities Press, 1997); Jeanne Shroeder, *The Vestal and the Fasces: Psychoanalytical and Philosophical Perspectives on the Feminine and Property* (Berkeley, University of California Press, 1997) and Peter Goodrich's, *Oedipus Lex: Psychoanalysis, History, Law* (University of California Press 1995). See also the special issue of the Cardozo Law Review on "Law and the Postmodern Mind" Vol. 16, Nos. 3–4 (1995) and in particular Drucilla Cornell, "Rethinking the Beyond of the Real", 16 *Cardozo Law Review* 3–4, 729–792 (1995). For a review of recent psychoanalytical jurisprudence, see Costas Douzinas, "Psychoanalysis Becomes the Law: Notes on an Encounter Foretold", 1997 *Legal Studies Forum* 323.

[2] Pierre Legendre, *Le Crime de Corporal Lortie* (Paris, Fayard 1989); *L'Amour du Censeur* (Paris, Seuil 1974); "The Other Dimension of Law", 16 *Cardozo Law Review* 3–4, 943–62 (1995). A Reader of Legendre's work was recently published in English: *Law and the Unconscious* (Peter Goodrich ed., London, Macmillan, 1997).

[3] Peter Goodrich, *Languages of Law* (Butterworths, 1993); *Oedipus Lex*, op.cit., supra n. 1; *Law in the Courts of Love* (London, Routledge, 1996).

Shroeder or of the Slovenian philosophers, Slavoj Zizek[4] and Renata Salecl,[5] has alerted us to the many links between law and the psyche. This Chapter will introduce, first, those aspects of psychoanalytical theory which have the greatest relevance for law and will examine critically the contribution psychoanalysis has made so far to our understanding of rights. It may be that, if the law expresses the power and the logic of institution, tradition and reason, it is our personal experience and history with its traumas, desires and symptoms, which determines the way we attach ourselves to the institution. In this sense, psychoanalyis could help explain the centrality of rights in modern law in a concrete way which takes account of personal differences: by combining institutional necessity and personal choice, rights represent the most characteristic legal expression of both social determination and personal desire.

I. FREUD AND THE GENESIS OF LAW

Psychoanalysis presents the birth of the law as a crime story. Freud's "mythological theory of instincts"[6] and of law's creation starts with the murder by his sons of the primordial father who had monopolised the females of the group. Freud uses the tribal ambivalence towards totemic meals, in which the slaughtering of the animal leads to ritual mourning and lamentation followed by festive and excessive rejoicing, to argue that the totemic animal is a substitute for the primal Oedipal father. At this point, Freud wonders whether this explanation can be used to extrapolate the first form of human organisation. His eclectic hypothesis brings together Darwin's "primal horde" theories and early anthropological evidence, gives them a psychoanalytical twist and creates a modern, "scientific" myth of the origins of law and society.

The primal horde, the first form of human organisation, was a band of roving males, ruled by a violent and jealous father who kept all females for himself and drove his sons away. One day, the sons, who hated their father because he blocked access to power and sex-

---

[4] Slavoj Zizek, *The Sublime Object of Ideology* (London, Verso 1989); *For they Know not what they do: Enjoyment as a Political Factor* (London, Verso, 1991); "Superego by Default" 16 *Cardozo Law Review* 3–4, 925–942 (1995).

[5] Renata Salecl, *The Spoils of Freedom* (London, Routledge 1995); "Rights in Psychoanalytic and Feminist Perspective", 16 *Cardozo Law Review* 3–4, 1121–1138 (1994).

[6] Sigmund Freud, *Why War* in *Civilisation, Society and Religion* (James Strachey ed. and trans., Penguin, 1985) 341, 359.

ual gratification, banded together and killed him. But after their hatred was satisfied, a sense of remorse and guilt overtook them and led to the establishment of the two laws of totemism, which eventually founded all law and sociality: the prohibitions of murder and incest. Incest expresses the fundamental desire of union with the mother, the desired and forbidden love object. The totemic prohibitions turned the primal horde into a fraternal clan which was later replaced by organised community. "Society was now based on complicity in the common crime; religion was based on the sense of guilt and the remorse attaching to it; while morality was based partly on the exigencies of this society and partly on the penance demanded by the sense of guilt".[7]

Freud presents his hypothesis as a "Just-So Story",[8] a tale which has "left indestructible traces upon the history of human descent".[9] Two elements emerge which will determine the legal proclivity of psychoanalysis. First, violence and crime lie at the beginning of humankind. Crime comes before the law and determines the nature of the law and its response. Secondly, Freud's story joins the great religious, philosophical and scientific attempts to go back to an *origo*, a time before history and memory at which human society was founded. For Freud, the law lies at the beginning of civilisation. Myth and law have a double function. Law is the progenitor and promoter of civilisation and without it humanity would not have come into existence. But the law also founds psychoanalysis. The "primal parricide" is the mythical explanation and the diachronic structure of the Oedipal drama. Psychoanalysis is the science which examines law's action and its transgression.

Freud links directly his analytical theory with the genesis of law in his late essays. In *Why War?*, he sets out to explain the causes of warfare in response to an invitation by Einstein.[10] The genealogy of law starts again with the "primal horde". Conflicts were resolved violently, and the most powerful member killed or subjugated his opponents through brute force. All law and right, Freud insisted, come from violence. The road from the might of the strongest to the legal institution passes through the victor's realisation that, if the defeated and weaker group members were to unite, they could challenge his

---

[7] Sigmund Freud, *Totem and Taboo* in *The Origins of Religion* (James Strachey ed. and Albert Dickson trans., Penguin 1985) 208.

[8] Sigmund Freud, *Group Psychology and the Analysis of the Ego* in *Civilisation, Society and Religion* supra n. 6, 154.

[9] ibid.

[10] Sigmund Freud, *Why War?*, supra n. 6.

domination. Law is therefore the replacement of individual violence by the organised violence of the community and is directed against those who resist it. The Hobbesian undertones of Freud's story are striking. Freedom is not the gift of civilisation and it was much greater, albeit unenforceable and impractical, before the law intervened. The desire for freedom is a sign of humanity's nostalgia for this original untamed personality, and mental illness the result of the resentment and hatred created by its suppression by civilisation. Law is the first and most powerful weapon in civilisation's attempt to restrain the satisfaction of instincts and desires. Freud goes on to admit that the "first requisite of civilisation is justice – that is the assurance that a law once made will not be broken in favour of an individual". But this is the positivist justice of legality, Freud adds. "[It] implies nothing as to the ethical value of such law".[11]

Communities are held together by shared emotional ties and by violence. Law's inability to resolve conflict in a community lacking communal feelings and emotional attachments leads to the extensive use of legal violence. Thus, the force which led to law's genesis is also found at the heart of its operations. A good example is the international community: it does not attract emotional ties of any kind and, as a result, war becomes the main means for resolving conflict.[12] The antidote to violence is nurturing those "emotional ties". They are of two types; people may share feelings of love towards each other but this is "more easily said than done". Alternatively, they share important interests and concerns which can draw them closer through their identification with the love object. The object Freud has in mind is chillingly clear. The "innate" and "ineradicable" inequality of men separates them into leaders and followers who "stand in need of an authority which will make decisions for them and to which for the most part they offer an unqualified submission. This suggests that more care should be taken than hitherto to educate an upper stratum of men with independent minds . . . whose business it would be to give directions to the dependent masses".[13] The father-chief-leader is the best substitute for violence and law's closest ally. In this transition from anthropology and myth to social psychology, law and politics acquire a menacing tone and a totalitarian potential.

---

[11] Sigmund Freud, *Civilisation and its Discontents* in *Civilisation Society and Religion* supra n. 6, 284.

[12] Recent controversies over Britain's position in Europe and the war in former Yugoslavia have made Freud's fears painfully topical and contemporary again.

[13] Sigmund Freud, *Why War?*, supra n. 6, 359.

II. LACAN AND THE NAME OF THE LAW

Freud's jurisprudence has been criticised on various grounds. Its emphasis on *anomie*, violence and the role of the leader have been explained as expressions of the catastrophic *maelstrom* of inter-war Europe. Moreover, Freud's prevarications as to the anthropological or mythological status of his political theory are usually attributed to the central conflict in psychoanalysis as to its "scientific" or hermeneutical nature. The anthropological evidence Freud used was scant and is now considered unsound. Additionally, the myth of law's genesis has been criticised for its logical flaws. If law and morality are the outcome of the murder, the sense of guilt experienced by the killer-sons cannot be explained. These inconsistencies made the French psychoanalyst and philosopher Jacques Lacan to turn Freud's story into a mythical structure and to read it, in a way similar to Levi-Strauss's explanation of the elementary structures of kinship, as an attempt to give narrative epic form to the structure of subjectivity and the operation of desire. The "novelty of what Freud brings to the domain of ethics",[14] according to Lacan, was the discovery of the structuring principle of subjectivity and the social bond. This enabled him to understand the reasons why the efforts of the finest minds and fieriest hearts over three millennia have failed to establish a successful moral code or an acceptable ethical practice, thus leaving civilisation drowning in its discontent.

In Lacan's reading, the murdered and cannibalised primal father is a symbol of the subject's internalisation of law. The parricide and its effect cannot be proven but, if we are to understand subjectivity and sexuality, its structure must be presupposed. While Freud, in common with all great system builders, and in particular his hero Moses, narrated the creation of law, Lacan closer to the concerns of anthropology, linguistics and structuralism, emphasises law's contribution to the constitution of human identity. Freudian psychoanalysis tried to explain the law as the necessary response of socialised personality to various needs, desires and instincts. Lacanian theory explains the desires, needs and identity of the subject through subjection to the law.

According to Freud's Oedipal structure, the subject comes into existence through the intervention of the father who disrupts the

---

[14] Jacques Lacan, *The Ethics of Psychoanalysis* (London, Routledge, 1992) 216.

mother-child dyad by prohibiting the child's desire for the mother. Lacan's "return to Freud" reads this "primal repression" in linguistic terms. The primal union between mother and child is broken and the subject comes into existence by entering the symbolic order, typically a combination of language and law. The symbolic separates the infant from the maternal body, "castrates" it, and this division inscribes loss, absence and lack in the midst of self. This lack is partially addressed through the infant's identification with signifiers, with words and images. In the famous "mirror stage", the infant between six and eighteen months experiences a sense of jubilation when she first recognises her image in the mirror or in the gaze of the mother and, through the reflection, comes to identify with a whole and complete body. But this image is external to the body and different from the child's sensual experience of a disjointed body and disobedient limbs. The biological reason for this disjuncture is that perceptual aptitudes develop well before motility and other motor functions. As a result of this stage, the first sense of identity is already external to the ego, an image of the ego, that becomes available visually. The ego does not precede the image but is made in the image of the image, its unity is imaginary, in the double sense of visual and illusionary, the result of a wholeness and anticipated completeness imagined through the projection of the uncoordinated body into an adorable visual other.[15] The body's coherence depends on the "future anteriority of the projection in that what has yet to be is imagined as already given".[16] Identity and bodily integrity are not given but are constructed through a mirroring process and the repeated recognition of self by the other, who looks complete and becomes the cause of the anticipated integrity.

The infant's encounter with liguistic signs works in a similar way. As Hegel, who strongly influenced Lacan, argued, language in its arbitrary connections between signifiers and signifieds and between words and things destroys, kills reality. "Say the word lion", writes Hegel, "and you create the lion *ex nihilo*, by abolishing the tangible thing".[17] "Say the word dog and you kill the real dog . . . the conceptual understanding of empirical reality is equivalent to a murder"

---

[15] See my "*Prosopon and Antiprosopon*: Prolegomena for a Legal Iconology" in Costas Douzinas and Lynda Nead (eds.), *Law and the Image: The Authority of Art and the Aesthetics of Law* (Chicago, University of Chicago Press, 1999) 36–67.

[16] Drucilla Cornell, *The Imaginary Domain* (New York, Routledge, 1995) 39.

[17] *Hegel and the Human Spirit: A Translation of the Jena Lectures on the Philosophy of the Spirit (1805–6) with Commentary* (L. Rauch trans.) (Detroit, Wayne State University Press, 1983) 89–95.

agrees Kojéve.[18] Say the word "elephants" adds Lacan and here comes a herd of elephants, present in its absence and filling up the room. The word nihilates the thing but creates the subject, whose unity is constructed by signifiers, a proper name, Phaedra or Costas. I come into being by being called Costas and, similarly, all other entities must become words and images to emerge into consciousness. This is the meaning of Lacan's famous statements that the "signifier represents a subject . . . (not a signified) – for another signifier (which means not for another subject)"[19] and "language before signifying something signifies for someone".[20] The subject speaks and comes to existence by being spoken in language, in other words by being alienated one more time from bodily and sensory experience into the cold world of the sign.

But an unsymbolisable residue of the primal union with the maternal body, which Lacan called the Real, survives this entry into the world of signs and drives the subject to go back and become the mother's presumed object of desire, the symbolic phallus. Becoming the mother's phallus, however, going back to the undifferentiated womb of the Real would be catastrophic. The law's function is therefore to separate the child from the mother through a rivalrous identification with the father. The name of the father, this representative of the symbolic, imposes a double prohibition: on incest – thus stopping the union with the mother – and on parricide – thus leading the male child to identify with the father. The law, the word of the father, confronts the omnipotence of the mother with the power of the word.[21] This separation from the mother and subjection to the law is Lacan's (in)famous "symbolic castration".[22] The phallus, elsewhere called the *petit objet a* (the little other object) symbolises the integrity or wholeness which has been lost, both impossible and prohibited through the action of language and law. This little other, the remnant of the Real after its ban by the symbolic, is the inner secret or "kernel" of the subject: it creates a ceaseless and destructive pressure to

[18] Alexandre Kojéve, *Introduction to the Reading of Hegel's "Phenomenology of Spirit"* (A.H. Nichols trans.) (Ithaca, Cornell University Press, 1989) 140–1.

[19] Jacques Lacan, "Radiophonie" 2/3 *Scilicet*, 1970, 65.

[20] Jacques Lacan, *Écrits* (Paris, Seuil, 1966) 82–3.

[21] Jacques Lacan, "The subversion of the subject and the dialectic of desire in the Freudian Unconscious" in *Écrits: A Selection* (Alan Sheridan trans.) (London, Routledge 1977) 292–325.

[22] For Lacan, access to the symbolic order is much easier for the girl-child who, in not having the penis, accepts with less difficulty the interdiction on becoming the mother's imaginary phallus. In this sense, men who harbour the ridiculous hope that the physical organ is identical with the symbolic position are "failed women".

return to the primal union (the death drive) which at the same time gives rise to an awesome, obscene enjoyment or *jouissance*.

In Lacan's version, therefore, the law creates the ego. The symbolic castration is a question of law and legitimate possession at all levels. The mother delivers the boy to the father through a symbolic contract. The boy-child identifies not with a father presumed to enjoy the mother, but with a father who has legal title to the phallus; he identifies with the signifier of the phallus, the "name of the father", or with the prohibited object of desire. The phallus, this absent, non-existent master signifier is a legal construct – Lacan calls it a "sceptre"[23] – acquired by the father through his own castration. "It is in the name-of-the-Father that we must recognise the support of the symbolic function which, from the dawn of history, has identified his person with figure of the law".[24] The symbolic castration represents the genealogical order by prohibiting imaginary and promoting symbolic identifications. Without submission to its law, the child cannot be separated from the mother and cannot be introduced to subjectivity. But by separating the subject from the love object and introducing him to lack, the law is also the creator of desire.

For psychoanalysis, therefore, the basic law or interdiction which creates humanity as a speaking species is that of division and separation: from the maternal body, through the Oedipal law of the Father, from one's own body through the narcissistic identification with its image, from the other as subject and object through their negation or nihilation in the sign. I must identify with my image in the mirror and with my name, those disembodied entities, those instances of otherness to become an ego. I must accept division and negativity, I must accept that I am what I am not, in Rimbaud's felicitous phrase that "Je est un autre". The ego from the start is alter, an other; it is born in its encounter with the Big Other, the linguistic and legal universe symbolised not by the Father or the paternal function, as in Freud, but by a sign which, Lacan calls, the master signifier or the Name of the Father.

When we turn from the law to *logos*, from the father to the linguistic rewriting of the Oedipus drama, legal metaphors proliferate

---

[23] "If this exchange must be described as androcentric . . . it is, M. Levi-Strauss tells us, because of the occurence of political power that make themselves felt in it, power that falls to men (sic) to exercise. It is therefore because it is also the sceptre that the fallus prevails – in other words because it belongs to the symbolic order". Lacan in unpublished Seminar X quoted by Mikkel Borch-Jacobsen, *Lacan: The Absolute Master* (Douglas Brick trans.) (Stanford University Press, 1991) 213.

[24] Lacan, *Écrits*, supra n. 21, 67.

again. Language both in its structure and action is homologous with the law. "No-one is supposed to be ignorant of the law; this somewhat humorous formula taken from our Code of Justice nevertheless expresses the truth in which our experience is grounded . . . No man is actually ignorant of it, since the law of man has been the law of language since the first words of recognition".[25] Again when glossing Levi-Strauss's structural interpretation of kinship and exchange, Lacan insists on the primacy of the law-language order:

> The marriage tie is governed by an order of preference whose law concerning the kinship names is, like language, imperative for the group in its forms, but unconscious in its structure . . . The primordial Law is therefore that which in regulating marriage ties superimposes the kingdom of culture on that of nature abandoned to the law of mating . . . This law, then, is revealed clearly enough as identical with an order of language.[26]

And if the order of language is identical with the order of law, speech or discourse acts like law. In Lacan's oracular aphorism:

> Thus it is from somewhere other than the Reality that it concerns that Truth derives its guarantee: it is from Speech. Just as it is from Speech that Truth receives the mark that establishes it in a fictional structure. The first words spoken (*le dit premier*) stand as a decree, a law, an aphorism, an oracle; they confer their obscure authority upon the real other.[27]

Reality, Speech, decree, the other. In this obscure formulation we can trace all the essentials of the rule of law according to Lacan. Law does not just constitute the subject but has wider redemptive qualities. Hegel's dialectics of desire can be traced in Lacan's legal formulations. Under the influence of the dialectic, Lacan turns the "discontents of civilisation" into desiring subjects who fight for the impossible love object unto death. In this dialectic of desire and death, law becomes a partial cure for the traumas of society, in a fashion not dissimilar to that applied to individuals in therapy.

III. LAW AND THE DIALECTICS OF DESIRE

Hegel believed that history will end when the spirit recognises itself in the world, and master and slave are dialectically overcome in the

---

[25] ibid., 61.
[26] ibid., 66.
[27] ibid., 305–6.

whole Man, the Citizen of the universal and homogeneous State.[28] But for the non–Marxist Parisian intellectuals of the inter-war period, this promised reconciliation was no longer historically credible and emphasis was placed on the agonistic aspect of intersubjectivity and desire. Hegelian theory, steeped in struggle, conflict and reconciliation, took a much darker inflection and influenced deeply the psychoanalytical school of Lacan. A key step in the transition from Hegel to Lacan is the influential interpretation of the *Phenomenology of Spirit* by the French philosopher Kojéve. Kojéve's influence on Lacan's "return to Freud" is well-documented.[29] Lacan used the Hegelian dialectic extensively to show how the Other and reflexivity construct self. But while the conflicts, turns and tribulations of the Hegelian self lead to self-consciousness, Lacan's reformulation presented the subject as split and decentred.

For Kojéve, Hegel's aim was to reconstruct the transcendental presuppositions and the necessary historical stages which have led to contemporary subjectivity and its historical and philosophical understanding. While the other's recognition is essential for the creation of subjectivity, Kojéve insisted that this dependence revealed a fundamental lack at the heart of self. The apparent types of desire for the other and for objects can be mediated only through another's desire. If desire is defined as the desire for the other's desire, it amounts to the desire to be recognised in one's individuality and is deeply narcissistic. Desire recognises itself in another desire, but what it discovers there is emptiness and lack, the essence of all desire. The mirror reveals desire's object to be nothingness, non-being. Death, Hegel's "absolute master", is the "truth" of desire and, as a result, history is competitive and violent.[30]

This analysis contains the mainsprings of the Lacanian theory of desire. Lacan was categorical about desire's turn towards the void of death, the catastrophic Real which has been exiled by the symbolic but lurks in the intense enjoyment of *jouissance*. Desire as the demand for recognition is a persistent and insatiable erotic request to be desired as a subject. The object of desire is a failed object, the pure

---

[28] Kojéve, supra n. 18, 44.

[29] See amongst many, Vincent Descombes, *Modern French Philosophies* (L. Scott-Fox and J.M. Harding trans.) (Cambridge University Press, 1980) Chapter 1; Borsch-Jacobson, *Lacan* op.cit., supra n. 23, Introduction; Michael Taylor, *Altarity* (Chicago University Press, 1987) Chapters 1 and 5; Slavoj Zizek, *The Sublime Object of Ideology*, op.cit., supra n. 4, passim.

[30] On Hegel's attitude to death, the "absolute master" see Costas Douzinas and Ronnie Warrington, "Antigone's *Dike*" in *Justice Miscarried* (Edinburgh University Press, 1994) Chapter 2.

negativity of a subject who desires herself and cannot be satisfied by objects, because they are what the subject is not and what desire lacks. Desire as the desire of the other is a pure desire of emptiness and bears witness to the subject's constitutive lack. Desire does not seek satisfaction but its own continuation, to go on desiring. But if desire desires itself as desire or as subject, it wants not to be an object, it wants not to be, it is a desire for death.

In Lacan's interpretation, the Oedipal scene is an attempt to shield the subject from the reality of this abysmal desire. The rivalry with the father becomes "the narrow footbridge thanks to which the subject does not feel invaded, directly swallowed up by the yawning chasm that opens itself to him as pure and simple confrontation with the anguish of death . . . indeed we know of that shield of intervention, or substitution that the father [forms] between the subject and the absolute Master – that is death".[31] It is preferable to identify symbolically and rivalously with the Other who bars enjoyment than be handed over to the abyss of radical absence. Thus the non object of desire becomes the target of repression. Non being cannot be represented, it is beyond presence and representation. But this desire of nothing organises itself in imaginary scenarios, it imagines and pictures itself in objects, Lacan's *little object a*, the cause and object of desire.

The little object is a remainder and reminder of the primal union, to which the subject clings and continuously returns in order to forget the separation and lack. This object may take different forms: the lost breast of the mother, a gaze, a particular voice are objects which belong to the Real and cannot be symbolised or substituted by language. But the subject also builds imaginary scenaria which trigger the return of the little object: fetishistic attachments, a sports car, a better job, greater recognition of the academic by the peer group. The attainment of the fantasy does not satiate desire however; it immediately attaches itself to a new object, an even faster car or further promotion *ad infinitum*. The cause of desire is interminable, entry to the Real is impossible and barred; the little object is always deferred, it has no name because it does not refer to some specific need or request but to something more or different from the object: the wish to become again complete or to be fully loved by the Other in a way that would fill the lack. But this is impossible: the little object as the remainder of the Real makes all fantasy scenaria

[31] Lacan in unpublished Seminar VI, quoted by Borch-Jacobsen, *Lacan* op.cit. supra n. 23, 94.

necessarily inadequate substitutes, always in search of something else or more or elsewhere.

Furthermore, the Other cannot offer what the subject lacks, because it is also lacking. The subject tries unsuccesfully to identify the desire of the Other and replaces lack with the little object. In its endless proliferation and diversification, desire emerges as the excess of demand over need, as something in every demand that cannot be reduced to a need. As Lacan argues, "desire is neither the appetite for satisfaction not the demand for love, but the difference which results from the subtraction of the first from the second, the very phenomenon of their splitting".[32] The little object, the insatiable excess of demand over need "represents what the other lacks in order to be absolute, represents the lack itself as the irreducible remainder in any signification".[33] Thus the little object "fills the lack, the split that traverses the subject after castration, but, on the other hand, the *objet a* prevents any object from really filling the lack".[34] The real object of desire cannot be present. It is always represented in inadequate and failing identifications and imaginary constructions raised on the ground of repressed jouissance. The imaginary identifications with objects and ideals are failing attempts to deny death. They both misrecognise desire and defend the self from the spectre of its morbidity.

IV. PSYCHONALYSIS AS JURISPRUDENCE

These imaginary identifications lead to intense competition for the love object and cause hostility, aggression and war. Lacan's solution brings the law back again. A contract lies behind speech and allows the social bond to operate. "This rivalrous, competitive base at the object's foundations is precisely what is surmounted in speech, insofar as it interests a third party. Speech is always a pact, an agreement; people understand each other, they agree – this is yours, that is mine, this is one thing, that is another".[35] To speak to another is to deny death, to delay and defer desire, to avoid addressing the absolute Other or Master. Speaking leads to a truce, rivalry is abandoned in order to participate in discourse and share our imaginary scenarios or

---

[32] *Écrits*, op.cit., 287.
[33] Bice Benvenuto and Roger Kennedy, *The Works of Jacques Lacan – An Introduction* (London, Free Association Books, 1986) 176.
[34] Renata Salecl, *The Spoils of Freedom*, op. cit., supra n. 5, 126.
[35] Jacques Lacan, *Seminar III: The Psychoses* (London, Routledge 1994) 50.

symbolic representations with the other. But speech is a lie, a denying, negating, deferring disourse which places the love-object, death
and its desire, (temporarily) in abeyance. But this lie is also the whole
truth. If, in Lacan's famous formulation, the subject is a signifier for
another signifier, we reveal ourselves in speech as beings which
always address an other. The act of speaking, the enunciation of discourse, is ontologically of greater importance than its contents.

> Let us set out from the conception of the Other as the locus of the sig-
> nifier. Any statement of authority has no other guarantee than its very
> enunciation, and it is pointless for it to seek it in another signifier,
> which could not appear outside this locus in any way. Which is what
> I mean when I say that no metalanguage can be spoken, or, more
> aphoristically, that there is no Other of the Other.[36]

But why do people down arms and enter into debate? We must
assume the existence of an initial pact, a hypothetical social contract
which supports subjectivity and sociality. This contract is minimal in
subject matter but far-reaching in consequences. The original pact
cannot be questioned or justified, it must be assumed to be true, a
fiction repeated in every act of speech. Its object is simply the agreement to speak, to exchange speech rather than blows and to conduct
the rituals and the struggle for recognition through discourse rather
than mortal battle. All speech, speaking itself before any content of
the utterance or intention to communicate, enacts the terms of this
contract.

The implications of this theory for jurisprudence are momentous.
Law is the social face of the inter-subjective contract of speech. It is
not the law that needs legitimacy; legitimacy is the product of a primordial legality. The most important aspect of the legal institution is
to guarantee the contract of speech, to offer a symbolic source or origin – the Sovereign, the Legislator, the Law – which announces that
law and speech have authority and must be obeyed.

> Every legitimate power always rests, as does any kind of power, on the
> symbol. And the police, like all powers, also rests on the symbol. In
> troubled times, as you have found, you would let yourselves be
> arrested like sheep if some guy has said *Police* to you and shown you a
> card, otherwise you would have started beating him up as soon as he
> laid a hand on you.[37]

---

[36] *Écrits,* op.cit., 310–1.
[37] Lacan, *The Seminar of Jacques Lacan,* Vol. 1 (John Forester trans.) (Norton, 1988) 201.

We should add parenthetically that the police are colloquially called the Law and that statements by the police and judges are law's "word". That the law exists and speaks is more important than what it is or says. The judge, confronted with an object – the legal materials – or another subject – the litigant – has as his first task to assert the completeness and gaplessness of the law through the performance of the legal ritual. The subject desires that the Other, the symbolic order, is whole, seamless, that it speaks and that it can tell the subject what it desires of her. The actual interpretation of the law, on the other hand, meets the secondary desire to ascribe definite legal meaning to the object thus turning it into a guarantee for the subject's lack. The judge must be seen to declare rather than make the law, to be the mouthpiece of the institution, because his declaration serves a double function: the pronouncement of the word, law's signifier, carries law's power; but this declaration expresses also the legal intention to seize the object (of dispute), to give it meaning, and thus make it witness the unity and completeness of the law and its subjects. Dworkin's "right answer" may have little to do with legal practice but its proclamation provides, despite its falsity, a necessary function for the fearful desiring subject.

The French legal historian, Pierre Legendre, turned the ontological power of the Lacanian "law-speech" into a complete juridical anthropology.[38] For Legendre, the legal system "institutes life",[39] it forms the "atomic bond" which binds the "primary material of man:

[38] The work of Pierre Legendre is quite unprecedented in legal historiography. In his many publications (supra n. 2) he has opened a new field of legal writing or legal poetics in which the love of the text (of law) and of medieval and patristic sources is accompanied by a highly literary and allusive – almost baroque – style. His genealogy of modern law and of its malady of technocratic rationalism, links the "revolution of the interpreters" in the 12th century with the incorporation of the key themes of canon law into civil law and challenges many of the assumptions of traditional historiography. Similarly, Legendre's historical and theoretical insight that the law captures the soul and by attaching body to spirit creates the subject, opens a large vista for jurisprudence and this writer has been considerably influenced by his captivating and seductive theory and prose. But a critical jurisprudence must question the conservative repercussions of his juridical anthropology, as presented for an English readership in his *Cardozo Law Review* essay, op.cit., supra n. 2. In these respects, Legendre joins the climate of the reactionary Catholic response to modernity. The critique of this aspect is indispensable for the development of a critical psychoanalytical jurisprudence which will profit greatly from an engagement with Legendre's work. Cf. supra n. 3; Anton Schutz, "Sons of Writ, Sons of Wrath" 16 *Cardozo Law Review* 3–4, 975–1012 (1995); and Peter Goodrich, "Introduction: Psychoanalysis and Law" in Goodrich (ed.), *Law and the Unconscious: A Legendre Reader* (Macmillan 1997). For a more critical approach see Alain Pottage, "The Paternity of Law" in Douzinas *et al* (eds), *Politics, Postmodernity, Critical Legal Studies* (Routledge, 1994).

[39] Legendre, "The Other dimension of Law", op.cit., supra n. 2, 943.

biology, the social, the unconscious".[40] The legal institution is functionally homologous to the law of the father or, in another version, it interprets and applies the original interdiction. In the same way that the name of the father introduces the subject into separation, lack and negativity, language and the institution "separate the subject from the fantasm of being whole".[41] But this separation needs a guarantor, a "sacred" inaccessible place which stages the origin or the cause of the subject's being. In pre-modern societies this role was played by totems, religions or mythical references to the divine or just foundations of law. In modernity it is "the state [which] is the sacred place of the Totem, wherever it takes hold, whatever its constitutional form may be, the religious or mythical space of the discourse called upon to guarantee the foundations without which the law would remain unthinkable".[42]

The law stages the totem or the interdiction around the father, more specifically around "the image of the substance of the Father, which is equivalent to the totemic principle in European civilisation".[43] The "juridical montages" of this image, God or Pope, Emperor or King, state or legislator, "giv[e] consistency to the founding discourse by representing the Other as a concept, in order to spread the effects of the Interdiction, that is to say, the juridically organised effects".[44] Again when Legendre turns to the mythical contract of speech, he interprets it in a legalistic way. The void that guarantees the social order – what Legendre calls the Reference – must be transmitted and validated legally, through patrilinear genealogy, juridical emblems and the reason of the law. This is the all important but neglected "other dimension" of law: "a body of discourses which, within any society, construct the founding image which is the subjects' marching banner . . . These are valorised institutionally; not according to their express content (which is a function of the declared intention of the author), but through the fact of being symbolically accorded a place within society as representations of the reference".[45] The "truth" and the function of the institution is, therefore, produced by "juridical reason as communicator of this non-juridical dimension of law, and manoeuvred through a function

---

[40] ibid., 954.
[41] ibid., 952.
[42] ibid.
[43] ibid., 959.
[44] ibid., 960.
[45] Legendre quoted in Alain Pottage, op.cit., supra n. 38, 165.

of paternity".[46] But how does psychoanalysis understand rights? The rest of the Chapter focuses on the insight that analytical theory can bring to the understanding of rights.

V. RIGHTS AS THE LITTLE OBJECT A

The continuous expansion (and contraction) of rights indicates their character as an evolving combination of language and law. Language facilitates the expansion while the law organises and delimits it. Law's involvement makes the Other's presence in the operation of rights apparent: rights are sets of signs which help define and underpin the identity of subjects in their relationship with the world. They achieve this by giving formal shape to people's desire for recognition by the Other: both the other person and the big Other, the law, language, the power structures and institutions, in a word, the symbolic order of the polity. In this sense, rights are a function for the subject, a way through which people are given to the world and formally relate to others. At the same time, the huge significance placed by political regimes of all colours and ideologies on the protection of human rights and the increasing mobilisation of international force in their name indicates that they are also an important function of the social organisation.

First, rights as a function for the subject. We have argued that rights legalise desire, that they organise an economy of wants and fears and give public recognition to the subject's wishes. Psychoanalysis, as a theory of desire, can help explain the function of rights in the psychic organisation of the subject and their link with the institution. We will proceed in two directions: we will examine, first, the link between desire and rights and, in the next Chapter, we will turn to the way in which rights operate for the subject and the social bond.

According to Renata Salecl, one of the few theorists to examine human rights from a psychoanalytical perspective, rights serve the same function for society that the little object a serves for the subject. In this sense, the symbolic organisation of modernity presupposes the concept of rights: rights allow us to express our needs in language by formulating them as a demand. Following the Lacanian definition of desire, Salecl argues that when we make a demand, we not only ask the other to fulfill a need but also to offer us his love. An infant, who

---

[46] Legendre quoted in Alain Pottage, op.cit., supra n. 38, 165.

asks for his mother's breast, needs food but also asks for the mother's attention and affection. Desire is always the desire of the other and signifies precisely the excess of demand over need. Each time my need for an object enters language and addresses the other, it becomes a request for recognition and love. But this demand for wholeness and unreserved recognition cannot be met by the other, either the big Other of the symbolic order (language, law, the state) or the concrete other person. The big Other is the cause and symbol of lack; it is symbolised by the name of the father. And as no further master-signifier exists outside the symbolic to turn it into a unified, complete and transparent order, the Other is always lacking. Similarly, the other person, whose love we crave, is subjected to the same castration and lack as ourselves. In this appeal to the other, we confront the lack in the other, a lack that can neither be filled nor fully symbolised. The little object a represents the excess of demand over need, what the other lacks to be complete, lack itself.

Salecl transfers the Lacanian analysis of castration, lack and desire to the social domain. The subject of modern democracies undergoes a "social symbolic castration" similar to that of the Oedipal scene. Before modernity, this indispensable function was carried out implicitly and silently by initiation rites. After the "invention" of democracy and human rights, it has become fully visible. The moderns are presented for the first time with a choice: either accept the social contract, sacrifice wholeness and freedom for security and enter community or be excluded from society. Through a massive translation of liberal political philosophy into Lacanian terms, Salecl concludes that this "choice" is homologous to that between entering the symbolic order and becoming a speaking subject or not and falling into psychosis. Both these choices are forced, and one should add that the concept of choice has little meaning here. It certainly does not refer to the intentional action of *mens rea* required by criminal and tort law, but to a retrospective responsibility implied by the fact that one has entered the social symbolic and has accepted, albeit unconsciously, its terms.

Rights are the substitute given to the subject, the little pleasure left or the reward offered for his subjection to the "fundamental prohibition" imposed by the social symbolic. In this sense, rights act like the little object a. As the remainder of a perceived social integrity and peace and as substitutes for lack, they are the cause and object of desire but, at the same time, they signify lack and prevent it from being filled. Rights give the impression that the subject and society can become whole: only if all the attributes and characteristics of the subject were to be given legal recognition, he would be happy; only if the demands of human dignity and equality were to be fully enforced by the law, the society would be just. But like the little object, rights both displace and fill the lack and make the desired wholeness impossible. The other's desire escapes the subject, always seeking something else, but the little that remains allows the subject to exist as a desiring being. Rights, like the little object, become a phantasmatic supplement that arouses but never satiates the subject's desire. Rights always agitate for more rights: they create ever new areas of claim and entitlement, but these prove without exception insufficient. We keep demanding and inventing new rights in an endless attempt to fill the lack, but this only defers desire.

> The discourse of universal human rights thus presents a fantasy scenario in which society and the individual are perceived as whole, as non-split. In this fantasy, society is understood as something that can be rationally organised, as a community that can become non-conflictual if only it respects "human rights".[47]

The debate on the recently introduced Human Rights Act 1998 can be used as an example: most commentators assume that all Britain needs for making human rights reality is to codify them in law and train the judiciary and the police.[48] This hope is based on the imaginary role of rights discourse and cannot be realised, because codification does not resolve the inherent volatility and endlessly deferred character of rights. The bombing of former Yugoslavia offers another chilling example of how the operation of human rights can occasionally become literally murderous. The bombs, which caused the death and injury of many civilians, including journalists, foreign nationals and fleeing refugees, were supposed to restore and guarantee the rights of the Kosovo Albanians. After every announcement of civilian deaths and the accompanying perfunctory apology, the bombing campaign was intensified. The principle appeared to be that the more we bomb the quicker will human rights triumph, the more

[47] Salecl, op.cit., supra n. 5, at 127.
[48] "The Human Rights Act marks the beginning of a new era in the quest to develop and protect human rights in the UK . . . it represents a new beginning and a fundamental shift to a right-based system of law", Keir Starmer, *European Human Rights Law* (London, LAG, 1999) 1. Jack Straw, the Home Secretary described it as "the first major Bill on human rights for more than 300 years" and "as a key component of our drive to modernise society and refresh our democracy". HC Debs, col 769, 782–3, 16 February 1998. The full introduction of the Act was delayed until October 2000 to allow for the training of legal officials.

civilians we kill (the inevitable "collateral damage" of the campaign) the better will the right to life be protected. And when the rights of Albanians were finally restored, after the NATO victory, their unhindered operation led to the murder, torture and cleansing of ethnic Serbs. These may be extreme cases, but they show the violence that underpins the desire of rights. To paraphrase a classical maxim, *jus juris lupus*.[49]

Salecl is particularly helpful in explaining the endless proliferation of rights-claims:

> Although we have rights, a right that would express the notion of rights does not exist. All we can do, in this regard, is to invent new rights perpetually, searching in vain for a right that would affirm us as non-split subjects . . . Human rights can never be fully described in language, as there will always remain a lack between positive, written rights and the universal idea of human rights.[50]

But the fruitful analogy between the *petit objet a* and rights becomes clouded by a rather unconvincing attempt to celebrate rights and by a rather hasty dismissal of the many criticisms of their operation, including Lacan's.[51] To develop her insight and rescue the Lacanian analysis from collapsing into a rather banal liberalism, for the defence of which one does not need psychoanalytical concepts, we must introduce some important qualifications and necessary corrections. To be sure, a liberal apologia for rights, from a Lacanian perspective, is a sissyphian undertaking and can be pursued convincingly only through a very idiosyncratic and eclectic reading of its theoretical sources.

The first difficulty in Salecl's approach refers to the idea of the "social symbolic castration", which the subject undergoes on entering modern society. The claim that societies go through processes similar to those of the individual is a rather massive and unargued assumption. Psychoanalysis is a theory of the subject. Any extension to social structures must be only by analogy and, as the difficulties of pscychoanalytical social theory show, it can only have the theoretical persuasiveness of analogy. What type of primal union exists, for example, between the subject and society, what kind of separation and alienation do people suffer when they enter social institutions? Salecl slides between the analogical (the subject acts as if a social

[49] The maxim is *homo hominis lupus,* man is a wolf to his fellow man.
[50] Renata Salecl, "Rights in Psychoanalytic and Feminist Perspectives", 16 *Cardozo Law Review*, 1121 at 1134 (1995).
[51] See Chapter 12 below.

castration has taken place) and the literal (a social castration necessarily takes place, its form has only changed from pre-modern societies) and, as a result, the exactness of Lacanian theory, which marvels in formulaic, mathematical and quasi-scientific concepts, is lost. More importantly, the necessary rhetorical and narrative tropes and strategies that accompany analogical arguments are absent.

This confusion is apparent in Salecl's claim that, because the subject chooses to enter society, albeit forcibly, she is "responsible" for words and deeds which violate the social contract. She draws an analogy with Freud's analysante Dora who, although subjected to many infamies in the hands of her immediate family and friends, was declared to be analytically "responsible" for her malady: "Psychoanalysis has always held the subject responsible for his or her jouissance, beginning with Freud who spoke of one's *choice* of neurosis . . . Analysis would be forever blocked if [the question of Dora's *jouissance* from victimhood and responsibility for it] was never posed, and the situation would be simply incomprehensible".[52] This ascription of responsibility may indeed be useful to the therapist in an analytical context. Salecl conveniently chooses hate speech as an area in which this type of strict responsibility should apply. "The subject 'chooses' to speak. Although the words may escape the subject's intentions, and he or she says more in slips of the tongue or between the lines, the subject cannot escape responsibility, even if this responsibility accounts for no more that the mere fact that he or she is a subject".[53] But extending this principle to the whole of law, as Salecl's discussion of rights implies, would be both impossible and catastrophic: one would be held "responsible" too for expressing "seditious" or "dissident" views since, by "accepting" the social symbolic castration, he has forcibly chosen the dominant social contract and is responsible for any deviations from it. By eliding therapeutic responsibility and legal liability, psychoanalysis sides with a type of liberalism which consistently acts in the most intolerant ways towards non-liberals. This rather quick combination of therapy and human rights is neither therapeutic nor liberal.

This confusion may be partly due to the absence of a clear distinction between law and language in Lacan's theorisation of the symbolic order and his lack of interest in positive law. This is not as big a problem for the analyst as it is for the legal theorist. Psychoanalysis can credibly explain the process of formation and the pathology of

---

[52] Salecl, *The Spoils of Freedom*, supra n. 5, 123.
[53] ibid.,123–4.

the psyche, but the transfer of its contested concepts from subject to society has not been successfully carried out yet, and one could argue is perhaps inappropriate. But this is not an insuperable problem in the context of rights. The primal interdiction against incest and parricide, which forms the legal component of symbolic castration, can be seen as the "naturalist" kernel of all legality. And as Legendre has argued, the indispensable function of legality, namely to separate and individuate the subject and reconcile it with lack, is carried out in modernity by positive law. In this approach, law and rights are a function for the subject, they help constitute it as legal and the massive transfer of psychoanalytical concepts to society is not necessary.

It was argued in Chapters 8 and 9, that the human subject is always accompanied, and occasionally even preceded, by the legal subject, a construction of the law and its institutional logic. We could analytically distinguish therefore between the subject, the speaking being, and the legal subject, the institutional being. If the subject comes to life by entering the symbolic order by acquiring language, the legal subject is born through entry to the law. There is no need to argue, therefore, for a massive and theoretically unsupported "social castration". The subject, already constituted through the symbolic, is introduced to legal subjectivity through a second subjection to the commands and procedures of positive law. The logic of the institution, with its ever-proliferating commands and regulations, prohibitions and permissions, duties and responsibilities, seizes and invests the subject with legal meaning. One could argue, therefore, that a "legal symbolic castration" complements the primary castration and introduces the subject to a secondary, law-induced lack of wholeness and a legal determination of even the most intimate aspects of life.

In this context, rights can be seen as a compensation for legal subjection, as the imaginary constructs which give the subject the sense of freedom or integrity. As imaginary complements of subjection, they keep desire going by acting in a way analogous to the fetishistic displacements of the little object a. Every success in the subject's fight for new rights leads to new and further claims in a spiral of desire that can never be fulfilled. Rights may meet real or imaginary needs and may, in a Hegelian fashion, extend recognition to people. But for psychoanalysis, their main task is to keep the legal subject in the position of desiring, in other words, to help maintain it as subject. The subject's relation to the little object a is ambiguous: it is the cause and object of the subject's desire but it must also be kept at a distance, it must not get too close or too far. "The subject comes into being as a defense against it, against the primal experience of pleasure/pain associated with it".[54] *Jouissance*, its satisfaction, is the desire of death; it would return the subject to psychosis or to the primal union and death.

Similarly with rights. As the subjects, following their desire, fight for more and more effective rights, political power comes under increasing pressure to acknowledge and codify them, and their protection has become the mark of civility of a society. But the success will always be limited. As we will examine in more detail in the next Chapter, no right can earn me the full recognition and love of the other and no Bill of Rights can complete the struggle for a just society. Indeed the more rights we introduce, the greater the pressure to legislate for even more, to enforce them better, to turn the person into an infinite collector of rights, and humanity into an endlessly proliferating mosaic of laws. As the law colonises life and the endless spiral of more rights and possessions and acquisitions fuels the subject's imagination, the Other of law dominates her symbolic and the other person's recognition becomes secondary. The ideological triumph of human rights is paradoxically consistent with the empirical observation that our epoch has witnessed their greatest violations.

We can conclude that psychoanalytical theory can offer many insights into the centrality and operation of human rights. But the formalism of liberal Lacanianism is not sufficient. If the little object a is the difference between the idea of human rights and their positive formulation, while human rights point to a future which is always still to be fought for, their legal formulation, which can only be historical and context bound, re-introduces in them the violence of the foundations of law. For psychoanalysis, this gap creates the paradox of rights, which are at the same time forward looking and hostages to the past, the joint between the futural imaginary domain and the backward leaning weight of the institution. Marking the point at which the imaginary impossibly defies the symbolic, human rights are the projection of the "not yet" into the "always there", a necessary but impossible promise.

---

[54] Bruce Fink, *The Lacanian Subject* (Princeton, Princeton University Press, 1995) 94.

12

The Imaginary Domain and the Future of Utopia

A map of the world that does not include Utopia is not worth even glancing at, for it leaves out the one country at which humanity is always landing.

Oscar Wilde

I. IMPOSSIBLE RIGHTS: HUMAN RIGHTS AND JOUISSANCE

The twin aims of the Enlightenment project were emancipation and self-realisation, domination and oppression the two evils it attacked. The struggle against tyranny, dictatorship and lack of effective participation in decision-making is still the first priority in many parts of the world. But in Western postmodern societies, self-realisation and self-fulfilment have become a central aspiration of self and polity. In a society where every desire is a potential right, it is forbidden to forbid. Could this be the subjective expression of the end of history? Self-realisation has been recently associated with the New Age movement and its jejune ideas of communing with an ineffable inner soul, or of unburdening the "real" self that lies concealed or overlaid by social conventions and laws. More generally, however, the claims to authenticity represented by lifestyle magazines and hedonistic consumerism, the exhortation to "be yourself", be free, not give in on your rights, desire etc. are inauthentic and narcissistic. They have created an ideological climate, in which all non-individualistic policies, from taxation to the regulation of the markets, are defined as limitations on freedom and as restrictions of rights, as the oppressive remnants of modernity.

Self-realisation is not merely liberation from external constraints and impositions, as Foucault has shown, and does not lead to the attainment of some "essential" identity. Self-realisation is a process of shaping the self, an aesthetic *poiesis* and care, which can only be carried out in relations with others and within a community. Other people, groups, and the law are aspects of our identity, the supports and constraints of our radical openness to the world. Being is being together, being with others. Viewed from this perspective, human rights acknowledge politically and legally the radical intersubjectivity of human identity, they involve the other and the law in the construction of self. The Hegelian tradition explains how rights are involved in the struggle for recognition and psychoanalysis adds that recognition passes through the desire of the Other, as symbolic order or as other person. The desire for integrity projects the Other as non-lacking but this gesture misfires, the other is as lacking as self. Let us examine this dialectic of lack as expressed in rights.

A right-claim involves two demands to the other: a specific request in relation to one aspect of the claimant's personality or status (to be left alone, not to suffer in his bodily integrity, to be treated equally) but, secondly, a much wider demand to have her whole identity recognised in its unique characteristics. In demanding recognition and love from the other person, we also ask the Big Other, the symbolic order, represented by the law, to recognise us in our identity through the other. When a person of colour claims, for example, that the rejection of a job application amounted to a denial of her human right to non-discrimination, she makes two related but relatively independent claims: the rejection amounts both to an unfair denial of the applicant's need for a job, but also to the denigration of her wider identity with its integral racial component. Every right therefore links a need of a part of the body or personality with what exceeds need, the desire that the claimant is recognised and loved as a whole and complete person.

Human rights violations offer the best illustration of the mutual implication of partial needs and identity. The reason is obvious: the non-recognition or violation of a human right puts on stage and emphasises the difficulties of the always fragile project of identity formation through other-recognition. We saw above, how torturers make their victim "betray" their comrades, thus severing the symbolic link with their community, which helps knot their identity together. With his imaginary identity unravelled, the victim can then be "turned", become useful to the police, an informant or politically inactive and harmless. The same analysis can help us understand why South African blacks reported feelings of deep personal hurt at even minor incivilities or violations of formal equality perpetrated by the white minority during apartheid. The smallest insult, the most secondary inconvenience, made the victim feel worthless in the eyes of the Big Other. Every denial of right was further confirmation that the polity does not recognise the identity of the person as a whole and, as a result, whatever partial compensations were offered, such as a higher standard of living than that of other African states, they were inadequate. But the attainment of identity through the desire and recognition of the other fails in different ways, even in those cases where human rights are successful on the surface and succeed in legalising desire.

Human rights redirect desire from its primary object, the primal union with the (m)other or the Real, into secondary and symbolic substitutes. In doing so, they both misrepresent the structure of radical desire or *jouissance* and they shield the subject from its catastrophic consequences. To have a right is to be recognised in some aspect of self and therefore to deny death, to delay and defer radical desire, to avoid speaking about the absolute Other. When exercising rights, we enter into a truce with others, we abandon rivalry in order to participate in discourse and share with them imaginary scenarios and symbolic representations. But right is also a lie, a denying, negating and deferring action which puts the object of desire (temporarily) in abeyance. If, in Lacan's famous formulation, the subject is a signifier for another signifier, in claiming and exercising our rights we reveal ourselves as beings addressed to an other. Having rights, living through rights, is therefore of greater ontological importance than the contents of these rights. Rights are our truthful lie. Their ever expanding potential is an expression of the intersubjective and insatiable character of desire. The subject of rights tries incessantly to find the missing object that will fill her lack and turn her into a whole being in the desire of the other. But this object does not exist the other does not "have" it, and it cannot be possessed. The impossibility of fulfilling desire leads into ever increasing demands for recognition, and every acknowledgement of right leads into a spiralling escalation of further claims. In this sense, the promise of self-realisation becomes the impossible demand to be recognised by others as non-lacking and all human rights partial expressions of the unattainable "right to be loved". Right-claims proliferate because legalised desire is insatiable. It looks as if the more rights and recognition we get, the more "in the deepest recesses of one's egocentric fortress a voice softly but tirelessly repeats 'our walls are made of plastic, our acropolis of papier-mâché' ".[1]

---

[1] Cornelius Castoriadis, "Reflections on Racism", 32 *Thesis Eleven* (1992), 9.

But the progressive legalisation of existence, in which increasing aspects of life become rights, keeps, like technological intervention, undermining the unity of self. While metaphysical humanism fixes the essence of humanity, the human being, turned into an object of technological and legal ordering, becomes an artificial totality. Technology dissects people into functions and limbs, factors and organs "each setting in motion a different technique, each to be handled separately while other aspects as kept out of the field of vision"[2] and then proceeds to reassemble them into continuously changing wholes. "Every human technique has its circumscribed sphere of action, and none of them covers the whole man", writes Jacques Ellul.[3] Each technique asserts innocently that it only works on one part of the body and leaves human integrity intact; effects on the rest are dealt with as side-issues put aside for further technical intervention. This leads to "the convergence in man of a plurality, not of techniques, but of systems or complexes of techniques. The result is operational totalitarianism; no longer is any part of man free and independent of these techniques".[4]

The same happens with rights. The law breaks down the body into functions and parts and replaces its unity with rights, which symbolically compensate for the denied and barred bodily wholeness. Encountering rights nihilates and dismembers the body: the right to privacy isolates the genital area and creates a "zone of privacy" around it; the mouth is severed and reappears "metonymised" as free speech which protects its communicative but not its eating function;[5] free movement does the same with legs and feet, which are allowed to move freely in public spaces while the whole person is given limited rights of abode and non-nationals none. Similarly, for Drucilla Cornell, "the denial of the right to abortion should be understood as a serious symbolic assault on a woman's sense of self precisely because it . . . places the woman's body in the hands and imaginings of others who deny her coherence by separating her womb from her self".[6]

---

[2] Zygmunt Bauman, *Postmodern Ethics* (Oxford, Blackwell, 1993), 193.

[3] Jacques Ellul, *The Technological Society* (J. Wilkinson trans.) (New York, Random House, 1964), 388.

[4] ibid., 391.

[5] William MacNeil, "Law's *Corpus Delicti*: The Fantasmatic Body of Rights Discourse" IX/2 *Law & Critique*, 37–57, 45–6 (1998). While freedom of movement and security of the person are treated as crucial civil liberties, no major human rights convention, including the European, creates a general right of residence. Some include no such right at all. Others restrict it to state nationals.

[6] Drucilla Cornell, *The Imaginary Domain* (New York, Routledge 1995) 38.

In the process of constructing legal subjects and of making humans, rights split and re-bind body and self and become companions and allies of the more obvious processes of biological, genetic, cybernetic etc. manipulation of bodies and selves. In his sense, the human can never be an individual, an un-divided and indivisible being. Individuals become flexible and malleable legal and technological syntheses. The self-identical subject of modernity, reflectively transparent to itself, a fiction according to most major philosophical schools, appears now as a highly precarious assembly of dismembered bodies and fragmented existences.

A main characteristic of technological intervention is that it deals with parts and organs of the body as if they were isolated and treats any adverse consequences on other organs or people as side-effects to be dealt with by further corrective intervention. As a result, the body is broken down and treated as a collection of processes rather than as an organic whole. Rights follow a similar strategy. A new right aimed at increasing the protection of free speech, fought for by the media, for example, makes private lives vulnerable to unnecessary disclosure. This, unwelcome to some effect, is defined as a threat to privacy and dealt through the creation of new rights for potential victims and more regulatory codes for the media. Again recent children legislation increased the rights of natural parents over their children and in order to deal with the numerous cases of abuse, it created help-lines where children can denounce their parents or gave children the right to go to court and ask to be removed from parental custody. It is part of the action of rights to create counter-demands and to lead to more legislation and new rights in order to combat their adverse consequences. Rights often create rather than address conflict.

The partial operation of rights is evident everywhere. A woman who is given civil and political rights, but does not have her gender recognised by the predominantly male definition of human rights, is not a complete person. An unemployed worker who wants to mobilise support against slum conditions and pollution in his council estate, but cannot do it because of lack of money and access to the media, feels frustrated in the most important project of his life. Gays or lesbians who are dismissed by the military because of their sexual orientation feel a key element of their personality denied. A refugee who is turned down in her application for political asylum, because the immigration officer believes that she lies, is not fully human. In these and a million other cases, the injury and insult caused by non-admission to the status of right-holder (the position of the legal subject) highlights the many ways in which the structures of domination and oppression withhold social recognition from what really matters to people. Human rights societies, by compartmentalising group characteristics, personal traits and individual entitlements, split the imaginary wholeness of self and body. They recognise some aspects of self (formal equality and dignity), withhold recognition from others (the necessary material preconditions for the effective enjoyment of dignity), finally, devalue or dismiss still others (sexual orientation and identity a prime example).

At the same time, each new and specialised right, the right to same-sex marriage for example, exposes the artificiality of the ego, by increasingly colonising its intimate parts. New rights remove activities and relations from their communal habitat and make them calculable, exchangeable, cheap. While rights are a compensation for the lack of wholeness, the more rights I get, the more I need to claim and, paradoxically, the greater the sense of disjointure of self. Rights are self-devouring; the "rights culture" turns everything into a legal claim and leaves nothing to its "natural" integrity. Desire and fear increasingly dominate all relationships and the action of community changes from being-in-common into beings attacking others and defending themselves. The concept of defensive medicine or defensive education is indicative of this process. Medicine is supposed to defend the patient from disease. Defensive medicine, on the other hand, by not taking risks, defends the doctor from anticipated attacks from the patient and his rights. This exposes another great paradox at the heart of rights culture: the more rights I have, the smaller my protection from harms; the more rights I have, the greater my desire for even more but the weaker the pleasure they offer.

This aggressive aspect of rights was recognised by the classics of psychoanalysis but has been forgotten by their liberal followers. For Legendre, contemporary law with its proliferating rights for various minorities has forgotten that the central task of institutions is to guarantee the genealogical binding or filiation of the subject, and has thus abandoned the main anthropological function of law. Courts which have legally recognised the new gender of sex change transsexuals and are prepared to have a child adopted by his hitherto mother who, after surgical intervention, became a man, suffer from a peculiar case of catastrophic institutional amnesia.[7] They have abandoned "thinking about the structure of the Interdiction . . . and given up on intro-

---

[7] Legendre refers to a Canadian case and one in the European Court of Human Rights, in "The Other Dimension of Law", 16 *Cardozo Law Review* 3–4, 943–962 (1995).

ducing the subject to the institution of the limit".[8] The law, lured by the "propaganda of science" and "our democratic ideals"[9] abandons its role and, by attacking the "montages of Interdiction", becomes an accomplice to the destruction of the symbolic order which hitherto "supported the life of the species".

Lacan, too, bemoaned the contemporary weakening of the laws traditionally used to displace the violence of imaginary identifications. The disenchantment with civilisation has been unleashed by a spiral of failing filiations and the progressive abandonment of speech in favour of sexual rivalry and violent competition. "We know in fact what ravages a falsified filiation can produce, going as far as the dissociation of the subject's personality".[10] Lacan, the man of the law, repeatedly diagnosed and castigated the various afflictions of legal civilisation: aborted genealogies, infelicitous filiations and incomplete Oedipal identifications are important failures in our societies, but they are not alone. They are accompanied by the weakening of every legal support of subjectivity and sociality, by a long list of broken laws and frustrated pacts. Borch-Jacobsen usefully catalogues,

> the insolvency and "narcissistic bastardising" of the father figure, the growing indistinguishability of the paternal function from the "specular double", the "tangential movement toward incest" in our societies and so on. In short, it is the competitive, rivalrous world, revealed as the great traditional ordering principles retreat, a world of doubles all the more identical for asserting their autonomy, all the more racked by guilt for declaring their emancipation from every law.[11]

This is a diatribe against a world contaminated by the endlessly proliferating claims to right and autonomy and a memorial for a past in which the symbolic had not exploded in a myriad of rights claims.

> The operation of the law through the symbolic castration and the introduction into language (the name of the father) is therefore a universal function which associates the father with the figure of the law . . . And when the Legislator (he who claims to lay down the Law) presents himself to fill the gap, he does so as an impostor. But there is nothing false about the Law itself or about him who assumes its authority.[12]

---

[8] ibid., 956.

[9] ibid., 957.

[10] Lacan, *Écrits: A Selection* (Alan Sheridan trans.) (London, Routledge 1977) 66–7.

[11] Borsch-Jacobsen, *Lacan: The Absolute Master* (Douglas Brick trans.) (Stanford University Press, 1991) 129.

[12] Lacan, *Écrits*, supra n. 10, 311.

In Lacan's vision, the proliferation of human rights and its challenge to the paternal function can be catastrophic. Indeed, in his one reference to human rights, Lacan gives an indication of how he would have explained their negative effects. In Seminar XIV, Lacan is explaining the idea that the *jouissance* which is sacrificed by the subject in symbolic castration does not get lost but is handed over to the Other and circulates outside of the self, in the realm of the symbolic. Literature, writing, science are fields in which this sacrificed *jouissance* is deposited and helps create and develop culture. Cultural artefacts, Lacan argues, often acquire a life of their own and when we come in contact with them, we receive back some of this sublimated creative surplus-pleasure. The principle is clear: "it is only insofar as we alienate ourselves in the Other and enlist ourselves in support of the Other's discourse that we can share some of the *jouissance* circulating in the Other".[13] At this point Lacan turns to rights:

> No jouissance is given to me or could be given to me other than that of my own body. That is not clear immediately, but is suspected, and people institute around this jouissance, which is good, which is thus my only asset, the protective fence of a so-called universal law called the rights of man: no one stops me from using my body as I see fit. The result of the limit . . . is that jouissance dries up for everybody.[14]

This passing remark, conveniently forgotten by liberal Lacanians, is extremely perceptive. Rights break up the various parts of the body and separate the subject from others, proclaiming his isolated sovereignty over his body parts and existence. But when relations atrophy and walls are built between self and other, *jouissance* dries up and, in the Lacanian idiom, culture and civilisation, the depository and work-place of sacrificed jouissance, are threatened. Law's ambiguous hostility towards art and literature is well-known.[15] But the excessive juridification of social life does not affect only artistic creativity. In a fully legalised community, the number and scope of rights would

---

[13] Bruce Fink, *The Lacanian Subject* (Princeton, Princeton University Press, 1995) 99.

[14] Lacan quoted in Fink, 101.

[15] Costas Douzinas, "Introduction" and "*Prosopon* and *Antiprosopon:* Prolegomena for a Legal iconology, in C. Douzinas and L. Nead, *Law and the Image* (Chicago, Chicago University Press, 1999) Chapter 1; Costas Douzinas, "Law's Fear of the Image" 19/3 *Art History*, 353-369, 1996. It is arguable, for example, that a strictly defined and applied right to intellectual property, which would turn into theft the incorporation in a work of art of all stylistic influences and innovations introduced by others, would increase the income of some artists but would undermine the creativity of everyone else.

keep increasing but the strictly demarcated pleasure they offer would dramatically decrease. [16]

Lacan and Legendre believe that the task of psychoanalysis is to underpin the law again, to bear witness to the "truth" of the speaking subject and strengthen the position of the father. Unlike their liberal followers, they adopted an authoritarian position and argued that we need a new social contract, which will oppose its fictitious truth to the lie of the imaginary and will "install (or reinstall) a rule of the game in the absence of any rule, at a time when truth, precisely, is no longer 'believable' ".[17] Such a rule in an age that does not believe in truths can only be accepted pragmatically, because it is backed by force, by gun and missile. In this sense, the bombing of Yugoslavia is, indeed, the first real humanitarian war in an age of uncertainty. As we will see in the next part, although the sovereign is not the origin of the law but a function of the law's operation on the psyche, he is indispensable. The legislator is an impostor but, according to the Lacanian story, this makes it even more imperative that his authority be asserted and the false truth of his law proclaimed. For the Lacanian, the legislator, the United States, NATO, the New World Order is the only hope we have and their violence is the necessary response to the catastrophic violence created by the absence of truth and the failure of the subject's quest for wholeness. When psychoanalysis turns from description to prescription its critical uses run out very quickly. But the bleak image it presents is a corrective to the excesses of human rights rhetoric.

II. LAW'S DESIRE: DO WE NEED THE SOVEREIGN?

Psychoanalytical theory is obsessed with the law. Individuals and societies come into existence through prohibitions and commands, through legal operations which create the world in the image of a non-existent but indispensable legislator. The struggle for recognition, the desire of the other is not addressed solely to the other person but also to the symbolic order, to law. Indeed, the other is often seen as the representative of the law and his recognition as the approval or bestowal of identity by the social order. The desire of the

---

[16] We can see this happening in the "rich men's ghettos" that spring in the metropolitan suburbs of the Western world. These security-induced enclosures give postmodern millionaires all the trappings of material wealth and the full protection of public law and privately-operated *cordons sanitaires* but, at the same time, trap them in their voluntary chosen prisons, away from danger and from human interaction and enjoyment.

[17] Lacan, *Écrits*, op.cit., supra n. 10, 130.

subject is the desire of law: the person takes his marching orders from law and, for this operation to succeed, the law must be seen as non-lacking, as a complete whole which knows, and has the answer to all problems of conflict. The desire of the Other as complete and non-lacking is therefore a function of the subject. I need the law to be gapless, to be Dworkin's "seamless web", in order to accept my subjection; I need the other person to be whole in order to accept that my desire and dependence on her are indispensable for achieving recognition and identity.

But the symbolic order and law cannot be complete; Dworkin's hope is the greatest liberal illusion. If we visualise the symbolic as a mathematical set, the law can be closed and the symbolic order complete only if a further master signifier exists outside the set, beyond the Name of the Father. A signifier which, by being outside of the symbolic, can act as the ultimate guarantee of law's completeness and allow the field to close. In psychoanalytical terms, such a transcendent signifier is called the other of the Other, a super or meta-master signifier, not included in the Other of the law and therefore able to make it complete. But the Name of the Father or the phallus are themselves signifiers, they belong to the symbolic field and cannot help it close around them, they are unable to make the law coherent and complete. There is no real Father behind the name, no God behind the word, no other of the Other.

The transcendent signifier or the sublime legislator is therefore both necessary and non-existent, impossible. Its role has been traditionally performed by God, Emperor, Sovereign or the Law, various patriarchal figures which, as Legendre has shown, have unerringly underpinned Western legality. The desire for an author standing behind the inescapable social institutions and bestowing authority on them animates law and legal scholarship. Its signs are everywhere: in the obsession of the common law with its sources; in the interminable and scarcely illuminating American debates about the strict or liberal construction of the Constitution and their pale English reflection in the so-called "literal" rule of interpretation; in the endless process of standard-setting and treaty-making of international institutions; finally, in the Hartian "rule of recognition", the Kelsenian grundnorm and other similar jurisprudential fictions. All these are attempts at what may be called "retrospective legitimacy": while laws and regulations, high norms and petty disciplines proliferate, the need to attribute them back to an authoritative person or text attests to this desire for a Father or law-maker who is outside the operation of law and infuses it with its majesty and justice or, in psychoanalytical terms, with its gapless and closed character.

In international law, the frenetic legislative activity indicates this desire at its strongest. Excessive law-making is a substitute for the obvious lack of a unitary legislator and credible implementation, a rather transparent attempt to claim that an author exists because otherwise so many texts would not have come into existence and so much progeny would have been orphaned. The negotiations to end the war in Yugoslavia were a good example. NATO and its allies imposed their terms upon the defeated Serbs, and later started negotiations with third states, members of the Security Council, to have the terms adopted by the Council. The force of war dictated terms to the defeated; their retrospective attribution to the United Nations, served more to establish the Council's position as the disinterested source of law, than to convince that it had much to do with the cessation of the conflict. We can now understand also why the US claim that they cannot be subjected fully to international law, as Kosovo and the war crimes tribunal episodes have shown, If international law is to be seen as universal and international politics as ethical, one power must be exempted from its operations and, through its forceful intervention and sovereign interpretation of the law, give it its desired seamlessness.

The law needs a law-maker, its inescapable presence creates the desire for a whole and undivided source. The Legislator, the King, the Sovereign, the Constitutional Court, the US or the Security Council are functions for the legal subject, guarantees that his subjection is not arbitrary, unnecessary, undesirable. Pierre Legendre argues that this function is necessary, that we need the montage or image of ineffable power and sovereignty, fake as it is, in order to domesticate the total otherness of death and accept the terrifying fact that there is nothing beyond the power of language and the commands of law. We can see this clearly in contemporary jurisprudence, still obsessed with sovereignty and rights, obligation and prerogative. The British constitutional debates around Europe and federalism or around the Bill of Rights and parliamentary sovereignty are replete with eighteenth century concerns and concepts. To paraphrase Foucault, in constitutional law the head of the king has not been severed yet. To paraphrase Legendre, even if severed, we must keep the head on the king's body and pretend he is still alive, like those experts in the power of symbols, the Soviets, who kept President Brezhnev's body long after his death as if alive, to ensure a smooth transition or to ensure, in psychoanalytical terms, that the master signifier never dies.

But as Lacan insisted time and again, there is no other of the Other, all these law-givers are impostors, there is nothing beyond language, its structures and interdiction and the law as much as the legislator are just a series of signifiers. There is nothing behind signs which can guarantee their completeness and nothing behind the law which can deliver its justice. God and King are not the cause but the effect of law. It is not so much that religion is the opium of the people, as Marx had it, but that religion is the desire of the people. But the paternal function is coming under attack in late modernity and cannot fulfil its role any longer. As the fatherly figures retreat, laughed out of court by women, ethnics, gays, transsexuals and all kind of minorities unwilling to accept the father's deceit, another signifier must occupy the impossible but indispensable position of the guarantor of the completeness of law.

One such is justice, the most discussed topic in Western philosophy, from Plato and the Sophists to Rawls and critical legal theory. In jurisprudential terms, justice is a synonym for the various forms of the Good, the principle or value that gives positive law its moral quality and makes it obligatory *moro conscientiae*. It has been successively defined as virtue (Aristotle), utility (Bentham), the law (Kant). But according to psychoanalysis, the social bond passes through our traumatic relation with the Other and is determined not by principles or simple pleasures and pains, but by our uncanny dependence on *jouissance*. For Lacan, one of Freud's great discoveries was that the Good is not an arrangement of virtues in the right order of reason, the absolute formal law of the Kantians or the two Rawlsian principles lexically ordered. Neither substance nor form, neither logos nor *lex*, individual or universal, the Good is the (M)other, the forbidden object of desire, and no other Good exists. All other goods and resources are distributed, arranged and used according to the demands of this supreme but unattainable Good.

Legal and moral attempts to define the supreme Good or achieve justice fail because the lack, the gap opened in the subject by the primal separation, the "symbolic castration", can never be filled. Freud repeatedly insisted, against the naiveté of jurisprudence, that "law was originally brute violence and that even to-day it cannot survive without the support of violence".[18] Law is inextricably linked with violence in a number of ways. Force stands at the origin of law and violence is law's tool. To restrict violence and destructive drives, the

[18] Sigmund Freud, *Why War*, in *Civilisation, Society and Religion* (James Strachey ed. and trans., Penguin, 1985) 355.

law incorporates both.[19] As an expression of the powerful, law can make no ethical claim other than the totally formal equal subjection of all to the same rule. Finally, in its attempt to limit desire and aggression which are "quite a natural thing, to have a good biological basis and in practice to be scarcely avoidable",[20] the law acts unnaturally and its success is inextricably bound with persistent failure. By exchanging pre-social fragile happiness for a civilised but pleasureless security, law contributes to the process of disenchantment. "The price we pay for our advance of civilisation is a loss of happiness through the heightening of the sense of guilt".[21] Whatever the type of social organisation, psychoanalysis insists that there is a residue, a "nonlinked thing"[22] or faultline in every community and law, beyond their control to which they remain hostage. It is analogous to an "unconscious affect", encountered in the "sharp and vague feeling that the civilians are not civilised and that something is ill-disposed towards civility" which "betrays the recurrence of the shameful sickness within what passes for health and betrays the 'presence' of the unmanageable".[23]

The only way for combating this violence, according to Freud, is to nurture "emotional ties" of love and identification. People should be encouraged to share important values and concerns and thus draw closer through their identification with the shared object, be it a leader, a party or the community of justice. Justice makes people identify with the totality. "I can be happy to be one of We, if We are just, because then We will treat Me as well as reasonably possible; and We will be happy to have Me as one of Us, because We know that I being just, will see things from Our point of view, and will not exclude wider considerations from my assessment of the situation". In the just society there is no "stasis, no dissension . . . no conflict",[24] justice, the other of Law, has finally guaranteed and closed law's empire.

But no such society exists; justice is not fully of this world. In psychoanalytical terms, this means that there is no other of the Other and a proclaimed Justice is, like the Legislator, fraudulent. Postmodern

---

[19] Walter Benjamin, "The Critique of Violence" in *Reflections* (E. Jephcott trans.) (New York, Schocken Books, 1978) 277–300 and Jacques Derrida's long commentary "The Force of Law; The 'Mystical Foundation of Authority' ", 11 *Cardozo Law Review* 919–1046 (1990).

[20] Sigmund Freud, *Why War*, supra n. 18, 360.

[21] Sigmund Freud, *Civilisation and its Discontents*, in *Civilisation, Society and Religion*, supra n. 18, 327.

[22] J.-F. Lyotard, "A l" Insy (Unbeknownst) in Miami Theory Collective ed. *Community at Loose Ends* (Minnesota University Press) 42–8, 46.

[23] ibid., 44, 43.

[24] J. R. Lucas, *On Justice* (Oxford, Clarendon, 1980) 18–9.

society lacks an ultimate ground or unity and, as a result of the centrality of human rights, theories of justice become increasingly extravagant and unrealistic. Their action gradually dissolves any remaining markers of certainty and "inaugurates a history in which people undergo the experience of a final indeterminacy as to the foundation of power, law, and knowledge, and as to the foundation of relations *between self and other*, at every level of social life".[25] The feeling of injustice, on the other hand, is the way through which people construct this sense of lack, incompleteness or disorder, the name given to the symptoms of social exclusion, domination or oppression. In this approach, justice is what society lacks and desires and has no other definition; rather, justice is the definition of the indefinable, the unconscious of the law, a trace that signifies a past trauma or a future union, always deferred and different. Theories of justice are the fantastical screen or frame philosophers, poets and lawyers have erected to shield ourselves and to explain away *jouissance* the unknown desire and fear of the other and of the impossible community. They answer the symptoms by negating their cause, they are failing attempts to forget and exorcise the terrifying trauma at the heart of the social. But the radical dissymmetry, the abyss of the other's desire and of lack perceived as injustice will always leave behind a remainder for which neither the law nor fantasy can fully account. Thus, while a huge amount of intellectual labour has been put into creating theories of justice, such theories are always bound to fail because justice forgets, it must forget injustice. This is the reason why the law always creates its critics and why critique always feeds off the law.

Human rights are the other obvious heir to the Father. The law and polity that proclaims them appears united coherent and civil, just and worthy of obedience. Governments, international and non-governmental organisations agree that human rights are the best, if not the only, way left for promoting the intrinsic value of a legal order. For the Western liberal, principles like nationalism or socialism, which have been used in the wake of religion to knot together various laws and polities, are aggressive, exclusionary and lead inevitably to ethnic cleansing and genocide. Only a law immersed in human rights is a law worthy of its name and, as in Yugoslavia, a law worthy of killing for. Psychoanalysis shows, however, that the promise of human rights to make the law whole or just, like that of religion or nationalism, cannot be delivered. The symbolic order and the law are just that, a series of

---

[25] Claude Lefort, *Democracy and Political Theory* (D. Macey trans.) (Minneapolis, University of Minnesota Press, 1988) 19.

signs open to negotiation and re-interpretation. Like all signs, those of religion or nationality are not intrinsically aggressive, and those of human rights are not inherently benign. This does not mean that a Western human rights state is not treating its citizens better than a fundamentalist theocratic one. It means that this type of comparison, if it can be made at all, is a matter of detailed observation and understanding of the different cultures and traditions and not of an axiomatic apriorism. Secondly, it means that Western human rights states can be as aggressive, murderous and barbaric as any type of regime. Our desire is law's desire: but the more our desire is achieved, the more the law appears closed, coherent and gapless around a grand legislator or principle, the more it becomes aggressive to outsiders and demands our unwavering and unreserved respect. In such a case, a porous nationalism may be more generous than a self-satisfiedly arrogant human rights culture. And in all cases, as Lacan insists "the legislator is an impostor", the law strives to be One, fully rational, a "seamless web", but cannot succeed.

We can provisionally conclude that while psychoanalysis is a powerful hermeneutic tool for understanding the persistence of critique and the emotional life of law, we need to re-interpret Lacan's Other ethically in order to address the inadequacies of the institution and the traumas of the social bond. Freud's story of law starts with violence and Lacan's story of the subject begins in separation and lack instituted by the law. But the persistent sense of injustice, and its attendant and unceasing critique, indicates that there is a thing which predates the law, an eros more primordial than the thanatos the law institutes as the object of desire. Feminist psychoanalysis calls this law before the law the "primal union with the Mother" (Irigaray)[26] or the "archaic mother" or "abject" (Kristeva).[27] In the ethical terms of Levinas, the trauma of the subject is created through its exposure to Otherness, in which the origin of law and language are "constantly submerged by pre-original substance".[28] In a paradoxical sense, psychoanalytical jurisprudence can be criticised for not being sufficiently erotic, for being unable fully to understand the nature of the "emotional ties" it places at the centre of the social and legal bond.

[26] Luce Irigaray, *Speculum for another Woman; An Ethics of Sexual Difference,* (Carolyn Burke and Gillian Gill trans.) (London, Athlone 1993); *I love to you* (Alison Martin trans.) (New York, Routledge 1996).

[27] Julia Kristeva, *The Abject: Powers of Horror* (Leon Roudiez trans.) (Columbia University Press, 1982); Part II, "Women, Psychoanalysis Politics" in *The Kristeva Reader* (Toril Moi ed.) (Oxford, Blackwell 1986) 137–320.

[28] Emmanuel Levinas, *Humanisme de l'Autre Homme* (Montpellier, 1972) 68. See Chapter 13, below.

An ethical and critical foundational myth of law would reinterpret the primal parricide by emphasising its erotic aspect. The brothers felt a sense of guilt before law and morality had arisen, because an ethical turning to the Other comes before the law and becomes its ground.[29] In this interpretation, the murder and the eucharistic meal of the dead symbolises not just the narcissistic Oedipal identification with the Father, but the original incorporation of alterity – as Death or the Other – at the heart of subjectivity. This love for the dead or unknowable Other is what will always infuse the passion for justice - although not its theory – and the vision of utopia – although not its practice. The most important ethical and political lesson of psychoanalysis would therefore be: resist all attempts to close the law in the name of human rights, justice or any other haughty principle; laugh at the imbecility of the petty bureaucrats and servants of power who tell us that they know the right of the law and the truth of justice; confront Emperor, Law or Sovereign, like the tale's child, with the truth about his new and most ancient clothes: they cover him and his symbolic majesty only because of our own imaginary needs and projections, and they can disintegrate, like a spider's web, in the lightest breeze of the real or in a child's cry. Our ethical obligation is to what in self and society is beyond the ego and the social body. This is the utopian heart of human rights.

III. THE IMAGINARY DOMAIN

A central premise of psychoanalytical theory is, as we saw, that the subject comes into existence by entering the symbolic realm and encountering language and law. Slavoj Zizek explains the paradoxical operation of language in the process of subjectification and subjection as follows:

> By means of the word, the subject finally finds himself . . . attains himself, posits himself as such. The price, however, is the irretrievable loss of the subject's self-identity: the verbal sign that stands for the subject – in which the subject posits himself as self-identical – bears the mark of an irreducible dissonance; it never fits the subject. This paradoxical necessity on account of which the act of . . . finding oneself . . . assumes the form of its opposite, of the radical loss of one's self-

---

[29] For an elaboration on these themes see Douzinas and Warrington, "The Force of Justice: A Jurisprudence of Alterity" (1994) 3 *Social and Legal Studies* 405 and *Justice Miscarried* (Edinburgh University Press, 1994) Chapters 2 and 4.

identity displays the structure of what Lacan calls "symbolic castration".[30]

Linguistic signification cuts the body away, symbolic castration replaces it with a name, prohibits the primal union and creates the "speaking subject", a split and lacking self who desires the prohibited Real. We have argued above, that something similar takes place perhaps with the operation of rights. If the encounter with language and the basic interdiction creates the subject, the encounter with positive law, becoming a bearer of rights, creates the legal subject. In this sense, the function of rights in the organisation of the psyche is associated with the effects of the symbolic castration and, more specifically, with what we have called secondary or legal castration. This second or socio-legal birth confirms the recognition rights give (I am a free and morally responsible agent with dignity and self-respect, I am formally equal in relation to basic civil and political entitlements etc.), introduces the person into adulthood and connects him with the representative of social and political power. The name of the father of the Freudian family drama is replaced here by what Legendre calls the Reference: God, King, the Law, the Sovereign, the ultimate source of all right, the locus from which all social power is assumed to proceed.

The symbolic castration and the mirror stage that follows it create a projected sense of bodily integrity, an imaginary completeness which replaces the feeling of fragmentation and lack of limb coordination. Let us turn now to the second or legal castration, the result of the entry into the legal symbolic. Becoming a legal subject denies in a similar fashion, as we saw, the bodily wholeness of the person and replaces it with partial recognitions and incomplete entitlements. Rights by their nature cannot treat the whole person; this is the reason why no right to rights exists. Such a right would be the right of a person to be himself or herself, a unique human being in common with others, a right that would defeat the whole purpose of having rights. In law, a person is never a complete being but a combination of various partial and often conflicting rights, the contingent holder of legal entitlements that punctuate life. The sum total of rights constructs the legal subject as a rather imbalanced vehicle for the differential investments of the law. If we were to imagine the portrait of the legal subject, it would have a passing resemblance with its

---

[30] Slavoj Zizek, *The Indivisible Remainder: An Essay on Schelling and Related Matters* (London, Verso, 1996) 46–7.

human sitter but it would also be strangely alien, as if painted in the style of Cubism: a huge ear, a minuscule mouth, one protruding and aggressive eye, an elephantine nose placed where the mouth should be. It would be a projection of a three-dimensional imago onto a flat and flattening canvas.

But the wholeness of the subject denied by the law and its rights returns in the imaginary projection of an ideal self. How does this projection operate? Drucilla Cornell's "imaginary domain" is useful as the starting point. Cornell argues that conflicts about abortion, pornography or sexual harassment should be understood in relation to the imaginary domain of women, the projected bodily integrity and sexual imago that the operation of the mirror stage installs in each of us early in life.[31] For Cornell, the "imaginary domain recognises that literal space cannot be conflated with psychic space and reveals that our sense of freedom is intimately tied to the renewal of the imagination as we come to terms with who we are and who we wish to be as sexuate beings. Since, psychoanalytically, the imaginary is inseparable from one's sexual imago, it demands that no one be forced to have another's imaginary imposed upon herself or himself in such a way as to rob him or her of respect for his or her sexuate being".[32] Cornell's emphasis on the imaginary nature of bodily integrity, which forms the indispensable basis of identity formation at the mirror stage and continues in adult life, is extremely useful in developing a jurisprudence of sexual respect and integrity. No legal intervention is legitimate, according to Cornell, if it violates the projected and anticipated bodily integrity of the person concerned. But as these projections differ from person to person, a universal position on these issues is impossible and a uniform response to the different and conflicting imaginary projections of women is morally wrong. If the law were to adopt, for example, the same attitude towards pro- and anti-abortion women, or towards an anti-porn feminist and a worker in the porn industry, it would necessarily violate the imaginary domain of at least one of the two parties.

Our project is wider however. If the future anteriority of bodily sexual integrity stems from the constitutive action of symbolic castration, the second or legal castration projects a coherent imaginary social identity, in which body and self are integrated and all aspects (not just sexual integrity) of a flourishing self are recognised by others. The imaginary domain of human rights is that of the complete human,

---

[31] Cornell, op.cit., supra n. 6, Chapter 1.
[32] ibid., 8.

rights are supported by a fantasy of wholeness which re-unites body and person into an integrated self. Behind the dismembered and legalised body parts, stands the image of a complete subject and a sutured body.

This imaginary existential integrity, which supports the sense of identity, is built on the desire of the other and is the opposite of the individualism of phoney "authenticity". It should be immediately added that the anticipated completeness of the imaginary domain, the projected future integrity that underpins present identity is, first, non-existent and impossible and, secondly, differs from person to person and from community to community. But despite the infinite number of ideal egos, the imaginary seems to have certain structural similarities. Whatever type of social recognition we may fantasise about, whatever dream of completeness gives us our sense of identity, they all include a claim to existential integrity: to the ability of self to be what it is, unique unrepeatable and different, an otherness as regards everything that is not itself, an entity unrestrained by necessity, free of determination and able to resist external imposition. The projection of existential integrity expresses the aspiration of being and of being perceived as an other, free from uniformity, common determinations and accepted or acceptable definitions. This imaginary wholeness and existential uniqueness which defines our place in the world exists equally in Western individualistic societies and in traditional communities and carries in it, albeit in different proportions, the hopes of freedom and equality, the central values of human rights. But our imaginary constructs these values as integral aspects of the uniqueness of the person and not as just semiotic outcomes of similarities with some and differences from others. To put it differently, while the postmodern subject has been pronounced split, decentred, lacking and plural, it is still held together through a fantasy of identity and a projection of completeness which creates fragile narratives of biographical coherence out of the many "subject positions" and disconnected fragments of our existence.[33] Our argument is that human rights play a central role in constructing this fantasy.

The imaginary domain of human rights is uncannily close to Ernst Bloch's definition of utopia and of radical natural law, in which the present foreshadows a future not yet and, one should add, not ever possible. The future projection of an order in which man is no longer a "degraded, enslaved, abandoned or, despised being" links the best traditions of the past with a powerful "reminiscence of the future".

---

[33] Ernesto Laclau and Chantal Mouffe, *Hegemony and Socialist Strategy* (London, Verso, 1985) *passim*.

It disturbs the linear concept of time and, like psychoanalysis, it imagines the present in the image of a prefigured beautiful future which, however, will never come to be. The anticipated bodily completeness of Lacan's imaginary draws its inspiration, like Bloch, from the future anteriority of the human identity and the "not yet" of the utopian chora. The imaginary domain is necessarily utopian, non-existing. As with all utopias, when the imaginary becomes real, the effects are catastrophic. And yet, this non-place or nothingness grounds our sense of identity, in the same way that utopia helps create a sense of social identity.

One could argue, therefore, that while human rights replace the body with linguistic and legal signs and split it into many disconnected parts, they also introduce the split subject to a utopian humanity, to an idealised self-image that brings together the various parts into its formal contours. Human rights construct both a dismembered self, dissolved in a plurality of entitlements, and the imago of a whole person which assumes "the recognition of the alterity of the future from which the self has been constituted, and, on which, through a projection, it depends for its survival as a self".[34] The space of the imaginary of rights is precisely between the legal disassembly of self and the fantasy scenario of a complete human, which comes from the future but colours our present self-understanding. For the Lacanians, this imaginary future anterior refers exclusively to the integrity of the sexuate body; from our perspective, it inscribes the utopian but indispensable promise of integrity onto self and the body politic.

But reviving the utopian imaginary and linking it with human rights is a difficult task. Not only have human rights been hijacked by governments and international committees and their early connection with the utopianism of radical natural law has been severed, but utopia also is not doing too well. It would not be inaccurate to say that our epoch has witnessed the demise of utopian hopes and that, additionally, the utopian motif has been suspended even in critical thought. The concept of utopia was dealt the first debilitating blow in the fifties and sixties when the Soviet gulags and mental asylums became widely known. It was deleted from the political dictionary with the collapse of communism. In this anti-utopian climate, Francis Fukuyama earned world-wide fame when he stated that "today, we have trouble imagining a world that is radically better than our own, or a future that is not essentially democratic and capitalist . . . We cannot picture to our-

---

[34] Cornell, supra n. 6, 41.

selves a world that is *essentially* different from the present one, and at the same time better".[35] As the individual and his rights became the universal religion, collective imagination seems to have dried out, the principle of hope either realised in liberal capitalism or extinguished.

Russell Jacoby, in his aptly called *the End of Utopia*, addressed recently the loss of nerve on the Left and concluded that "at best radicals and leftists envision a modified society with bigger pieces of pie for more customers. They turn utilitarian, liberal and celebratory. The left once dismissed the market as exploitative; it now honours the market as rational and humane".[36] The statement charts accurately the way from Clause Four to new Labour. But it also alludes to the wider cultural moment of the *fin-de-siècle*, shared by the Left, in which grand theories and meta-narratives have been discredited and the politics of multiplicity, difference and pluralism have replaced the promise of a perfect future. The demise of communism has created on the Left a grudging respect for liberalism and its failing attempts to create a rational scheme for justly negotiating interactions amongst individuals whose desires and interests are inevitably in conflict.

And yet no century has been more murderous and genocidal than the twentieth, and the "end of history" has not signalled the end of genocide. Jacques Derrida has helpfully catalogued the limitations of the "new world order" and of the

> discourse on human rights that will remain inadequate, sometimes hypocritical, and in any case formalistic and inconsistent with itself as long as the law of the market, the "foreign debt", the inequality of techno-scientific, military and economic development maintain an effective inequality as monstrous as that which prevails today, to a greater extent than ever in the history of humanity. For it must be cried out, at a time when some have the audacity to neo-evangelise in the name of the ideal of liberal democracy that has finally realised itself as the ideal of human history: never have violence, inequality, exclusion, famine, and thus economic oppression affected as many human beings in the history of the earth and of humanity.[37]

As the millennium draws to a close, Fukuyama's complacency makes Jacoby's diagnosis too painful for everyone who wants to deny the infamies of the present in the name of the future.

Does that mean that we are left with no hope, that we are condemned both individually and collectively to tinkering with the

---

[35] Francis Fukuyama, *The End of History and the Last Man* (London, Penguin, 1992) 46.
[36] Russell Jacoby, *The End of Utopia* (New York, Basic Books, 1999) 10.
[37] Jaques Derrida, *Spectres for Marx* (P. Kamuf trans.) (New York, Routledge, 1994) 85.

margins of the social system, private and privatised by the forces of global culture? This was always the advice or threat of the apologists of power and of the pragmatists of the common sense, against whom natural law consistently rebelled. The "end of history" thesis, the celebration of the present for its presence, has accompanied every historical period, more as a warning of imminent change than as celebration of stability, surfacing usually at the point at which history was about to enter a radically new phase. What is interesting about our present prophesies of the "end" is that, unlike previous periods, they are accompanied by the powerful utopian imagination of human rights which, the new order has positivised, tamed and co-opted to a large extent, but which retains a huge creative and explosive potential. While theories of justice are the longest failure of Western thought, symbolic attempts to appease the discontent of civilisation created by the symbolic order, the sense of injustice and the utopian hopes associated with it, have always acted as a social imaginary domain, as if societies have an imagination of wholeness analogous to that of individuals.

We saw how Ernst Bloch blended together utopia and natural law. In a more melancholic mood, Theodor Adorno emphasised the central paradox of all utopian hope. On the one hand, "the only philosophy which can be responsibly practiced in the face of despair is the attempt to contemplate all things as they would present themselves from the point of redemption. Knowledge has no light but that shed on the world by redemption. All else is reconstruction, mere technique". On the other, the utopia is "also an utterly impossible thing, because it presupposes a standpoint removed, even though by a hair's breadth, from the scope of existence . . . the more passionately thought denies its conditionality for the sake of the unconditional, the more unconsciously, and so calamitously, is delivered up to the world".[38] Utopian thought is caught in a double bind: by denying the determined character of thought, "even by a hair's breadth", in order to raise itself above the infamies of the present and open a critical distance, it risks forgetting the determinations of thought or the subjection of the subject thus letting the impositions of power work undetected. We cannot stop criticising the present and we cannot do that without adopting the position of the future; but, similarly, we can never remove ourselves sufficiently from our here and now to adopt the redemptive position. Utopian hope is necessary and impossible; a gen-

[38] Theodor Adorno, *Minima Moralia: Reflections from Damaged Life* (E. Jephcott trans.) (London, Verso, 1991) 247.

eral utopian plan, if imposed on people, risks becoming a blueprint for worse oppression and domination. As Thomas Nagel argued in a more prosaic style, the problem with utopia is that "it presents an ideal of collective life, and it tries to show people one by one that they should want to live under it", that it forces people to be free.[39]

It is here that Bloch's combination of natural law and social utopia can be developed in a postmodern perspective. If a fantasy of integrity, supported by the discourse of human rights, helps construct our radically inter-subjective social identity, this fantasy is inextricably bound with the desire of the other. Existential completeness, the negation of domination and oppression, impossible as it is, helps build our sense of uniqueness which can exist only in relation to unique others. Similarly, if all human activity is relational, our actions address directly or indirectly another before becoming objectified into events, facts or rights. A just relationship does not attack the ontological constitution or undermine the existential integrity of the related entities. The utopia projected by the human rights imaginary would be a social organisation which recognises and protects the existential integrity of people expressed in their imaginary domain. The postmodern utopian hope has ontological importance: it protects the integrity of unique beings in their existential otherness, by promoting the dynamic realisation of freedom with others. While the individual imaginary helps build an other-dependent identity, the social imaginary supports a social organisation in which human relationships will respect and promote the uniqueness of the participants.

In the social imaginary, memories of fear, tales of pain and suffering and the experience of oppression have a key role. During the Yugoslav wars, when people were presented with images which brought to the surface the memories and emotions of the Nazi concentration camps, the reaction was immense horror and willingness to act. Although most people today do not have first hand experience, the Holocaust has formed a central part of our moral imagination, and these communal resources can be mobilised by the utopian hope. The imaginary domain of each society is partly constructed as a reaction to specific injustices and multiple instances of major and petty dominations and oppressions, it draws its force from the *a priori* pain of human life. When the struggle against injustice takes the form of human rights, they become invested with the energy and creativity of this imagination.

[39] Thomas Nagel, *Equality and Partiality* (New York, Oxford University Press, 1991) 23.

The postmodern "best polity" or the human rights utopia – to coin two paradoxical phrases – promises to shelter human relations from reification, from being turned into the non-relation of subjection, dependence and mastery of one over others. Subjection makes a relationship unavoidable and therefore destroys the existential freedom of the participants, of both master and subjected. The utopian hope promotes social relations in which the people experience their lives as if they were free from necessity. But unlike theories of justice, which go for the high ground and from top to bottom reform, utopian thought has always been filled with suppressed popular images and reminiscences, untold dreams and stories, lowly memories and emotional affects projected into an adorable future. In this sense, the utopianism of human rights is the opposite of the classical utopias which hoped to create a "new man" to fit the collective plan. Like classical utopianism, it is the prefiguration of a future in which people are not degraded, despised or oppressed, the anticipation of a completeness in which the desire of the other would be erotic and not just competitive and destructive. And while, like all utopias, its realisation is always deferred, turning human rights from governmental triumphalism and diplomatic somnobulism into utopian hope would be the greatest contribution of our political culture to the new millennium. Human rights can fill the non-place of the postmodern utopia: they generate a powerful political and moral energy, unlike any other ideology; they draw their force from past memories and future hopes; their promise exists hidden beyond conventions, treaties and bills in a variety of inconspicuous cultural forms. Human rights, based as they are on the fragile sense of personal identity and the – impossible – hope of social integrity, link integrally the individual and the communal. Like all utopias, they deny the present in the name of the future, which means that they paradoxically deny the rights of laws and states in the name of the plural humanities yet to come.

But Adorno's warnings are justified. The hope of the future must not conceal the infamies of the present and the distance necessary for critique must not become the gap of detachment. The postmodern principle of hope, as represented by human rights, is perhaps aporetic rather than utopian: caught between the dismembering action of law which splits the body physical and politic (the work of the symbolic), and the redeeming future of existential integrity (the work of the imaginary), human rights are both the malady and its cure, both the poison and its antidote, a veritable Derridean *pharmakon*.[40]

[40] Jacques Derrida, "Plato's Pharmacy" in *Dissemiantions* (B. Johnson trans.) (London, Athlone Press, 1981) 61–171.

13

The Human Rights of the Other

Concern with human rights is not the function of the state. It is a non-state institution inside the State – an appeal to humanity which the State cannot accomplish.

Emmanuel Levinas

As we are coming to the end of our journey through the philosophy of rights, two central arguments have emerged. Rights exist only in relation to other rights, right-claims involve the acknowledgement of others and their rights and of trans-social networks of mutual recognition and arrangement. There can be no free-standing, absolute right, because such right would violate the freedom of everyone except its bearer. There can be no positive right, because rights are always relational and involve their subjects in relations of dependence on others and responsibility to the law. Rights are a formal recognition of the fact that before my (legal) subjectivity always and already has come another. Linked with that is the recognition that human rights have the ability to create new worlds, by continuously pushing and expanding the boundaries of society, identity and law. They keep transferring their claims to new domains, fields of activity and types of (legal) subjectivity, they construct ceaselessly new meanings and values, and they bestow dignity and protection to novel subjects, situations and people. Paradoxically, however, this expansion weakens the social bond. Human rights come to institutional existence in their performative declaration, which declares what it creates and creates the ground upon which it stands. A human rights society turns this experience into a main principle of organisation and legitimation.[1] Human rights are the recognition of the world-making power of groundlessness which turns the experience of ontological freedom into a principle of law and politics.

[1] For the Heideggerian roots of this argument see Jean-Luc Nancy, *The Experience of Freedom* (B. McDonald trans.) (Stanford University Press, 1993).

Human rights do not "belong" only to the citizens of states which explicitly, even if ineffectively, recognise them. After their ideological and rhetorical triumph, postmodern human rights define the fluid relation between power blocs and the contested identities of individuals and groups. In a strange almost metaphysical way, human rights "exist", even when they have not been legislated. When the American civil rights activists asserted the right to equality, when torture victims all over the world claim the right to be free in their integrity, when gays and lesbians in homophobic cultures proclaim the dignity of their identity or, when an abandoned lover demands his "right to love", they are acting strictly within the human rights tradition, even though no such legal rights currently exist or are likely to be accepted. The dissident, the rebel, the melancholic lover, the green or the anti-corporations protester belong to a long and honourable lineage: the eighteenth century revolutionaries, the nineteenth century political reformers and this century's economic, social and cultural protesters, share the common determination to proclaim and thus bring into being new types of entitlement and forms of existence against received wisdom and the law. The absence of legislative approval, often the legislator's opposition to the new claims, is their structural characteristic. In this sense, human rights have a certain independence in relation to the context of their appearance. Legal procedures, political traditions and historical contingencies may be part of their constitution, but human rights retain a critical distance from law and stretch its boundaries and limits. Indeed, their rhetorical nature, proclamatory enunciation and regular defiance of state law are aspects of their ability to transcend and redefine their contextual boundaries. Legal and social contexts are part of the definition of concrete rights; but it is also in the "essence" of right to suspend any reference to the vagaries of time and the exigencies of place.

The approach to the discourse of rights adopted so far has been resolutely anti-metaphysical. We have examined various unsatisfactory definitions of humanity and summarised Heidegger's critique of metaphysical humanism. But the persistence of the gap between humanity and (legal) rights, or between the utopian moment in human rights and law, indicates that their force and rebelliousness may be related to a metaphysical or redemptive urge which lay dormant but has acquired renewed significance in postmodernity. At the end of the most atrocious century, it is too late in history to return to the concepts of human nature and free will of classical liberalism. Marxist critique has showed how the common "human nature" conceals political and social exclusions, and the deconstruction of sub-jectivity has indicated the historical and particular character of this most powerful discourse of the universal. After Hegel, nature must be seen as historical and intersubjective instead of eternal and solitary. In the aftermath of existentialism, human essence cannot be perma-nent and essential but fluid and becoming. After Freud and Lacan, the human subject lacks and desires the Other. In the wake of structural-ism, the subject must be theorised as context dependant, both sub-jected and free.

We mobilised these philosophies of suspicion to deconstruct the uni-versalism of rights and the historicism of cultural relativism. They both share a common characteristic with Western philosophy and ethics: they reduce the distance between self and other and return the differ-ent to the same. As Heidegger argued, philosophy has put the meaning of Being at the centre of its concerns, since classical Greece, and has claimed that the question of Being is governed by the protocols of rea-son. Universal *logos* reflects and reveals the structure of reality since the ontological realm follows the demands of theoretical necessity. The traces of this ontological totalitarianism litter the body of philosophy. In its modern version, individual consciousness has become the starting point of all knowledge and, as a result, what differs from the self-same has been turned into a cognitive question, into the exploration of the conditions under which the other's existence can be known; this way, the other becomes my knowledge of the other.

The Cartesian and Kantian subject constituted the other and the world according to the subject's own schemata and categories with-out which, they claimed, the other cannot be reached. Hegel's strug-gle for recognition assumed that a symmetrical reciprocity exists between the two parties and posited the end of dialectics as the moment when the same becomes the synthesis of the same and the different. But the unique other cannot be sublated; otherness is not just a moment in the dialectic of the same and the different but the moment of its transcendence, what the system cannot sublate. For phenomenology, again, the ego acquires knowledge through the intentionality of consciousness and its adequation with the phenome-nal world. Husserl asserted the primacy of self-perception and claimed that the world discloses itself fully to consciousness. According to Manfred Frank, "the being that stands across me in the circle of reflec-tion is *my* Being" which has been mistaken for Being as such.[2]

---

[2] Manfred Frank, *What is Neostructuralism?* (S. Wilke and R. Gray trans.) (Minneapolis, University of Minnesota Press, Press, 1989) 297.

Heidegger, on the other hand, emphasised the historical and social nature of self. Self is not constituted before its implication with others. "By 'Others', we do not only mean everyone else but me – those over against whom the 'I' stands out . . . but those among whom one is . . . The world is always one I share with others".[3] There is no life which is not life with others. Self does not postulate the other in its own image but, in discovering itself, it simultaneously recognises the other. Heideggerian ontology, however, by privileging the relationship between beings and Being abandons ethics in favour of the primordial *ethos*. For Heidegger, self and the other are equal participants in the "we" through which we share the world. Inevitably, all speculation as to the meaning of Being starts from the examination of my own being and returns to ontology's preoccupation with self. Sartre, on the other hand, accepted that the other is a subject before me but thought that the separation between self and others was so radical as to preclude any possibility of genuine knowledge of the other. The other fixes his gaze on me and turns me into an object before I can establish myself as a gazing, objectifying subject. The shame of being looked at and judged makes me want to objectify the other in turn, and ends by discovering hell in the face of others. The epistemology of modernity has followed suit: the world corresponds with its representations built by the subject and truth is the approximation between private mental images and theories and the world. What all these theories have in common is an exaggerated belief in the idea of the sovereign self, the claim that the otherness of the world and of the other person can be domesticated in the immanence of self to itself.

When ontological philosophy turns to ethics, it must supplement Being with the postulate of a free will, a faculty absent from the empire of pure reason. In this way, the universal *logos* which provides the criteria establishing moral validity becomes both necessary and morally obligatory. In Kantian moral philosophy, the subject legislates the law he obeys, but, to do that, he must postulate a universal community of beings who are similar if not identical in reason and inclination with the ego. The move from ontology to ethics and the passage from theoretical necessity to the realm of praxis passes through the freedom of the universal rationality of form. To obey the *logos* is therefore to be autonomous.[4] Reason reveals the structure of

---

[3] Martin Heidegger, *Being and Time* (J. Macquarrie and E. Robinson trans.) (New York, Harper & Row, 1962) 144–5.

[4] Simon Critchley, *The Ethics of Deconstruction. Derrida and Levinas* (Oxford, Blackwell, 1992).

reality and subsumes individual cases and moral dilemmas to the imperative of universality which necessarily reduces the singularity of the individual person. But the starting and concluding point of this universal moral law is the ego, the knowing and willing subject, who finds within himself all the resources necessary in order to turn the formal injunction to universalise into a concrete moral norm. In reducing the other to the same "man shuts himself up like a monad".[5]

In the universal community of reason, which acts as the horizon for the realisation of the law, the other, the alien, the third and unrepresentable is turned into the same, the critical distance between self and other is reduced and the experience of value of moral conscience is grounded solely on the representation of the other by the knowing and willing ego. The alternative is the other's exclusion, banning or forgetting. But the other who approaches me is singular and unique; she cannot be reduced to being solely an instance of the universal concept of the ego, nor can she be subsumed as a case or example under a general rule or norm. The law of modernity based on self's right and the subject's empire is strangely immoral as it tries to assimilate and exclude the other. The other side of the universal legal subject, of equality and autonomy, of law's formalism and its imperative (the categorical command) is the necessary inequality and the lack of autonomy of the alien and the enemy of nation. The discourse of universality is necessarily a white mythology: the enthronement of free will as the principle of universal legislation is achieved only through the exclusion, disfranchisement and subjection without free subjectivity of the other. Communitarianism and cultural relativism, on the other hand, can often become "mythologies of colour": local and usually much more aggressive reflections of the exclusions of universalism. The essentialism of individualism, universal rights and the power of "reason" are not far removed from the essentialism of community, the localism of duties and the power of tradition and the past.

And yet it is arguable that an ethical residue can be detected in the long history of natural law and can still be traced in popular attitudes to human rights. The continuous flight of meaning which creates ever-new rights could perhaps be anchored on an ethics, the groundlessness and world-making power of freedom on a moral foundation. If my right has meaning only in relation to another, whose action or entitlement are presupposed in the recognition or exercise of my

---

[5] Emmanuel Levinas, *Collected Philosophical Papers* (A. Lingis trans.) (The Hague, Nijhoff, 1987) 144.

right, the right of the other always and already precedes mine. The (right of the) other comes first; before my right and before my identity as organised by rights, comes my obligation, my radical turn towards the demand to respect the existential integrity of the other. The non-essential essence of human rights, the fleeting universal involved in all particular right-claims could be the recognition of the priority of the other person whose existence before mine makes me ethically bound and opens to me the domain of language, intersubjectivity and right. This other cannot be the universal "man" of liberalism nor the abstract and formalistic "subject" of law. The other is always a unique, singular person who has place and time, gender and history, needs and desires. If there is something truly "universal" in the discourse of human rights, if a metaphysical trait survives their deconstruction, this could perhaps be the recognition of the absolute uniqueness of the other person and of my moral duty to save and protect her.[6]

I. THE ETHICS OF ALTERITY AND HUMAN RIGHTS

This non-essential essentialism is associated with the phenomenology of Emmanuel Levinas, which has challenged the ontological, epistemological and moral assumptions of philosophical modernity.[7] The "ethics of alterity" starts with the other and challenges the various ways in which the other has been reduced to the same. For Levinas, the other is not the self's extension or *alter ego*. Nor is the other the negation of self in a dialectical relation which can be totalised in a future synthesis. Heidegger correctly emphasised the historical and social nature of self; but the other is not similar to self. Self and other are not equal partners in a Heideggerian "we" in which we share our world, nor is the other the threatening externality and radical absence of Sartrean existentialism which turns self into an object.

---

[6] This argument is pursued further both in its critical and constructive aspects in Douzinas and Warrington *Justice Miscarried* (Edinburgh University Press, 1994) *passim*.

[7] Emmanuel Levinas, *Totality and Infinity* (A. Lingis trans.) (Pittsburgh, Duquesne University Press, 1969); *Otherwise than Being or Beyond Essence* (A. Lingis trans.) (Kluwer, 1991). For uses of the ethics of alterity in law, see Douzinas and Warrington, "A Well-Founded Fear of Justice: Ethics and Justice in Postmodernity", Vol. II/2 *Law and Critique*, 115–47 (1991); "The Face of Justice: A Jurisprudence of Alterity", 3 *Social and Legal Studies*, 405–25 (1994); *Justice Miscarried* (Edinburgh University Press, 1994); Marinos Diamantides, "Ethics in Law: Death Marks on a 'Still Life' ", VI/2 *Law and Critique*, 209–28 (1995).

The other comes first. (S)he is the condition of existence of language, of self and of the law. The other always surprises me, opens a breach in my wall, befalls the ego. The other precedes me and calls upon me: where do you stand? Where are you now and not who you are. All "who" questions have ended in the foundational moves of (de)ontology. Being, or the I of the Cartesian *cognito* and the Kantian transcendental subject start with self and create the other as an *imitatio ego*. In the philosophy of alterity, however, the other can never be reduced to the self or the different to the same. Nor is the other an instance of otherness or of some general category, an object to a subject that can become a move in dialectics.

The sign of another is the face. The face is unique. It is neither the sum total of facial characteristics, an empirical entity, nor the representation of something hidden, soul, self or subjectivity. The face does not represent an absent presence, and cannot therefore become a cognitive datum. Nor is the face the epiphany of a visage, or the image of a substance. The face eludes every category. It brings together speech and glance, saying and seeing, in a unity that escapes the conflict of senses and the arrangement of the organs. Thought lives in speech, speech is (in) the face, saying is always addressed to a face. The other is her face. "Absolutely present, in his face, the Other – without any metaphor – faces me".[8] In its uniqueness, the face gets hold of me with an ethical grip "myself beholden to, obligated to, in debt to, the other person, prior to any contracts or agreements about who owes what to whom". In modernity, to comprehend is to make something my own. But the face of the Other cannot be domesticated or consumed. Alterity remains outside, quasi-transcendental, unique, frail like the face of a child that demands that I accept my responsibility. The face is a fundamental ontological fact which however cannot be systematised; in its orientation towards me the face turns into an ethical fact by addressing me. In the face-to-face, I am fully, immediately and irrevocably responsible for the other who faces me. A face in suffering issues a command, a decree of specific performance: "Do not kill me", "Welcome me", "Give me Sanctuary", "Feed me". The only possible answer to the ethical imperative is "an immediate respect for the other himself . . . because it does not pass through the neutral element of the universal, and through respect, in the Kantian sense for the law".[9]

---

[8] Levinas quoted in Jacques Derrida, "Violence and Metaphysics" in *Writing and Difference* (A. Bass trans.) (London, Routledge, 1978) 100.

[9] Derrida, ibid., 96.

The demand of the other and my obligation to respond are the "essence" of the ethics of alterity. But this "essence" is based on the non-essence of the other who cannot be turned into the instance of a concept, the application of a law or the particularisation of the universal ego. "The other arises in my field of perception with the trappings of absolute poverty, without attributes, the other has no place, no time, no essence, the other is nothing but his or her request and my obligation".[10] As the face of the other turns on me, she becomes my neighbour, but not that of the neighbour principle of negligence law. My neighbour and proximate is, at the same time, the most strange and foreign. It is this situated encounter and unrepeateble, unique demand which assigns me to morality and makes me a bound and ethical subject. Our relationship is necessarily non-symmetrical and non-reciprocal as her unique demand is addressed to me and me alone. Equity is not equality but absolute dissymmetry.

The other is incomparably unique; she is external to categories, norms, principles and rules, in her face humanity is annulled to leave her the only one of her kind, bearer of all the dignity in the world, the most equal amongst equals. "It marks the absolute identity of a person, a uniqueness beyond the individuality of multiple individuals".[11] But at the same time, the total uniqueness of the other creates my own identity, as the addressee, respondent and hostage to the demand. If my identity is intersubjective, it is not as the outcome of a struggle for recognition; if I am subjected to the Other, it is not done initially through laws and structures. I am unique because I am the only one asked by the singular other to offer my response and responsibility here and now to his demand. The appeal of the other is direct, concrete and personal; it is addressed to me and I am the only one who can answer it. Against moral philosophy, the demand does not depend on absolute reason or universal law, but on the concrete historical and empirical encounter with the other. On this bedrock of total uniqueness which has nothing to do with the selfishness of individualism or the safety and certainty of community, both abstract universalism and particular relativism find their inescapable limit.

The ontology of alterity is therefore based on the absolute proximity of the most alien. When self comes to constitute itself, it faces

[10] Jean-François Lyotard, *The Differend* (G. Van Den Abbeele trans.) (Manchester, Manchester University Press, 1988) 111.

[11] E. Levinas, "The Rights of Man and the Rights of the Other" in *Outside the Subject* (M. Smith trans.) (London, Athlone Press, 1993) 116–25.

before the I, I's relationship with the other; the structure of subjectivity is the outcome of this opening, an opening which is also fully historical. Each time I turn to the concrete other, my self takes a new direction, I become who I am. My *principium individuationis* is my unavoidable call to responsibility. My uniqueness is the result of the direct and personal appeal the other makes on me and of my subjection not to the law but to the other. It is me that the other addresses and not a universal ego or a legalistic personhood, as Antigone discovered.[12] This radical passivity precedes my ontological freedom and makes it ethical, the acceptance of a vocation to which I alone can respond when called. To be free is to do what none else can do in my place.

In the ontology of alterity the ego is elected; I am always persecuted by the refugee and seek asylum from the exile, but (s)he always comes back, always before me, a step behind or a step in front, the not yet which is the always has been. Closer than the air I breathe and further away than the starry sky, the other calls on me but the encounter can never be fully consummated. Against the concepts and strategies of traditional philosophy, the other is both the ground who, by calling me to my unique responsibility assigns me my singular subjectivity, but also the conceptuality that escapes all systematicity. In this sense, the other has always and already been within self, (s)he dispossesses and decentres self. The face is a trace of otherness inscribed on the "ground" of self. And if such is the case, all return to self from otherness is exposed to this exteriority which leaves its trace but can never be fully internalised. Self is always followed by the other's demand, never able to return home fully, always an internal exile.

The ethics of alterity is as powerful a metaphysics as any humanism. But this is a humanism of the other person; unlike the ontological emphasis of liberalism and the abstract nature of the (legal) subject, it carries the strongest historical commitment to the unique needs of the concrete other. If one wants to maintain the world-shaping urge that animates the metaphysics of subjectivity, if one wants to find an – admittedly contested – basis for the absolute, non-historical character claimed for human rights, one must turn to the other-dependent kernel of individuality. The most irreducible element in subjectivity is the non-coincidence of self, its constitutive openness to exteriority, Rimbaud's *Je es un autre*. "The main task", writes Levinas, "consists in thinking of the Other-in-the-Same

---

[12] Costas Douzinas, " 'Law' birth and Antigone's Death: On Ontological and Psychoanalytical Ethics", 16 *Cardozo Law Review*, 1325–1362 (1995).

without thinking of the Other as another Same".[13] All humanity and every right proceed from this primacy of ethics over being and of obligation over need or interest. Such obligatory turning away from self is the sign of an incarnate transcendence, of a fundamental cut the other imposes on me or, if you will, of the fundamental duty upon which all other rights and duties depend. But this duty is also the manifestation of freedom; in putting myself in the service of the other's right, a duty that cannot be transferred or delegated, I become a unique, concrete unsubstitutable being. At that moment, humanity is eclipsed by the face of the other who becomes its unique representative. Human rights are therefore concretisations of the right of the other person and of my duty, my freedom, before becoming antagonistic to that of others, is the freedom of responsibility and fraternity. One could argue that the naturalist claim that right exists *a priori,* independently of any legislative conferral or state authorisation, is perhaps an oblique recognition of this priority of the other and of the consequent uniqueness of the called upon self; an ethical uniqueness which does not depend on semiotic similarities and differences.

But while the fundamental duty of self and right of the other are the outcome of this original responsibility, a "third" soon enters the scene. In the social world, my neighbour is faced by his own neighbour who is also close to me; the other becomes "they", and a limit to responsibility must be introduced to take account of the conflicting demands. The social world is that of egotism, citizenship, political and legal order and human rights. "In the ethical position 'I' is distinct from the citizen and from that individual who, in his natural selfishness precedes all order, yet from whom political philosophy, from Hobbes on, tries to derive – or derived – the social and political order of the City".[14] The conflicting demands upon me by the other and the third require comparison, calculation and balancing, the procedures of reasoning, justification and the law. The unique other is turned into a citizen, she is put on the scales of justice, her demands are synchronised and thematised under the categories of law and compared with those of others. Every balancing, by reducing uniqueness, is an act of injustice, every comparison of the incalculable is violent. Injustice is never removed from the operation of state law and from the legal implementation of human rights. "Justice" says Levinas

[13] Quoted in Alain Renaut, *The Era of the Individual* (M.B. DeBevoise trans.) (Princeton, Princeton University Press, 1997) 147.

[14] Emmanuel Levinas, *La Souffrance inutile,* quoted in Zygmunt Bauman, *Postmodernity and its Discontents* (Cambridge, Polity, 1997) 48.

"means constant revision of justice, expectation of a better justice" and the same can be applied to human rights.[15] The paradox of human rights appears in a new formulation: human rights are both the creation of this first fundamental ethical duty and a distortion of the moral imperative, an acknowledgement of the uniqueness of the other which gives way however to the need of accommodating the many.

In this ethical sense, rights can be seen as universal companions of human nature both in democratic and in totalitarian regimes, both in sleepy first world states and in revolutionary or reactionary second and third world ones. Social contracts, universal and local declarations, legislation and case-law, commissions and courts are just expressions of their historical character. Their force does not depend on their legislation and is not weakened by historical deviation or geographical contingencies. Right refers to what is proper to human beings on account not of their abstract humanity but of a concrete dignity, opened through ethical submission. Rights, the most timely of human inventions, paradoxically partake also of a strange timelessness and placelessness, both in and of history and outside or standing in judgment of history.

Morality is not synonymous therefore with human rights and does not derive from them. Ethical responsibility precedes rights, gives them their force and legitimacy and becomes the judge of their and of state action. Human rights are the instrument of ethics. According to this phenomenology, a human rights state has been subjected to ethical considerations and has accepted limits and restrictions to its political action out of ethical care. While this is not sufficient for constructing a general ethical theory of rights, it helps explain in part the recent ethical concern for the distant other, shown in popular campaigns and political pressure to prevent and stop the human rights violations of people far away. But the ethical stance of Western public opinion, which responded with outrage to the plight of the Kosovo Albanians or the East Timorese, must be distinguished from that of governments. The arguments canvassed above against the proclaimed morality of governmental foreign and military policy scarcely apply to ordinary people. Their reaction indicated that the suffering of unknown victims has started mobilising the sense of moral proximity which has underpinned recent human rights awareness.

One way of conceptualising this awareness is to say that in caring for the starving, the ethnically cleansed, the refugee or the tortured,

---

[15] Quoted in Bauman, supra n. 14, 50.

who are not my other in a face-to- face encounter, but whose plight enters my consciousness, we concretise (and to a certain extent dilute) the ethical responsibility for the unique other into a wider moral feeling of duty to alleviate the pain of many suffering others. The fundamental moral responsibility remains the ground or horizon of human rights and is translated in politics and law, from an infinite responsibility for my neighbour into a finite obligation to save many others whom I have never faced. The scope of this duty has become much wider than my responsibility to my neighbour but its content and demands have narrowed. In this sense, human rights become the postmodern version of the idea of justice or rather the expression of the sense of injustice. If right derives its force from ethics, postmodern human rights are linked with an individual and collective sense of vulnerability – my being hostage to the other, my openness and subjection to the social and natural environment with its fears and dangers, my sense of interdependence in the world – for which I have the duty, the moral and even legal obligation to respond. Solidarity, according to Bauman, involves "the recognition of other people's misery and suffering as one's own responsibility, and the alleviation and eventually the removal of misery as one's own task".[16] In this approach, human rights are not based on the *a priori* free will of the subject, but on her *a priori* pain and suffering which marks subjectivity not as fearful and antagonistic but as ethical.

A paradoxical link exists therefore between freedom and ethics. Kant's ethical universalism was the first to propose the paradox of ethical obligation realised as the performance of freedom. But the co-ordination of free wills and subjects in the Kantian "kingdom of ends", of which the law of human rights is a secular approximation, often suppresses the ethical duty to the other. The human rights mentality assumes a community of antagonistic subjects; rights are necessary in order to organise a conflictual economy of need and desire, they make personality dependent on the absence of the other. In this sense, the expanding right-claims express the human ability to transcend the contextual – natural or social – limits placed upon the exercise of interests and rights and, secondly, the capacity of *logos,* as language, reason and law, to transfer meaning and value from known to new instances and to re-define its concepts and boundaries. But at the same time, right expresses and presupposes a community of duties to others in their absolute singularity. Embedded within the commu-

---

[16] Quoted in Bauman, supra n. 14, 63.

nity of external relations between egos, of limits and boundaries, prohibitions and restrictions placed around antagonistic subjects exists another community: a community of love and proximity, where I am turned towards the other, I am for the other, and my own self, uniqueness and freedom are the result of my answering the demand of the other that is only addressed to me. The community of human rights is also a community of hostages to the other:

> There is a goodness in peace, which is also the exercise of freedom, and in which the *self* frees itself from its "return to self," from its auto-affirmation, from its egotism . . . *to answer for the other*, precisely to defend the rights of the other man . . . My freedom and my rights, before manifesting themselves in my opposition to the freedom and rights of the other person, will manifest themselves in the form of responsibility, in human fraternity.[17]

This "goodness", unlike the *agathon* of the classical tradition, does not depend on and indeed rejects all ideas of a shared horizon of *teloi* and virtues. Unlike the modern tradition, it does not just follow the law and it does not turn the other into an instance of generalised human nature or personhood. It is a "goodness" that does not exclude any other and does not try to impose the preferences of self upon the stranger. This radical sensitivity and responsibility is the postmodern moral substance. A non-essential substance, always on the move, as it follows the shifting boundaries of the social and answers the singular demands of the suffering other.

After the death of God, transcendence must be situated in history but must avoid the pitfalls of historicism. International law and jurisprudential theories of human rights cannot avoid the problem, as they vacillate between ahistorical universalism and historicist localism. The experience of otherness can perhaps provide this historically grounded transcendence. We discussed in the previous Chapter the utopian element that human rights inject in individual fantasies and the social imaginary. We can now take the same idea further in a different direction.[18] The (rights of the) other are already constitutive of the I, exteriority lurks in the intimacy of self. The other who defines me gives me also paradoxically a "gleam of exteriority or of transcendence". "A dimension of openness to an otherness – in effect, a dimension of transcendence – must be recognised as constitutive of

---

[17] Levinas, "The Rights of Man", op.cit., supra n. 11, 124–5.

[18] The possible links between the radical conceptions of the other in Lacan and Levinas have been recently noted in Sarah Hansym (ed.), *Levinas and Lacan: The Missed Encounter* (Albany, State University of New York Press, 1998).

the subject, [and] the self-sufficiency or independence of the subject/monad turns out to be an illusion (or, more precisely turns out to be the prototype of the metaphysical illusion concerning the Self)".[19] Radical otherness lies beyond totality and conditions it, it takes totality to the point where is breaks up. The other and the other's trace in self is an immanent principle of redemption, an empirical and historical transcendence which marks law and self. Rights, by reducing the uniqueness of the other and turning her into the case of a rule or the instance of a category, are unjust. But as the finite presentation of the infinite and as distorted applications of the fundamental right, they can become perhaps the basis of another judgment which criticises or replaces the judgments of law and history, when they forget otherness for the norm or destroy singularity under the dictates of the universal reason. This would be a utopian judgement carried out in the name of redemption which, despite the efforts of governments, lawyers and philosophers, still operates in the realm of fantasy and still comes from the place of the other.

Human rights are therefore a paradoxical double discourse which recognises two types of intersubjectivity and community. They allow the experience of freedom and the openness of language to become a political strategy and operate on the social. But at the same time, they institutionalise the ethics of alterity and the duty to respect the singular and unique existence of the other. The experience of groundlessness and freedom makes it impossible to define, describe or delimit a human rights society. Such a society always looks to re-definitions and re-conceptualisations, to new possibilities and subjectivities. The time of such societies is the future because their principle is always-still to be declared and met. But a society of human rights operates also a – non-essential – theory of the good, and becomes a community of obligation to the singular, unique other and her concrete needs.

II. HUMAN RIGHTS, THE REFUGEE AND THE OTHER

It seems that a man who is nothing but a man has lost the very qualities which make it possible for others to treat him as a fellow man.

Hannah Arendt

---

[19] Renaut, op.cit., supra n. 13, 141.

We argued in Chapter 11, that for psychoanalysis the self is split, that the subject comes to existence by being separated from the mother and by being introduced to lack, to an otherness which marks a deep trauma but also founds subjectivity and desire. This constitutive and catastrophic trauma is rejected and prohibited but it does not go away, it lurks in us unbeknown and returns in violent and repetitive symptoms, the cause of which is forgotten because they never entered consciousness. Freud calls the dread created by this return uncanny. This abject uncanny has been compared to a stranger, who being already inside the psyche, threatens their boundaries. Faced with this inscrutable fear and desire, the subject erects symbolic and imaginary scenaria of wholeness. Something analogous happens with the nation-state and its law. The original separation and exclusion of other people and nations we examined in Chapter 5 introduces a lack at the heart of the polity, which cannot be fully represented or managed and always comes back, in xenophobia and racism, in hatred and discrimination and remains intractable to politics, which keep inventing myths and celebrating a fictitious unity. Whatever the type of social organisation, there is always a residue, a faultline, analogous to the individual unconscious trauma and the recurring symptoms, beyond the control of community and law to which however they remain hostage.

Aliens are the other of subjectivity, the symptom of the subject and the refuge of the state, what the state needs in order to declare its sovereignty and dignity. This analysis applies to all aliens. What makes it specific to refugees is that their arrival at the borders is experienced as the symptom of the trauma, as the return of the repressed, the sign of the lack in the heart of the citizen. The exclusion of foreigners is, by analogy, as much constitutive of national identity as it is of human subjectivity. In asking to be recognised, refugees bring back the exclusion and repression at law's foundation, and demand of us to accept the difficulty we have to live with the other in us, to live as an other. The law treats the refugee as a returning symptom and uses a number of strategies of disavowal and denial in an attempt to shelter subject and community from the recognition of its constitutive trauma.

Similar conclusions can be derived from the ethics of alterity. When the other, every other, comes to me, he appears as a foreigner, indeed as a refugee who "is not autochthonous, is uprooted, without country, not an inhabitant, exposed to the world and the heat of seasons".[20] But the metaphor of a homeless refugee captures also the

[20] Emmanuel Levinas, *Otherwise than Being or Beyond Essence* (A. Lingis trans.) (Kluwer, 1991) 81.

way in which the other places an absolute obligation to self, a demand which persecutes the ego and threatens homely existence. We cannot escape the other and rid ourselves from the stranger. The refugee is the representative of total otherness and the symbol of our own exile, the sign that ego cannot find peace and security in a secluded and protected existence. In this sense, there is no greater reminder of the demands of ethics than the request of asylum by the persecuted, and no stronger empirical incarnation of the other than the actual refugee. This is the reason why the refugee is seen as such a threat. Her arrival reminds us that we too, in our safe houses, are never at home, that the self is never identical with itself but contains the trace of otherness and that our complacent enjoyment of rights is predicated on the exclusion of others.

The foreigner is the political pre-condition of the nation-state and the other the ethical pre-condition of identity. The refugee is the absolute other. She represents in an extreme way the trauma that marks the genesis of state and self and puts to the test the claims of universalisation of human rights. There is a great paradox therefore in asking the law to protect the refugee. The law divides inside from outside and is then asked to heal the scar or bandage it by offering limited protection to its own creations. The strategies of rejection adopted by the receiving community offer a vivid case-study into the consequences of identifying someone as the terrifying absolute, total Other, the symbol of contamination that otherness may bring upon community and identity. English law and courts when confronted with the threatening and moving foreigner have used three strategies of denial and displacement: First, the denial of the trauma by making the symptom – the refugee – an object of cognition or interpretation. Secondly, the denial of the trauma through the effacement of the face of the other and, finally, the assertion of the wholeness and unity of the nation and its law or the denial of symbolic castration. In developing these defensive mechanisms, the law is not necessarily in violation of human rights; indeed, courts have insisted that they scrupulously honour the obligations of the state, as expressed in international treaties and domestic undertakings. At this point, the problem with historicism becomes apparent and it is here that the utopian tribunal that hails from the place of the other puts the law to judgment.

First, reification. The case of *R. v. The Secretary of State for the Home Department, ex parte Sivakumaran*,[21] involved a number of Tamil asy-

---

[21] [1988] 1 All ER 193, HL.

lum seekers fleeing an offensive by the Sinhalese Government and the Indian Army against the Tamil areas of Sri Lanka. Their applications had been denied by the Home Office, and the House of Lords was asked to determine the circumstances when a "well-founded fear of persecution for reasons of race, religion, nationality, membership of a particular social group or political opinion" exists, the necessary precondition under international and British law for establishing an asylum claim. The Court of Appeal had held that the test for finding a "well-founded fear" should be largely subjective. It would be satisfied by showing that the refugee had (a) actual fear and (b) good reason for this fear. Unless an applicant's fear could be dismissed as "paranoid", "fear is clearly an entirely subjective state and should be judged accordingly".[22] The House of Lords reversed. According to the Lords, a genuine fear of persecution could not suffice. The fears should have an "objective basis" which could be "objectively determined".[23] Justified fear should be based on "true", "objective facts" which, as such, could be ascertained by an objective observer like the Home Secretary or the immigration officers. The authorities were entitled to decide not only "on the basis of the facts known to the applicant, or believed by him to be true" but also on "unknown facts" which would help assess whether "subjective fear was objectively justified".[24] The Home Secretary had taken into account various reports from relevant sources (the refugee unit of the Home Office, press articles, information supplied by the Foreign Office) and had concluded that while army activities "amounted to civil war" and "occurred principally in areas inhabited by Tamils", they did not "constitute evidence of persecution of Tamils as such . . . nor any group of Tamils".[25] He was therefore justified in dismissing the fear of persecution and rejecting the asylum application, because on the basis of the "objective" facts known to him, the applicant had been or was likely to be subjected to persecution.

In this encounter with the refugee, the role of the judge or the administrator has gradually changed. He starts as the recipient of the refugee's request but, in stating the facts, he now claims to be on the same plane as the refugee, able to understand his predicament. In other words, the past pain of the refugee and his fear of future torture have been translated into an interpretable, understandable

22 ibid., 195.
23 ibid., 196.
24 ibid., 202.
25 ibid., 199.

reality that, like all reality, is potentially shareable by judge and victim. But if interpretation is the possibility of constructing interpersonal realities in language, pain, death and their fear bring interpretations to an end. In the idiom of cognition, fear is either reasonable and can be understood by the judge but cannot lead to the granting of asylum, or is irrational and therefore non-existent as non-reason is the very thing the law does not recognise. In the first instance, it is the excess of knowledge and reason on the part of the judge that disqualifies the fear, in the second, it is the excess of fear that disqualifies itself. But this translation of fear into knowledge assumes that the judge can occupy the place of the refugee and share the pain. Fear, pain and death however are radically singular and timely; they resist and at the limit destroy language and its ability to construct shared worlds. The refugee suffers fear and violence, first, in the hands of the torturer and, secondly, in the administrative/judicial claim that his intimate fear can be translated into shareable knowledge. For the law, this translation of the unique feelings into knowable realities is necessary. It restores its ability to pass sentence, an ability temporarily disturbed by the encounter with reason's other (feeling, pain, death) and cognition's other (the refugee). But at the same time this translation objectifies the other. It negates the temporal and situated character of fear and turns its timeliness into another, allochronic time, a time disqualified when compared with the temporal stasis of truth and the timelessness of the law.

A second instance of reification is apparent in the amendments to Social Security regulations introduced into law in 1996. Under the new regulations, income support, housing benefit and miscellaneous other benefits were withdrawn retrospectively from those applying for asylum after entering Britain, those who become trapped in this country as a result of a change of conditions in their home country, and those appealing against refusal of their asylum application. According to refugee organisations, these categories cover the great majority of all asylum seekers in this country.[26] The Court of Appeal

---

[26] The justification given at the time, by Peter Lilley, the Social Security Secretary, for these changes was quite characteristic. The "after entry" exception is justified because such applications have "less merit" that those submitted at a port of entry. But in the period between 1992–5, 3445 "after entry" applicants were allowed to stay and only 1385 port applicants. Those trapped because of a "change of circumstances" would be exempted from benefit withdrawal, if the Secretary of State declares that their country has undergone a "fundamental change" but not as a result of a change in their individual circumstances. Finally, benefits were withdrawn from appellants against rejection, because only a small percentage of rejections are overturned on appeal. This may say something about the effectiveness of

found these regulations "less generous towards foreigners than at Napoleonic times". The policy contemplated for these refugees, "a life so destitute that no civilised country can tolerate it". The regulations were overturned on the procedural grounds that they would have annulled the intention of Parliament to give rejected applicants a right of appeal. Appellants would be faced with the "intolerable dilemma" of either abandoning their appeal or having to starve while awaiting its determination. Specific rights created by statute could be withdrawn constitutionally, and income support for refugees could be removed, only by means of primary legislation rather than ministerial diktat passed under a different statute.[27] But this procedural victory was short-lived. The sovereign Parliament immediately rushed through legislation, described as "the most draconian piece of legislation this century", overturned judicial generosity and retrospectively withdrew benefits from some 10,000 applicants who had benefited from the earlier judgement. In a related case, the High Court ruled that local authorities were under a duty to grant emergency aid to "after entry" asylum seekers under the National Assistance Act 1948. "I find it impossible", argued the judge, "that Parliament intended that an asylum seeker lawfully here should be left destitute, starving or at risk of grave illness and even death because he could find none to provide him with the bare necessities of life".[28]

These cases exemplify the two most common ways of objectifying the other. The refugee is turned either into a fully transparent object of knowledge or into a quasi-human entity deprived of the minimum requirements for survival, and abandoned to the discretions of public benevolence or private charity. In the first instance, when the law is confronted with a traumatised and trauma producing other, it adopts a cognitive attitude and tries to make her fully transparent, to deny her trauma and translate her into the idiom of an objective and manageable truth, an instance of political mastery through the will to knowledge. For the knowing subject, knowledge and its objects stand in perfect harmony. But the other, the concrete person, cannot be subsumed to universal essences nor can she solely be turned into

the measures put into place to discourage applicants from appealing and reduce the number of successful applications, but it does nothing for those exercising their lawful entitlement to appeal and having to live an average of ten months – the time between rejection of application and determination of appeal – without any money at all.

[27] *R. v. Secretary of State for Social Security ex parte J.C.W.I* [1997] 1 WLR 275.

[28] *R. v. Hammersmith and Fulham LBC ex parte M. and R.*; *R. v. Westminster City Council ex parte A.*, *The Times*, February 19, 1997; (1997) 9 Admin LR 504.

the instance of a norm. The other, in the uniqueness of her dignity and vulnerability, remains exterior to concept and essence. As Levinas puts it, knowledge as complete comprehension is "a way of approaching the known being such that its alterity with regard to the knowing being vanishes".[29] He adds that this is the foundation of domination. "The surrender of exterior things . . . does not mean in all innocence their comprehension, but also their being taken in hand, their domestication, their possession".[30] But this domestication has catastrophic results for the knowing subject too. By refuting the exteriority of the absolute other, the subject blocks the openness of his own desire towards the other and the forward looking character of his identity. He thus returns to the misery of fearful existence and misses the world making and self shaping promise of human rights.

In the second instance, refugees are not treated as subjects but as the subject's contrary or opposite, either as non-subjects or as objects. If they are objects, they are not human beings therefore they are not entitled even to the minimum requirements of life, such as food, shelter, clothes, a refuge. If they are non-subjects, they have no rights or entitlements; the law owes them nothing, their survival is at the discretion of state benevolence or private philanthropy. The "bare necessities of life" offered reluctantly against the fear of destitution and death are not a recognition of their humanity but an advertisement of the humane nature of the law always liable to cancellation.

The second strategy denies the trauma by effacing the face of the other. Our case involved four applicants who were refused asylum by the immigration authorities and wanted to challenge that decision.[31] Under the Immigration Act 1971, illegal entrants, those without visa and those refused refugee status at a port of entry, should leave the country and appeal against the refusal from abroad. The Act's remarkable assumption that people fleeing persecution will not experience some difficulty in obtaining visas paved the way for the courts' subsequent actions. The refugees argued that under the UN Handbook of Refugee-Determination Procedures, they had a right to appeal against the refusal of asylum and that their removal would frustrate that right. The House of Lords responded by stating that the Handbook had "no binding force in either municipal or international law". The applicants were illegal entrants and to allow them to stay, while other visitors denied leave to enter could only appeal after leav-

---

[29] Levinas, *Totality and Infinity*, supra n. 7, 42.
[30] Levinas, *Collected Philosophical Papers*, supra n. 5, 50.
[31] *Budgaycay v. Secretary of State for the Home Department* [1987] 1 All ER 940, HL.

ing, would be "plainly untenable".[32] "Where the result of a flawed decision may imperil life or liberty a *special responsibility lies on the court in the examination of the decision-making process*".[33] The dignity of the process should be protected at all costs. Here the traumatic other is used to underpin the superiority of the law (and) of belonging. The fairness, worth and justice of the law is proved and its attractiveness "as a haven" justified even when – especially when? – it turns the refugee away and sends him back to his fate.

This second strategy is associated with the fact that the refugee moves. He crosses borders and territories, he has left home and he does not have a home, he may even not want a home other than a temporary refuge. But home and dwelling, the safety of community and tradition is what shelters self and community from the "unspeakable other". This other is always elsewhere, not where I am, where consciousness is and speaks. "Where it was you will be" is the way Freud defines the primary trauma. The refugee defies the propriety and property of self, he denies home, hearth and national territory by having no shelter and anchor. He is roaming, nomadic, delirious and threatening. By sending him away, we ensure that we and the law will not come face to face with the trauma and will avoid the face. A face in fear or pain comes, in its singularity, to haunt its neighbours as much as its persecutors. The trauma must be denied, it must be sent away to its place which is also a non place, the unconscious. The executioner covers the head of the executed as a defence against the face upon which suffering gets indelibly and indescribably inscribed and which, after disposal or death, persecutes the persecutor. To come to the law, the refugee comes to the port of entry, the physical and metaphorical door of the law. But to face the law, the refugee must leave both the country and its law. The coming foreshadows the going, the law is present and makes its presence felt only to the absent. The refugee is brought to the law by being removed, the exclusion at the foundation of the law is both repeated and repressed. Our community and the law will not come face to face with our injustice.

The final strategy can be called the assertion of unity or the denial of castration. The case, *M v. Home Office*,[34] is one of the most famous refugee cases. Its most important element is that the refugee, under

---

[32] ibid., 947.
[33] ibid., 951.
[34] [1992] 2 WLR 73, CA [1993] 3 All ER 537, HL.

the initial M for murder,[35] is only a prop in the proceedings, absent, silent, dead. M is the initial for a Zairian refugee who sought asylum in this country claiming that he had been extensively tortured as a result of anti-government and trade union activities. The Home Secretary, based on his "objective reports", turned down his application and ordered his removal to Zaire. As a result of a last minute application for judicial review, a judge ordered a stay of the deportation until further medical reports were obtained. In a series of events never fully explained, the Home Secretary, Kenneth Baker, decided to disobey the court order because he thought that in constitutional law a mandatory order against the Crown was beyond the jurisdiction of the court. M was released from the British Embassy in Kinshasa and was never heard of again. The issue before the courts, in a subsequent application for judicial review, was whether the Home Secretary had acted in contempt of court by disobeying the court order.

In this case more than any other, law's desire comes to the fore. Faced with the absent, silent probably dead other, the law comes out in its most grandiose and absurd. Death is the most uncanny of fears and the strongest desire of the unconscious. The death of the refugee mirrors this fear and desire and indicates in the strongest possible fashion the lack, the gap at the heart of the subject and the polity. The courts deny the traumatic object facing them by offering one of the most elaborate defences of the spiritual unity of the Crown and of the eternal validity of the common law. The action of the minister, if found in contempt, would be a challenge "against the fundamental supremacy of law".[36] But the Home Secretary, as a Minister of the Crown and an integral part of the unwritten constitution, cannot have offended the supremacy of the law or the dignity of its administration. The Crown, this most fictitious of entities, is the fount of justice, an image of eternal unity, of emotional bonds and immemorial trust. It cannot be in contempt of its own creation and attribute.

Law's strategy is clear: the more threatening the exclusion and the fear, the stronger does the court deny them by proclaiming the wholeness and the integrity of the political community, and by offering a paean to the supremacy of the law, the residual trust between government and the courts, and the unity of crown and the nation it represents. The trauma is denied through the erection of an imagi-

---

[35] See Peter Goodrich's insightful rhetorical analysis of the case in *Oedipus Lex: Psychoanalysis, History, Law* (University of California Press, 1995) 210–222.

[36] [1992] 2 WLR 73, at 98.

nary scenario of a complete law and a unified polity. The desire is to deny castration, to forget the violence and exclusion present at its foundation and re-enacted when the refugee is sent to his death, to present the body politic and the *corpus juris* as immune from otherness and fear.

We can conclude that legal responses to the refugee indicate her real nature. Lack of community and total absence of rights turn the refugee into the absolute, total threatening other. Beyond the embrace of family and group, and outside the protection of the law, the refugee is reduced to the status of naked, abstract humanity, an exemplum of universal human nature before it becomes concrete through the individualising action of community and equalising effect of the law. The refugee is so radically different from us that no similarity can be found or equivalence constructed. She is the symbol of difference as such, she represents nothing but her own absolutely unique individuality, which deprived of all recognition or protection is as deadly as death is totally singular. The refugee is a frightening symbol of the totalisation of difference and of the denial of affinity and points to those realms which civilisation cannot change and has a tendency to destroy.

Confronting the refugee raises the possibility that we, too, are refugees, which means that I am asked not just to accept the other but to accept that I am another, to extend the notion of the itinerant foreigner to the foreignness that lies deep in me and the political community. The refugee is within us. When we are fighting the refugee we are fighting our unconscious, this improper place in the midst of our own and proper. The refugee is the dark side of our identity. When he arrives our individual and collective consciousness experiences the uncanny. By sending him away, we think that we deny the trauma, that we shield ourselves from the horrible recognition that the other, the refugee is in us, and that we cannot avoid living as others.

Freud teaches that if we detect foreignness in ourselves, we will not hound it outside of us. The refugee is within me, we are all refugees from another place, the unconscious for psychoanalysis or the other for Levinas, which is not a *patria*, the place of the father, but a *matria*. In a paradoxical sense, the law of asylum, so selectively offered to refugees, attests to that. There has been no convincing normative argument in favour of extending asylum to refugees. The only possible moral ground for offering refuge to someone who lands in Dover, although we have no obligation to the same person a few

miles away in the Channel, is that in landing in the territory, in facing us in the face, she has become the symbol of our own Otherness
and this proximity of presence opens the ethical obligation that exists
towards the face in pain and suffering who is also my own.

III. HUMAN RIGHTS AND THE JUSTICE OF THE LAW

Let us finally turn to the place and function of human rights in law,
from the perspective of the "humanism of the other person". It is not
just the trace of the other that determines my own right; to the extent
that right is defined, regulated and restricted by positive law, the law
is launched in me, more accurately, it is the law's regulatory presence
or constitutive absence that shapes my right and identity. But if no
right is ever positive, it follows that no freedom is ever absolute and
no identity closed. Identity is marked by negativity, by the constitutive absence of the other and of the law. Identity is therefore contingent and relational, based on the various claims of others on me, and,
secondly, on the determinations of the legal system, which may
appear fixed at first, but which are also partly contingent. Human
rights introduce an element of unfixity at the heart of the subject and
do not permit the final completion of the project of subjectification.
Two absences, two types of negativity are launched at the centre of
modern (legal) identity; otherness, what is not self, and the law. If
subjection to the self-legislated law is the key element of autonomy
and identity, as Kant insisted, it involves the recognition of the non-
essential character of human nature, the indeterminacy at the heart of
the subject and the openness of the social.

But the law attempts to fix, police and regulate the parameters of
society, to fill and irrevocably define identity. The proclamation of
rights symbolises the freedom and groundlessness of modernity, but
the action of law in sanctioning and enforcing them returns rights to
logos, not as language but as the order of practical reasoning, argumentation and justification. Legal reason as a rational order of principle and argument which determines the application of right,
distinguishes between justified and unacceptable restrictions and consistently controls the extension of right from known to new
instances. The domain of practical reason is where the legal subject
resides and the concept is sovereign. The expansion from the given
to the new will follow the protocols of pure calculation, of equivalence and addition, of negation and contradiction.

There is no need to engage in an extensive critique of legal argumentation. The claim that legal reason can control its own operation has been extensively and convincingly deconstructed by the legal realists and their successors. Suffice to say, following the American critical legal scholars, that the legal principles of human rights adjudication are beset by squatting parasitic counter-principles (for example, free speech against national security or the protection of privacy).[37] The inherent reversibility of the opposed pairs undermines the hope of rational reconciliation and no meta-principle exists to help rational choice. Reason cannot create the common framework for arbitrating between conflicting claims and interpretations, because legal principle and reason itself are caught in the polysemies of the written archive as much as the substantive texts of law and are constructs of legal history, tradition and practice as much as the claims that come before the law. There can be no clear and unambiguous principle of interpretation in cases of conflict of right. As Rolando Gaete has argued, "man" is the key interpretative value that permeates the discourse of human rights. "Man provides the Archimedean point, the decisive principle of reason that can check the excesses of rhetoric and can correct practices, grounding the distinctions and differences made within the human rights discourse, Man is the 'unwritten Constitution' which takes misreadings and renders determinate the indeterminacy of the Bills of Rights".[38] But "man" cannot become the principle of interpretation precisely because the discourse and practice of human rights aims at partially fixing the meaning of this empty signifier.

The texts of human rights are supposed to control their own interpretations but the ever-expanding right-claims lead to an unstoppable will to interpret. The quest for a legal hermeneutical grail duplicates within the law, law's attempt to discipline the openness of the social. The introduction of human rights inscribes their symbolic and rhetorical character in law and opens it to its own continuous transcendence. The limited power of reason is supplemented by the infinite possibilities of rhetoric.[39] Practical reason is a limited and

---

[37] See generally Allan Hutchinson (ed.), *Critical Legal Studies* (Totowa NJ., Rowman and Littlefield, 1989).

[38] Rolando Gaete, *Human Rights and the Limits of Critical Reason* (Aldershot, Dartmouth, 1993) 107.

[39] The *locus classicus* on the relationship between law and rhetoric is Peter Goodrich P., *Legal Discourse* (London, Macmillan, 1988) and *Oedipus Lex*, op.cit., supra n. 35, which presents the rhetorical construction and analysis of the legal text in terms of a symptomatology of the institutional unconscious. See also Douzinas and Warrington with McVeigh *Postmodern Jurisprudence*, Chapter 4.

regional only part of the faculty of judgement, which Fish has called law's "rational rhetoricism": the practice of "allowing an apparently rational discourse to unfold with no acknowledgement . . . of the 'non-rational' determinations that reside at its heart".[40] When human rights become law, the law can no longer claim to be the exclusive domain of reason or to follow exclusively the protocols of logic. *Logos* as reason is accompanied by *logos* as language, and their linkage brings together both the necessity of the concept and the contingency of freedom.

Human rights find an uncomfortable place in the text of the law, national or international. To the extent that they become positivised legal discourse and join law's calculation, thematisation and synchronisation, they share the quest for subjecting society to a unique and dominant logic which necessarily violates the demand of justice. But at the same time, they are the promise of a justice always still to come: they are the figure of the negative and the indeterminate in the person and the state, and of the proximity of self and other upon which the universal and the abstract rise. The undecidability between the strict requirements of legal *logos* and the indeterminacy of human rights is both a structural characteristic of legal discourse and the moral element in the operation of the legal system. Human rights cannot be reduced to categorisation and classification, their content is not given to categorical presentation. We have a sense of being surrounded by injustice without knowing where justice lies. Human rights represent this denunciation of injustice and they remain necessarily and radically negative both in their essence and in their action. For a polity that protects human rights, injustice would be the attempt to crystallise and fix individual and group identities, to establish and police the boundaries of the social, to make it co-extensive and close it around some figure of authority or law. For a law that protects human rights, injustice would be to forget that humanity exists in the face of each person, in her uniqueness and unrepeated singularity and that human nature (the universal) is constituted in and through its transcendence by the most particular.

The justice of human rights therefore does not offer a definition and description of the just society or a prescription of its conditions of existence. This lack of definition which is also the definition of lack is logically necessary and ethically unavoidable. Sloterdijk calls, in a reference to the dog-philosopher Diogenes, a "kynic" someone

---

[40] S. Fish, "Dennis Martinez and the Uses of Theory", 96 *Yale Law Review* 1773–1800 (1987) at 1784.

who adopts not the standpoint of universal reason but of "*a priori* pain", not the detached position of disinterestedness but that of proximity, closeness and concern for the other, not cold irony but warm satirical laughter and the politics of sensuality and the body.[41] It is in this "kynical" sense, that a society of human rights accepts that person and rights are radically contingent and that this contingency founds a strong ethical obligation; that the subject of rights is internal to rights discourse and has no external determination or ground; finally, that a defence of rights must be based on the concrete needs of she who comes before the law. Human rights have no proper place, time or ideology, they cannot be assigned to any particular epoch or party. They are open to application to new areas and fields now following the logic of continuity and principled development and now the operations of rhetorical play that allows their unstoppable extension to contiguous fields. This is the dynamism of *logos*; but rights express also a primordial passivity towards the demand of the other and the proximity of the one for the other.

When the law attempts to halt the openness of the social and to fix identity, human rights denounce it for injustice. When the law forgets the suffering of the person who comes before it, in the name of reasoned consistency and formal equality, human rights denounce its immorality. Justice as human rights is not critical only of totalitarian or dictatorial attempts to deny them; even more important is their challenge and overtaking of the limits of self and law. Their symbolic importance is that they inscribe futurity in law. Their ethical importance is the demand that each person be treated as sole incarnation of humanity and her need as the responsibility of me first and then of the law. Caught between the symbolic and the ethical, paradoxically ensnared in the indeterminacy of the future and the concreteness of the present, lies the postmodern aporia of justice. Human rights can never triumph; they can suffer and even be temporarily destroyed. But their victory and their justice will always lie in an open future and in a fleeting, but pressing present. It is in this sense, that human rights are our utopian principle: a negative principle which places the energy of freedom in the service of our ethical responsibility for the other.

---

[41] Peter Sloterdijk, *Critique of Cynical Reason* (M. Eldred trans.) (London, Verso, 1988) xv and 101–28.

14

The End of Human Rights

If rights are what historically subjugated peoples most need, rights may also be one of the cruelest social objects of desire dangled above those who lack them.

Wendy Brown

The historical, philosophical and psychoanalytical approaches to human rights we examined have helped us to a fuller understanding of the operation of rights and develop a number of critiques of the shortcomings of liberal rights theory. Burke attacked the abstraction and rationalism of rights. From Marx and the Marxists, we learnt that human rights are political constructs which both conceal important ways in which power is exercised and can also be used to challenge oppression and domination. Hegel argued *contra* Kant that rights are institutional expressions of the struggle for mutual recognition; they make an important contribution to the creation of identity and are radically intersubjective rather than individualistic. Psychoanalysis taught us that the law is deeply implicated in the constitution of persons, and rights are one way through which people negotiate the fundamental prohibitions and restrictions which are the price for entry into language and society. The natural lawyers and the dissident Marxists argued that societies which lose a vision of a future without exploitation and oppression, communities without utopias, have lost their dynamism and have been abandoned to the "grey on grey" of an overwhelming past and a conformist present. We learnt that rights are grounded on human discourse and nothing more solid, like nature or humanity. They are therefore essentially unlimited, in other words inessential, the dissolution of all guarantees of certainty.

Human rights construct humans. I am human because the other recognises me as human which, in institutional terms, means as a bearer of human rights. Slaves or animals are not humans because they have no human rights. Nothing in their essence either stops them from having rights or guarantees them. Slavery was abolished only when the difference between free and slaves was re-interpreted, against the Aristotelian tradition and through long political struggles, not as an instance of natural difference between the races but as the most extreme case of unacceptable domination and oppression. The campaigns of extermination and genocide of the last fifty years show that the formal admission of humans to the dignity of humanity is not irreversible. The inmates of the German, Cambodian, Rwandan or Serbian concentration camps were constructed as non-human vermin, as beings so inferior and dangerous to the fully humans that their extermination was a natural necessity. If we turn to animals, their lack of a developed language means that they are not socially born through entry into the symbolic order. But while they cannot become human subjects, nothing stops them from becoming legal subjects, if they are given rights and legal protections, as environ-mentalists and animal liberation campaigners argue.

As we have sadly learnt after the atrocities and genocides of this last and worst century of the second millennium, the recognition of humanity is never fully guaranteed to all. Let us repeat that it is not so much that humans have rights but that rights make human. Humanity has many shades and types. The poor, whose life expectancy in sub-Saharan Africa is some 30 years lower than that of the average Briton, are lesser humans. The 5,000 Iraqi babies who die every month as a result of the Western embargo and the African babies who suffer from infant mortality seventeen times more than Europeans infants are an even lower part of humanity, barely at its threshold.[1] Those who are persecuted for their sexual orientation or race are defective humans, since a large part of their identity and self-esteem is deleted or becomes the cause of victimisation. Subjectivity according to law is a fragile achievement; it can be easily undermined and destroyed under physical and symbolic attack. Humanity is therefore a graded and ranked status with many shades and tiers between the "superhuman" Western, white, heterosexual male at the one end and the non-human, the concentration camp inmates or the fleeing refugee, at the other. Becoming more or less human through the policed distribution of rights is the modern way of creating the subject as social animal. Technological and genetic developments accompanied by the necessary institutional extensions and adjust-

---

[1] In 1990, life expectancy at birth was 50 in sub-Saharan Africa and 75 in the UK Infant mortality was 136 per 1000 live births in Africa and 7 in the UK *The Guardian*, 12 June 1999, 16.

ments may still remove the human person's centrality. In such a case, the reverse of the slave society's exclusion of some biological humans from humanity will emerge. Cyborgs, clones and genetically modified humans will be added to the group of speaking subjects; they will be given rights and protections which will make them legally human. Foucault was severely criticised for arguing that the figure of "man" or of the subject may be nearing the end of its brief sojourn in history, that it may be swept away like a sand drawing on a beach disappearing as the tide comes in. Prophesy is always a risky business. But law's participation in the making of the human is highly volatile: legal subjectivity can be given and taken away and there is no guarantee that the "natural" and the legal human will coincide.

In psychoanalytical terms, the subject of rights is a symbolic construct, the result of the action of language and the law on the body. The subject is always split, free and subjected, origin and determined, willing and oppressed, autonomous and heteronomous, the cosmopolitan representative of the species human and the citizen of a state. Authority and autonomy are both part of it, for even if autonomy is subjection to the law and this subjugation is called freedom, "it is attributed to man not to woman, to human not to animal, to adult not to child. The virile strength of the adult male, father, husband or brother dominates the concept of the subject".[2] The legal subject is the creation of positive law and the accompaniment of its rules, the sovereign plaything and its potential critic, the autonomous centre of the world as well as the dissident and rebel. Its outline may change as a result of political struggle, elements of difference may be introduced to the deformed drawing, but its imaginary integrity will be guaranteed only in the future, always not just yet; even so, this imaginary future inscribes itself as the horizon of the person and the polity, a prefiguration of a state of grace always still to come but also already present as a trace in what passes. In psychoanalytical terms, this is the result of law's deceit; we see it also as the other side of the desire for impossible integrity, as the paradoxical and utopian element of human rights.

***

Liberal jurisprudence claims that rights and human rights are historically, structurally and politically indistinguishable. Most human rights textbooks introduce their topic by presenting the standard liberal

---

[2] Jacques Derrida, "Eating Well" in E. Cadava, P. Connor and J.-L. Nancy (eds), *Who Comes after the Subject?* (New York, Routledge, 1991) 114.

theories of rights, as if there is no theory of human rights independent of rights theories. But we must resist this equalisation of rights (the building blocks of every positivism) and human rights, which are the promises of a future and the critique of all positive law and system of rights. It is a sign of the moral poverty of jurisprudence and of its neglect of the imaginary domain that the most advanced discourse and practice of transcendence is approached exclusively on the basis of a banal understanding of the existent. Legal thinking has abandoned transcendence, has condemned natural law to the history of ideas, has tamed justice and has become an accountancy of rules.

The positivisation and globalisation of human rights marks the end of political modernity in the same way that globalised economy marks the end of Leviathan. Their triumph is the recognition of the lack that constitutes human identity. Desire is moved by lack, by the desire and fear of the other. If for Hobbes, the unleashing of desire to organise modern society leads to the establishment of the absolutist state made in the image of the emancipated individual, in Locke the fear of death leads to a limitless endeavour to accumulate and to shape the polity and the world according to the dictates of bottomless desire. The Sovereign and human rights are the twin causes and objects of legalised desire. The Sovereign, built on the principle of unlimited individual desire but assuming the mantle of the party, the class or the nation, can turn its desire into murderous rage and the denial of all right. Our century has repeatedly witnessed this descent of group or national right into the affirmation of the rights of death. From the Holocaust to the Gulags and from Hiroshima to the killing fields of Vietnam and Cambodia, from Bosnia to Rwanda and Kosovo the rights of absolute desire have been confirmed time and again. When the Sovereign is devised according to the characteristics of the desiring self, it has the ability, empirically denied to individuals, to frustrate all human desire and surrender people to the horrors it was made to protect them from.

The globalisation of the principle of sovereignty and the aggressive legitimation of state power by reference to morality and human rights leaves no-one and nothing untouched. Human rights have become the *raison d'être* of the state system as its main constituents are challenged by economic, social and cultural trends. It is no coincidence that human rights "triumphed" at a point of maximum angst about life chances and malaise about the collapse of moral certitudes and political blueprints. The enormous potential for diversity released by the demise of Communism was accompanied by an unprecedented desire for unity and order. Its signs are apparent all over the world. They are expressed as despair about the loss of state authority, national virility and parental, specifically paternal and male, power; as grave concern about the increase of broken and non-standard families, of "scroungers" and "welfare mothers"; as hatred against "bogus" refugees and criminal chidren, muggers and corrupt police-men; as fear about nationalist warlords, ex-communist mafias and juvenile thugs; or, as millenarian angst, identity crisis and *fin-de-siècle* blues. If modernity created the moral panic, in postmodernity it is moral to panic. There are many postmodern nightmares and visions of horror, but they are all are haunted by the ideal of a new united, homogeneous grouping, a new Single genetically modified Power which will mobilise and unite the fragments again under a novel immanent reason, deep structure or metaphysical principle. The tribe, the group, the believers, a re-packaged nation are asked to replace state and society and to re-assert authority for fake tradition.

As institutional practice, human rights often express the imagina-tion of the one and homogeneous world society, in which the exten-sion of formal equality and negative freedom and the globalisation of Western capitalism and consumerism will equate society with its "ideal" picture drawn by governments and international law experts. Institutional human rights are mobilised in the name of global cul-ture, the values and principles of which are an attempt to close soci-eties and impose on them a unique logic. Whether that logic is Western or otherwise is secondary; the point is that it follows a prin-ciple of unity against the ideas of social indeterminacy and existential self-creation promised by the radical history of natural rights. But human rights are also a powerful popular imaginary open to diverse identities, to heterogeneous and suppressed traditions. Human rights as a principle of popular politics express the indeterminacy and open-ness of society and politics. They undermine the attempt to police some social identities and sanction others and their indeterminacy means that the boundaries of society are always contested and never coincide fully with whatever crystallisations, power and legal entitle-ment impose. Human rights enclose both a principle of unity and homogeneity and its opposite, the former symbolised by the legal form the latter by the struggles of people under the ill-defined ban-ner of humanity.

Institutionally, human rights are both a principle of state aggran-disement and a protective principle against the bottomless pit of state desire. Individually, they are the mechanism for shaping identity and life according to the dictates of desire (of the other) and the trauma of separation and lack. Human rights are fissured; they both offer limited protection against the society of desire, against the threatening state and the fearsome other, but they also express the way in which identity is arranged in shifting relations of fear, affection and care towards the other. There is no guarantee that affection will win over fear. Experience tells us however that when the fear of the other, the foreigner, the Jew, the refugee, becomes their institutional logic, human rights lose their protective value against the state. An alternative, already visible in the politically liberal part of our globalised world, is that the devouring potential of fearsome desire in its legal form will go on colonising the social world. The final outcome will be the fracturing of community and of the social bond into a monadology, in which some people will be able to assert their final and absolute sovereignty while others will be reduced to the status of the perpetually oppressed underclass. But a fully sovereign individual is a delusionary and rather farcical simulacrum of Leviathan. In both instances, positivised human rights and legalised desire, based on the fear of the other, coincide and their world and the self-creating potential of existential freedom is extinguished.

★★★

What is the end of human rights?

The first part of this book presented an alternative history of the idea of natural right and sketched the continuities and breaks between classical natural law, natural rights and human rights in order to rescue them from their dubious respectability. Historiography cannot avoid a degree of backwards projection. The past is a foreign country, its language dead. We read the past from our position in the present and we write history, consciously or unconsciously, with current interests and concerns in mind. Anachronism is not a defect; it is an unavoidable virtue which becomes problematic only when it hides behind a smokescreen of objectivity and detachment. We write for a purpose, even if that is simply the pleasure of writing; writing the history of human rights is doubly involved in the duplicity of a backward look that is firmly established in the politics of the future. Natural law, the progenitor and companion of human rights, unlike other classical theories and practices, does not belong fully to any one epoch. It violates the constraints of time, not in the sense of preaching eternal law in place of a fallen temporal positivity, but of judging the present according to the protocols of the past in the name of the future.

Natural right inhabits the boundaries of history, it is a trace of the past and a prefiguration of the future in the present. It has often acted as an imaginary revelry and vision, suspended between myth and utopia, immemorial past and unreachable future. Natural right looks backwards to a golden age, a mythical state of absolute freedom, unrestricted equality and edenic bliss, and forwards to an age where redemption and peace will come to this world. As myth and utopia, it expresses the power of imagination, the poetic energies of societies where the present cannot gag the future and what exists is judged in the court of what will never be. But natural law is Janus-like in another way too: a tradition that opposes the present in the name of the future, has also triumphed many times. But in its transition from dream to reality and from imagination to institutional design, the present and existent has often silenced the futural and absent, the sign of the cross or the hammer and sickle have mutated from witnesses to martyrdom, resistance and redemption to symbols of empire, obedience and domination. Natural law has both subverted and upheld the existing order, its history caught between the long past and the infinite future, between the dream and its realisation, which often coincides with its betrayal. The unceasing quest for natural right offers the most consistent map of the human ability to disrupt the empirical world and pass beyond the given, in the hope that the present can and must be pushed aside in order to liberate the future. Its inevitable failure, the inescapable betrayal of utopia, shows humanity to be an incomplete project fired by the injustices and infamies of this world but unable to reach the state of grace.

For natural right, the future has a dynamic pull. Reality is never complete and all honest realism includes the not yet, the future or utopia in its heart. "There is no realism worthy of the name if it abstracts from the strongest element in reality, an unfinished reality".[3] In this, utopian thought may be assisted by Hegelian and psychoanalytical insights. Hegel opened the *Philosophy of Right* with the justly infamous claim that "the rational is real; the real is rational". It has been repeatedly interpreted, as we saw, as the most telling symbol of the historicism and conservatism of Hegelian philosophy. The Prussian State was the first to be identified with the world spirit and its rationality. But this was a rather lame affair and there was much mileage and millions of dead still left in history. More recent pronouncements of the end of all conflict, of the final victory of liberal

---

[3] Ernst Bloch, *The Principle of Hope* (Oxford, Blackwell, 1986) 624.

capitalism and of the death of utopia are more convincing – and more menacing. From the perspective of the victors of the Cold War, all critique is dismissed as irrational and unreal. Utopia has been branded intellectually bankrupt, a morally repugnant gloss of communism. From the perspective of the prophets of the end, free markets and human rights are the non-ideological ideologies left, final proofs of the pragmatic benevolence of the American way. Yet, the Hegelian real does not coincide with the immediately given and the dialectical identification of reality and rationality is neither present nor guaranteed but a future-looking trend and possibility. The rational-as-real marks the unity of essence and existence, of essence that can be realised only as historical becoming, of history that judges the sedimentation of reason. In this sense, the identification does not signify an achieved or given state of affairs but a normative postulate, according to which the real must become rational and the essence of historical movement must be united with its empirical realisation. Once the petty accountancy of trade agreements and the narcissistic sycophancy of intellectual nouveau riches and political arrivistes supported by bombers have been set aside, the Hegelian principle appears as precisely the opposite of that of the historians of the "end": the only way in which the future union of real and rational can come together is by resisting the real in the name of the rational. When we combine this with the post-Hegelian critique of rationalism, we could formulate a postmodern dialectical principle: resist the real in the name of the many rationalities to come.

Derrida calls the disturbance of the present by the future, a "messianism without a messiah": he describes the messianic experience as an apprehension, a straining forward towards the coming event which is the most irreducibly heterogeneous otherness, "an irreducible amalgam of desire and anguish, affirmation and fear, promise and threat . . . Messianicity mandates that we interrupt the ordinary course of things, time and history here-now; it is inseparable from an affirmation of otherness and justice".[4] Derrida wants to distinguish the Jewish messianic hope, which he considers to be a universal structure of experience independent of any religious messianism, from the Greek utopian tradition with its expectation of a perfect collective future. He disagrees with Frederick Jameson's view that the messianic is another name for his "persistent utopianism" but he accepts that utopianism could not exist without the experience of the messianic

---

[4] Jacques Derrida, "Marx & Sons" in *Ghostly Demarcations: A Symposium on Jacques Derrida's "Spectres for Marx"* (Michael Sprinkler ed.) (London, Verso, 1999) 249.

disruption. Our argument has been that the imaginary domain, by bringing together the future anteriority of human identity and of the human rights society, links the structure of subjectivity with that of social utopia or, in Derrida's terms, makes utopia the social aspect of the messianic experience.

Similarly, in psychoanalytical terms, the Real, threatening or promising, lies unrecognised and yet all-powerful at the heart of psychic reality. *Jouissance,* the constitutive and catastrophic force of the Real, disturbs the linear temporality of daily reality. As the retrospective explanation of passions and pathologies, it creates the past in the image of the present and makes it the present's cause. As an imaginary projected beautiful form, it prefigures the future in the present. Here again, the identification of what exists with the good or the true is the blockage, the disease. But if the futural aspect of human rights is to be reinforced, it must be anchored in an ethical interpretation of the (desire for the) other which the weak ethics of psychoanalysis cannot support.[5] This is how the utopian presents the power of natural right:

> It is rectified – but never refuted by the mere power of that which, at any particular times, is. On the contrary it confutes and judges the existent if it is failing and failing inhumanely; indeed first and foremost it provides the standard to measure such facticity precisely as departure from the Right; and above all to measure it immanently: that is, by ideas which have resounded and informed from time immemorial before such a departure, and which are still displayed and proposed in the face of it.[6]

Bloch alerts us to the links between natural law and human rights. Human rights descend from this tradition, they are the utopian element behind legal rights. However unlike classical utopias, they do not draw their force from a predicted and described future perfection, but from the pain and contempt felt by the citizens of the states

---

[5] Freud comments that the Christian command "to love thy neighbour" is the most obscene principle he knows. Lacan formulates the ethical principle of psychoanalysis as "never give up on your desire". While these "ethical" principles may be of use when addressed to the participants of the therapeutic encounter, they are expressions of a self-centered view of ethics which, if generally applied, can have catastrophic consequences. In the Lacanian canon, acting fully on your desire means following the death drive over erotic desire. The murderous results of the death drive have littered the history pages of the twentieth century too many times. See Costas Douzinas, "Law's Birth and Antigone's Death: On Ontological and Psychoanalytical Ethics", 16 *Cardozo Law Review*, 1325–62, 1995.

[6] Ernst Bloch, *The Philosophy of the Future* (J. Cumming trans.) (New York, Herder and Herder, 1970) 91.

which have proclaimed their triumph. Human rights are the necessary and impossible claim of law to justice. They draw their force from the suffering of the past and the injustices of the present and act as parasites on the body of rights, consuming the host and projecting a future out of a rather bland legal history. Many of the authors we have examined insist on the radical break between natural right and human rights, and historiography may be on their side. But natural law and human rights share also a common tradition of resistance and dissent from exploitation and degradation and a concern with a political and ethical utopia, the epiphany of which will never occur but whose principle can stand in judgement of the present law. When human rights lose that element, they remain an instrument for reform and, occasionally, a sophisticated tool for analysis but they stop being the tribunal of history.

The triumph of human rights and the accompanying "end of history" may conceal a final mutation in the long trajectory of natural law, in which the call of nature has turned from a defence against conventional wisdom and institutional lethargy into the legitimating device of some of the most sclerotic regimes and powers. As human rights start veering away from their initial revolutionary and dissident purposes, as their end becomes obscured in ever more declarations, treaties and diplomatic lunches, we may be entering the epoch of the end of human rights and of the triumph of a monolithic humanity. If human rights have become the "realised myth" of postmodern societies, this is a myth realised only in the energies of those who suffer grave and petty violations in the hands of the powers that have proclaimed their triumph. Human rights are the negative principle at the heart of the social imaginary. The end of human rights, like that of natural law, is the promise of the "not yet", of the indeterminacy of existential self-creation against the fear of uncertainty and the inauthentic certainties of the present. When the apologists of pragmatism pronounce the end of ideology, of history or utopia, they do not mark the triumph of human rights; on the contrary, they bring human rights to an end. The end of human rights comes when they lose their utopian end.

Bibliography

ADORNO, THEODOR *Negative Dialectics* (E. B. Ashton trans.) (London, Routledge, 1990)

—— *Minima Moralia: Reflections from Damaged Life* (E. Jephcott trans.) (London, Verso, 1991)

ADORNO, THEODOR and HORKHEIMER, MAX *Dialectics of Enlightenment* (J. Cumming trans.) (London, Verso, 1979)

ALSTON, PHILIP *The European Union and Human Rights* (Oxford, Oxford University Press, 1999)

ALTHUSSER, LOUIS *For Marx* (B. Brewster trans.) (London, Allen Lane, 1969)

—— "Ideology and Ideological State Apparatuses", in *Lenin and Philosophy and other Essays* (B. Brewster trans.) (London, Verso, 1971)

—— "Marx's Relation to Hegel", in *Politics and History* (B. Brewster trans.) (London, New Left Books, 1972)

ST AQUINAS, THOMAS *On Law, Morality and Politics*, W. Baumgarth and R. Regan (eds.) (Indianapolis, Hackett, 1988)

ARENDT, HANNAH *The Origins of Totalitarianism* (San Diego, Harvest Books, 1979)

ARISTOTLE *Nicomachean Ethics* (J. A. K. Thomson trans.) (London, Penguin, 1976)

—— *Politics* (H. Rakham trans.) (Cambridge Mass., Loeb, 1990)

—— *The Art of Rhetoric* (H. C. Lawson-Tancred trans.) (London, Penguin, 1991)

—— *Metaphysics* (D. Bosctock trans.) (Oxford, Clarendon, 1994)

—— *Physics* (D. Bosctock trans.) (Oxford, Oxford University Press, 1996)

ARMSTRONG, MARK, "Face to Face with Child Abuse: Towards an Ethics of Listening", 1999, X/2 *Law and Critique*, 147–73

ARNAUD, A-J. "Women in the Boudoir, Women at the Pools: 1804, the History of a Confinement", in A-J. Arnaud and E. Kingdom *Women's Rights and the Rights of Men* (Aberdeen, Aberdeen University Press, 1990)

ARNAUD-DUC, NICOLE "Women Entrapped: from Public Non-existence to Private Protection", in A-J. Arnaud and E. Kingdom *Women's Rights and the Rights of Men* (Aberdeen, Aberdeen University Press, 1990)

AUGUSTINE *De Civitate Dei* (M. Dods, J. J. Smith and G. Wilson trans.) (Edinburgh, 1872)

BADINTER, R. *L'Universalité des Droits de l'Homme dans une Monde Pluraliste* (Strasbourg, Conseil d'Europe, 1989)

BALIBAR, ETIENNE "Citizen Subject", in E. Cadava, P. Connor and J. L. Nancy (eds.) *Who Comes after the Subject* (New York, Routledge, 1991)

—— *Masses, Classes, Ideas: Studies on Politics and Philosophy before and after Marx* (J. Swanson trans.) (New York, Routledge, 1994)

—— "Subjection and Subjectivation", in Joan Copjec (ed.) *Supposing the Subject* (London, Verso, 1994)

BARRET-KRIEGEL, BLANDINE *Les droits de l'homme et le droit naturel* (Paris, P.U.F., 1989)

BAUMAN, ZYGMUNT *Postmodern Ethics* (Oxford, Blackwell, 1993)

—— *Postmodernity and its Discontents* (Cambridge, Polity, 1997)

BENJAMIN, WALTER "Theses on the Philosophy of History", in *Illuminations* (H. Zohn trans.) (New York, Schocken, 1969)

—— "Critique of Violence", in *Reflections* (E. Jephcott trans.) (New York, Schocken Books, 1978)

BENTHAM, JEREMY *Anarchical Fallacies; being an examination of the Declaration of Rights issued during the French Revolution*, in Jeremy Waldron (ed.) *Nonsense upon Stilts* (London, Methuen, 1987)

BENVENUTO, BICE and KENNEDY, ROGER *The Works of Jacques Lacan – An Introduction* (London, Free Association Books, 1986)

BERGSMO, MORTEN and TOLBERT, DAVID "Reflections on the Stature of the I.C.C." (1999) 11 *Wig & Gavel* 21

BERNSTEIN, JAY "Rights, Revolution and Community: Marx's 'On the Jewish Question' ", in Peter Osborne (ed.) *Socialism and the Limits of Liberalism* (London, Verso, 1991)

BIGONGIARI, DINO "The Political Ideas of St Augustine", in St Augustine, *The Political Writings*, Henry Paulucci (ed.) (Washington D.C., Gateway, 1962)

BLACK, V. "On connecting natural rights with natural law", (1990) *Persona y Derecho* 183–209

BLOCH, ERNST *The Philosophy of the Future* (J. Cumming trans.) (New York, Herder and Herder, 1970)

—— *The Principle of Hope* (N. and S. Plaice and P. Knight trans.) (Oxford, Blackwell, 1986)

—— *Natural Law and Human Dignity* (Dennis J. Schmidt trans.) (Cambridge Mass., MIT Press, 1988)

BOBBIO, NORBERTO *The Age of Rights* (Cambridge, Polity, 1996)

BORCH-JACOBSEN, MIKKEL *Lacan: The Absolute Master* (Douglas Brick trans.) (Stanford, Stanford University Press, 1991)

BOURGEOIS, BERNARD *Philosophie et droits de l'homme: de Kant à Marx* (Paris, P.U.F., 1990)

BOURKE, JOANNA *An Intimate History of Killing: Face to Face Killing in 20th Century Warfare* (London, Granta, 1999)

BROWN, WENDY "Rights and Identity in Modernity: Revisiting the 'Jewish

Question' ", in A. Sarat and T. Kearns (eds.) *Identities, Politics and Rights* (Ann Arbor, University of Michigan Press, 1997)

BROWNLIE, IAN (ed.) *Basic Documents on Human Rights* (Oxford, Clarendon, 1994)

BRUDNER, ALAN *The Unity of the Common Law: Studies in Hegelian Jurisprudence* (Berkeley, University of California Press, 1995)

BUCHAN, JAMESA "Inside Iraq" (1999) 67 *Granta* 169

BURKE, EDMUND *A Philosophical Enquiry into the Origins of the Sublime and the Beautiful* J. T. Boulton (ed.) (Notre Dame, University of Notre Dame Press, 1958)

—— *Reflections on the Revolution in France* J. G. A. Pockock (ed.) (Indianapolis, Hackett, 1987)

BURNET, J. *Early Greek Philosophy* 4th ed. (London, A & C Black, 1930)

CAMPOS, PAUL *Jurismania: The Madness of American Law* (Oxford, Oxford University Press, 1998)

CAPUTO, JOHN *Demythologising Heidegger* (Bloomington, Indiana University Press, 1993)

CARLSON, DAVID "Duellism in American Jurisprudence" *Cardozo Law Review* (forthcoming 2000)

CASSESE, ANTONIO *Human Rights in a Changing World* (Cambridge, Polity, 1990)

CASSIRER, ERNST *The Philosophy of the Enlightenment* (F. C. A. Koelln and J. P. Pettegrove trans.) (Princeton NJ, Princeton University Press, 1968)

CASTORIADIS, CORNELIUS "Reflections on Racism" (1992) 32 *Thesis Eleven* 9

CAUDILL, DAVID *Lacan and the Subject of Law: Toward a Psychoanalytic Critical Legal Theory* (New Jersey, Humanities Press, 1997)

CHOMSKY, NOAM "A letter to Santa Claus" *The Times Higher* (19 February 1999) 23

—— *The Umbrella of U.S. Power* (New York, Seven Stories, 1999)

CICERO *De inventione* (H. M. Hubbell trans.) (London, Heinemann, 1949)

—— *De Officiis* (M. T. Griffin and E. M. Atkins trans.) (Cambridge, Cambridge University Press, 1991)

—— *De natura deorum* (R. W. Walsh trans.) (Oxford, Clarendon, 1997)

—— *De Legibus* (N. Rudd trans.) (Oxford, Oxford University Press, 1998)

—— *Republic* (N. Rudd trans.) (Oxford, Oxford University Press, 1998)

CIORAN, E. M. A. *A Short History of Decay* (R. Howard trans.) (London, Quartet Books, 1990)

COPPELL, J. *The Human Rights Act 1998* (London, John Wiley & Sons, 1999)

CORNELL, DRUCILLA "Rethinking the Beyond of the Real" (1995) 16 *Cardozo Law Review* 3, 729

—— *The Imaginary Domain* (New York, Routledge, 1995)

CORNELL, DRUCILLA, ROSENFELD, MICHEL and CARLSON, DAVID *Hegel and Legal Theory* (New York, Routledge, 1991)

CRANSTON, MAURICE *What are Human Rights?* (London, Bodley Head, 1973)

CRITCHLEY, SIMON *The Ethics of Deconstruction: Derrida & Levinas* (Oxford, Blackwell, 1992)

—— "Prolegomena to any Post-Deconstructive Subjectivity", in S. Critchley and P. Dews (eds.) *Deconstructive Subjectivities* (New York, S.U.N.Y. Press, 1996)

DALLMAYR, FRED *The Other Heidegger* (Ithaca, Cornell University Press, 1993)

DANIEL, J. O. & MOYLAN, T. (eds.) *Not Yet: Reconsidering Ernst Bloch* (London, Verso, 1997)

DE LA PRADELLE, G. *L'Homme Juridique* (Paris, Maspero, 1979)

DE ROMILLY, JACQUELINE *La Loi dans la pensée Grecque: des origines à Aristote* (Paris, Les Belles Lettres, 1971)

DE TOCQUEVILLE, ALEXIS *L'ancien régime et la révolution* (Paris, Gallimard, 1967)

DE ZALUETA, F. (ed.) *The Institutes of Gaius* (Oxford, Oxford University Press, 1946)

DELEUZE, GILLES "Coldness and Cruelty", in *Masochism* (J. McNeil trans.) (New York, Zone Books, 1989)

DEMOSTHENES *"Peri Stephanou"* ("On the Crown", C. Vince and J. Vince trans.) (London, Heinemann, 1974)

DERRIDA, JACQUES *Of Grammatology* (G. Spivak trans.) (Baltimore, The Johns Hopkins University Press, 1974)

—— "Violence and Metaphysics", in *Writing and Difference* (A. Bass trans.) (London, Routledge, 1978)

—— "Plato's Pharmacy" in *Disseminations* (B. Johnson trans.) (London, Athlone Press, 1981)

—— *Glas* (J. Leavy and R. Rand trans.) (Lincoln, University of Nebraska Press, 1986)

—— *Of Spirit: Heidegger and the Question* (G. Bennington and R. Bowlby trans.) (Chicago, University of Chicago Press, 1989)

—— "Devant la Loi", in A. Edoff (ed.) *Kafka and the Contemporary Critical Performance: Centenary Readings* (Bloomington, Indiana University Press, 1989)

—— "The Force of Law; The 'Mystical Foundation of Authority' " (1990) 11 *Cardozo Law Review* 919

—— "Eating Well", in E. Cadava, P. Connor and J. L. Nancy (eds.) *Who Comes After the Subject* (New York, Routledge, 1993)

—— *Spectres for Marx* (P. Kamuf trans.) (London, Routledge, 1994)

—— "Marx & Sons", in *Ghostly Demarcations: A Symposium on Jacques Derrida's "Spectres for Marx"* Michael Sprinkler (ed.) (London, Verso, 1999)

DES FORGES, ALISON *Leave None to tell the Story: Genocide in Rwanda* (New York, Human Rights Watch, 1999)

DESCOMBES, VINCENT *Modern French Philosophies* (L. Scott-Fox and J. M. Harding trans.) (Cambridge, Cambridge University Press, 1980)

DIAMANTIDES, MARINOS "Ethics in Law: Death Marks on a 'Still Life' " (1995) VI/2 *Law and Critique* 209

DICEY, A. V. *Introduction to the Study of the Law of the Constitution* (London, 1885; 10th edition, 1959)

DONNELLY, JACK *Universal Human Rights in Theory and Practice* (Ithaca, Cornell University Press, 1989)

DOUZINAS, COSTAS "Antigone's Death and Law's Birth: on Ontological and Psychoanalytical Ethics" (1995) 16 *Cardozo Law Review* 1325

—— "Law's Fear of the Image", 1996, 19/3 *Art History*, 353–69

—— "Psychoanalysis Becomes the Law: Notes on an Encounter Foretold" (1997) *Legal Studies Forum* 323

—— "Eros and Thanatos", in D. Manderson (ed.) *Courting Death* (London, Pluto, 1999)

—— "Human Rights at the End of History" (1999) 4/1 *Angelaki* 99

—— "*Prosopon and Antiprosopon*: Prolegomena for a Legal Iconology", in Costas Douzinas and Lynda Nead (eds.) *Law and the Image: The Authority of Art and the Aesthetics of Law* (Chicago, University of Chicago Press, 1999)

DOUZINAS, COSTAS & WARRINGTON, RONNIE "Domination, exploitation and suffering: Marxism and the opening of closed systems of thought" (1986) 4 *Journal of the American Bar Foundation* 801

—— "Posting the Law: Social Contracts and the Postal Rule's Grammatology" (1991) IV/11 *International Journal of the Semiotics of Law* 115

—— "A Well-Founded Fear of Justice: Ethics and Justice in Postmodernity" (1991) II/2 *Law and Critique* 115

—— *Justice Miscarried* (Edinburgh, Edinburgh University Press, 1994)

—— "The Face of Justice: A Jurisprudence of Alterity" (1994) 3 *Social and Legal Studies* 405

DOUZINAS, COSTAS and WARRINGTON, RONNIE with MCVEIGH, SHAUN *Postmodern Jurisprudence: The law of text in the texts of law* (London, Routledge, 1991, 1993)

DUGUIT, LEON *Traité de Droit Constitutionnel* (Paris, 1921)

DUMONT, LOUIS *Essays on Individualism: Modern Ideology in Anthropological Perspective* (Chicago, University of Chicago Press, 1986)

DUPRE, LOUIS *Passages to Modernity* (New Haven, Yale University Press, 1993)

DWORKIN, RONALD *Taking Rights Seriously* (London, Duckworth, 1977)

—— "Law as Interpretation", in W. J. T. Mitchell (ed.) *The Politics of Interpretation* (Chicago, University of Chicago, 1983)

—— *Law's Empire* (London, Fontana, 1986)

EDELMAN, BERNARD *Le Droit saisi par la photographie* (Paris, Maspero, 1973)

EDELMAN, BERNARD *The Ownership of the Image* (E. Kingdom trans.) (London, Routledge and Kegan Paul, 1979)

ELLUL, JACQUES *The Technological Society* (J. Wilkinson trans.) (New York, Random House, 1964)

EVANS, TONY (ed.) *Human Rights: Fifty Years On* (Manchester, Manchester University Press, 1998)

FARIAS, VICTOR *Heidegger and Nazism* J. Margolis and T. Rockmore (eds.) (Philadelphia, Temple University Press, 1989)

FEINBERG, JOEL *Rights, Justice and the Value of Liberty* (Princeton NJ, Princeton University Press, 1980)

FELDMAN, DAVID *Civil Liberties and Human Rights in England and Wales* (Oxford, Oxford University Press 1993)

FERRY, LUC *The New Ecological Order* (Carol Volk trans.) (Chicago, University of Chicago Press, 1992 or 1995)

FERRY, LUC and RENAUT, ALAIN *From the Rights of Man to the Republican Idea* (Franklin Philip trans.) (Chicago, University of Chicago Press, 1992)

—— *Heidegger and Modernity* (F. Philip trans.) (Chicago, University of Chicago Press, 1990)

FIGGIS, JOHN *The Divine Right of Kings* (Bristol, Thoemmes Press, 1994/1914

FINER, S., BOGDANOR, V. and RUDDEN, B. *Comparing Constitutions* (Oxford, Clarendon, 1995)

FINK, BRUCE *The Lacanian Subject* (Princeton NJ, Princeton University Press, 1995)

FINNIS, JOHN *Natural Law and Natural Rights* (Oxford, Clarendon, 1980)

FISH, S. "Dennis Martinez and the Uses of Theory" (1987) 96 *Yale Law Review* 1773

FOUCAULT, MICHEL, *Discipline and Punish: The Birth of the Prison* (London: Penguin, 1979)

—— "Two Lectures: Lecture Two: 14 January 1976", in *Power/Knowledge* (C. Gordon ed., K. Soper trans.) (New York, Pantheon, 1980)

—— *History of Sexuality, Volume I: An Introduction* (London, Penguin, 1981)

FRANK, MANFRED *What is Neostructuralism?* (S. Wilke and R. Gray trans.) (Minneapolis, University of Minnesota Press, 1989)

FREUD, SIGMUND *Why War?, Group Psychology and the Analysis of the Ego, Civilisation and its Discontents*, in *Civilisation, Society and Religion* James Strachey (ed.) (Albert Dickson trans.) (London, Penguin, 1985)

—— *Totem and Taboo*, in *The Origins of Religion* James Strachey (ed.) (Albert Dickson trans.) (London, Penguin, 1985)

FUKUYAMA, FRANCIS *Have we reached the End of History?* (Santa Monica Ca., Rand Corporation, 1989)

—— *The End of History and the Last Man* (London, Penguin, 1992)

GADAMER, HANS-GEORG *Truth and Method* (London, Sheen and Ward, 1975)

GAETE, ROLANDO *Human Rights and the Limits of Critical Reason* (Aldershot, Dartmouth, 1993)

GAUCHET, MARCEL *La Révolution des droits de l'homme* (Paris, Gallimard, 1989)

GEOGHEGAN, VINCENT *Ernst Bloch* (London, Routledge, 1996)

GEWIRTH, ALAN *Reason and Morality* (Chicago, University of Chicago Press, 1978)

—— *Human Rights* (Chicago, University of Chicago Press, 1982)

—— *Self-Fulfilment* (Princeton NJ, Princeton University Press, 1998)

GIERKE, OTTO *Natural Law and the Theory of Society* (Ernest Baker trans.) (Cambridge, Cambridge University Press, 1934)

GLENDON, MARY ANN *Rights Talk: The Impoverishment of Political Discourse* (New York, Free Press, 1991)

GOLDMAN, LUCIEN *The Philosophy of the Enlightenment* (H. Maas trans.) (London, Routledge and Kegan Paul, 1973)

GOODRICH, PETER *Reading the Law* (Oxford, Blackwell, 1988)

—— *Legal Discourse* (London, Macmillan, 1988)

—— *Languages of Law* (London, Weidenfeld and Nicolson, 1990)

—— *Oedipus Lex: Psychoanalysis, History, Law* (Berkeley, University of California Press, 1995)

—— *Law in the Courts of Love* (London, Routledge, 1996)

—— *Law and the Unconscious: A Legendre Reader* (London, Macmillan, 1997)

—— "Social Science and the Displacement of Law" (1998) 32/2 *Law and Society Review* 473

GOTHHELF, ALAN "Aristotle's Conception of Final Causality" (1976) 30 *Review of Metaphysics* 226

GREEN, KATE and LIM, HILLARY "What is this Thing about Female Circumcision" 1998, 7/3 *Social and Legal Studies* 365–87

GROTIUS *De Jure Beli et Pacis Libre Tres* ("Law of War and Peace", F. Kelsey trans.) (Indianapolis, Bobbs-Merrill, 1962)

GUZZONI, UTE "Do we still Want to be Subjects?", in S. Critchley and P. Dews (eds.) *Deconstructive Subjectivities* (New York, S.U.N.Y. Press, 1996)

HABERMAS, JURGEN *Theory and Practice* (London, Heinemann, 1974)

HANSYM, SARAH (ed.) *Levinas and Lacan: The Missed Encounter* (Albany, State University of New York Press, 1998)

HARDIE, W. F. R. *Aristotle's Ethical Theory* (Oxford, Oxford University Press, 1980)

HART, H. L. A. *The Concept of Law* (Oxford, Clarendon, 1979)

—— "Are There Any Natural Rights?" (1955) 64 *Philosophical Review* 175

HARVEY, DAVID *Justice, Nature & the Geography of Difference* (Oxford, Blackwell, 1996)

HAYEK, F. A. *Law, Legislation, Liberty* Vol. 2 (London, Routledge and Kegan Paul, 1976)

HEGEL G. *Philosophy of Right* (T. M. Knox trans.) (Oxford, Oxford University Press, 1967)

—— *Natural Law* (T. M. Knox trans.) (Philadelphia, University of Pennsylvania Press, 1975)

—— *The Phenomenology of Spirit* (A. V. Miller trans.) (Oxford, Oxford University Press, 1977)

—— *System of Ethical Life (1802–3)* and *First Philosophy of Spirit (1805–6)* (H. S. Harris and T. M. Knox trans. and ed.) (Albany, S.U.N.Y. Press, 1977)

—— *Hegel and the Human Spirit: A Translation of the Jena Lectures on the Philosophy of the Spirit (1805–6) with Commentary* (L. Rauch trans. and ed.) (Detroit, Wayne State University Press, 1983)

HEIDEGGER, MARTIN *An Introduction to Metaphysics* (R. Mannheim trans.) (New York, Doubleday Anchor, 1961)

—— *Being and Time* (J. Macquarrie and E. Robinson trans.) (New York, Harper and Row, 1962)

—— "The Anaximander Fragment", in *Early Greek Thinking* (D. F. Crell and F. Capuzzi trans.) (New York, Harper and Row, 1975)

—— "The Age of the World Picture", in *The Question Concerning Technology and Other Essays* (W. Lovitt trans.) (New York, Harper and Row, 1977)

—— "Letter on Humanism", "The Question Concerning Technology", in *Basic Writings* D. F. Krell (ed.) (HarperSan Francisco, 1977)

HELLER, AGNES *Beyond Justice* (Oxford, Blackwell, 1987)

HENKIN, LOUIS *The Age of Rights* (New York, Columbia University Press, 1990)

HERMITTE, MARIE-ANGELE "Le concept de diversité biologique et la création d'un status de la nature", in *L'homme, la nature, le droit* (Paris, Bourgeois, 1988)

HIRST, PAUL *Law and Ideology* (London, Macmillan, 1985)

HOBBES, THOMAS *Leviathan* Richard Tuck (ed.) (Cambridge, Cambridge University Press, 1996)

—— *Dialogue between a Philosopher and a Student of the Common Law of England*, Crospey, J. (ed.) (Chicago, University of Chicago Press, 1997)

HODGE, JOANNA *Heidegger and Ethics* (London, Routledge, 1995)

HOFFMAN, P. *La Femme dans la Pensée des Lumières* (Paris, Orphys, 1977)

HONNETH, AXEL *The Struggle for Recognition* (J. Anderson trans.) (Cambridge, Polity, 1995)

HUMPHREY, JOHN *Human Rights and the United Nations* (Epping Bowker, 1984)

HUNT, LYNN (ed.) *The French Revolution and Human Rights: A Brief Documentary History* (Boston, Bedford Books, 1996)

HUSSERL, EDMUND *The Paris Lectures* (The Hague, Nijhoff, 1964)

HUTCHINSON, ALLAN (ed.) *Critical Legal Studies* (Totowa NJ, Rowman and Littlefield, 1989)

IRIGARAY, LUCE *Speculum for another Woman; An Ethics of Sexual Difference* (Carolyn Burke and Gillian Gill trans.) (London, Athlone, 1993)

—— *Thinking the Difference* (K. Montin trans.) (New York, Routledge, 1994)

—— *I love to you* (Alison Martin trans.) (New York, Routledge, 1996)

JACOBY, RUSSELL *The End of Utopia* (New York, Basic Books, 1999)

JAMES, C. L. R. *The Black Jacobins: Toussaint d'Ouverture and the San Domingo Revolution* (New York, Vintage, 1980)

JAY, MARTIN "Must Justice be Blind", in Costas Douzinas and Lynda Nead (eds.) *Law and the Image* (Chicago, University of Chicago Press, 1999)

JELLINEK, GEORG *La Déclaration des droits de l'homme et du citoyen* (G. Fardis trans.) (Paris, 1902)

KANT, IMMANUEL *Critique of Practical Reason* (London, Macmillan, 1956)

KANTOROWICZ, ERNST "The Sovereignty of the Artist: A note on Legal Maxims and Renaissance Theories of Art", in *Selected Studies* (New York, J. J. Augustin, 1965) 352–65

KAUFMANN, DAVID "Thanks for the Memory: Bloch, Benjamin, and the Philosophy of History", in J. O. Daniel and T. Moylan (eds.) *Not Yet: Reconsidering Ernst Bloch* (London, Verso, 1997)

KEARNY, RICHARD *The Wake of Imagination* (London, Hutchinson, 1988)

KELLY, JOHN MAURICE *A Short History of Western Legal Theory* (Oxford, Oxford University Press, 1992)

KELSEN, HANS "The Metamorphoses of the Idea of Justice", in P. Sayre (ed.) *Interpretations of Modern Legal Philosophies* (New York, Oxford University Press, 1947)

—— *General Theory of Law and State* (Cambridge Mass., Harvard University Press, 1949)

KINGDOM, ELIZABETH "Gendering Rights", in A-J. Arnaud and E. Kingdom *Women's Rights and the Rights of Men* (Aberdeen, Aberdeen University Press, 1990)

KIRCHHEIMER, OTTO "The *Rechsstaat* as Magic Wall", in *The Rule of Law Under Siege* W. Scheuerman (ed.) (Berkeley, University of California Press, 1996)

KLUGER, RICHARD *Simple Justice* (London, Andre Deutsch, 1977)

KOJEVE, ALEXANDRE *Introuction to the Reading of Hegel* (A. H. Nichols trans.) (Ithaca, Cornell University Press, 1989)

KRISTEVA, JULIA *The Abject: Powers of Horror* (Leon Roudiez trans.) (New York, Columbia University Press, 1982)

—— "Women, Psychoanalysis, Politics", in *The Kristeva Reader* Toril Moi (ed.) (Oxford, Blackwell, 1986)

—— *Strangers to Ourselves* (Leon Roudiez trans.) (New York, Columbia University Press, 1991)

KRISTEVA, JULIA *Nations without Nationalism* (Leon Roudiez trans.) (New York, Columbia University Press, 1993)

LACAN, JACQUES *Écrits* (Paris, Seuil, 1966)

—— "The subversion of the subject and the dialectic of desire in the Freudian Unconscious" in *Écrits: A Selection* (Alan Sheridan trans.) (London, Routledge, 1977)

—— *The Seminar of Jacques Lacan* Vol I. (John Forester trans.) (Norton, 1988)

—— *The Ethics of Psychoanalysis* (London, Routledge, 1992)

—— *Seminar III: The Psychoses* (London, Routledge, 1994)

—— "Radiophonie" (1970) 2/3 *Scilicet* 65

—— "Kant avec Sade" (Winter 1989) 51 *October* 55

LACEY, NICOLA *Unspeakable Subjects* (Oxford, Hart, 1998)

LACLAU, ERNESTO *New Reflections on the Revolution of our Time* (London, Verso, 1990)

—— *Emancipation(s)* (London, Verso, 1996)

LACLAU, ERNESTO and MOUFFE, CHANTAL *Hegemony and Socialist Strategy* (London, Verso, 1985)

LACOUE-LABARTHE, PHILIPPE *Heidegger, Art and Politics* (C. Turner trans.) (Oxford, Blackwell, 1990)

LARKS, STEPHEN "From the 'Single Confused Page' to the 'Decalogue for Six Billion Persons': The Roots of the Universal Declaration of Human Rights in the French Revolution" (1998) 20 *Human Rights Quarterly* 459

LAUREN, P. G. *Power and Prejudice: The Politics and Diplomacy of Racial Discrimination* 2nd edition (Oxford, Westview Press, 1996)

LEFORT, CLAUDE *The Political Forms of Modern Society* John Thompson (ed.) (Cambridge, Polity, 1986)

—— *Democracy and Political Theory* (D. Macey trans.) (Minneapolis, University of Minnesota Press, 1988)

LEGENDRE, PIERRE *L'Amour du Censeur* (Paris, Seuil, 1974)

—— *Le Désir politique de Dieu: Études sur les montages de l'État et du Droit* (Paris, Fayard, 1988)

—— *Le Crime de Corporal Lortie* (Paris, Fayard, 1989)

—— "The Other Dimension of Law" (1995) 16 *Cardozo Law Review* 3–4, 943

LESTER, ANTHONY and PANICK, DAVID *Human Rights Law and Practice* (London, Butterworths, 1999)

LEVINAS, EMMANUEL *Totality and Infinity* (A. Lingis trans.) (Pittsburgh, Duquesne University Press, 1969)

—— *Humanisme de l'Autre Homme* (Montpellier, 1972)

—— *Collected Philosophical Papers* (A. Lingis trans.) (The Hague, Nijhoff, 1987)

—— *Nine Talmudic Readings* (Bloomington, Indiana University Press, 1990)

—— *Otherwise than Being or Beyond Essence* (A. Lingis trans.) (Kluwer, 1991)

—— "The Rights of Man and the Rights of the Other", in *Outside the Subject* (M. Smith trans.) (London, Athlone Press, 1993)

LEVY, ERNS "Natural Law in Roman Thought" (1949) 15 *Studia et Domenta Historiae et Juris*

LEWIS, NORMAN "Human rights, law and democracy in an unfree world", in Tony Evans (ed.) *Human Rights Fifty Years on: A reappraisal* (Manchester, Manchester University Press, 1988)

LINOWITZ, SOLM and MAYER, MARTIN *The Betrayed Profession* (Baltimore, John Hopkins University Press, 1994)

LISSKA, ANTHONY *Aquinas's Theory of Natural Law* (Oxford, Clarendon, 1996)

LIVINGSTONE, STEPHEN and OWEN, TIM *Prison Law* (Oxford, Oxford University Press, 1993)

LOCKE, JOHN *Second Treatise of Government* P. Laslett (ed.) (Cambridge, Cambridge University Press, 1960)

—— *An Essay Concerning Human Understanding* P. H. Nidditch (ed.) (Oxford, Clarendon, 1975)

LOUGHLIN, MARTIN *Public Law and Political Theory* (Oxford, Oxford University Press, 1992)

LUCAS, J. R. *On Justice* (Oxford, Clarendon, 1980)

LYOTARD, JEAN-FRANCOIS *The Postmodern Condition: An Essay on Knowledge* (Manchester, Manchester University Press, 1984)

—— *The Differend* (G. Van den Abbeele trans.) (Manchester, Manchester University Press, 1988)

—— *Heidegger and the "jews"* (A. Michel and M. Roberts trans.) (Minneapolis, University of Minnesota Press, 1990)

—— "The Other's rights", in *On Human Rights* Stephen Shute and Susan Hurley (eds.) (New York, Basic Books, 1993)

—— "A l'Insy (Unbeknownst)" in Miami Theory Collective (ed.) *Community at Loose Ends* (Minneapolis, University of Minnesota Press, 1996)

LYOTARD, JEAN-FRANCOIS and THEBAUD, JEAN-LOUP *Just Gaming* (W. Glodzich trans.) (Manchester, Manchester University Press, 1985)

MACNEIL, WILLIAM "Law's *Corpus Delicti*: The Fantasmatic Body of Rights Discoutse" 1998 IX/2 *Law & Critique* 37

MANITAKIS, A. *The Subject of Constitutional Rights* (Athens, Sakoulas, 1981)

MARCEL, GABRIEL *Creative Fidelity* (R. Rosthal trans.) (New York, Farrar, Strauss & Co), 1964)

MARCUSE, HERBERT *Eros and Civilisation* (Boston, Beacon Press, 1966)

MARITAIN, JACQUES *The Rights of Man and Natural Law* (D. Anson trans.) (New York, Charles Scribner's Sons, 1951)

MARSHALL, GEOFFREY "Patriating Rights – With Reservations", in *Constitutional Reform in the United Kingdom* (Cambridge, Centre for Public Law, 1998)

MARTINEAU, HARRIET (ed. and trans.) *The Positive Philosophy of Auguste Comte* Vol. 2, 3rd ed. (London, 1893)

MARX, KARL *Theories of Surplus Value* (J. Cohen trans.) (London, Lawrence and Wishart, 1972)

—— "On the Jewish Question" in *Early Texts* (D. McLellan ed. and trans.) (Oxford, Blackwell, 1971) 85–114

—— *Critique of Hegel's Philosophy of Right* in *Early Texts* (D. McLellan ed. and trans.) (Oxford, Blackwell, 1971) 115–29

—— "Critique of the Gotha Programme", in David McLellan (ed.) *Selected Writings* (Oxford, Oxford University Press, 1977)

MATHIEZ, ALBERT *La Révolution et les étrangers* (Paris, La Renaissance du Livre, 1928)

MATSUDA, MARI, LAWRENCE, CHARLES III, DELGADO, RICHARD and CRENSHAW, KIMBERLEY (eds.) *Words that Wound: Critical Race Theory, Assaultive Speech and the First Amendment* (Boulder, Westview Press, 1993)

McINERNY, RALPH "Natural Law and Natural Rights", in *Aquinas on Human Action* (Washington D.C., Catholic University of America Press, 1992)

McINTYRE, ALASDAIR *After Virtue* (London, Duckworth, 1980)

MELVERN, LINDA "How the system failed to save Rwanda" *The Guardian* (7 December 1998) 10

MILLER, FRED *Nature, Justice, and Right in Aristotle's Politics* (Oxford, Oxford University Press, 1995)

MITCHELL, W. J. T. *Iconology* (Chicago, University of Chicago Press, 1986)

MURPHY, W. T. *The Oldest Social Science? Configurations of Law and Modernity* (Oxford, Oxford University Press, 1998)

NAGEL, THOMAS *Equality and Partiality* (New York, Oxford University Press, 1991)

NANCY, JEAN-LUC *The Inoperative Communtiy* (Minneapolis, University of Minnesota Press, 1991)

—— *The Experience of Freedom* (Stanford, Stanford University Press, 1993)

NARAGHI, EHSAN "The Republic's Citizens of Honour", in *1789: An Idea that Changed the World* (June 1989) *The UNESCO Courier* 13

NEUMANN, FRANZ "The Concept of Political Freedom", in *The Rule of Law Under Siege* W. Scheuerman (ed.) (Berkeley, University of California Press, 1996)

NIETHAMMER, L. *Posthistoire. Has History Come to an End?* (London, Verso, 1992)

NIETZSCHE, FRIEDRICH *Philosophy in the Tragic Age of the Greeks* (M. Cowan trans.) (Chicago, Regnery, 1962)

—— *The Will to Power* (W. Kaufmann and R. J. Hollingdale trans.) (New York, Vintage, 1968)

NINO, CARLOS *The Ethics of Human Rights* (Oxford, Clarendon, 1993)

—— *Radical Evil on Trial* (New Haven, Yale University Press, 1996)

NORRIE, ALAN *Crime, Reason and History* (London, Weidenfeld and Nicolson, 1993)

NUSSBAUM, MARTHA "The Betrayal of Convention: A reading of

Euripides' *Hecuba*", in *The Fragility of Goodness* (Cambridge, Cambridge University Press, 1986)

PAINE, THOMAS *The Rights of Man, Being an Answer to Mr. Burke's Attack on the French Revolution* H. Collins (ed.) (London, Penguin, 1969)

PERRY, MICHAEL *The Idea of Human Rights* (New York, Oxford University Press, 1998)

PETERSON, V. S. and SISSON, RYAN, A. *Global Gender Issues* (Boulder, Westview Press, 1993)

PILGER, JOHN "Under the influence" *The Guardian* (21 September 1999) 18

PLATO, *Gorgias* (W. Hamilton trans.) (London, Penguin, 1960)

—— "Epistle VII", in *Phaedrus and Epistles VII and VIII* (W. Hamilton trans.) (London, Penguin, 1973)

—— *Republic* (D. Lee trans.) (London, Penguin, 1974)

—— *The Laws* (T. J. Saunders trans.) (London, Penguin, 1988)

POTTAGE, ALAIN "The Paternity of Law", in C. Douzinas et al (eds.) *Politics, Postmodernity, Critical Legal Studies* (London, Routledge, 1994)

POULANTZAS, NICOS *State, Power, Socialism* (London, New Left Books, 1978)

RADIN, MARGARET JANE *Reinterpreting Property* (Chicago, University of Chicago Press, 1993)

RAWLS, JOHN *A Theory of Justice* (Oxford, Oxford University Press, 1972)

RENAUT, ALAIN *The Era of the Individual: A Contribution to a History of Subjectivity* (M. B. DeBeviose and F. Philip trans.) (Princeton NJ, Princeton University Press, 1997)

ROBINSON, FIONA "The limits of a rights–based approach to international ethics", in Tony Evans (ed.) *Human Rights Fifty Years on: A reappraisal* (Manchester, Manchester University Press, 1998)

ROBINSON, J. M. *An Introduction to Early Greek Philosophy* (Boston, Houghton Mifflin, 1968)

RORTY, RICHARD "Human Rights, Rationality and Sentimentality", in Stephen Shute and Susan Hurley (eds.) *On Human Rights* (New York, Basic Books, 1993)

ROSENBERG, MICHEL (ed.) *Constitutionalism, Identity, Difference and Legitimacy* (Durham, Duke University Press, 1994)

—— *Just Interpretations* (Berkeley, University of California Press, 1998)

—— "Hegel and the Dialectics of Contract" (1989) 10 *Cardozo Law Review* 1199

ROUSSEAU, JEAN JACQUES *The Social Contract*, in *Political Writings* F. Watkins (ed.) (London, Nelson, 1953)

—— *The First and Second Discourse* (R. and J. Masters trans.) (New York, St. Martin's Press, 1964)

—— *Emile or on Education* (A. Bloom trans.) (London, Penguin, 1991)

SALECL, RENATA *The Spoils of Freedom* (London, Routledge, 1994)

SALECL, RENATA "Rights in Psychoanalytic and Feminist Perspective" (1995) 16 *Cardozo Law Review* 3–4, 1121

SARTRE, JEAN-PAUL *Existentialism and Humanism* (P. Mairet trans.) (London, Methuen, 1980)

SCARRY, ELAINE *The Body in Pain* (Oxford, Oxford University Press, 1985)

SCHLAG, PIERRE *The Enchantment of Reason* (Rudham, Duke University Press, 1998)

—— "The problem of the Subject" (1991) 69 *Texas Law Review* 1627

—— "The empty Circles of Liberal Justification" (1997) 96 *Michigan Law Review* 1

SCHWAB, GAIL and JEANNENEY, JOHN (eds.) *The French Revolution of 1789 and its Impact* (Westport, Greenwood Press, 1995)

SCOTT, JOAN *Only Paradoxes to Offer: French Feminists and the Rights of Man* (Cambridge Mass., Harvard University Press, 1996)

SEVE, LUCIEN *Man in Marxist Theory* (Sussex, Harvester Press, 1978)

SHKLAR, JUDITH *The Faces of Injustice* (New Haven, Yale University Press, 1990)

SHROEDER, JEANNE *The Vestal and the Fasces: Psychoanalytical and Philosophical Perspectives on the Feminine and Property* (Berkeley, University of California Press, 1998)

SHROEDER, JEANNE and CARLSON, DAVID "The Subject is Northing" (1994) 5 *Law and Critique* 93

SINGER, PETER "Rights for chimps" *The Guardian* (29 July 1999) 9

SINGER, PETER and CAVALIERI, PAOLA (eds.) *The Great Ape Project: Equality before Humanity* (London, Fourth Estate, 1993)

SLOTERDIJK, PETER *Critique of Cynical Reason* (M. Eldred trans.) (London, Verso, 1988)

SOPHOCLES, *Antigone* in *Three Theban Plays* (R. Fagles trans.) (London, Penguin, 1984)

STARMER, KEIR *European Human Rights Law* (London, LAG, 1999)

STEINER, HENRY and ALSTON, PHILIP *International Human Rights in Context* (Oxford, Clarendon, 1996)

STONE, CHRISTOPHER "Should Trees have Standing? Towards Legal Rights for Natural Objects" (1972) *Southern California Law Review* 553

STRAUSS, LEO *Natural Law and History* (Chicago, University of Chicago Press, 1965)

—— *What is Political Philosophy* (Chicago, University of Chicago Press, 1988 or 1959)

TAYLOR, CHARLES *Hegel* (Cambridge, Cambridge University Press, 1977)

—— *Multiculturalism: Examining the Politics of Recognition* (Princeton NJ, Princeton University Press, 1994)

TAYLOR, MICHAEL *Altarity* (Chicago, Chicago University Press, 1987)

TIERNEY, BRIAN *The Idea of Natural Rights* (Atlanta Georgia, Scholars Press, 1997)

TSAITOURIDES, CHRIS "Leviathan-Moby Dick: The Physics of Space" (19978) VIII/2 *Law and Critique* 223–43

TUCK, RICHARD *Natural Rights Theories* (Cambridge, Cambridge University Press, 1979)

TULLY, STEVE "A vain Conceit? The Rome Stature of the I.C.C. and the Enforcement of Human Rights" (1999) 11 *Wig & Gavel* 16

ULLMAN, WALTER *A History of Political Thought: The Middle Ages* (London, Penguin, 1965)

—— *The Individual and Society in the Middle Ages* (Baltimore, The John Hopkins University Press, 1966)

URMSON, J. O. *Aristotle's Ethics* (Oxford, Blackwell, 1988)

VARIKAS, E. "Droit naturel, nature féminine et égalité des sexes" (1987) *Revue Internationale des Recherches et des Synthèses en Sciences Sociales* 3

VARTIER, JEAN *Les procès des animaux du Moyen Age à nos jours* (Paris, Hachette, 1970)

VATTIMO, GIANNI *The End of Modernity* (Cambridge, Cambridge University Press, 1988)

—— *The Transparent Society* (Cambridge, Polity, 1992)

VERNANT, J. P. and VIDAL-NAQUET, P. *Myth and Tragedy in Ancient Greece* (New York, Zone Books, 1990)

VILLA, DANA *Arendt and Heidegger: The Fate of the Political* (Princeton NJ, Princeton University Press, 1996)

VILLEY, MICHEL *Lecons d'Histoire de la Philosophie du Droit* (Paris, Dalloz, 1962)

—— *La Formation de la Pensée Juridique Moderne* (Paris, Montchrétien, 1968)

—— *Seize Essais de Philosophie du Droit* (Paris, Dalloz, 1969)

—— *Histoire de la Philosophie du Droit* 4th ed. (Paris, P.U.F., 1975)

—— *Le droit et les droits de l'homme* (Paris, P.U.F., 1983)

—— "Abrégé du droit naturel classique" (1961) 6 *Archives de Philosophie du Droit* 27

—— "La philosophie du droit de Burke", in *Critique de la pensée juridique moderne* (Paris, Dalloz, 1975)

VINING, J. *Legal Identity* (New Haven, Yale University Press, 1978)

WADDINGTON, C. H. *The Ethical Animal* (London, Allen & Unwin, 1960)

WADE, WILLIAM "The United Kingdom's Bill of Rights", in *Constitutional Reform in the United Kingdom* (Cambridge Centre for Public Law, 1998)

WALDRON, JEREMY "Nonsense upon Stilts? – a reply", in J. Waldron (ed.) *Nonsense upon Stilts: Bentham, Burke and Marx on the Rights of Man* (London, Methuen, 1987)

WALZER, MICHAEL *Just and Unjust Wars: A Moral Argument with Historical Illustrations* (London, Penguin, 1980)

—— *What it Means to be an American* (New York, Marsillio, 1992)

WEBER, MAX *Economy and Society: An outline of Interpretative Sociology* G. Roth and C. Wittich (eds.) (Berkeley, University of California Press, 1978)

WILLIAMS, PATRICIA *The Alchemy of Race and Rights* (Cambridge Mass., Harvard University Press, 1991)

YOUNG, IRIS MARION *Justice and the Politics of Difference* (Princeton NJ, Princeton University Press, 1990)

ZIZEK, SLAVOJ *The Sublime Object of Ideology* (London, Verso, 1989)

—— *For they know not what they do: Enjoyment as a political factor* (London, Verso, 1991)

—— *The Indivisible Remainder: An Essay on Schelling and Related Matters* (London, Verso, 1996)

—— "Superego by Default" (1995) 16 *Cardozo Law Review* 3–4, 925

Index